INTRODUCTION TO COMPUTER SCIENCE

INTRODUCTION TO COMPUTER SCIENCE

ALAN J. PERLIS
Yale University

*A preliminary edition
of this title was published
in 1972.*

Harper & Row, Publishers
New York   Evanston   San Francisco   London

Cover Photo: Howard Leiberman

Sponsoring Editor: George J. Telecki
Project Editor: Brenda Goldberg
Production Supervisor: Will Jomarrón

INTRODUCTION TO COMPUTER SCIENCE

Library of Congress Cataloging in Publication Data
Perlis, Alan J
     Introduction to computer science.
     Includes bibliographical references and index.
     1. Electronic digital computers—Programming.
I. Title.
QA76.6.P46   001.6'42   75-4643
ISBN 0-06-045128-9

To Sydelle

CONTENTS

3 LANGUAGES   153

4 DATA STRUCTURES   265

5 SYSTEMS 319

6 THEORY 357

PREFACE

Computer science is a young science. As such it has many fewer scientists, courses of instruction, and textbooks than do the more mature sciences such as physics, chemistry, and biology. For most college students a high-school level course in computer science has not been generally available. Certainly it is true that standard courses at the high-school level have not yet been defined. Consequently, much of the material in this book will appear new in purpose, terminology, and technique. Much will seem more difficult than it really is.

Programming has become a highly useful skill. Many students choose a first course in computer science merely to acquire the ability to use a programming language. However, programming involves much more than language skill. We do not program the content of ordinary human discourse; we program methods of solving problems, and we express these programs in logical and symbolic form. We do so because there is no other way to get computing machines to execute the programs. Thus, language skill is necessary but not sufficient for mastering the use of computers. Precise expression of symbolic concepts stated in a programming language is required. Although the arsenal of mathematical theory used in this book does not go beyond high-school level mathematics, students must develop a willingness to absorb notations and to express relations in symbolic form.

Learning a language *is* important. However, the choice of language is less important. In acquiring a competence in one language, students must see that they are developing the ability to acquire competence in computer languages in general. Learning about language, programming, and the computer should make us aware of the shifting and shadowy boundaries between them. Technology dictates how this boundary shifts; education prepares us for the eventuality of the shift.

A university course in computer science has several goals which this book attempts to achieve:

1. To give students practice in expressing problem-solving methods in the form of executable computer programs.

2. To give students an appreciation of the computer: its logical simplicity, its ingenious structural complexity, and its awesome potential.

3. To give students experience in the use of programming languages.

4.   To give students an appreciation of programming systems, not so much as they are encountered during use of the computer, but as they are shaped and built for the students' own purposes.

5.   To give students some contact with the emerging theory of computation.

Some readers may question the use of Algol60 and APL as the programming languages in this text. Certainly they are neither the most popular nor the most advanced. They are, however, enormously influential in shaping trends, and an understanding of them makes the more popular and newer languages simpler to understand and master.

For most college students this text aims to support their first and only course in computer science. Computers play a part in all of our lives. Education reveals that the computer's role is shaped by people and not by the machine itself. In all probability, computers ultimately will become as common-place as the ubiquitous electric motor. This is as it should be. In our world the computer is a basic tool that we reach for at progressively earlier stages, in our search for solutions to our pressing societal, scientific, and personal problems. Thus, it is my conviction that an introduction to computer science must be significantly more than mere drill in the use of a popular programming language. It must provide students with a *pou sto*.*

All the material in this book can be easily covered in a two-semester course. With judicious selection by the instructor and serious study by the student, a one-semester course also can be organized. The notes for this book have been used at Yale for the past three years in a one-semester course for students who either have had a previous elementary programming course, or who intend to study computer science or expect to have prolonged contact with the computer during and after their academic years.

Much of the philosophy that guided the selection and organization of the material in this book was developed during the period 1957–1970, while the field of computer science was developing and I was teaching an introductory course on this subject at Carnegie-Mellon University. I owe much to the students and faculty of that institution for providing a stimulating environment in which to develop the material and its pedagogy.

I particularly wish to thank my son Robert for typing the current manuscript into the computer and performing editing on it there and my daughter Andrea for her help. The Yale PDP-10 and its interactive editing system aided immeasurably in reducing the tedium involved in editing and reprinting during the manuscript's development.

Alan J. Perlis

* A term used by Archimedes. It is a platform on which to stand in order to pry up the world—if only one had a lever that were long enough.

INTRODUCTION TO COMPUTER SCIENCE

CHAPTER 1

ALGORITHMS

1

INTRODUCTION

In this book you will meet a number of what may appear to be new concepts, since they are presented in the context of a new technology—the technology of electronic digital computers. Actually the concepts are not totally foreign to you, you have been using some of them intuitively since childhood: *language* in which to express commands, and *algorithms* by which tasks are to be accomplished. What will be new is the attachment of algorithms and languages to a machine—the *electronic digital computer*—which is the agent commanded to perform (to do, to accomplish) *algorithms* expressed in *language*.

It is this trinity and the relationships among its parts and the relationship of them to us that determine the content of this book.

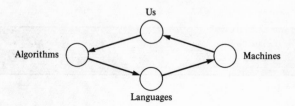

Let us agree to name this diagram the "cybernetic dialogue" (between us and machines).

A number of questions should occur to you and should be answered here: What is all the fuss about? Why isolate among human experiences this dialogue for study? Why is it important to understand it? Why has a technology been created by and for the dialogue? Why does it flourish?

Like all important questions, these are not easy to answer, perhaps because the answers lie within various classical studies of human society: history, economics, sociology, psychology, and the natural sciences. Nevertheless, I shall be so bold as to attempt answers, sketchy though they must be.

For two hundred years western society has been engaged in a continual (though by no means systematic) development of successively more complex and artificial environments. Later environments appear capable of supporting the more rapid development of new environments than did earlier ones; that is, the process of development is an accelerating one. This development is characterized by heavy investment in tools, extensive training for their widespread use, and the definition of systematic technologies both to expedite these processes and to provide directions in which new environments can more rapidly occur. Although this evolution is not guaranteed a perpetuity, no counterdevelopment of any real content has appeared that can support society at the levels of population and choice to which man has become accustomed.

Thus in our society we have a background and foundation of increasing complexity and showing an increasing rate of change. We may observe two growth laws. First, the increase in the population trained to use tools and in the number of tools available for their use implies that the potential for tool utility grows as a product rather than as a sum. Second, the amount of composition—that is, the number of uses of tools to produce new tools—grows as a part of the product and thus assures an even greater overall growth in tool use.

The understanding and the management of tool use is organized through the use of abstract models realized in nothing more substantial than language, such as mathematics. Like the tools and tool use they describe, the models have so increased in complexity *that they too have come to require management,* and it is here in model management that computers have come to be so necessary and useful.

I might mention that among the tools coming into common use are those which perform automatically at great speed and whose management must also perform in the same way. Here the computer is *essential* because of the need for quick response.

So stylized has the set (tools, tool use, modeling, and control) become, that the study of the set has acquired a special name: *system theory.*

Computers are thus the offspring of the increasing complexity in our tools and affairs and the requirement of a rapid response in the performance of many of their activities.

While the history of the computer is very short, less than three decades, its development in that brief period has followed that of other tools, but in an incredibly compressed period of time and for reasons that underscore the computer's importance.

Not only can computers accomplish much in a short time, but also they can be used for modeling extremely diverse phenomena, and one computer can be diverted from one activity to another quite rapidly: computers exhibit enormous "plasticity." It is said, with a great deal of truth, that computers are general-purpose instruments.

The production of computers depends on a sophisticated technological base in electronics and mechanical engineering. This dependency has resulted in a mutually reinforcing development: advances in the support technology are quickly absorbed into computer technology, and the expanding requirements of computers set important goals of development for the support technologies.

The computer field has become accustomed to speak of its ladder of goals and attainments as having rungs separated by "orders of magnitude" (powers of ten) rather than factors!

The computer is an object of great value and complexity. While its potential is enormous, that potential can be delivered only by organizing a pattern of precise work statements (a program) that commands the computer to perform a desired task. The computer is designed to be general purpose, but it is after all only a machine, having but a finite capacity for holding patterns of activity—far fewer than the patterns we (ultimately) require it to hold. This apparent contradiction between generality of demands and finiteness of capacity is resolved by making use of the "building-block" or "tinker-toy" approach we find so successfully used in nature. The computer is inherently capable of performing only a few tasks (several hundred). All other tasks are woven from patterns of these. It is as though each task is a large protein molecule which we "program" from a few basic components.

The act of organization called programming, though often called an art, is an infant technology and must be understood as such. It is mastered through practice and application of intelligence in the careful use of tools.

ALGORITHMS

A number of terms that have been introduced now need some explanation. Let us look at algorithms. A proper starting point is a dictionary definition.

> **Algorithm:** a rule or procedure for solving a recurrent mathematical problem.

The definition reveals an algorithm to be a process (something that is carried out), a term for which we have a number of synonyms. *Recipe*, one such synonym, is a method of synthesizing a thing from its components; it usually includes a declaration of the components followed by a description of the steps to be taken to effect the synthesis. Careful attention is paid to sequencing: some parts are to be performed before others, and others can be performed in any order.

A *mathematical procedure* is another synonym for an algorithm; numbers or other symbolic data are manipulated by the rules of mathematics to produce one or more symbolic results. Here the accent is on the symbolic nature of the input and output and the careful delineation of the operations that may be performed on the symbolic data. Most of the examples of algorithms in this chapter are mathematical procedures.

Although all the algorithms participating in the cybernetic dialogue show the standard features of careful attention to sequencing, manipulation of symbolic information, and utilization of mathematical—indeed, arithmetical—operations, we must become aware of the profound consequences of algorithms' being performed by a machine, the digital computer. An algorithm is a finite sequence of elementary tasks, each performable by a computer in a finite amount of time. Let us consider some aspects of algorithms and their relation to machines.

1. Every task that we want the computer to perform, and that it is capable of performing, we can state as an algorithm.

2. All the tasks that we know can be done in a finite amount of time can be stated as algorithms and thus will take a finite amount of time to perform on a computer.

3. The written description of an algorithm should not be required to have a length proportional to the number of actions to be performed in the algorithm; otherwise, because of the enormous disparity between our rate of algorithm creation (how many marks can we write in a second?) and the rate of algorithm execution on a computer (about 10^6 operations in a second), we should soon find that the computers never had any work to do. Actually, we seek algorithms whose description length is approximately independent of the number of actions to be performed. Hence some part of every algorithm is "read" and executed many times by the computer.

4. Advantage should be taken of the great speed of the machine; algorithms usually involve tasks requiring large numbers of operations. Furthermore, the algorithm execution should not require human intervention to "stoke it" too often. A computer performs about 10^6 operations each second, and human intervention can seldom be accomplished in less than 10 seconds. Thus we attempt to devise algorithms in which the effect of human intervention, where essential, can be obtained within the algorithm itself in substantially less than 10^7 operations. Some interventions exist whose human response requires but a few seconds yet which would require an order of magnitude more than 10^7 operations from within the algorithm. Language translation on computers is one application in which frequent human intervention has proved to be essential if quality translation is to be obtained.

5. Algorithm execution should be reproducible. The same algorithm on the same machine should always give the same result.

Thus far nothing has been said about what algorithms cause to be manipulated by and within digital computers. Cookbook recipes apply operations such as cutting, storing, cooling, and heating to foods in containers. Our study of algorithms will be limited to those which apply the operations of arithmetic to numbers, because that is what, and all, computers do.

One might think this to be a significant limitation, but it is not. If we wish to manipulate characters from the extensive alphabets found in print (letters, figures, fonts, and sizes), they all can be represented as numbers. Any operations we should wish to perform on these characters can be replaced by collections of arithmetical operations on the numbers representing the characters and their properties. We usually say that we have *encoded* the characters into numbers, and the numerical results obtained by the algorithm then will be *decoded* into interpretations of and about characters.

We shall limit our consideration of algorithms to those involving the manipulation of symbols, represented by numbers, since such algorithms are the ones directly performed on computers.

The attachment of devices to the computer makes it possible to extend our view of algorithms to include those involving control of physical acts, such as observing temperatures, scanning a visual scene, and causing motion of objects. However, adding this capability to the computer only apparently enlarges the scope of algorithms, nothing has been added to their fundamental properties, and no fundamental increase in their capabilities has occurred.

We shall not further consider such extensions except in a most primitive way: input and output of symbolic data.

Let us list a few important properties of our symbolic algorithms:

1. An algorithm has a unique starting point, and its execution proceeds from one step to another, until it reaches a halting point.

2. Each step of the algorithm is simple and unambiguous, so that it can be correctly performed by a machine whose only knowledge of the algorithm is that step. The execution of an algorithm utilizes the worm's-eye view: only a single step is under consideration at any one time. Furthermore, each step must be executable in a finite amount of time.

3. Since parts of the description must be read and executed more than once, indeed many many times, an algorithm contains at least one cycle; that is, certain sequences of steps reoccur during the algorithm execution. Since the algorithm is to terminate after a finite number of steps, there must be a way of terminating every cycle. Put another way, there must be at least one step in every cycle whose function is to choose *which* step is to be its successor. Thus every cycle must include at least one step that makes the choice of either continuing the cycle or of leaving it. It is sufficient that it make a choice from among two possible successors, since more choice can be obtained by a sequence of such binary choices.

4. Every algorithm must contain at least one variable whose domain of values is reasonably extensive. If an algorithm had no variables, hence only constants, a single execution would yield the only result it would ever produce, and that result would thereafter suffice. The algorithm need never be executed again. Actually, this is not strictly true, since it is conceivable that an algorithm produces a result of such descriptive complexity that it would be better to

produce the result each time it is needed than to remember it. However, algorithms generally have variables.

5. Algorithms have, among their variables, some whose values are initialized as *input*. Input provides a means of focusing an algorithm's execution on values of particular interest. The values of certain variables, when the algorithm is terminated, are specified as *output*. It is in this sense, of transforming inputs to outputs, that algorithms are often viewed as functions.

6. Algorithms generally contain at least one variable of complicated structure: one identifying a set of variables. Usually this set has a variable number of elements, and this number changes from one execution of the algorithm to another. The component variables are members of the set because they share some common property. The variability of their number makes it difficult to give a unique and simple name to each, so that the elements are usually identified relative to the variable identifying the set. By using a numeric index it is possible to identify arbitrarily many elements by using arithmetically constructed names. Indeed, by using a variable index it is possible to identify an arbitrary element and hence, any element. For example, if x is 2, 3, . . . , 100, 101, then $x[3]$ is 4, $x[997]$ is 998, and $x[i]$ is the element in the ith position; x is a set of variables, and $x[i]$ identifies the ith member. Two names, x and i, can now identify any from among a *variable number of variables*.

Let us consider an example of an algorithm to see why the preceding six points were made. Suppose I have a list of N integers and I wish to find the largest. Let us proceed by invoking a dialogue between ALG, the algorithm creator, and PROB, the problem proposer.

PROB: Do you understand the problem?

ALG: Of course, but isn't it a bit silly, since you can tell the answer by looking?

PROB: Really, N can be very, very large; for example, 10,000,000.

ALG: O.K. If I'm going to describe how to do it, I must have names for each of the numbers in the list, else I can't talk about these numbers. Ah, I see. The list is an example of a structured piece of data. So I'll call my numbers $A[1]$, $A[2]$, . . . , $A[N]$.

PROB: No objections. But what are you going to do?

ALG: Simple. Find the largest of $A[1]$ and $A[2]$. Oh, I need a variable to name the largest of these two. I'll use W.

PROB: Go on.

ALG: Then I'll repeat what I did to $A[1]$ and $A[2]$, but on W and $A[3]$. Then on W and $A[4]$. Then on W and $A[5]$. Then on W and $A[6]$, etc. Do I make myself clear?

PROB: You sound like a broken record. And what does "etc." mean?

ALG: Surely you can't expect me to drone on and on until I've said "Then on W and A something" for all N numbers? It would take much too long and, besides, my description would have to be changed each time you changed N. Thank heavens I don't have to change it each time you give me a new list of numbers. Ah, I see. This is why algorithms have cycles and variables. This is going to be subtle, so follow me carefully. I am going to give you a description that tells you to reread it until the description itself tells you to stop reading!

>Read: Make W the largest of W and $A[I]$.
>Increase I by 1.
>If $I \leq N$, then read this paragraph again; else STOP, W is your answer.

PROB: When I start, what is W, and what is I, since you haven't told me?

ALG (triumphantly): My you're dense. Let W start with the value $A[1]$, I mean the number whose name is $A[1]$, and start I at 2. Of course you will input the values to N, $A[1]$, $A[2]$, . . . , $A[N]$. You see, I've used all your six points, and even a fool who knows just a little arithmetic could understand what to do.

PROB (sadly): You should look before you leap. What do you do if $N = 1$? Then there is no $A[2]$, is there?

ALG: Well, if you're going to be that way, I'll just reorder the steps:

>First, read in the numbers N, $A[1]$, . . . , $A[N]$.
>Second, let W be $A[1]$ and I be 2.
>If $I \leq N$, then make W the largest of W and $A[I]$, and then increase I by 1, and then read this sentence again; else STOP, and W is your answer? OK?
>I need a better way to describe algorithms. Writing sentences that control sequencing in English is painful.

PROB: I'm satisfied.

REPRESENTATION OF ALGORITHMS

We note that algorithms specify not only actions but also the order in which they are to be performed. Thus there is an initial action and, since there are only finitely many actions to be performed, there is a last action.

The description of an algorithm is a static portrayal through which a sequence of actions progresses. Thus there are both lexicographic and temporal interpretations that can be given to the words *next, before, after, subsequent, preceding, following, initial, final, starting, last, predecessor,* and *successor.* In this text we shall use *next, before, after, later, predecessor, successor, starting,* and *last* to represent temporal relations, and *following, above, below, subsequent, preceding, initial,* and *final* to represent lexicographic relations among the steps of an algorithm. See (1.1).

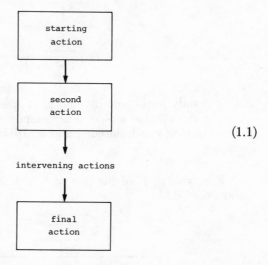

(1.1)

The ↓ in (1.1) means "then do." Rather than tag the actions as starting or last, we always include two special actions, START and STOP; see (1.2).

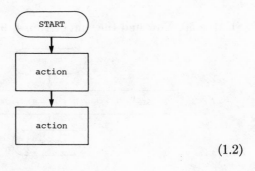

(1.2)

intervening actions

An initial view of an algorithm might be that each action except STOP has one successor and every action except START has one predecessor. Thus, all algorithms would look like

and differ only in the number and kind of actions specified.

The describable actions are compounded from those of the hundred or so of which the computer is capable. Let us consider some examples.

Example 1:   Find the sum of 1, 5, 4, 9, 16, and 24, and name the answer SUM:

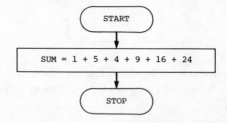

SUM is 59. Now find the sum of 1, 5, 4, 9, 16, 24, 56, and 11.

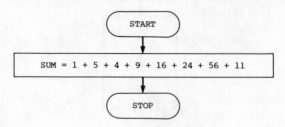

SUM is 126.

These algorithms, though simple, clear, and correct, are unsatisfactory, since (a) for each new set of numbers the algorithm must be rewritten, and (b) the number of characters in the algorithm specification grows in size as the number of operations (here additions) grows.

We must be aware that a simple process is being hidden by including in the algorithm the specific set of numbers we wish to sum. This hidden process is exposed through the use of variables—symbols for which values may be substituted. A variable is associated with a *set* of quantities, called its *domain* or *type*, any one of

which the variable has as its value at a given examination. The set
may be finite as, for example, 1, 3, 6, 7, 52,

> or infinite: {the positive integers: 1, 2, 3, . . .}
> or heterogeneous: {1, abc, 9, 2d, 143, z$2}
> or structured, in that some elements in the set may themselves
>   be sets:

$$\{\{1, a, 2\}, \{1, 2, ab\}, \{1, 2, 3, . . .\},$$
$$\{a, b, \{c, d, e\}, 3, g\}, . . .\}$$

The sets are not necessarily ordered. Of those that are, the most important are called *arrays*. Arrays are both ordered and homogeneous.

A word should also be said here about heterogeneity. The set
$(1, abc, 9, 2d, z\$2)$ is labeled heterogeneous because its elements are
from different domains. In one sense this is a fictitious distinction,
because all domains arising in algorithms are collections of integers
or, to be more specific, can be so represented. We can take the last
set and identify the domains of the elements:

(I, A, I, IA, IAC)

where I is the domain of integers, A is the domain of Roman letters,
IA is the domain of both Roman letters and integers, IAC is the
domain of both IA and the set of characters variously used as
punctuation, special markers, and so on.

Domains may be encoded as integers in numerous ways, and
the encoding is chosen to make the desired operations on the data
required by the algorithm easiest to describe and perform. Making
the correct choice is one of the most important tasks in programming.

One encoding approach is to map all alphabets onto the simplest alphabet, the binary alphabet, containing only two characters
denoted by 0 and 1. Individual characters from an arbitrary alphabet map into the words, called *bytes*, of this binary alphabet. Even
the ten ordinary decimal digits can be so mapped. The length of a
byte is called its *bit length;* that is, a byte has so many binary digits,
or bits.

There are 2^k distinctive bytes of k bits. Thus, if $k = 3$, the
eight distinct bytes are

000   001   010   011   100   101   110   111

Thus, if an alphabet contains M characters, each character can be
uniquely represented in a byte containing no more than k bits, where

$$k = \Gamma(\log_2 M), \text{ where } \Gamma X$$
$$= \begin{cases} X, \text{ if } X \text{ is an integer} \\ \\ \text{otherwise, the integer next largest to } X \end{cases}$$

For example:

M	k
10	4
26	5
64	6
88	7

While human communication uses alphabets of enormous size, it has become standard practice to limit our algorithms to an alphabet of 128 characters, and hence a byte will standardize to a length of 7 bits. The alphabet in the table is called the ASCII alphabet and

TABLE 1.1 ASC II ALPHABET

Character	Byte	Character	Byte	Character	Byte
Space	040	@	100	`	140
!	041	A	101	a	141
"	042	B	102	b	142
#	043	C	103	c	143
$	044	D	104	d	144
%	045	E	105	e	145
&	046	F	106	f	146
'	047	G	107	g	147
(	050	H	110	h	150
)	051	I	111	i	151
*	052	J	112	j	152
+	053	K	113	k	153
,	054	L	114	l	154
−	055	M	115	m	155
.	056	N	116	n	156
/	057	O	117	o	157
0	060	P	120	p	160
1	061	Q	121	q	161
2	062	R	122	r	162
3	063	S	123	s	163
4	064	T	124	t	164
5	065	U	125	u	165
6	066	V	126	v	166
7	067	W	127	w	167
8	070	X	130	x	170
9	071	Y	131	y	171
:	072	Z	132	z	172
;	073	[	133	{	173
<	074	\	134	|	174
=	075	]	135	}	175
>	076	↑	136	~	176
?	077	←	137	delete	177

is an international standard. The byte code is obtained by extending the number of bits to 9 and fixing the two leftmost bits at 0. The 9 bits are represented as 3 octal (base 8) digits. The alphabet for the octal number system is 0, 1, 2, 3, 4, 5, 6, and 7. For example, q is 161 (octal) is 001 110 001 (binary). Its 7-bit representation is 1 110 001.

While this has become a standard mapping of characters into bytes, others are possible. For example, we may require all representations to be of the same length to facilitate counting off. When a string of characters maps into a string of bytes, the transform of the lth character is found by a simple multiplication, the lth character is bits $7 \times (l - 1) + 1$ through $7 \times l$. However, we could map characters into words of different length with lengths proportional to the frequency of occurrence of the characters in texts. Savings in the number of bits required to represent a long text can be achieved at the expense of ease of locating the character in the lth place. Such a coding is treated in Chapter 4.

The same problem presents itself when we encounter any nonhomogeneity in organization of data: nonhomogeneity requires either:

1. An imbedding in a homogeneous representation with the resultant waste of bits but providing ease of access through a simple arithmetic pattern or
2. An efficient use of bits in representation coupled with a more difficult task of identifying and locating the separate parts.

This problem of efficient representation is so fundamental to algorithm organization that we will call it the *data representation problem*, and we will return to it repeatedly, since it exposes the trade-off between time (ease of locating) and storage (number of bits used) whose management is a major engineering component of all algorithm design.

We are not going to give more of a formal definition to homogeneity of data than to say that a collection of data is homogeneous of order P if each datum in the collection has $K \geq P$ properties and there are P properties having identical values for all the data.

A variable whose domain consists of arrays is called an array variable. Each entry in the array is called a component. An example of an array value is (1, 5, 7, 11), and to emphasize the array character (ordered and homogeneous) we use the notation [1, 5, 7, 11] for the value. Another example is [[1, 2], [2, 4], [5, −6]], which we often write as a *matrix:*

$$\begin{bmatrix} 1 & 2 \\ 2 & 4 \\ 5 & -6 \end{bmatrix}$$

Suppose we have an array variable x whose value is [1, 5, 9, 11]. We write: x is [1, 5, 9, 11]. If we wish to give x a new value, we write $x \leftarrow [2, -7, 10, 4]$. We often wish to focus on one of the components of the value of x, and we use subscripts for this. Thus, if x is $[2, -7, 10, 4]$, then $x[3]$ <u>is</u> 10. If each component of x is itself an array, we use two subscripts to focus on each value. Thus,

$$\text{If } x \text{ is } \begin{bmatrix} 1 & 5 & 6 \\ 2 & -4 & 10 \\ 3 & 11 & 4 \end{bmatrix}, \text{ then } x[2, 3] \text{ } \underline{\text{is}} \text{ } 10.$$

Clearly, this approach can be extended to situations in which x is an array whose components are arrays, and so on. The use of arrays is most facilitated by the use of subscripts, which are *themselves* variables, whose domain is the integers. Thus suppose x <u>is</u> $[2, 27, 10, 4]$ and i <u>is</u> 3, then $x[i]$ is $x[3]$ <u>is</u> 10. Consequently, assigning different values to i permits us to focus on different components of x by virtue of their positions in the array.

　　Now let us return to the algorithm for summing integers. We may now write an algorithm for summing any collection of N integers (the value of N tells us how many integers we wish to sum) organized as the components of an array X (Algorithm 1).

Algorithm 1:

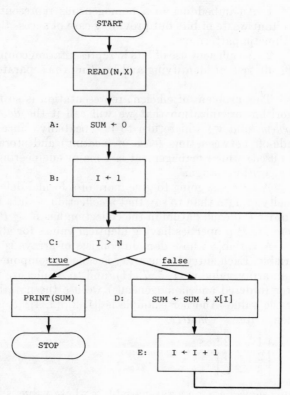

Algorithms may be represented in many ways as flowcharts. When the number of steps is small and the eye can easily scan the chart, the representation given by Algorithm 1 is the one most commonly used. For very complicated charts and for those in which the individual actions are quite complex the representation given by Figure 1.1 is often used as, for example, for Algorithm 1.

The advantage of this notation is that the statements may be quite lengthy and still not obscure one's view of the flow of control in the algorithm. This representation will prove to be particularly useful when we first sketch out an algorithm and are not quite sure precisely how we wish to express a particular action. Associated with the algorithm is an organized commentary:

1. Input the value of N and the values of the N numbers $X[1]$, $X[2]$, . . . , $X[N]$.
2. The variable SUM is initialized to 0.
3. The variable I is simultaneously a counter, telling how many values have been added, and an index, identifying which component of X is to be added. Its initial value is 1, so that step 6 will initially utilize $X[1]$.
4. If $I > N$, then we will have summed all N numbers, and we should print the result, the value of SUM, and STOP as shown in step 5.

```
1.  READ (N,X)
2.  SUM ← 0
3.  I ← 1
4.  I > N
5.  PRINT (SUM)
6.  SUM ← SUM + X[I]
7.  I ← I + 1
```

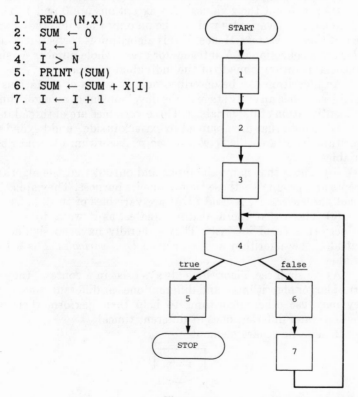

Figure 1.1

6. If we are not done, SUM should be augmented by the value $X[I]$.
7. Having added the Ith component of X, $X[I]$, augment the index by 1 to deal with the next element of X, following which we go back to step 4.

The reader must become aware sooner or later that flowcharts are not what computers execute. Computers execute programs written as text organized in a sequence of sentences. However, the text is often easiest to create from a flowchart. In that sense a flowchart is a convenient intermediate representation for the description of algorithms. Flowcharts have so few distinctive "parts of speech" that their understanding is not dependent on their notation. While several "standards" have been proposed, none are widely accepted, and each reader might wish to develop his own flowchart notation. That which is used here is merely exemplary of the wide variety of available notations.

Let us pay close attention to Algorithm 1, for if we understand it, programming will become possible for us; if we do not, programming will remain a mystery.

1. Note that, with two exceptions, only variables appear in the algorithm, and not their values. The exceptions are 0 and 1. These are the names of variables which take on only the value they name. We call them *constants*. Hence, if this algorithm is correct, it will be so for *every* collection of N integers for every whole number N, since no special mention is made of the individual members.

An algorithm can be described only in terms of operations on variables. Hence an early stage in the development of an algorithm is the identification of its variables. These variables are of three kinds:

(a) Those that are assumed to exist "outside" and beyond the algorithm. They are called *global variables*. Algorithm 1 has no global variables.

(b) Those that name the input and output that the algorithm accepts and produces—those that define its purpose. They are called *formal parameters*. N, X, and SUM are variables of this kind.

(c) Those that the algorithm creates, as it were, to assist in the performance of its task. They generally have no significance "outside" the algorithm and are called *local variables*. I is a local variable.

As we shall see, algorithms always exist in a context, they are part of larger algorithms—and different ones at different times—and they may use other algorithms to help them perform their own function—and different ones at different times!

2. The flowchart element

presents a choice between two alternatives. If $I > N$, then the true path is followed, else the false path is followed.

3. The use of variables and choices permits the existence of a cycle or loop in the algorithm so that the length of the description of the algorithm is not necessarily proportional to the number of steps executed. Indeed, the steps labeled D and E in Table 1.1 are written once and executed N times. We will observe that a good many of the loops we encounter contain an initialization, a test (or choice), and an increment or decrement on the value of the variable initialized and participating in the test.

4. The variable SUM accumulates the sum of the N integers, adding to itself one new value each passage through the loop, until all N numbers have been added.

The structures that appear in flowcharts are as follows.

Any number of ↓ can enter any of the last three named structures. The "action" is the assignment of a (new) value to a variable, the reading (entering) of input, or the producing (printing) of output. A fourth action, called *execute procedure* or, more briefly, *procedure call*, or *call* for short, will soon be introduced. The "relation" is between the values of two arithmetic expressions.

A fifth structure, called a goto or *jump*, often proves useful. Imagine that every flowchart structure can have a unique label attached to it, represented as

Then 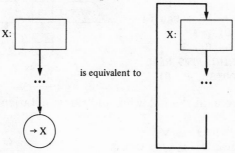 meaning goto X, is equivalent to an entry arrow to the action labeled by X. For example,

The goto is quite useful in the creation of *switches*. Let us define a switch as a vector of labels, such as FAN ← ONE, IMAG

NULL, NORMAL. Then 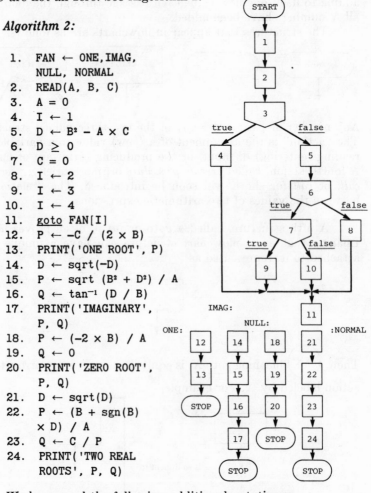 → FAN[J]   will cause a goto ONE or

goto IMAG or goto NULL or goto NORMAL, depending on whether J is 1, 2, 3, or 4, respectively.

Consider an algorithm for computing the two roots P and Q of a quadratic equation $Ax^2 + 2Bx + C = 0$. Assume that A, B, and C are not all zero. See Algorithm 2.

Algorithm 2:

```
1.  FAN ← ONE,IMAG,
    NULL, NORMAL
2.  READ(A, B, C)
3.  A = 0
4.  I ← 1
5.  D ← B² – A × C
6.  D ≥ 0
7.  C = 0
8.  I ← 2
9.  I ← 3
10. I ← 4
11. goto FAN[I]
12. P ← –C / (2 × B)
13. PRINT('ONE ROOT', P)
14. D ← sqrt(–D)
15. P ← sqrt (B² + D²) / A
16. Q ← tan⁻¹ (D / B)
17. PRINT('IMAGINARY',
    P, Q)
18. P ← (–2 × B) / A
19. Q ← 0
20. PRINT('ZERO ROOT',
    P, Q)
21. D ← sqrt(D)
22. P ← (B + sgn(B)
    × D) / A
23. Q ← C / P
24. PRINT('TWO REAL
    ROOTS', P, Q)
```

We have used the following additional notation:

$$sqrt(f) \text{ is } \sqrt{f}$$
$$(y \text{ is } tan^{-1} (f)) \text{ is } (f \text{ is } tan (y))$$

An interesting issue is raised in the formula tan (D/B). If

$B = 0$, then Q is $\pi/2$, but D/B cannot be defined. Hence it would be appropriate to test B *before* defining Q.

$$sgn(f) \text{ is } \begin{cases} 1 \text{ if } f > 0 \\ 0 \text{ if } f = 0 \\ -1 \text{ if } f < 0 \end{cases}$$

The switch provides a nice means of separating the cases that must be considered one by one. Use of goto structures allows every algorithm to be "linearly" represented, which turns out to be important in enabling computers actually to execute algorithms.

Where do algorithms come from? Laying out an algorithm is only possible if we have one, and we really don't have one if we can't lay it out! An algorithm is a synthesis whose development proceeds apace with some description of it. This process, involving both inductive and deductive thought, is not identical for all people. Algorithms are not, for a given problem, unique. This makes it very difficult—nevertheless important—to be able to compare different algorithms for performing the same task. The comparison is only partly quantitative. Properties we tend to compare include the following.

1. EXECUTION TIME. How many "steps" are required to execute the algorithm? This is usually given as a function of the data of the algorithm.

2. STORAGE. How many variables are required during the execution of the algorithm? In particular, what is the maximum number of variables required at any stage of the algorithm execution?

3. DESCRIPTION LENGTH. How long is the description?

We tend to compare also some less quantitative properties:

4. HOW DOES IT GENERALIZE? Almost every algorithm created for solving one task can be modified to solve a more general task, including the original task as a special case.

5. HOW DOES IT FIT? Almost every algorithm is useful as a part of some "larger" algorithm. Or, put another way, every task is potentially a subtask for some as yet undetermined larger task. One often is reminded that "everything is a special case of something more general." However, generality is not obtained without cost. We acquire generality through the replacement of constants by variables; each increase in the generality requires an assignment of value to these same variables, and this assignment adds to the work of the algorithm. Very often this is revealed as an initialization, or "fitting" phase, of an algorithm.

Programming—the creating of algorithms—is a complex activity that has interrelated synthetic and analytic phases. No adequate set of rules exists that, if followed, creates good, correct algorithms, just as no rules exist that, if followed, guarantee the solution of problems. Still, there are some rules that help.

1. Comprehend the problem. Sometimes the comprehension isolates a more general problem easier to solve than the original and whose solution includes that of the original.

2. Isolate an algorithm and represent it.

3. Test it on some sample data to justify its correctness, and attempt to show it is correct by some method of proof that does not explicitly depend on the choice of the test data. Testing may reveal the presence of errors, but it rarely shows their complete absence.

4. Part of the comprehension of the problem is arrived at through the awareness that a problem is solved by solving sub-problems and that an algorithm is composed of subalgorithms. In this way problems are solved through decomposition and recom-position. Rules 1 to 3 are applied to the whole, to its parts, and possibly to their parts, etc.

5. At some stage in the development of the algorithm repre-sentation, or program, one becomes aware of the vicissitudes of choice—the many ways to skin a cat. Some programmers respond by choosing programs that are clever and unusually compact, by using, for example, one variable to represent unrelated quantities at different stages of the algorithm execution. Others are motivated by clarity and an exposure of structure, so that understanding, im-provement, and extension are most easily forthcoming. In the last analysis the resolution of these conflicts isolates an esthetics of programming.

6. In acquiring experience we shall develop a multitude of techniques for handling commonly occurring algorithmic situations. Error-free use of these techniques should be one of our goals.

Let us consider the case of cycles or loops. We shall find that many of our cycles involve a counter and have the following:

An initialization of the counter
An increment (or decrement) of the counter
A test of the counter against an upper (or lower) limit
A computation around which the above are organized; an example of a typical cycle is given in (1.3).

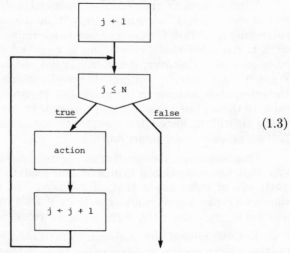

(1.3)

Now note that we go through the cycle N times for $N \geq 0$. In particular, we go through it zero times for $N = 0$. Often it is convenient to combine the three cycle actions into one box:

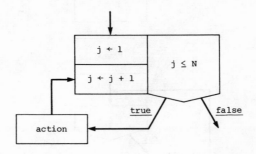

Now let us consider a few examples that contain cycles:

Example 1: To compute a^n for n, an integer.
Since n, though an integer, is variable, we cannot write

$$a \times a \times a \times \cdots \times a$$

The $\cdots$ are not legal. What does it mean after all? To clarify, we develop a cycle by observing the pattern

$$P_0 \leftarrow 1$$
$$P_1 \leftarrow P_0 \times a$$

and finally

$$P_n \leftarrow P_{n-1} \times a$$

Since we compute these values sequentially and each P_k, $1 \leq k \leq n$, is used only in the very next step, we may write:

$$P \leftarrow 1$$
$$P \leftarrow P \times a \qquad \text{repeated } n \text{ times}$$

that leads to the flowchart Figure 1.2.

Loops surround an algorithmic form whose computational structure is invariant with respect to the number of times the loop is traversed. This invarient captures the purpose of a loop. Thus, in Algorithm 1 the invariant is $\text{SUM} \leftarrow \text{SUM} + X[i]$, and in the last flowchart it is $P \leftarrow P \times a$.

Suppose, however, $n < 0$. Then the algorithm grows a tail, as in Algorithm 3. NOTE: $|n|$ is the absolute value of n.

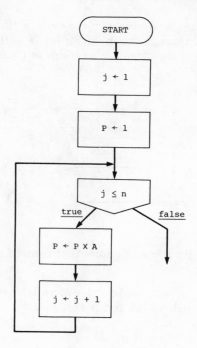

Figure 1.2

Algorithm 3:

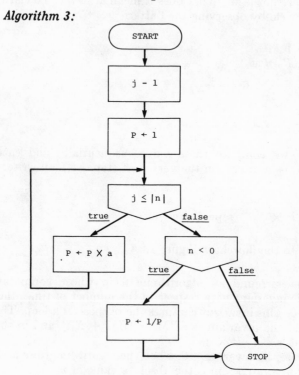

The condition that controls a loop may not explicitly depend on a counter variable. The loop may terminate as soon as a relation becomes <u>false</u>. The structure of such a loop is:

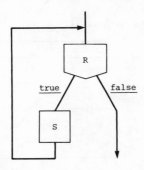

We shall call such a loop a *while* loop: it represents <u>while</u> R <u>do</u> S, since cycling continues while the relation R remains true. For example, Newton's method for computing the square root of a number $a \geq 0$ to an approximation E is describable by Figure 1.3 by utilizing a *while* loop.

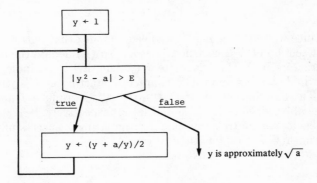

Figure 1.3

Example 2: Suppose we have a character string U. We wish to find where another character string V first occurs in U.

An example helps. Suppose U <u>is</u> CATATARAN and V <u>is</u> ATAR. V certainly occurs in U. To know where it first occurs, it is sufficient to give the leftmost position in U where the match with V begins. Thus we give 4 as the answer, it being reasonable to number the positions in U and V from left to right and starting at 1. However, suppose V had been ATRA. Then no match with U would have been possible. In such case we shall use the convention: Give 0 as the answer.

The simplest way to solve the problem is to slide V along U, V being compared to successive 4-character sections (substrings) of U, until a match is found or it is determined that no match exists.

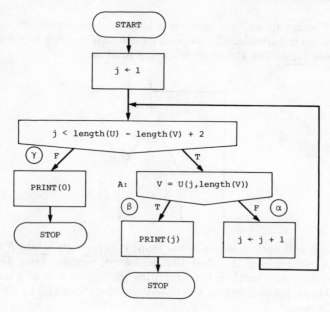

Figure 1.4

Since we slide V along U, we need an index that tells where the current section of U commences. Let length (V) denote the number of characters in V. Let us write $U(j, \text{length}(V))$ to indicate the section in U having length(V) characters starting at U's jth character. The flowchart is Figure 1.4. NOTE: We introduce T and F as obvious abbreviations for <u>true</u> and <u>false</u>, respectively.

The loop α controls the slide for comparing V successfully with $U(1, \text{length}(V))$, $U(2, \text{length}(V))$, etc.

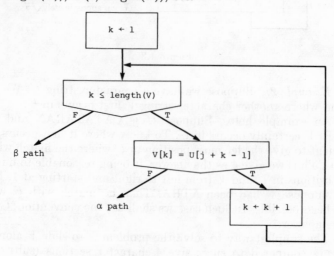

Figure 1.5

The exit β occurs for the first j at which a match is possible.

The exit γ occurs when all feasible j values have been exhausted (in our example there is no point in testing $j > 6$).

The box A contains a test that we can (and often must) further decompose so that we test only equality of characters and not strings. We may replace box A by a loop, as shown in Figure 1.5.

We exit on the β path if *all* characters of V equal their corresponding characters in the U segment. We exit on the α path if at least one character of V does not equal its U correspondent. This is a typical loop structure that arises when we are testing for a "conjunction": a is true and b is true and c is true, etc., where a, b, and c are conditions.

The approach to developing a flowchart by successive expansions of actions and conditions, the "outsider-in" approach, is of great value in organizing algorithms for complicated problems.

Example 3:   In how many ways may one make N cents from coins of denomination 1, 5, 10, 25, and 50 cents?

As in the previous example, we seek a pattern for solving this problem as a sequence of simpler problems that have the same structure as the original. To what problems do we already know the answers? Clearly, one may make N cents from 1¢ pieces in just one way for any $N > 0$. How about using only 1¢ and 5¢ pieces? If N were 17, and if we were to use, say, three 5¢ pieces, then $N - 15$ is the amount to be made by using only 1¢ pieces. Now we have before us the gist of the solution. To express its general form requires the use of some notation. Let $X(N, q)$ mean the number of ways of making N cents from coins of denomination $\leq q$ cents. Then the problem asks us to find $X(N, 50)$. Using this notation, we can express our solution as

$$X(N, 50) = X(N, 25) + X(N - 50, 25) + \cdots$$
$$+ X(N - K \times 50, 25)$$

This equation says that what we seek is the sum of the number of ways using

$$0 \text{ half-dollars: } X(N, 25)$$
$$\text{and} \quad 1 \text{ half-dollars: } X(N - 50, 25)$$
$$\text{and} \quad 2 \text{ half-dollars: } X(N - 100, 25)$$
$$\cdots$$
$$\text{and} \quad K \text{ half-dollars: } X(N - K \times 50, 25)$$

There are those $\cdots$ again, and what is K? Clearly, K is the largest integer satisfying

$$K \times 50 \leq N < (K + 1) \times 50$$

Here K is the largest number of 50¢ pieces, the value of which is $\leq N$; K is the integer quotient of $N/50$. We often write this as $[N/50]$ or entier $(N/50)$ or $\lfloor N/50$. Actually, if $N = k \times 50 + R$,

$0 \le R < 50$, then the last term in the sum is $X(N - K \times 50, S)$, where S is the largest coin $\le R$. If $R = 0$, then $X(N - K \times 50, 0) = 1$. (Why?) Our flowchart is:

Algorithm 4:

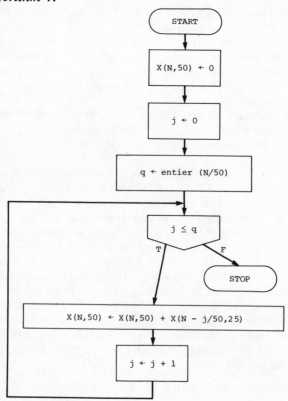

The flowchart looks reasonable, but is it?

To compute $X(N, 50)$ we must have *already* computed $X(N - 50, 25)$, $X(N - 100, 25)$, etc. But each of these computations requires the *same* flowchart as $X(N, 50)$ with 25 replacing 50 and $N - 50$ replacing N, etc. And, of course, when we process the flowchart for $X(N - 50, 25)$, we will need to compute, among others, $X(N - 50 - 25, 10)$, etc. This repeated postponement of the required result while we "descend" to do similar subproblems is called, in programming, the use of *recursion*. Within a flowchart a required computation of the same function as that which the whole flowchart computes indicates that the flowchart describes a recursive computation. In order that this descent may not spiral indefinitely, there must be at least one path in the chart leading to the STOP that does not require a reinitiation of the entire flowchart on the same function, albeit with different arguments. Recursion requires "descent" followed by "ascent," the latter occurring when we have found for our problem the $X(U, V)$ for some U and V that we had needed but did not yet have. In using our recursive model we have gained simplification at the expense of an added complication: while it is true that each "descent" uses the same elevator, as it were, we must remember, when we go down, to which floor to return when we go back up, that is, to what subproblem we have just found a solution.

A little thought will show us that we *always* ascend (return) with the answer to the last problem that forced us to descend: the elevator stops at every floor on the way up.

To keep matters straight, we must remember with which N, J, and q we are contending. To see that there are several of each of these variables, imagine that you can "explode" the algorithm by substituting for $X(N - j \times 50, 25)$ the algorithm that computes it, properly removing the new START and STOP that have been introduced. Now there are two of each of the variables! We shall shortly see that it is very easy to keep track of which version of j we are dealing with by using something called a "stack." To capture the idea of descent and ascent let us extend our flowchart notation somewhat, as follows.

In place of START let us permit the use of the box ENTER $F(U, V, W)$, meaning: The chart that follows computes the function F with the values of the parameters U, V, and W to be supplied whenever we wish to execute the function F. Then we can merely say, in some flowchart box, $F(R, S, T)$, and the values of R, S, and T will be assigned to U, V, and W, respectively, and the flowchart for F will be executed with these assignments.

In the action

$$X \leftarrow W + F(R, S, T) \times V$$

the multiplication cannot be done until the value of $F(R, S, T)$ has been obtained. That value will be supplied as the result of the execution of $F(R, S, T)$, after which the multiplication and then the addition may be done. To specify the result of F the STOP in its flowchart will be replaced by RETURN (H), meaning that on arrival at this box the current flowchart execution terminates with its result the value of H. Thus, when a RETURN (H) is reached, the value H is returned as the result of the execution of F that led to the RETURN in question.

Let us then rewrite Algorithm 4 as Algorithm 5. Next smallest (C) is the largest coin smaller than C; for example, next smallest $(50) = 25$, next smallest $(10) = 5$, next smallest $(5) = 1$. Note that if $C = 1$, next smallest (C) will never get executed, so next smallest (1) need not be defined!

While this flowchart is structurally simple, following its course of action is tedious, but not terribly difficult if we use a programming structure called a *stack*. We shall explore the role of a stack as it is used in this example. Let us list the variables of the flowchart: N, C, P, j, and q, and the result, in this case the argument associated with

Algorithm 5:

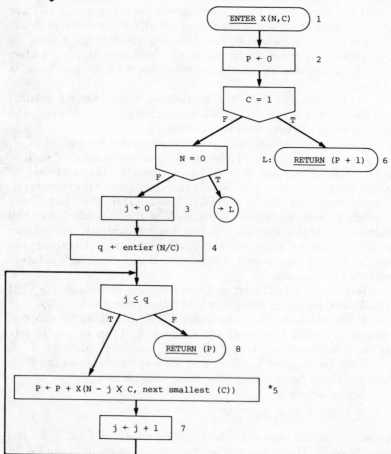

RETURN. Each time we suspend execution of the flowchart to start over again (in the box tagged with *), a new *incarnation* of these variables is created. The values of the previous incarnation are hidden away or shadowed, only to be resumed when the new incarnation is no longer needed or, that is, when the execution in which the current incarnation was created has been completed. Let us make a table where (a) each row denotes a step in the computation and (b) the variables are named as column heads and the table entries are values of the variables, the name of the step being executed and an integer representing the incarnation. Let us call the original incarnation 0 and trace through the calculation of $X(17, 10)$. We can see that the calculation follows a pattern:

$$X(17, 10) = X(17, 5) + X(7, 5)$$
$$X(17, 5) = X(17, 1) + X(12, 1) + X(7, 1) + X(2, 1) = 4$$
$$X(7, 5) = X(7, 1) + X(2, 1) = 2$$
$$\therefore X(17, 10) = 6$$

Examination of this pattern reveals why there are two <u>RETURN</u> boxes in the flowchart. One is for completing the computation $X(N, 1)$ whose value is 1 (box 6) for any N, and the other (box 8) is for completing the evaluation of the sum

```
X(N, next smallest (C)) + X(N - C, next smallest (C))
+ · · · X(N - j × C, next smallest (C)) + · · · +
X(N - ⌊(N/C) × C, next smallest (C))
```

The final result is 6, as Table 1.2 shows.

There is not only one variable P, but one for each incarnation or, as we say in programming, one for each *level of recursion*. Let us look at the "history" of the variable P. Each time we do $X(N, C)$, a new P is defined or, as we say in programming, *declared*. Each time we return from an execution of $X(N, C)$, having completed a round-trip excursion as it were, the *previous* incarnation of P is reinstated with its attached value, and all incarnations extant during the excursion are gone, erased, wiped out, destroyed, and expunged. At any one time *only one* value of P is accessible; earlier ones are shadowed, and later ones have been destroyed. This birth-death behavior is neatly captured in a stack. The appropriateness of this term can be appreciated by visualizing the cafeteria stack used for holding plates, as diagrammed in the figure.

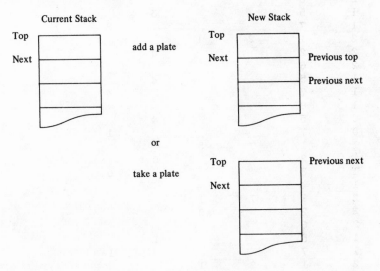

In this problem, how many incarnations can exist? Examining Table 1.1 we see that in the computation of $X(N, C)$ the maximum number of incarnations, n, is the number of coins less than or equal to C. For the Example 3 incarnations (0, 1, 2) are required for the 10¢, 5¢, and 1¢ coins.

Since we know the (maximum) possible number of incarnations of all the variables, we can actually construct a flowchart that does

TABLE 1.2

Incar- nation	Flow- chart Step	N	C	P	j	q	Result Returned
0	1	17	10				
0	2			0			
0	3				0		
0	4					1	
1	1	17	5				
1	2			0			
1	3				0		
1	4					3	
2	1	17	1				
2	2			0			
2	6						1
1	5			1			
1	7				1		
2	1	12	1				
2	2			0			
2	6						1
1	5			2			
1	7				2		
2	1	7	1				
2	2			0			
2	6						1
1	5			3			
1	7				3		
2	1	2	1				
2	2			0			
2	6						1
1	5			4			
1	7				4		
1	8						4
0	5			4			
0	7				1		
1	1	7	5				
1	2			0			
1	3				0		
1	4					1	
2	1	7	1				
2	2			0			
2	6						1
1	5			1			
1	7				1		
2	1	2	1				
2	2			0			
2	6						1
1	5			2			
1	7				2		
1	8						2
0	5			6			
0	7				2		
0	8						6

not use <u>ENTER</u> and <u>RETURN</u>, because we can fold in the flow-chart for computing $X(N, C)$ into box * in Algorithm 5, and this will require 8 insertions for $X(17, 10)$, whereas if we were to compute $X(35, 25)$, then 26 insertions would be required. However, this is a fruitless exercise, because the flowchart itself expands with different values of N and C. Hence Algorithm 5 must be changed into a flowchart that is both not recursive and does not change with N and C; see (1.4).

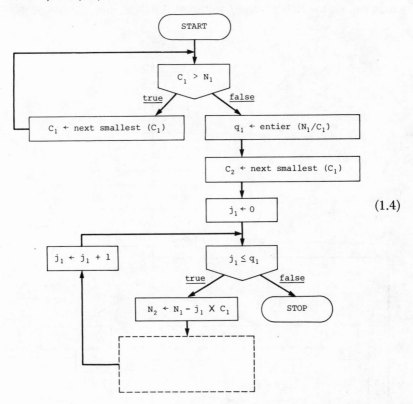

(1.4)

The interior of the dashed-line box accumulates the value of the terms $X(N_1, \text{next smallest } (C_1)) + X(N_1 - C_1, \text{next smallest } (C_1)) + \cdots + X(N_1 - q_1C_1, \text{next smallest } (C_1))$, one at a time. Each of those is computed by the same algorithm and, of course, each is the same, as we have already seen, as the entire Algorithm 5 with the value of N and C in $X(N, C)$ being different, which difference we emphasize by the use of subscripts in N_2, C_2, C_3, etc. Furthermore this folding into the dashed-line box continues until next smallest $(C_4) = 1$, when the box becomes merely $P \leftarrow P + 1$. Let $M(C)$ be the number of coin denominations. Hence this flow-chart "nests" within the dashed-line box exactly $M(C) - 2$ times as the full algorithm and once as $P \leftarrow P + 1$ and does not otherwise depend on the initial values of N and C.

But this is still unsatisfactory, since whenever we change M, that is, go to a new denominational system, a new flowchart must be constructed. However, this too can be corrected, since all nestings (except the innermost) are the same. Let us just introduce a counter j that tells which coin denomination we are considering and make all variables, except P and j, vectors having $M - 1$ components. Let index denote which coin (through its position in the vector C) is the largest to be used from among the elements of C. In the next flowchart the vector K holds the j values at different incarnation levels.

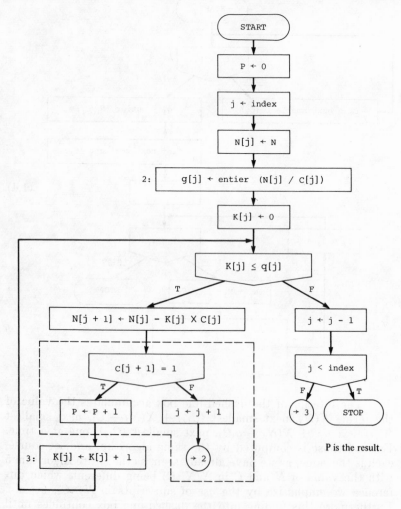

P is the result.

An even shorter algorithm using only one stack variable, $M[j]$, can be derived from the preceding one; see Algorithm 6. We have explicitly included READ and PRINT actions in this algorithm. This algorithm lacks *comment*. We supply comment by adding three levels of information, as follows.

Algorithm 6:

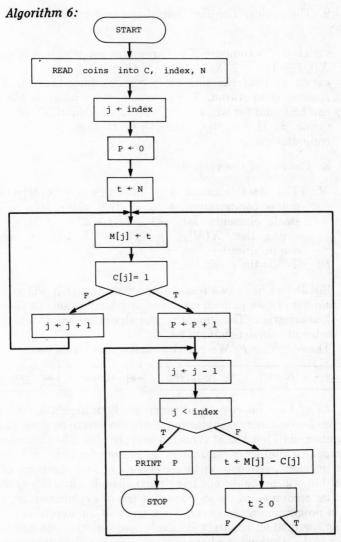

1. The algorithm (via an example: N is 11, index is 3, and C is 50, 25, 10, 5, 1) computes:

$$X(11, 10) = X(11, 5) + X(1, 5)$$
$$X(11, 5) = X(11, 1) + X(6, 1) + X(1, 1)$$
$$X(11, 1) = 1$$
$$X(6, 1) = 1$$
$$X(1, 1) = 1$$
$$X(11, 5) = 3$$
$$X(1, 5) = X(1, 1)$$
$$X(1, 1) = 1$$
$$X(1, 5) = 1$$
$$X(11, 10) = 3 + 1 = 4$$

2. The cycles: The flowchart has three cycles denoted α, β, and γ.

CYCLE α: To compute $X(t, j)$ requires computation of each of $X(t, j + 1)$, $\cdots$ $X(t, n)$, where $C(n)$ is 1.

CYCLE γ: Find the smallest $j \geq$ index for which an $X(t, j)$ requires computation. The algorithm stops when no $j \geq$ index can be found for which $X(t, j)$ requires computation.

CYCLE β: If $t = M[j] - C[j] \geq 0$, then an $X(t, j)$ requires computation.

3. The role of the variables:

M: The stack element $M[j]$ indicates that $X(M[j], j)$ requires computation; t carries that value $M[j]$ to other stack elements $M[j + 1]$, $M[j + 2]$ $\cdots$ $M[n]$, indicating that $X(M[j], j + 1)$ $\cdots$ $X(M[j], n)$ require computation:

P: Totals the result.

Finally we have two reasonable algorithms that will work for any number of coin denominations of any kind as long as there is a unit denomination. The inputs to the algorithm are N and C and the vector of coin denominations.

The output is P. We can thus make of it a function:

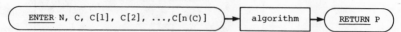

As we have improved and generalized our algorithm, its structure has become more complicated, more obvious to us since we have programmed it, but less obvious to everyone else. The algorithm has undergone a number of mutations, the reasons for which are obvious only through participation in its evolution; and the users of this algorithm will probably not have participated. Thus the evolution must be accompanied by an increased use of explanation or, as we say in programming, *comment*. Most users of an algorithm are unwilling, or unable, to study its evolution, but they do appreciate access to descriptions of what is occurring in the algorithm they use. While some commentary exterior to the algorithm is always required, commentary within the algorithm description is very valuable. What should it say and where should it be placed?

Too much comment is almost as painful as too little comment is frustrating. Comment that is limited to a rephrasing of local actions is a useless bore. But, then, what guides the creation of good comment? The answer is simple: a good algorithm, if we agree that by "good" we mean "clearly understandable." Very often the other use of *good*, meaning "efficient," works against easy understanding, as the preceding algorithm development illustrates.

A useful approach is to start the creation process from the commentary from which the specific algorithm is ultimately created: an algorithm that is amply explained is simply structured. Commentary can aid the creator as well as the ultimate user. Like algorithms, commentary can also be created as an "exploding structure."

Comment should be tied to important changes in the information state of an algorithm: where a crucial variable attains a new value, where a control branch occurs, or where a call on a function occurs. Cycles should be clearly isolated so they may be parenthesized by pithy comment. The practice of jumping into the interior of cycles other than through their beginnings should be discouraged.

In some sense an efficient algorithm may be characterized as one in which each step participates in a large number of control paths. Such an algorithm may also be a bad algorithm in the sense that it would be difficult to comment on it clearly.

Really there are only two tests of good commentary: (a.) Can another programmer create the program (or one like it) from some level of supplied commentary, and not necessarily have to create it in the same language as that in which the algorithm is written? (b.) Can a nonprogrammer who understands the problem follow the algorithm in, at least, its grossest details?

Any algorithm describes how a task is accomplished, but it does not tell why it is being accomplished or what is being accomplished. Answers to these questions are to be found, if at all, in larger algorithms that utilize the given one. Similarly, in creating the comment for an algorithm, several representations are useful, each possibly accenting a different aspect of the algorithm. Let us consider a commentary of Algorithm 6.

The data are the set of coins, M in number, ordered in decreasing values, index, the index of the largest coin that may be used, and N, the amount in coin units from which we are to compute P, the number of ways of making N coin units from coins of denomination $C[index]$, $C[index + 1]$, $\cdots$ $C[M]$.

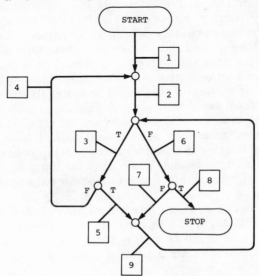

1. P, j, and $N[j]$ have been initialized.

   Example: j is index is 3 $N[j]$ is $N[3]$ is 17.

2. The number $q[j]$ is the number of coins of denomination $C[j]$ contained in $N[j]$; $K[j]$ is initialized to 0, that is, we take no coins of type $C[j]$.

   Example: $C[j]$ is $C[3]$ is 10, $N[j]$ is 17, and $q[j]$ is $q[3]$ is 1.

3. $N[j + 1]$ is the remainder after using $K[j]$ coins of denomination $C[j]$ to make $N[j]$.

   Example: j is 4, $K[4]$ is 2, $N[j]$ is $N[4]$ is 17, and $N[5]$ is 17.

4. $C[j + 1]$ is not 1, so we know that $N[j + 1]$ is not 1 and must now be calculated; that is, for a new j, $q[j]$ must be computed.

5. $C[j + 1]$ is 1, hence $N[j + 1]$ is 1, hence P is augmented.

6. We are unable to use an additional coin $C[j]$ in making $N[j]$. We would not reach this point unless $X(N[j], C[j])$ were completely calculated and absorbed into P. Hence we proceed to a previous level, $j \leftarrow j - 1$.

7. The new level, with its $N[j]$, $K[j]$, and $C[j]$, may require further removals of a $C[j]$.

8. The new level is < index and hence requires no computation, and we are finished.

9. Prepare to subtract one more $C[j]$ from $N[j]$.

Comment is made in language, usually English. Flowcharts are graphical descriptions of the actions to be performed under the control of the chart. It seems reasonable to use stereotyped statements of control in English to provide an early commentary to an algorithm. We shall underline these control words to emphasize their dual function in commentary. We shall apply these notational ideas in the next example and the next section, where we shall consider in more detail the powerful methods of backtracking and of recursion.

When we turn to the computer to execute our algorithms, exceptional circumstances that might arise due to erroneous input, unusual values of variables that rarely occur, etc., must be processed by the algorithm. How do we develop an algorithm to handle "special" cases? Since there is no general method, some insight will be gained by treating an example: develop an algorithm to compute the score of a tenpin bowling game when the input is a sequence of numbers, that we shall call *drops*, representing the number of pins struck down on successively thrown balls.

For example, we might give the sequence 4, 3, 6, 4, 10, 10, 8, 1, 7, 3, 9, 0, 10, 10, 5, 5, 8. It is natural to represent the data as a vector that we shall call D; $D[7]$ is 8.

The rules for scoring a bowling game are generally given in

terms of frames and drops, and the score is accumulated frame by frame. Hence it seems reasonable that we give an algorithm for partitioning the drops among successive frames.

Algorithm A:

```
Let the current frame be the first frame.
While there are frames to fill, do let the current
frame be filled and move to the next frame.
If the 10th frame is a strike, then let the 11th and
the 12th frames be the next two drops.
Else if the 10th frame is a spare, then let the 11th
frame be the next drop.
```

Algorithm A is expressed in sentential form. The underlined words are control words that have a specific sequencing function. Thus Algorithm A has the flowchart representation shown.

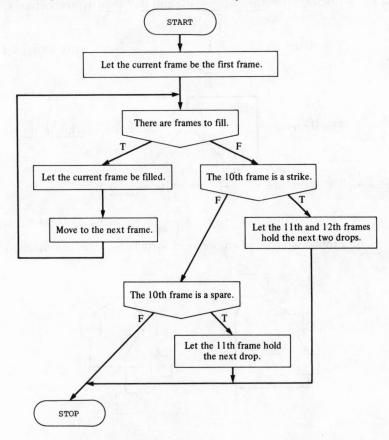

Early in our study of algorithms we commented on the importance of sequencing in an algorithmic description. The use of ordinary English was felt to be cumbersome, primarily because of the difficulty in establishing the precise rules of execution and succession, whereas flowcharts provided us with a representation that emphasized sequencing but had little concern with the contents of the various boxes or steps that were connected together.

Flowcharts emphasized for us both the importance and the simplicity of necessary controls. We can now return to a sentential form of algorithm description that underlines certain words as having a specific control connotation.

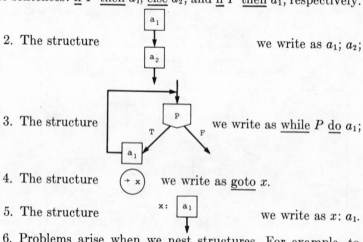

1. The structures   we shall write

as the sentences: $\underline{if}\ P\ \underline{then}\ a_1,\ \underline{else}\ a_2$; and $\underline{if}\ P\ \underline{then}\ a_1$; respectively.

2. The structure   we write as $a_1;\ a_2$;

3. The structure   we write as $\underline{while}\ P\ \underline{do}\ a_1$;

4. The structure   (→ x)   we write as $\underline{goto}\ x$.

5. The structure   x: [a_1]   we write as $x:\ a_1$.

6. Problems arise when we nest structures. For example, to

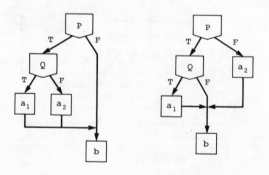

which of the two charts shown does $\underline{if}\ P\ \underline{then}\ \underline{if}\ Q\ \underline{then}\ a_1\ \underline{else}\ a_2$ $\underline{else}\ b$ correspond? We shall introduce either indenting or bracketing to clarify. The former chart would be written

if P then   if P then begin if Q then
    if Q then a_1 or a_1 else a_2 end;
    else a_2; b;
b;

and the latter as

if P then
    if Q then a_1;   or   if P then begin if Q then a_1 end
else a_2;   else a_2;
b; b;

begin end brackets surrounding a set of actions cause them to be considered a *single* action. Note that we use the semicolon as a sentence terminator.

The structure 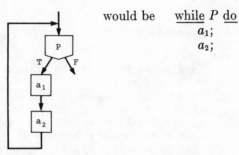 would be   while P do
                                                    a_1;
                                                    a_2;

or while P do begin a_1; a_2 end.

An obvious advantage of the sentential form of the algorithm is that it is written in the form of linear text with indenting and/or begin end playing a control role. Using Algorithm A and begin end we would have the following.

Let the current frame be the first; while there are frames to fill do begin let the current frame be filled; let us move to the next frame end; if the 10th frame is a strike then let the 11th and 12th frames hold the next two drops else if the 10th frame is a spare then let the 11th frame hold the next drop.

The next step in developing our algorithm is to introduce variables and to describe actions on these variables in arithmetic terms. Denote the following:

The sequence of drops by the array $D[1:N]$
The pointer to the current drop by the integer i;
The sequence of frames by the array $B[1:2, 1:N]$;
The pointer to the current frame by the integer f.

We shall use hereafter the following abbreviations:

$x \leftarrow y$ to stand for let x be y,
$x = y$ to stand for x is y.

We may rephrase Algorithm A in more arithmetical terms:

```
i ← 1; f ← 1;
while f ≤ 10 do begin
B[1,f] ← D[1];
if D[i] = 10 then begin
f ← f + 1; i ← i + 1 end
else begin B[2,f] ← D[i + 1];
i ← i + 2; f ← f + 1 end end;
if B[1,10] = 10 then begin B[1,11] ← D[i];
if B[1,11] = 10 then B[1,12] ← D[i + 1]
else B[2,11] ← D[i + 1] end
else if B[1,10] + B[2,10] = 10 then B[1,11] ← D[i] ed
```

Having assigned the drops to frames, we can append the algorithm to compute the score as follows.

Algorithm B:

```
denote the score by the integer s:
s ← 0; f ← 1;
while f ≤ 10 do begin
if B[1,f] = 10 then begin
if B[1,f + 1] = 10 then s ← s + 20 + B[1,f + 2]
else s ← s + 10 + B[1,f + 1] + B[2,f + 2] end
else if B[1,f] + B[2,f] = 10 then s ←
s + 10 + B[1,f + 1]
else s ← s + B[1,f] + B[2,f];
f ← f + 1 end
```

Instead of Algorithms A and B we can compute the score directly from the drop sequence D and bypass the need for the frame array B, giving Algorithm C.

Algorithm C:

```
s ← 0; f ← 1; i ← 1;
while f ≤ 10 do begin
if D[i] = 10 then begin s ← s + 10 + D[i + 1] +
D[i + 2];
i ← i + 1 end
else if D[i] + D[i + 1] = 10 then begin
s ← s + 10 + D[i + 2]; i ← i + 2 end
else begin s ← s + D[i] + D[i + 1]; i ← i + 2 end;
f ← f + 1 end
```

By combining some common computations, we get another algorithm.

Algorithm D:

```
s ← 0; f ← 1; i ← 1;
while f ≤ 10 do begin
t ← D[i] + D[i + 1];
s ← s + t;
if D[i] = 10 then begin s ← s + D[i + 2];
i ← i + 1 end
else if t = 10 then begin s ← s + D[i + 2];
i ← i + 1 end
else i ← i + 2; f ← f + 1 end
```

Suppose it is possible that the drop sequence does not represent a legal bowling game. For example,

if D contains . . . 7, 4, 10
$$\uparrow$$
$$i$$

the game is not legal if the preceding drops form the beginning of a legal game. A legal game may have anywhere from 11 to 21 drops. What errors may we ask our algorithm to expose?

1. When our algorithm reaches for $D[j]$. It may not be there.
2. A $D[j]$ may not be legal as the jth drop.
3. There may be more drops than needed for a legal game.

We may write an algorithm that merely signals the presence of an error but does not reveal its type or cause.

Algorithm E (skeleton):

```
q ← true;
s ← 0; f ← 1; i ← 1;
while f ≤ 10 ∧ q do begin
{same body as Algorithm D but with a check for errors}
if q then PRINT (s) else PRINT ('ERROR').
```

Here q is called a *logical variable*, and it takes on the value *true* or *false*. The expression $f \leq 10 \wedge q$ has the behavior that it is true only when both $f \leq 10$ and q are true. Any occurrence of an error in the algorithm body will lead to the execution of $q \leftarrow$ *false*. We now give Algorithm E in detail:

Algorithm E:

```
READ(N,D); s ← 0; f ← 1; i ← 1; q ← true;
while f ≤ 10 ∧ q do begin
if i > N − 1 then q ← false
else begin t ← D[i] + D[i + 1]; s ← s + t;
if D[i] = 10 then begin
```

```
if i ≤ N - 2 then begin
s ← s + D[i + 2]; i ← i + 1 end
else q ← false end
else if t = 10 then begin
if i ≤ N - 2 then begin
s ← s D[i + 2]; i ← i + 2 end
else q ← false end
else if t < 10 then i ← i + 2 else q ← false;
f ← f + 1 end end;
if q then PRINT(s)
else begin PRINT('ERROR'); PRINT(i) end
```

Two types of error have been isolated: first, insufficient number of drops and, second, a frame that is not a strike has its two drops totalling more than 10. How could you test for the case of too many drops?

This example nicely illustrates a useful paradigm of algorithm development:

1. Describe the algorithm, using controlled English text.
2. Define the organization of the data and the algorithm variables that identify the data.
3. Define the algorithm in terms of logical and arithmetic operations on the algorithm variables, assuming no errors occur in the data or its processing.
4. Define the error conditions that might arise, and introduce into the algorithm tests for them.

TWO PARADIGMS OF PROGRAMMING: BACKTRACKING AND RECURSION

Programming is the art of organizing computations. When one knows exactly what is to be programmed, a natural strategy is to develop the program by using what is known as a top-down strategy: develop the program as a tree of specializations. As we go deeper in the tree, we make decisions that are more and more detailed but that affect proportionately less and less of the tree. Conversely, as we go up the tree toward the root, we find ourselves generalizing and dealing more abstractly. From the root (the original goal, or what the program is to do), as we move deeper into the tree, nodes represent points of decision and bindings of choice. Ultimately, at the end nodes of the tree, everything is expressed in some algorithmic language in whose terms the program may be executed. The decisions of design are at an end. The die is cast. Of course the refinement must be in all aspects of programming: choice of algorithm, choice of language, and choice of data representation, to say nothing of choice of computer.

Although there are many paradigms for fashioning algorithms

available to the programmer, and we have already used iterative programming, we shall focus our attention on two additional useful paradigms: backtrack programming and recursive programming.

Backtrack programming is a powerful technique to use in solving problems when a simple analytic solution is not known: there is no simple formula whose evaluation will give us the answer. We will appreciate the method by applying it to a well-known problem.

Given a standard 8×8 chessboard, where may we place 8 chess queens upon the board so that none is in a position to be taken by another? Knowing a little chess, we interpret the condition as stating that no row, column, or diagonal is to have more than one queen in it. At least one solution exists, as shown, and it is known

	column number							
	1	2	3	4	5	6	7	8
row number 1				Q				
2						Q		
3								Q
4		Q						
5							Q	
6	Q							
7			Q					
8					Q			

that there are 11 other essentially different solutions. Where did this solution come from? A simple method of solving the problem occurs to us at once.

1. The number of board configurations is finite:

There are 64 places for the first queen,
$\times 63$ " " " second queen
$\times 62$ " " " third queen, . . .

$. . .$
$\times 57$ " " " eighth queen

We write this number as $\sim 1.78 \times 10^{14}$

2. Generate all the board configurations, and select those that satisfy the constraint.

Backtracking is a method of controlled generation of cases that can make it possible to generate *only a small fraction of the alternatives*, but within which a solution, if one exists at all, will be found.

We observe that in the 8-queens problem there are 8 independent columns in which we may assign one or more queens. Let

X_i be the number of the row in which we place the queen in the ith column. The number of configurations is now at most $8^8 = 2^{24}$. We now define a predicate $P(X_1, X_2, \ldots, X_k)$, or $P(k)$, for the first k columns, that tells us whether or not we have a feasible distribution of queens on the first k columns, $1 \leq k \leq 8$. Let $P(k)$ be <u>true</u> if the disposition is acceptable; otherwise, <u>false</u>.

Suppose we have already obtained an acceptable disposition for $k - 1$ columns; then an acceptable choice for X_k leads to $P(k) = P(k - 1) \wedge (X_k \neq X_1) \wedge \cdots \wedge (X_k \neq X_{k-1}) \wedge (|X_k - X_1| \neq k - 1) \wedge \cdots \wedge (|X_k - X_{k-1}| \neq 1)$.

To find a value of X_k for which $P(k)$ is true, we search among the 8 values for X_k. One of two conditions will arise: a value is found that makes $P(k)$ <u>true</u>, or none of the 8 values makes $P(k)$ <u>true</u>. In the first case we progress from k to $k + 1$; we move to the next column. In the second case we regress to column $k - 1$ and seek a different value for X_{k-1} so that $P(k - 1)$ is true and then attempt $P(k)$ again. Of course there may be no acceptable value for X_{k-1} and we must then regress to column $k - 2$, etc.

To prevent repeating unsuccessful trials on successive *regresses* to column j, no value of X_j should be chosen more than once, and every value that X_j may take should be accessible to trial.

The process will terminate in either a *regress* from $k = 1$, which means there is no solution, or a *progress* from $k = 8$, which means we have found a solution. We can now sketch our algorithm:

```
Procedure Q1
k ← 1;
while k ≤ 8 ∧ k ≥ 1 do begin
initialize column (k);
while (~P(k)) ∧ choice available (k) do next (k);
if ~ choice available (k) then regress (k)
else progress (k) end;
if k > 8 then X₁, X₂, . . . ,X₈ is a solution
else "no solution can be found";
```

The algorithm is expressed now in terms of understood, but vaguely defined, actions: initialize column (k), progress (k), regress (k), choice available (k), next (k), "$X_1, X_2, \ldots, X_8$ is a solution" and "no solution can be found." We have already exhibited an expression for $P(k)$ though we may wish to reexpress it.

At some stage of algorithm development it becomes necessary to focus on the representation of data. The programmer may:

1. Choose the representation and directly express, within the algorithm, operations upon it—the algorithm and the representation become interdependent.
2. Leave the issues of data representation and manipulation within the actions that manipulate them. Then changes in data representation will not affect the algorithm.

The second choice is preferable on many grounds: ease of understanding, recovery from errors in choice of representation, ease of generalizing the algorithm, etc.

An obvious data representation is an 8×8 array B to represent the board; $B[i, j] = 1$ if there is a queen in the ith row and jth column and 0 otherwise.

However, the constraints with which $P(k)$ is concerned are easier to compute if we choose a more parsimonious data representation.

Let R be a vector of 8 components:
If there is a queen in row i, then $R[i]$ is 1, else $R[i]$ is 0.

The first ( ) term in $P(k)$ becomes simple. There is a j, $1 \leq j \leq 8$, for which $R[j] = 0$. The second ( ) term in $P(k)$ that computes the diagonal constraint is slightly more complicated to arrange. The square in the ith row and jth column lies on 2 diagonals: $i + j$ = constant (/ diagonal) and $i - j$ = constant (\ diagonal). Hence let us define two vectors, NESW[2:16] and NWSE[−7:7].

If there is a queen in diagonal $i + j = s$ and $i - j = r$, then NESW[s] = NWSE[r] = 1.

In terms of the three vectors R, NESW, and NWSE, $P(k)$ is:

$$P(k - 1) \wedge (\text{There is a } 1 \leq j \leq 8 \text{ for which}$$
$$R[j] = 0 \wedge \text{NESW}[j + k] = 0 \wedge \text{NWSE}[j - k] = 0)$$

With these data choices we see that, working on column k, we march j from 1 to 8, testing $P(k)$. We keep a record of our choice j in $X[k]$ so that, if regress should occur, we need merely do $X[k] \leftarrow X[k] + 1$ to make sure we will never retry a previously used value of $X[k]$ on successive regresses.

We can now write:

```
action initialize (k)
X[k] ← X[k] + 1
predicate P(k)
if R[X[k]] = 0 ∧ NESW[X[k] + k] = 0
∧ NWSE[X[k] - k] = 0 then true
else false
action choice available (k)
X[k] ≤ 8
action next (k)
X[k] ← X[k] + 1
action regress (k)
X[k] ← 0
k ← k - 1
R[X[k]] ← NESW[X[k] + k] ← NWSE[X[k] - k] ← 0
action progress (k)
R[X[k]] ← NESW[X[k] + k] ← NWSE[X[k] - k] ← 1
k ← k + 1
action 'X,  , X₂ . . . . .X₈ is a solution'
PRINT (X)
action 'no solution can be found'
PRINT ('NO SOLUTION EXISTS')
```

We can now produce a rendition of Q1 in which the data representation is explicitly used by every action in the algorithm:

```
Procedure Q2
vectors X,R[1:8], NESW[2:16], NWSE[-7:7];
comment We may assume that X, R, NESW, and NWSE are all
initially zero;
k ← 1;
while k ≤ 8 ∧ k ≥ 1 do begin
X[k] ← X[k] + 1;
while (R[k] = 0 ∧ NESW[X[k] + k] = 0 ∧
NWSE[X[k] - k] = 0 ∧ X[k] ≤ 8) do
X[k] ← X[k] + 1;
if X[k] > 8 then begin comment regress;
X[k] ← 0;
k ← k - 1;
R[X[k]] ← NESW[X[k] + k] ← NWSE[X[k] - k] ← 0 end
else begin comment progress;
R[X[k]] ← NESW[X[k] + k] ← NWSE[X[k] - k] ← 1;
k ← k + 1 end; end;
if k > 8 then PRINT(X)
else PRINT ('NO SOLUTION EXISTS')
```

In more general terms, the backtracking method is applied to problems that can be described as follows:

We have a finite number of sets of objects $A_1, A_2, \ldots, A_N$, each of which has a finite number of elements. We seek a selection a_1 from A_1, a_2 from A_2, . . ., a_N from A_N, for which a predicate $P(a_1, a_2, \ldots, a_N)$ is true.

We construct a set of N partial predicates

$$P(1) = P_1(a_1)$$
$$P(2) = P_2(a_1, a_2)$$
$$\cdots$$
$$P(N) = P_N(a_1, a_2, \ldots, a_N) = P(a_1, a_2, \ldots, a_N)$$

that satisfy

if $P_2(a_1, a_2)$ then $P_1(a_1)$
$\cdots$

and ultimately,

if $P(a_1, a_2, \ldots, a_N)$, then $P_{N-1}(a_1, a_2, \ldots, a_{N-1})$

The selection process is now

choose an a_1 in A for which $P_1(a_1)$ is true

With that a_1 choose an a_2 in A_2 for which $P_2(a_1, a_2)$ is true, etc. The chain of conditions says that if there is an $a_1, a_2, \ldots, a_k$ for which $P(k)$ is true, then $P(k - 1)$ was true with $a_1, a_2, \ldots, a_{k-1}$. Hence, if there is a solution, this method will find it, if we are capable of generating all possible choices of a_i from A_i.

However, note the important fact:

if $\sim P_k(a_1, a_2, \ldots, a_k)$ then $\sim P(a_1, a_2, \ldots, a_N)$

There is no point in extending choices that fail, for some k, to satisfy $P(k)$. This is the secret of the value of this method. Thus if A_1 has 10 elements, A_2 has 10 elements, A_3 has 10 elements, and if, for some a_1 in A_1, $P_1(a_1)$ is false, we need never look at $10 \times 10 = 100$ cases.

It may well be that for a choice of $a_1, a_2, \ldots, a_k$

$P_k(a_1, a_2, \ldots, a_k)$ is <u>true</u>

but no a_{k+1} exists for which

$P_{k+1}(a_1, a_2, \ldots, a_{k+1})$ is <u>true</u>

It is this case for which backtracking is necessary.

The general backtracking algorithm can now be given:

```
Initialize choices for all sets
k ← 1
while k > 0 ∧ k ≤ number of sets do
X[k] ← next member of set(k)
while (~P(X[k]) ∧ choice available (k) do next (k)
if ~ choice available (k) then regress (k)
else progress (k)
if k > number of sets then X[1], X[2], . . . ,
X [number of sets] is a solution.
else there is no solution.
and
regress (k)
initialize choice for set (k)
k ← k - 1
undo consequences of choice of X[k]
and
progress (k):
X[k] is the kth choice
Compute consequences of this choice
k ← k + 1
```

Backtracking is a very general technique, and there are many problems for which it is really the only technique available. However, backtracking algorithms can be very time consuming and should be used with care. Often backtracking algorithms contain special subalgorithms to select the choices on both the progress and regress branches of the algorithm.

Suppose the problem being solved is known to have M solutions. The backtracking algorithm can easily be modified to yield them all. For, having found one solution, merely backtrack to find the next. But often one can find a new solution more easily, given the existence of a solution, than by merely backtracking.

RECURSION

One version of the coin algorithm was recursive: it employed itself, as it were, in its own execution. Many algorithms are most naturally and simply expressed as recursive algorithms. Let us give some examples.

A famous ancient problem is called the Tower of Hanoi. N disks are stacked on one of three spindles. The disks are of decreasing diameter with the largest at the base. Moving but one disk at a time, all N disks are to be transferred to one of the other spindles, but at no step may one find, on any spindle, a disk of smaller diameter lying below one of larger diameter. The accomplishment of this task may be concisely described by a recursive algorithm:

```
algorithm transfer (how many, source, auxiliary,
destination);
if how many = 1 then δ: move top one (source,
destination);
else: α: transfer (how many - 1, source, destination,
          auxiliary);
      β: move top one (source, destination)
      γ: transfer (how many - 1, auxiliary, source,
          destination);
```

The words "how many" specify the number N of disks to be moved from the spindle "source" to the spindle "destination" via the "auxiliary" spindle; "move top one (source, destination)" has the obvious meaning "move the top disk on the spindle 'source' to the spindle 'destination'."

Note that we have underlined the control words *algorithm*, *if*, *then*, and *else*. Indentation has been used to define the set of actions that are consequences of control decisions, though we could have used *begin* and *end* for that purpose. We have inserted labels α, β, γ, and δ as aids in following the recursion.

Examine the algorithm carefully. Note that, while the formal parameters always remain the same on each use of the algorithm, the actual parameters shift. Let us call the three formal parameters (representing the three spindles) I, II, and III, and examine what happens when how many is 3. Let s, a, and d denote source, auxiliary, and destination, respectively, when occurring as actual parameters:

Recursion Level	Action	How Many	I	II	III
0	entry	3	s	a	d
1	α	2	s	d	a
2	α	1	s	a	d
3	δ		s		d
2	β		s		a
2	γ	2	d	s	a
3	δ	1	d		a
1	β		s		d
1	γ		a	s	d
2	α	1	a	d	s
3	δ		a		s
2	β		a		d
2	γ	1	s	a	d
3	δ		s		d

Recursion Level   Tree

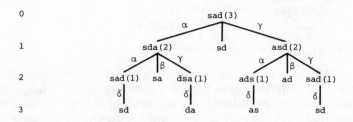

Figure 1.7

The recursion can also be illustrated by a "tree," as in Figure 1.7. The three branches emanating from the root $sad(3)$ are followed in the order of the algorithm, α then β then γ, and each of these is the root of its own tree that must be followed to its completion before the next branch to the right on its level is followed. The tree enables one to follow easily the movement of the disks, since the top disk on a spindle is the only one ever moved, and it is moved only on step δ or β.

From the algorithm we can compute how many moves are required. If $M(n)$ is the number of moves for n disks, then

$$M(n) = \begin{cases} 2M(n-1) + 1 & n > 1 \\ 1 & n = 1 \end{cases}$$

and $M(n) = 2^n - 1$ satisfies this "recurrence relation."

Let us consider another example. Suppose we wish to compute n factorial, $n!$ We know that $n! = n(n-1)(n-2) \ldots (2)(1)$. To be rid of the . . . we may define a number of algorithms for computing factorial (n), as we shall call it.

```
(a) algorithm factorial (n)
return (if n = 0 then 1 else n × factorial (n - 1))
```

or

```
(b) algorithm factorial (n)
m ← 0
h ← 1
while m ≠ n do
m ← m + 1
h ← m × h
return (h)
```

or

```
(c) algorithm factorial (n)
m ← n
h ← 1
while m ≠ 0 do
h ← m × h
m ← m - 1
return (h)
```

or

```
(d) algorithm factorial (n)
algorithm intermediate (s)
return (if n = s then 1 else (s + 1) ×
   intermediate (s + 1)
return intermediate (0)
```

All these algorithms compute factorial (n), but they do it in somewhat different ways. Two are recursive, (a) and (d), and two use explicit cycles, (b) and (c), and are called iterative algorithms. Note that algorithm (d) is an example of an algorithm inside which another algorithm, intermediate (s), is defined. This inner algorithm could not be defined outside factorial (n), because it has the global variable n that is a formal parameter supplied to factorial. The two iterative algorithms utilize local variables h and m to accumulate explicitly the result and count, respectively, while recursion enables us to dispense with these variables.

Algorithm (a) describes the computation of factorial (n) in much the same way that we first encounter its definition in mathematics. Algorithm (a) requires no local variables and no programmed looping. The control is subsumed by the nature of a recursive algorithm: in $n \times$ factorial $(n - 1)$ the multiplication is performed, once factorial $(n - 1)$ has been computed, etc.

As another example consider the following interesting problem. Draw a sphere of radius $\sqrt{R}$ about the origin; see Figure 1.8. We wish to count the number of points inside and on the sphere that have integer coordinates. These are called *lattice points*. Put another way, we wish to find how many points $W = (x, y, z)$ satisfy

1. $R \geq x^2 + y^2 + z^2$
2. x, y, z are integers

We may count up these points in many ways, but we shall do it recursively. First we observe that a line may be considered a

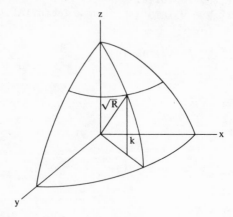

Figure 1.8

one-dimensional sphere and a circle a two-dimensional sphere. Furthermore, we can count the points in the sphere by summing the points lying in longitudinal planes with integer altitudes. Because of symmetry we need only count the planes in the northern hemisphere twice and add in the contribution of the equatorial plane. While we are interested in the case $N = 3$, (the ordinary sphere) we shall write the algorithm for general N, where N is the number of dimensions.

```
algorithm point (R, N):
if N = 0 then return (1)
else
count ← equatorial count ← point (R, N - 1);
determine initial latitudinal plane; while latitudinal
planes remain to be counted do begin count ← count +
2 × point (radius of the current latitudinal circle,
N - 1); choose next latitudinal plane end;
return (count)
```

We make use of the fact that the "equatorial plane" is a "sphere" of one less dimension than the given one, but with the same radius.

We now have the flow of control and comments and we can fill in the computational details. The kth latitudinal plane for $N = 3$ is a circle,

$$R - k^2 = x^2 + y^2$$

and for $N = 2$ is a line segment,

$$R - k^2 = x^2$$

We can now write:

```
algorithm point (R,N)
if N = 0 then return (1)
else
count ← point (R, N - 1);
k ← 1;
while k² ≤ R do begin
count ← count + point (R - k², N - 1);
k ← k + 1 end;
return (count)
```

We note that this algorithm generalizes nicely to higher dimensional spheres (arbitrary integer N).

Let us consider another example of the use of recursion. Suppose we are given two sequences of digits X and Y. We wish to transform X into Y by a sequence of operations, any of which are either (a.) delete a digit or (b.) insert a digit and no other kind of operation is permitted. What is the *minimum* number m of operations required?

Let us draw straight lines from every digit d in X to all digits in Y equal to d. Let us define a match set as any collection of lines that do not cross. Let R = maximum number of lines (matches) in any match set. Then m = length of X + length of $Y - 2 \times R$, since we may construct Y by no more than length of X deletions followed by length of Y insertions, and a deletion and an insertion may be saved by each match.

Thus we must compute R. Let $G(1, 1)$ be the maximum number of matches possible in the sequence commencing with $X[1]$ and $Y[1]$, R is $G(1, 1)$. We either do or do not include $X[1]$ in the maximum match set, and this gives us the recursion formula:

$$G(1, 1) \text{ is maximum } (1 + G(2, j + 1), G(2, 1))$$

where j is the leftmost position in Y for which $X[1] = Y[j]$.

This formula must be modified because there may be no $j \geq 1$ for which $X[1] = Y[j]$. So we write

```
G(1, 1) is
find (j);
if 1 ≤ j ≤ length(Y) then u ← 1 else u ← 0;
z ← maximum (u + G(2, j + 1), G(2, 1));
return (z)
```

This is not yet a useful recursive definition, because we really need a definition for $G(h, k)$, the maximum number of matches commencing with $X[h]$ and $Y[k]$, since we need to compute $G(2, j + 1)$ and $G(2, 1)$, etc.

It is easy enough to write $G(h, k)$, using $G(1, 1)$ as a model:

```
G(h, k) is
find (j);
if k ≤ j ≤ length(Y) then u ← 1 else u ← 0;
z ← maximum (u + G(h + 1, j + 1), G(h + 1, k));
return (z)
```

But we need to give a value for $G(h, k)$ when either $h > \text{length}(X)$ or $k > \text{length}(Y)$, and that value is 0:

```
G(h, k) is
if h > length(X) ∨ k > length(Y) then return (0)
else begin
find (j);
if k ≤ j ∧ j ≤ length(Y) then u ← 1 else u ← 0;
z ← maximum (u + G(h + 1, j + 1), G(h + 1, k));
return (z) end
```

The "find (j)" depends on h and k and obtains j. We need only look for $j \geq k$, and hence we note that $k \leq j$ is always true.

```
find (j) is
j ← k;
while j ≤ length(Y) ∧ X[h] ≠ Y[j] do
j ← j + 1;
```

Our final algorithm is

```
G(h,k) is
if h > length(X) ∨ k > length(Y) then return (0)
else begin
j ← k;
while j ≤ length(Y) ∧ X[h] ≠ Y[j] do
j ← j + 1;
if j ≤ length(Y) then u ← 1 else u ← 0;
z ← maximum (u + G(h + 1, j + 1), G(h + 1, k));
return (z) end
```

SAMPLE DATA:

X is 1,2,3,4,3,2,
Y is 2,1,3,4,1,4,3,2,4

The preceding recursive algorithm is somewhat inefficient because $G(h, k)$ will be recomputed many times for the *same* h and k. There is a simple trick to avoid this recomputation: Define an array $H[1:\text{length}(X) + 1, 1:\text{length}(Y) + 1]$ and compute $H[h, k] \leftarrow G(h, k)$. Then one never recomputes $G(h, k)$ if $H[h, k]$ has already been evaluated.

We can guarantee that $H[h, k]$ is computed *exactly* once by organizing our sequencing properly. Look at the key recurrence equations written in terms of the array H:

```
H[h, k] ← Max (H[h + 1, k], if X[h] = Y[k] then
1 + H[h + 1, k + 1] else H[h, k + 1])
for h = 1; 2, . . . , length(X), k = 1, 2, . . . ,
length(Y)
```

We define $H[1 + \text{length}(X); k] = 0$ for $k = 1, 2, . . . , \text{length}(Y)$ and, similarly, $H[h, 1 + \text{length}(Y)] = 0$ for $h = 1, 2, . . . , \text{length}(X)$.

Since $H[1,1]$ is the desired result, the above recurrence equation tells us that if we compute the H elements one row at a time in order of *decreasing* h, and each row in order of decreasing k, no element of H need be computed more than once.

For the preceding example the H array is:

h \ k	1	2	3	4	5	6	7	8	9	10
1	5	5	4	4	4	3	2	2	1	0
2	[5]	4	4	4	4	3	2	2	1	0
3	4	4	[4]	3	3	3	2	1	1	0
4	3	3	3	3	3	[3]	2	1	1	0
5	2	2	2	2	2	2	[2]	1	1	0
6	1	1	1	1	1	1	1	1	[1]	0
7	0	0	0	0	0	0	0	0	0	0

Almost half of the entries need not be directly computed since, once a $k = k_0$ is found on the hth row for which

$$H[h, k_0] = \text{length}(X) - h + 1 = c$$
then $H[h, k] \leftarrow c$ for all $1 \leq k \leq k_0$.

The boxed elements in the array show the k_0 values for the various rows. A similar result holds for the columns.

From the H array it is easy to find the sets of entries from X and Y that participate in a maximum match.

The maximum match set is

X is 1, 2, 3, 4, 3, 2

Y is 2, 1, 3, 4, 2, 4, 3, 2, 4

and $H[1, 1]$ evaluates to 5.

The algorithm was developed by using a combination of the problem-solving strategies:

1. Using recursion to organize the sequencing through sub-problems.
2. Abstracting an initial special-case algorithm to the general-case algorithm.
3. Completing a reasonable, but incomplete, algorithm.
4. Establishing higher-level before lower-level details.
5. Improving the algorithm's efficiency.

SUMMARY

The content of the preceding sections should have provided the reader with some attitudes about, and techniques for handling, algorithms:

1. Problems do not possess unique algorithms. The choice of algorithm depends upon many factors: efficiency, generalizability, and ease of understanding, to name but a few. It is most important to discover and understand one algorithm.

2. An algorithm is not really at hand until we have described it in an algorithmic notation. But what is an algorithmic notation? Let us say merely that it is a notation akin to that of the flowchart. It describes in its steps explicit manipulation of symbolic data and unambiguous rules for giving the order in which the steps are to be performed. The algorithms in this chapter have been deliberately described in several notations. It is important that the programmer not be constrained to write and think in a fixed algorithmic notation once he has learned to use one well. As will be seen in the subsequent chapters, the nearer an algorithm moves to the computer for execution, the more rigid the algorithmic notation must become.

3. Finding algorithms is the process of problem-solving. Some problems we solve from the top down, and some algorithms

are written that way. Some problems we solve by "jigsawing" together algorithms we have already created, perhaps for other purposes. In either event we search for the proper cycle and recursion structure organized around data that itself is structured.

4. Algorithms manage complexity in control of sequencing by the use of recursion, and complexity in data organization by the use of stacks and arrays.

5. Probably one should solve difficult subproblems before solving easy ones. Solution of the former may suggest or require extensive algorithm reorganization. Completion of too many of the latter creates an appreciable inertia against fundamental reorganizations.

6. No algorithm is ever really final.

7. It appears easier to write algorithms than to read them. Yet we must use the algorithms of others when we turn to solving complex tasks. Then you will appreciate the value of commentary. So include adequate commentary in your own algorithms.

8. Algorithms should always be accompanied by examples. Man has an ability to abstract (one man's constant is another man's variable) and to generalize (everything is a special case of something more general). Real examples aid both thinking activities.

9. Algorithms should not founder on special cases. It is one thing knowingly to restrict input data—all real algorithms do this in one way or another—but it is another to assume more from an algorithm than it can deliver.

10. Correct performance on a small set of test cases does not constitute an argument of correctness.

11. Algorithms rarely divide their execution times equally among their parts. The algorithm writer should always know, or empirically determine, where an algorithm spends its time. In improving efficiency the programmer should dedicate most of his efforts to those parts of the algorithm where execution causes most time to be spent.

REFERENCES

A vast amount of literature has been produced within the last decade probing the relationships between man and computer. In almost every area where man organizes his efforts either individually or in groups the role of the computer is enlarging. Each profession is developing its own technical literature on the subject of computers. However, the author would like to recommend the following books that provide both wit and insight into the symbiotic relationship between man and his computer.

Jacques Ellul, *The Technological Society* (Alfred A. Knopf, New York, N. Y., 1964).

Martin Greenberger, ed., *Management and the Computer of the Future* (MIT Press, Cambridge, Mass., 1962).

Elting Morison, *Men, Machines, and Modern Times* (MIT Press, Cambridge, Mass., 1968).

An interesting book in which wariness of the computer and its effects on human society is the predominant attitude is

Robert M. Baer, *The Digital Villain* (Addison-Wesley, Reading, Mass., 1972).

For the paranoic this book will be immensely reassuring.

The large numbers of books on algorithms and programming range from introductory to advanced texts. Introductory texts tend to interlace the study of programming with that of one or more specific programming languages. The author particularly recommends the following. The first treats the Algol60 and FORTRAN programming languages and their use in representing algorithms. The second treats the systematic development of algorithms using the language PASCAL developed by Wirth and his students. The third focuses on the development of algorithms by using the top-down approach. Algorithms are expressed in PL/I and a dialect, PL/C.

John K. Rice and John R. Rice, *Introduction to Computer Science* (Holt, Rinehart and Winston, New York, N. Y., 1969).

Niklaus Wirth, *Systematic Programming: An Introduction* (Prentice-Hall, Englewood Cliffs, N. J., 1973).

Richard Conway and David Gries, *An Introduction to Programming, A Structured Approach Using PL/I and PL/C* (Winthrop Publishers, Cambridge, Mass., 1973).

The books by George Polya on problem-solving, primarily in mathematics, are an important source of insight into programming even though the computer does not explicitly participate in any of his treatments:

G. Polya, *How to Solve It* (Anchor Book A93, Doubleday, New York, N. Y., 1957).

G. Polya, *Mathematical Discovery* (John Wiley, New York, N. Y., 1962, two volumes).

A more abstract view of algorithms than that given here is found in the excellent introductory text:

Marvin Minsky, *Computation, Finite and Infinite Machines* (Prentice-Hall, Englewood Cliffs, N. J., 1967).

A good study of the development of programming techniques for one kind of algorithmic specification, the Markov algorithm, is given in

B. Galler and A. J. Perlis, *A View of Programming Languages* (Addison-Wesley, Cambridge, Mass., 1970).

The multivolume work by Knuth is an indispensable reference for the serious computer-science student. It requires of the reader a level of mathematical maturity that is indicative of that expected from the computer scientist:

Donald Knuth, *The Art of Computer Programming* (Addison-Wesley, Cambridge, Mass., 1968, 7 volumes).

Backtracking is described in a beautiful article:

S. Golomb and L. Baumert, *"Backtrack Programming"* (*Journal of the ACM*, 12, 516–524, 1965).

The professional organization of computer scientists is the Association for Computing Machinery (ACM). This association publishes a number of periodicals containing research results, new techniques, reviews of the field, and surveys of progress in the field:

Communications of the ACM (published monthly).
Journal of the ACM (published quarterly).
Computing Surveys (published quarterly).

PROBLEMS

1. Suppose we have a recursive relation,

$$y_{k+1} = a_0 y_k + a_1 y_{k-1} + \cdots + a_r y_{k-r}, \ k \geq r$$

that computes y_{k+1}, given the $r + 1$ previous values. $y_k, y_{k-1}, \ldots, y_{k-r}$. The a_i are positive integer constants. Suppose we are given $y_0, y_1, \ldots, y_r$ to start with. Find an algorithm that computes y_N for some $N \geq r + 1$ and does not require storage that grows with N. Can you find an algorithm that does not require shifting previously computed y values?

2. The natural logarithm of a number $X > 0$ can be defined as

$$\ln X = \lim_{n \to \infty} 2^n (X^{1/2^n} - 1)$$

Thus we could approximate the logarithm by taking n large enough. However, we run into a severe problem if we do that. Why? Can you transform the definition so as to give a way of approximating the logarithm that avoids the problem? The quantity $X^{1/2^n}$ means the n-fold iteration of the square root of X:

$$\sqrt{\cdot \sqrt{\sqrt{X}}}$$

3. Find an algorithm to list and count the solutions to the following problem: How can I buy 100 fowl, at least one of each kind, for

$100 if the prices are 1 duck for $2, 1 hen for $1, 2 doves for $1, and 10 sparrows for $1? Generalize your algorithm to treat the case when one is given an N component vector of unit prices, a required number of units W, and an amount K to spend.

4. For an angle $0 < \alpha < \pi/2$ we may imbed a chain of inscribed and tangential circles. If we are given an integer N and a fraction $0 < r < 1$, what is the least possible diameter of the largest circle in the chain so that no more than the fraction r of the area of the sector $OACB$ lies outside the circles? Can you "invert" your algorithm to find the largest possible angle $0 < \alpha < \pi/2$ if the diameter of the largest circle is given instead?

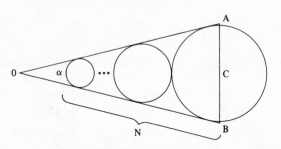

5. Imagine that the managers of the Rockefeller Plaza in New York City decide to replace the usual Christmas evergreen tree by a "tree" constructed from soft-drink cans (all having the same diameter and the same height). An initial design for the tree is as shown.

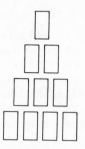

    a. Give an algorithm that assumes that a variable N contains a positive integer value and that assigns to NC the total number of cans needed to construct a tree containing N rows.

    b. Suppose that the managers have a total of only NN cans from which to construct the "tree." How many rows will the largest possible tree constructed from NN cans have? Give an algorithm that assigns this value to a variable called NR.

    c. Because the "tree" is rather uninteresting, it has been suggested that each row be replaced by a radial arrangement of cans so that there will be S radial arms on the "tree." Below is a diagram of the third level from the top of a "tree" having three radial arms (the dashed lines represent the positions of the cans in the second level from the top). Give an algorithm that computes the total number of cans needed to build a tree that has S radial arms and N levels. Assume that N and S both are positive integers and that the value in S is greater than 1. Assign the total number of cans needed to the variable NCS.

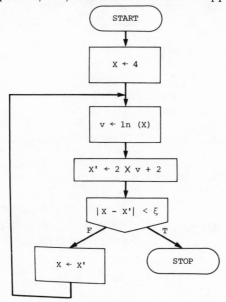

    d. Give an algorithm that assigns to NL the total number of levels a "tree" having S radial arms and built from NN cans will have.

    e. It has been suggested that, since there are five boroughs in the City of New York, and the city is in New York State, the "tree" should be constructed with six radial arms. Is this possible?

6. The accompanying flowchart computes the approximate solution of an equation, i.e., when two successive approximations X

and X' are closer to each other than E, one of them is taken as the desired solution. What is the equation? (NOTE: ln (X) is the natural logarithm of X.)

7. The following algorithm prints a table of a certain function of X for values of X from 1 to 20.

```
X ← 1
B ← 6
C ← 5
D ← 6
while X ≤ 20 do begin
PRINT(X, B)
X ← X + 1
C ← C + D
B ← B + C end
```

What is the function of X whose values are being printed? Give it in closed form as, for example, $e^{2X} + \cos X$, or $9X^5 + 14/X$, etc.

8. COVERINGS: Suppose you are given N line segments that are portions of the positive X axis. These segments may be overlapping. Suppose the segments were laid down on the axis; we can say they "cover" part of the axis. See the accompanying diagram. Starting at the origin, how far does the "cover" extend before a break in the cover is met? Informally, how far could you "walk" along the segments before a hole were reached?

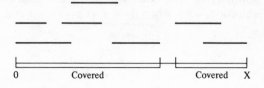

Assume that the line segments are given by two one-dimensional arrays START and LENGTH; the ith segment begins at START[i] and ends at START[i] + LENGTH[i]. For example, if segment 2 extends from $X = 4.2$ to 5.0 inclusive, then

$$\text{start [2] = 4.2}$$
$$\text{and} \quad \text{length [2] = 0.8}$$

9. Given the integers $1 \leq P \leq 20$ and $1 \leq N \leq 30$ and the set of numbers $D_1, D_2, \ldots, D_N$, the numbers $A(X, Y)$ are defined by

$$A(X, Y) = \sum_{Z=1}^{Y} A(X + 1, Z) \qquad X = 1, 2, \ldots, P - 1$$
$$= D_Z \qquad\qquad\qquad X = P; Z = 1, 2, \ldots, N$$

It is desired that the sum

$$S = \sum_{Y=1}^{N} A(1, Y)$$

be computed by two different procedures: (a) by computing in increasing order of X by using a stack and (b) from the "bottom up" in decreasing order of X.

Procedure (a). Initially the counter S is set to zero and the stack elements X_1 and Y_1 are set to 1. On entry, the top of the stack contains two integers X_k and Y_k. New elements are added, until finally some $X_k = P$. This incrementation of the stack follows the pattern:

$$\begin{aligned}
A(1, 1) &= A(2, 1) = A(3, 1) = \cdots = A(P, 1) = D_1 \\
A(1, 2) &= A(2, 1) + A(2, 2) \\
&= A(2, 1) + (A(3, 1) + A(3, 2)) \\
&= A(2, 1) + (A(3, 1) + (A(4, 1) + A(4, 2))) \\
&\quad \text{etc.}
\end{aligned}$$

When $X_k = P$, we compute $\sum_{Z=1}^{Y_{k-1}} D_Z$ and add this quantity to S. Then we move back up the stack until some $Y_k \neq Y_{k-1}$, at which point we set $Y_k = Y_k + 1$ and move down once again. The process is completed when $k = 1$ and $Y = N$.

Procedure (b). A little algebra will show that the sum S may be written in closed form as

$$S = D_N + \sum_{m=1}^{N-1} D_m \times \prod_{r=1}^{N-m} (P - 1 + r)/r$$

Two cycles suffice to compute S.

Note that the $A(X, Y)$'s can be written as an array, where each $A(X, Y)$ can be written as the sum of the elements $A(X + 1, Z)$ from $Z = 1$ to Y in the row immediately below.

Give algorithms for both procedures.

Here is an example in which two algorithms are given. Which should be used, and why?

10. From a sequence S of N numbers subsequences may be obtained by blotting out some elements of S. Identify a subsequence X that is the longest one whose successive members are monotone increasing in value. For example,

$$\begin{aligned}
S: &\quad 1\ 3\ 2\ 4\ 21\ 1\ 6\ 9\ 37\ 4 \\
X: &\quad 1\quad\ 2\ 4\quad\quad 6\ 9\ 37
\end{aligned}$$

11. A sequence of N digits

$$X_0 \underline{\text{is}}\ d_N, d_{N-1}, \ldots, d_1$$

is thought of as a decimal integer. What is the longest sequence of integers

$$X_k > X_{k-1} > \cdots > X_0$$

that can be fabricated from the digits of X_0?

12. A region of two-dimensional space is divided into square cells of area 1. Each square is colored "white" or "black." The black cells are connected in the sense that any black cell is at least touched on a side or corner by another black cell. Find the area of a white region R containing a given cell X, that is, the area of white cells that have at least sides in common. Put another way, every cell in R can be reached from X by horizontal and vertical movement through white squares.

13. You are given a square of side L with two gaps A and B in the base, each of length δ. Assume a particle is fired from a point on the base, x units from the left side, at an angle $0 < \theta < \pi$. The particle rebounds elastically from the walls. Compute the distance d traveled by the particle before it exits through one of the gaps. If the particle will not exit through one of the gaps in K reflections, set d to 0. HINT: Consider space filled by stacks of identical boxes with perfectly ethereal walls.

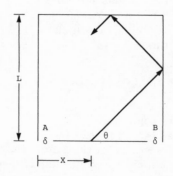

14. Parts (a.) through (e.) that follow form a unified sequence of problems. In general, the solution to each part is useful as a sub-algorithm in the parts that follow it in sequence. Before starting the problems we give some definitions:

Two line segments *intersect* if they have exactly one point in common; they *overlap* if they have a line segment in common. A line segment always has nonzero length, so that a point is not a segment.

A *polygon* (or *n*-gon) is a set of n line segments (that is, sides) such that one can trace a closed path along the segments that (a) passes through each endpoint half as many times as the endpoint appears in a list of the segments and that (b) passes along each segment exactly once.

Examples

Polygons

Nonpolygons

a. Given a line segment L_{ab} defined by the coordinates (X_a, Y_a), (X_b, Y_b) of its endpoints, determine whether the point $P = (X, Y)$ lies *on* the segment (between a and b), and set variable ONLINE to true; otherwise, set it to false.

b. Given two line segments L_1 and L_2 defined by the coordinates of their endpoints, compute the coordinates (X, Y) of their point of *intersection*, and set the variable INTERSECT to be true. If, however, L_1 and L_2 do not intersect (within their lengths), then set INTERSECT to false and X and Y to 0.

Assume that the two line segments have *at most* one point in common; that is, they do not *overlap*.

c. You are given j line segments $L_1, L_2, \ldots, L_j$ represented by the coordinates of their endpoints; thus, for each $i = 1, \ldots, j$, L_i is represented by $((X_{1_i}, Y_{1_i}), (X_{2_i}, Y_{2_i}))$. Find all points P of intersection of pairs of segments L_a, L_b from the given set. Your result should include the number m of such intersections and a list of their coordinates in the following order:

1. If $a < c$, then P_{ab} is listed before P_{cd},
2. If $b < d$, then P_{ab} is listed before P_{ad}.

As in part (b), assume that no segments overlap.

d. Given J line segments $L_1, L_2, \ldots, L_j$ represented as in part (c), determine whether they form a polygon (N-gon) when all N segments are included, and set a variable ISAPOLYGON to true accordingly. To determine whether the segments do form a polygon (according to the definition given earlier) you must traverse the segments in some order. If the segments do form a polygon, your program must not only set ISAPOLYGON to true but also reorder the segments to correspond to the order in which you traced them. It should also exchange endpoints of segments in the reordered list $L_1, L_2, \ldots, L_j$, if necessary, so that the second endpoint of each segment L_k coincides with the first endpoint of the next segment L_{k+1}.

e. Given j line segments as in part (d), compute N, the greatest integer such that an N-gon can be constructed from some subset of the given segments. Thus, not all given segments need be used, and $0 \leq N \leq J$. Examples are shown in the figure.

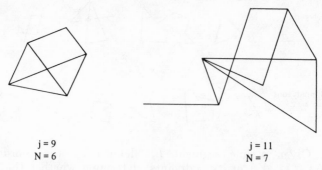

$$j = 9$$
$$N = 6$$

$$j = 11$$
$$N = 7$$

15. THE TRIANGLE PROBLEM. You are given N line segments $L_1, \ldots, L_N$ defined by the coordinates of their endpoints. Find the first triangle, if any, that is formed from intersections of these segments. We define "first" by the ordering:

(L_a, L_b, L_c) comes before (L_d, L_e, L_f)
    if $a < d$
    or if $a = d$ and $b < e$
    or if $a = d$ and $b = e$ and $c < f$

If no triangles can be formed, set a variable NONE to true.

16. You are given the vertices of two triangles A and B, such that triangle A encloses triangle B. Compute d, the minimum distance from any point on A to any point on B.

17. Given a nonreentrant polygon of N sides defined by the N vertices $(X_1, Y_1), \ldots, (X_N, Y_N)$ and a point $P = (X, Y)$, determine whether P is inside or outside the polygon. (A polygon is nonreentrant if no side intersects any other side except at vertices.)

18. You are given a sequence of M numbers $X_1, X_2, \ldots, X_M$. From these your algorithm should select a subsequence of N numbers: $X_{i_1}, X_{i_2}, \ldots, X_{i_N}$. The subsequence must satisfy all of the following conditions:

1. Adjacent numbers have opposite signs:

$$X_{i_k} \times X_{i_{k+1}} < 0 \quad \text{for } k = 1, 2, \ldots, N - 1$$

2. The order of the original set is preserved:

$$i_p < i_q \quad \text{if and only if } p < q$$

3. The difference between largest and smallest members,

$$\max_k(X_{i_k}) - \min_j(X_{i_j})$$

must be as large as possible.

Furthermore, the value you use for N must be the largest integer for which properties 1, 2, and 3 hold. Given M and $X_1, \ldots, X_M$, your algorithm should compute N and $i_1, \ldots, i_N$.

19. THE CALENDAR PROBLEM. Give an algorithm to compute how often the Fourth of July falls on a Thursday. Assume a calendar with the following properties: 365 days per year with 7 days per week, starting at year 1:

1. Every Lth year is a leap year (that is, it has 366 days, the extra day being February 29), except:
2. Every $(L \times M)$th year is an ordinary year (that is, not a leap year), except:
3. Every $(L \times M \times P)$th year is a leap year.

This calendar is simply a generalization of our Gregorian calendar that uses $L = 4$, $M = 25$, $P = 4$.

Suppose we number the days of the week as follows:

Sun Mon Tue Wed Thu Fri Sat
 0   1   2   3   4   5   6

With this information, we may state the exact problem:

For the span of years 1, 2, . . . , $(L \times M \times P)$, and assuming the Fourth of July falls on day D in year 1, compute how many times the Fourth of July falls on a Thursday.

Notice that in the special case in which L, M, and P have the values for our Gregorian calendar, the following are true:

1. The product $L \times M \times P$ is 400. The answer to the problem is not simply 400/7, because, for example, this is not an integer. In other words, the Fourth of July does not fall with equal frequency on each day of the week.
2. Over the entire 400 years there are the same numbers for each day of the week. In other words the Gregorian calendar is cyclic; it repeats itself every 400 years (but not sooner!). Thus, the same answer would result regardless of the year with which it started.

20. Find a "stable" set of marriages for a given group of N boys and N girls. Each boy has ordered the girls according to his preferences, and you are given the results as an array BOY in which BOY_{ik} = (the number of the girl who is the kth choice of boy i). Similarly, the girls have indicated their preferences in an array GIRL, in which $GIRL_{ik}$ = (the number of the boy who is the kth choice of girl i). A set of marriages is unstable if a man and woman exist who are not married to each other but prefer each other to their actual mates. If there are no such discontented couples, then the set of marriages is stable.

One possible algorithm for solving this problem is contained in the following article:

D. Gale and L. S. Shapley, "College Admissions and the Stability of Marriages" (*American Mathematical Monthly*, 69 (January 1962), pp. 9–15).

21. Given N circles C_1, C_2, . . . , C_N defined by triplets (X_1, Y_1, R_1), . . . , (X_N, Y_N, R_N) giving the coordinates of the centers and the radii, compute the area of the smallest square that encloses all N circles.

22. Given two squares A and B defined by the coordinates of their vertices, compute their common area.

23. Given N, count the number of primes $\leq N$.

24. In the following each letter is to be assigned a different one of the digits 0, 1, 2, 3, 4, 5, 6, 7, 8, 9, so that the substituted equations are arithmetically correct:

a. FORTY   b. CATS
    TEN $\times$ 9
 + TEN   LIVES
 SIXTY

25. Find an algorithm that will create a sequence of distinct puzzles of the form

$$\frac{\begin{array}{r} \alpha_1\alpha_2\alpha_3\alpha_4 \\ \times \alpha_5 \end{array}}{\alpha_{10}\alpha_9\alpha_8\alpha_7\alpha_6}$$

where each α_i is to be assigned a different letter and the resulting assignment of a unique digit to each letter makes the form a correct arithmetic statement. How could you arrange for the puzzles to use legal English words?

26. In procedure Q1 show that regress(k) will never regress more than twice in succession.

27. In procedure Q1 show that if a solution exists, Q1 will find it.

28. Modify procedure Q1 so that it will produce *all* 92 solutions of the 8-queens problem.

Create algorithms to solve the following problems,

29. Find a chessboard distribution of N queens satisfying the following:

1. No queen can "take" any other.
2. The addition of one queen anywhere on the board places some queen under attack.
3. N is the smallest integer for which (a) and (b) hold.

30. Given an integer $N > 0$, find a sequence $a_1a_2 \cdots a_N$ satisfying:

1. $a_i = 0$ or 1 or 2
2. No adjacent subsequences are the same. Put another way, for no j, $k > 0$ is it the case that
   a. $j + 2k + 1 \leq N$
   b. $a_ja_{j+1} \cdots a_{j+k} = a_{j+k+1}a_{j+k+2} \cdots a_{j+2k+1}$

31. Generate a string of 2^k bits (0 or 1), a_i, and imagine them laid out in a circle:

The string is to satisfy the property that every one of the possible k-bit sequences occurs as consecutive values $a_j a_{j+1} \cdots a_{j+k-1}$ (modulo the circle). For example:

$$k = 2 \qquad\qquad k = 3$$

$$\begin{matrix} & 0 & \\ 1 & & 0 \\ & 1 & \end{matrix} \qquad 0 \; 0 \; 1 \; 0 \; 1 \; 1 \; 1 \; 0$$

(NOTE: there are 2^k different sequences of k bits.)

HINT: The pattern for $k = 3$ can be derived from that for $k = 2$ by backtracking:

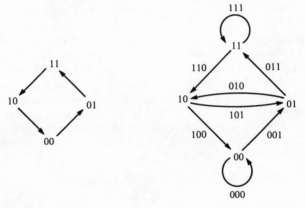

32. Suppose we have a set of sets of integers where

A is $(A_1, A_2, \ldots, A_k)$
A_1 is $(a_{11}, a_{12}, \ldots, a_{1n_1})$
A_2 is $(a_{21}, a_{22}, \ldots, a_{2n_2}),$ $\qquad a_{ij} =$ an integer
$\cdots$
A_k is $(a_{k1}, a_{k2}, \ldots, a_{kn_k})$

Determine whether there is a set D of *distinct representatives* for A, that is, a set of $k(d_1, d_2, \ldots, d_k)$ integers, all distinct, and such that d_j is a member of A_j for $j = i, 2, \ldots, k$. For example,

a. $A_1 = (1, 3, 4)$ b. $A_1 = (1, 3, 4)$
    $A_2 = (1, 3)$ $A_2 = (1, 3)$
    $A_3 = (1, 3)$ $A_3 = (3, 4)$
     $D = (4, 3, 1)$ $A_4 = (1, 4)$

                    There is no D.

33. A knight in chess may move from X to any of the marked positions 1 to 8 that are on the 8-by-8 chessboard. A knight's tour is a sequence of 63 moves starting from any square and then touching every other square on the board. Find a tour commencing from some arbitrary square.

	2		1	
3				8
		X		
4				7
	5		6	

34. A set S of integers is said to be sum-free if x, y in S guarantees that $x + y$ in S. The following are two obviously related problems.

a. Given the integers $1, 2, 3, \ldots , N$, find the *smallest* number of sets $\sigma(N)$ into which the N integers can be distributed such that each set is sum-free.

b. Given the integer n, find the *largest* number $N(n)$ such that the integers $1, 2, \ldots , N(n)$ can be distributed among n sum-free sets.

Can you create a single algorithm that will solve either problem? (NOTE: It is known that $[(n + 1)!e] \geq N(n + 1) \geq 3N(n) + 1$.)

35. In the text example that computed the maximum number of matches between two sequences of digits we did not retain the record of which digits participated in the maximum match set. Extend the algorithm so that the record of participating digits is retained, for example, as two integer vectors U and V for which it is true that $\text{length}(U) = \text{length}(V) = G(1, 1)$ and

$$X[U[k]] = Y[V[k]], \quad k = 1, 2, \ldots , \text{length}(U)$$

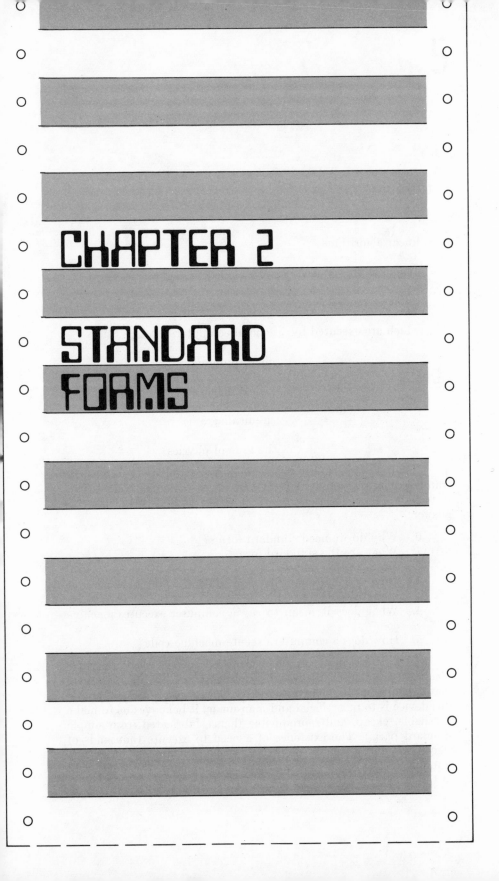

CHAPTER 2

STANDARD FORMS

2

INTRODUCTION

general algorithms
↓
linear algorithms
↓
symbolic programs
↓
numeric codes
↓
which are executed by   general computer
↓
microcomputer
↓
logical diagrams
↓
circuit diagrams
↓
the laws of physics

Before flowcharts can be executed by computers they must be translated into a standard form known as "machine code." This restriction raises questions which it is the goal of this chapter to answer:

0. Why do we need standard forms?
1. What are the standard forms?
2. How are they related?
3. How and by whom does an arbitrary flowchart get put into standard form?
4. What does it mean to say a computer executes machine code?
5. How does a computer execute machine code?

Why do we need standard forms? You will recall that our specification of an algorithm as a flowchart had the ultimate goal that a device (indeed many devices) could execute the algorithm. If this device is to be artificial and man-made, it behooves us to make it reliable, cheap, and reproducible (hence fabricated from simple standard parts). The existence of a need to execute thousands of algorithms millions of times has led to the development of an outstanding technology whose economic development is strongly tied to the intelligent invention and use of standard parts.

Our choices of standard forms should be such that:

1. Any algorithm will run on some computer or, even better,
2. A computer will be capable of executing any algorithm,
3. An understanding of, and ability to work in, the standard form of one computer will make it relatively easy to do the same with any other computer, and
4. All computers having the same standard form are interchangeable.

We are going to establish this transformation of an algorithm, represented in flowchart form, into its representation in machine code by a sequence of steps, each of which brings the representation closer to machine code, itself a particular kind of flowchart representation. The reduction process has the following steps.

1. LINEARIZATION. To reduce the more convenient two-dimensional flowchart representation to a linear form as a simply ordered sequence of algorithm steps.

2. SIMPLIFICATION. The contents of the algorithm boxes are simplified, if necessary, by introducing additional boxes.

3. ARITHMETIZATION 1. The content of each box is simplified so as to be represented by a nonnegative integer, and each integer uses no more than M decimal digits to represent it, for some constant M.

4. ARITHMETIZATION 2. Each integer is represented in the binary number system.

We now proceed to take up the reductions one step at a time.

LINEARIZATION OF A FLOWCHART

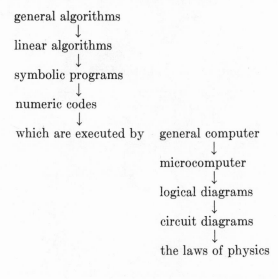

general algorithms
↓
linear algorithms
↓
symbolic programs
↓
numeric codes
↓
which are executed by   general computer
↓
microcomputer
↓
logical diagrams
↓
circuit diagrams
↓
the laws of physics

1. We eliminate all junctions (points having more than one directed arrow impinging on them) by cutting all but one path entering the junction, affixing a unique label to the box immediately following the junction point and appending at the end of each severed path a box of the form goto X, where X is the label attached to the junction point. If more than one label has been affixed to a box, replace all the occurrences of these labels by a single label. For example,

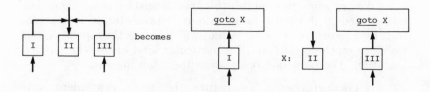

2. Branching occurs only at condition boxes. Alter all condition boxes as follows. Affix a unique label, say X, to the box to which the T path leads, sever the T path, and add a box goto X at the severed end. For example,

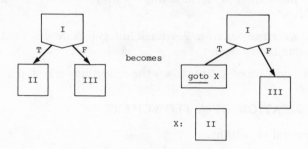

3. Alter all subalgorithm boxes of the form

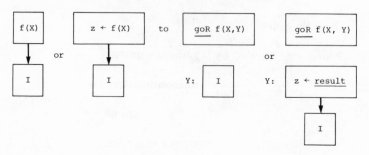

respectively, where Y is a unique label and X is the actual parameter of the function call, and alter the algorithm identified by f:

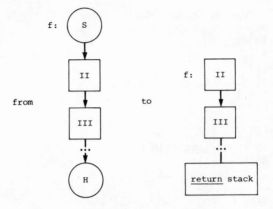

The operation $\text{go}R\ f(X,\ Y)$ stands for goto f with X as parameter and return upon completion of f to the box labeled Y with the result $f(X)$, if any, as the value of the variable *result*.

The return stack holds as its surface value the label to which return is to be made, that value being placed there by the $\text{go}R$ action. return stack specifies that the next box to be executed is not stack but that box whose label is stored at the top of the stack.

4. We shall now proceed to list the contents of the boxes, each on a separate line, in the order in which they are encountered when we commence with (the unique) START and follow the directed arrows.

All condition boxes such as

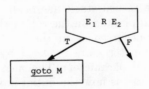

are listed as if $E_1\ R\ E_2$ then goto M, where R is some arithmetic relation such as $<$ or $>$ or $=$.

If the box is labeled, say, with X, the line description commences with X:. For example, X: if $E_1\ R\ E_2$ then goto M.

If the path terminates and some boxes of the flowchart have not yet been listed, take any box that has no arrow coming into it and continue the listing with the contents of the box and those connected to, and following from, it.

When there are no more paths to follow and no boxes remain unlisted, the process is terminated. Rather than list START, it is deleted, and the line following is assigned the label START.

The flowchart of the coin algorithm in linear form and with box outlines deleted, is:

```
START: READ N, Coins into C, index
P ← 0
j ← index
t ← N
L1: M[j] ← t
if C[j] = 1 then goto L2
j ← j + 1
goto L1
L2: P ← P + 1
L3: j ← j - 1
if j < index then goto L4
t ← M[j] - C[j]
if t ≥ 0 then goto L1
goto L3
L4: PRINT P
STOP
```

The list we have obtained we shall call a program.

It is relatively easy to describe how to execute a program:

1. We always commence with the line labeled **START**.
2. When we are executing a line, we always know which line to execute next:
   a. If it is an *assignment*, READ, or PRINT, the following line is next.
   b. If it is a goto X, the next line is that labeled by X.
   c. If it is goR̄ $f(X, Y)$, the determination of the next line has been preceded by two actions:
      1. The return stack has been "pushed," and Y has been planted on the top of the return stack.
      2. All occurrences in the f algorithm of its formal parameter v are replaced by references to X (the actual parameter). The successor step of the goR $f(X, Y)$ is now the initial box in the description of algorithm f.

         Note that each invocation of f (call on f) will cause these steps to be reenacted with the particular X and Y used in the call.
   d. If it is a condition of the form if $E_1 \ R \ E_2$ then goto X, test the condition $E_1 \ R \ E_2$. If the condition is not true, the line following is next; otherwise, that line labeled X is next.
   e. If it is a halt or stop, the execution ceases.
   f. If it is a return stack, the next line is that one whose label is the value currently at the top of the stack. The stack is also "popped," so that a new value appears from below to become the new top of the stack.

The preceding is the paradigm of the execution cycle of computers. We shall see it repeated in each of the ensuing transformations on programs. The paradigm will ultimately be described in purely arithmetic terms.

SIMPLIFICATION

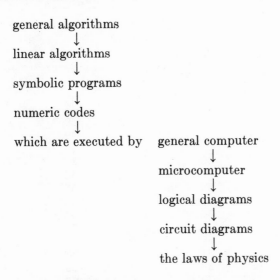

general algorithms
↓
linear algorithms
↓
symbolic programs
↓
numeric codes
↓
which are executed by   general computer
↓
microcomputer
↓
logical diagrams
↓
circuit diagrams
↓
the laws of physics

We shall now proceed to the next stage: simplification. An obvious candidate for simplification is the type of data we will permit in our reduced flowcharts. All symbols will name integers or real numbers (reals) or arrays of one dimension; we have called such arrays *vectors*. Since we have already agreed in Chapter 1 to limit the data of our algorithms to reals, integers, logical values (booleans), character strings, and arrays of these types, we must establish how these types simplify: that is, how each data type in our general algorithm is represented among the reduced data types of our simplified algorithms.

The correspondences to be established are listed below. It will be clear in what follows that our choice of alphabet will not affect in any important way the choices we make in representing characters, strings of characters, and arrays of characters.

	GENERAL	REDUCED
1.	integer	integer
2.	real	real
3.	logical	logical
4.	character string	vector of character strings
5.	array	vector

Items 1, 2, and 3 are unchanged.

The reductions of character strings is accomplished as follows.

How many different allowable characters are there? This question asks for the size of the alphabet from whose characters strings can be created. For our purposes we will set this figure at 64, though the standard alphabet (called ASCII) has 128 characters. Indeed, we shall use the following alphabet:

Number	Character	Number	Character	Number	Character
0	0	22	M	43	≠
1	1	23	N	44	≥
2	2	24	O	45	>
3	3	25	P	46	+
4	4	26	Q	47	−
5	5	27	R	48	×
6	6	28	S	49	/
7	7	29	T	50	↑
8	8	30	U	51	←
9	9	31	V	52	.
10	A	32	W	53	,
11	B	33	X	54	;
12	C	34	Y	55	:
13	D	35	Z	56	'
14	E	36	(	57	$_{10}$
15	F	37	)	58	∧
16	G	38	[	59	∨
17	H	39	]	60	∼
18	I	40	<	61	≡
19	J	41	≤	62	$
20	K	42	=	63	⊔ (blank)
21	L				

Suppose we have a character string X of N characters. We shall represent it as a vector, say Z of $1 + \text{entier}\ ((N + 2)/3)$ components. $Z[1]$ will always be N, the integer specifying the number of characters in the string (the length of the string), and $Z[2]$, $Z[3]$, . . . , etc. will each hold up to 3 characters. If the last component holds 1 or 2 characters as, for example, 'G' or 'TU', its representation is 'G⊔⊔' or 'TU⊔', respectively.

We shall follow the practice of delimiting character strings by a single apostrophe (') in reading them into an algorithm or employing them as constants. The representation of a single quotation mark in a string will be two quotation marks. The printing and the representation of a character string will strip away the bounding quotation marks and replace every internal pair by a single quotation mark. The character in the Kth position of X will be found as the Jth character in the Lth component of Z, where

```
L = 2 + entier ((K - 1)/3)
J = 1 + rem ((K - 1)/3)
```

It will be recalled that entier (X) is the largest integer $\leq X$, and rem (a/b) is the remainder upon division of a by b.

For example, suppose X is a character string $'TC''' \; D\sqcup\$'''$. Hence N is 7. Z has four components: $Z[1]$ is 7. $Z[2]$ is TC'. $Z[3]$ is $D\sqcup\$$. $Z[4]$ is $'\sqcup\sqcup$. The fourth character in X, D, is found as the rem $(4/3)$ character in the $2 +$ entier $((4-1)/3)$ component of Z, the first character in the third component of Z.

We shall subsequently examine the technique by which we can isolate, extract, insert, and delete characters from a string represented as a character vector.

Let us next consider arrays of numbers. Each such array is to be represented as a vector. To see how the correspondence is made, suppose we are given the array $A[3:5, -2:2]$. The notation provides the information that A has two subscripts (A is of rank 2), the first subscript taking values 3, 4, and 5, and the second values of -2, $-1, 0, 1$, and 2. It has $3 \times 5 = 15$ elements, so that the corresponding vector B will have fifteen components also. For example, suppose

$$
A \text{ is } \begin{array}{ccccc}
1 & 2 & 3 & 4 & 5 \\
6 & 7 & 8 & 9 & 10 \\
11 & 12 & 13 & 14 & 15
\end{array}
$$

then B is 1 2 3 4 5 6 7 8 9 10 11 12 13 14 15.

The element in the Ith row and Jth column of A, denoted by $A[I, J]$, is the Kth element of B, where

$$
\begin{aligned}
K &= (I-3) \times (2-(-2)+1) + J - (-2) + 1 \\
&= 5I + J - 12
\end{aligned}
$$

In general, if A has the shape $[r_1:r_2, \; c_1:c_2]$, then B will have the shape $[1: \; (r_2 - r_1 + 1) \times (c_2 - c_1 + 1)]$ and $K = (I - r_1) \times (c_2 - c_1 + 1) + J - c_1 + 1$.

Since c_1, c_2, r_1, and r_2 are constant for a given array, while I and J will change from reference to reference, we may first compute

$$
\begin{aligned}
a &\leftarrow c_2 - c_1 + 1 \\
b &\leftarrow 1 - c_1 - r_1 \times a
\end{aligned}
$$

and then, for any desired I and J,

$$
H \leftarrow aI + J + b
$$

Example: For the array A defined above, $A[4, 1]$ is $B[5 \times 4 + 1 - 12] = B[9]$ is 9.

Suppose that we have an array A of strings. Again a correspondence between A and a vector B is to be made.

Create the array C of the same shape as A, the value of whose general element $C[i, j]$ is the subscript position in B where the string representation of element $A[i, j]$ is to begin. For example, if

```
        HELEN   TROY
A is    HORSES  SOLDIERS
        GREEK   TRAGEDY
```

it has six elements and the components of B, $B[2]$, . . . , $B[7]$ will contain the mapping of the array elements of C:

```
        8   11
C is    14  17
        21  24
```

$B[1]$ will contain the total number of numbers required by this representation of A. Therefore B is 27, 8, 11, 14, 17, 21, 24, 5, HEL, EN⊔, 4, TRO, Y⊔⊔, 6, HOR, SES, 8, SOL, DIE, RS⊔, 5, GRE, EK⊔, 7, TRA, GED, Y⊔⊔.

Actually the mapping is quite straightforward when written as an algorithm. Let the shape of A be $[r_1:r_2, c_1:c_2]$. Let length $(A[I, J])$ be the number of characters in the string $A[I, J]$.

Algorithm 6:

```
START: K ← 2
M ← 2 + (r₂ − r₁ + 1) × (c₂ − c₁ + 1)
I ← r₁
L4: if I > r₂ then goto L1
J ← c₁
L3: if J > c₂ then goto L2
P ← length (A[I,J])
B[K] ← M
B[M] ← P
N ← M + entier ((P + 2)/3)
B[M + 1] . . . B[N] gets the characters of A packed 3
to each component of B
M ← N + 1
K ← K + 1
J ← J + 1
goto L3
L2: I ← I + 1
goto L4
L1: B[1] ← M −1
Halt
```

With this representation it is straightforward to find in B any of the strings and/or their characters, that were in A:

1. What components of B contain the string that is the value of $A[I, J]$? Using the previously established correspondence for arrays of numbers,

$$a \leftarrow c_2 - c_1 + 1$$
$$b \leftarrow 1 - c_1 - r_1 \times a$$

The notation $t \leftarrow B[aI + J + b]$ indicates where, in B, the string translation of $A[I, J]$ commences. The translation itself occupies components $B[t]$, $B[t + 1]$, . . . , $B[t + \text{entier } ((B[t] + 2)/3)]$.

Example: The string in $A[3, 1]$ leads to the values

```
a is 2
b is -2
t is B[6] is 21
```

The translation occupies components:

$B[21]$, $B[22]$, $B[23]$

2. Which component contains the Rth character of the string in $A[I, J]$, and where is it in that component? Compute:

```
L ← t + 1 + entier ((R - 1)/3)
H ← 1 + rem ((R - 1)/3)
```

Then the Rth character of $A[I, J]$ is in $B[L]$, where it occupies the Hth character position.

3. On examining the Hth character at $B[L]$, which entry in $A[I, J]$ is being examined?

Let K be the index of the component among the first $1 + (r_2 - r_1 + 1) \times (c_2 - c_1 + 1)$ components of B that holds the largest value $\leq L$.

```
Then K - b - 2 = aI + J = 1
so that I ← entier ((K - 2 - b)/a)
and J ← I + rem ((K - 2 - b)/a)
specifies the position in A, A[I, J].
```

The first stage of the simplification process is completed: All data on which our algorithms operate have structures no more complicated than vectors.

We shall agree to list in an algorithm each such vector and its extent, the number of its components, in the form

$X:$ VCT m

stating that X is a vector of m components, $X[i]$ selects the ith component, and $1 \leq i \leq m$. Each such entry is called a *declaration*.

The second stage of the simplification process will arrange for the simplification of the contents of the unit steps (boxes or lines) of an algorithm.

Let us first consider the assignment statement. An assignment statement is of the form $X \leftarrow$ expression, where X is an algorithm variable, as A or BETA[6] or $C[i + J - 1]$, etc., and an expression unites (values of) variables and constants under the rules of arithmetic and logic. The order in which dyadic (two-operand) operations are performed within an expression is determined by:

1. A ranking or precedence rule.
2. Placement of parentheses.
3. Left-to-right examination.

Thus, (a.) $y + z/t$ is the same as $y + (z/t)$ but different from $(y + z)/t$, since / "outranks" + in its "pull" on operands, and (b.) $y - z - t - w$ is the same as $((y - z) - t) - w$ but different from $y - (z - t) - w$ since, of k successive operators of equal rank, that one to the left has greater "pull" on operands than any to its right.

The customary ranking, in decreasing order, is:

7.   ↑ (exponentiation)
6.   × /
5.   + −
4.   = < > ≠ ≤ ≥   (2.1)
3.   ∧
2.   ∨
1.   ←

A monadic operator such as − outranks any binary operator. Sub-algorithm or Procedure calls may be considered monadic operations. In a chain of successive monadic operators the rightmost outranks those to its left.

By using these rules the evaluation of any expression can be reduced to a sequence of evaluations of very simple expressions. Thus the evaluation of

$$m \leftarrow y - (w + cx - z{\uparrow}u)/(r - s \times u)$$

can be reduced to that of

1. $t_1 \leftarrow - z$ (monadic − outranks dyadic ↑)
2. $t_1 \leftarrow t_1 \uparrow u$
3. $t_1 \leftarrow c \times t_1$
4. $t_1 \leftarrow w + t_1$
5. $t_2 \leftarrow s \times u$
6. $t_2 \leftarrow r - t_2$
7. $t_1 \leftarrow t_1 / t_2$
8. $t_1 \leftarrow y - t_1$
9. $m \leftarrow t_1$

The t_1 and t_2 are often called "temporary or intermediate variables" since they are used only during the evaluation of the expression.

An additional simplification we shall make is to require that in each of the expressions one of the operands be a particular "universal variable" called the "accumulator." Furthermore, the result of each operation is to reside in the accumulator. We shall denote the accumulator by @. Then we get:

1. @ ← - z
2. @ ← @ ↑ u
3. @ ← @ × c
4. @ ← @ + w
5. t ← @
6. @ ← s   (2.2)
7. @ ← @ × u
8. @ ← r - @
9. @ ← t / @
10. @ ← y - @
11. m ← @

It is convenient to introduce a general reversal operator Φ which, when preceding an operator, reverses its operands. Using Φ in the operation above we get

5. @ Φ ← t
8. @ ← @ Φ - r
9. @ ← @ Φ / t
10. @ ← @ Φ - y
11. @ Φ ← m

In each of these operations @ occurs *always* to the left of ← and, if it occurs a second time, always to the immediate right of the ←.

Let us now examine condition boxes. They are of the form

        if expression₁ R expression₂ then goto M
or   if expression₃ then goto M

where M is some label and R is one of the six arithmetic relations $<, \leq, =, \neq, \geq, >$, and expression₁ and expression₂ are *arithmetic* expressions: they utilize only the dyadic arithmetic operations (ranks 5, 6, and 7) in (2.1) and the monadic minus $(-)$. Expression₃ is a logical expression whose value is <u>true</u> or <u>false</u> and which may contain the additional dyadic operations $\wedge$ and $\vee$ and the monadic operation $\sim$. Two examples follow.

Example 1: <u>if</u> $x + 7 > u \times V - t$ <u>then</u> <u>goto</u> M meaning <u>if</u> $(x + 7) > ((u \times V) - t)$ <u>then</u> <u>goto</u> M

Example 2: <u>if</u> $c \wedge y > 4 \vee d \wedge \sim (x + y > p)$ <u>then</u> <u>goto</u> M meaning <u>if</u> $(c \wedge \overline{(y > 4)}) \vee (d \wedge (\sim ((x + y) > p)))$ <u>then</u> <u>goto</u> M

Let us agree to represent <u>true</u> by the integer 1 and <u>false</u> by the integer 0. We shall reduce all condition boxes to the form

    <u>if</u> @ = 1 <u>then</u> <u>goto</u> M

which says: <u>if</u> @ $=$ <u>true</u> <u>then</u> <u>goto</u> M.

Indeed, consider Example 2. In the same spirit as the reduction of the arithmetic expression (2.2), Example 2 is reduced to:

1. $@ \leftarrow y$
2. $@ \leftarrow @ > 4$
3. $@ \leftarrow @ \wedge c$
4. $@ \leftarrow t$
5. $@ \leftarrow X$
6. $@ \leftarrow @ + y$
7. $@ \leftarrow @ > p$
8. $@ \leftarrow \sim @$
9. $@ \leftarrow @ \wedge d$
10. $@ \leftarrow @ \vee t$
11. if $@ = 1$ then goto M

We should pause to say a word about vector components that may appear in expressions. Thus, in expression$_1$ $\times$ B[expression$_2$], we may reduce expression$_2$ (as above) with its result as the value of the accumulator and follow with

$$@ \: \phi \leftarrow t$$
$$\iota \leftarrow t$$

followed by the reduction of expression$_1$ with $@$ finally holding its value. Then

$$@ \leftarrow @ \times B, \: \iota$$

This second universal variable, denoted by ι, is called an *index variable*. It will generally take on an integer value, and its value will be used to *select* a component from B, that component whose position in B is the value of the universal variable ι. For example, if ι holds the value 7, then

$$@ \leftarrow @ \times B, \: \iota$$

will set $@$ to the product of the previous value in $@$ and the value in $B[7]$. B is the label of the (nonexistent) zeroth component of the ·vector B, and B, 7 means $B + 7$, the label of the seventh component of B.

Let us now turn our attention to the simplification of procedure or subalgorithm calls. The linearization phase left all such calls in the form

goR $f(X_1, X_2, \: . \: . \: . \: , X_n, Y)$

where Y labels the next step to be done when the procedure f has completed its execution and where $X_1, X_2, \: . \: . \: . \: , X_n$ are the actual parameters to be used in this call of f. We shall adopt the rule that all calls on a subalgorithm will utilize the same (required) number of actual parameters. Naturally, f will know this number, since it requires that many! However, f does not know, in the case of any particular call, what the parameters are, and we must solve the problem of how to pass this information to f in such a way that the method we will use is independent of f, independent of the number of actual parameters, and independent of their type and values.

We will wiggle out of this problem by always passing precisely one piece of information on a call to f, the label Y. If f requires a single parameter, it will be assumed to be the value of @. If f requires more than one parameter, we have to make use of an idea towards which we are heading and will shortly justify. Briefly put, if two boxes *follow each other* in a linearized algorithm, and we correspond the second of the two boxes—for example, that box having label Y, with an integer M, then we correspond the first box, *regardless of its label*, to the integer $M - 1$, and the one before that to $M - 2$, etc. Subroutines will communicate by using these label correspondences, and it will be in the sense of these correspondences that we will use labels Y, $Y - 1$, $Y - 2$, $Y - 4$, etc. Thus, if $Y \leftrightarrow M$, then $Y - 2 \leftrightarrow M - 2$.

Now suppose that subalgorithm f requires three parameters. Then

$$\underline{\text{goR}} \ f(X_1, \ X_2, \ X_3, \ Y)$$
$$Y:$$

will be transformed into the set of lines known as a *calling sequence:*

	$\underline{\text{goto}} \ T$ ①
$Z_1:$	lines evaluating the first actual parameter with the label of the result held in @
	$\underline{\text{return}}$ stack
$Z_2:$	lines evaluating the second actual parameter with the label of the result held in @ ②
	$\underline{\text{return}}$ stack ③
$Z_3:$	lines evaluating the third actual parameter with the label of the result held in @
	$\underline{\text{return}}$ stack
$T - 3:$	$\underline{\text{goto}} \ Z_1$
$T - 2:$	$\underline{\text{goto}} \ Z_2$ ④
$T - 1:$	$\underline{\text{goto}} \ Z_3$
$T:$	$\underline{\text{goR}} \ f$
$Y:$	. . . the continuation of the algorithm

The nature of this transformation can be understood by following it step by step. Certainly it is an enormously important transformation, since its role is that of a magical membrane coupling together two independent algorithms so they become (temporarily) one! The circled integers 1 to 4 refer to the comments that follow.

Comments

① The steps between this line and that at T compute the values of the actual parameters used in this call and provide links between their need by the formal parameters of f during its execution and their evaluation in the calling program.

② This set of steps evaluates the second actual parameter and leaves in the accumulator the label of the box where the result is to be found.

③ Once the second actual parameter is evaluated, the result assigned to some box, and the label of the box where it is kept assigned to the accumulator, the return stack accomplishes the return to that point within f from where the request for the actual parameter value had been issued.

In keeping with the ultimate goal of representing algorithms as sequences of integers, each the contents of a "box," boxes will also be the repository for values of variables. The box label will thus be the name of a variable whose successive values the box will successively hold.

④ Before commencing the actual parameter evaluation, f planted on the return stack the label to return to in f when the parameter had been evaluated. After putting it there, one of the lines $T - 3$, $T - 2$, or $T - 1$ is executed, depending upon which actual parameter is to be evaluated. All processing associated with the second parameter is confined to line $T - 2$ and the lines commencing with label Z_2 up to, but not including, Z_3.

How does f know where to plant the return so as to establish the link to the code at Z_2? It is so that the go$\overline{R}$ in T itself plants a $T + 1$ (the integer corresponding to Y) on the top of the return stack and then executes a goto f. Now the subroutine f has access to $T + 1$, and hence to $T - 2$ for the link to the algorithm for evaluating the second actual parameter.

Next, let us examine how the subalgorithm itself is organized. Its form is like that of any other algorithm except that it has formal parameters that are to take on values determined by their corresponding actual parameters in any call for the subalgorithm's execution. When the HALT of the subalgorithm is reached, the sequencing of the calling program execution is to continue from the point following the call on the subalgorithm. Thus may a line of the algorithm behave as though it were an entire, arbitrarily complicated algorithm. Execution of a procedure will always commence with the first line of the procedure. The HALT in the procedure will be replaced by the line

    return stack

All that remains is to indicate how the formal parameters are linked to their actual counterparts. Where can a formal parameter occur in the subalgorithm? The answer is obvious: Anywhere that a variable could occur in an algorithm:

1. In an arithmetic or logical capacity,
2. As a variable to which a value is to be assigned,
3. As a label, as in a goto or goR capacity,
4. As the name of a subalgorithm,

since one algorithm, in calling a subalgorithm, can dictate a second subalgorithm for the first sub-algorithm to call upon in performing its function.

Let us consider how an occurrence of the pth formal parameter of the subalgorithm is treated.

Let n be the number of formal parameters of the subalgorithm f. Then, if the occurrence is as an operand, as a label or as a subalgorithm, we have the following.

1. As an operand X:

> $\iota \leftarrow$ return stack $-$ (n + 2)
> γ: goR p, ι

> The integer of the line holding the value of X is the value of @ at this point:

> γ + 1:

2. As a label:

> $\iota \leftarrow$ p $-$ (n + 2)
> γ: return stack

> The actual parameter computation performs the goto dictated by the actual parameter.

3. As a subalgorithm identifier:

> $\iota \leftarrow$ return stack $-$ (n + 2)
> γ: goR 0, ι

> At this point the variable @ contains the integer corresponding to the first line of the subalgorithm to be called.

> γ + 1: $\iota \leftarrow$ @
> γ + 2: goR 0, ι

> Communication is now focused between the two subalgorithms until their intercourse is completed, after which primary communication is reestablished between the original caller and the first subalgorithm.

> T: goR 0, ι

We can now display the entire process in one diagram:

CALL SIDE · SUBALGORITHM SIDE

<u>goto</u> T: a call on f is to be made · f: First line of f

Z_1: computation of first actual parameter: the location of this value is in @. · comment on a need for the second actual parameter

· $\iota \leftarrow$ <u>return</u> stack $- (n + 2)$

<u>return</u> stack

Z_2: computation of second actual parameter: the location of this value is in @ · γ: go R 2, ι the jump is to $T - 2$ with $\gamma + 1$ planted on the top of the return stack

<u>return</u> stack

· $\gamma + 1$: $\iota \leftarrow$ @
$m \leftarrow q \times (0, \iota)$ the value of the actual parameter is multiplied by q, etc.

Z_3:
· · ·

· · ·

<u>return</u> stack · · ·

$T - 3$: <u>goto</u> Z_1
$T - 2$: <u>goto</u> Z_2 · λ: a subsequent use of
$T - 1$: <u>goto</u> Z_3 · $\lambda + 1$: second parameter from line λ
T: go R f
Y: upon completion of f continue from here

· ·

<u>goto</u> W
H_1:

<u>return</u> stack

H_2: · <u>return</u> stack return to the calling program, for example, either to Y or Q

<u>return</u> stack

H_3:

<u>return</u> stack
a second
$W - 3$: <u>goto</u> H_1 call on f
$W - 2$: <u>goto</u> H_2 from the
$W - 1$: <u>goto</u> H_3 "main"
algorithm
W: go R f
Q: upon completion of f, continue from here

We can see from the foregoing that the use of procedures is both convenient and expensive. Each actual parameter takes several lines of linkage. Each formal parameter requires three lines to prepare and use actual parameters. However, the communication has an elegant simplicity, since only one value need be transmitted in a call, and that will always be the label of the next line to be executed. With the go$R$ it can be done implicitly so that only the algorithm being called need ever be explicitly identified in this communication pattern.

ARITHMETIZATION 1

general algorithms
↓
linear algorithms
↓
symbolic programs
↓
numeric codes

which are executed by   general computer
↓
microcomputer
↓
logical diagrams
↓
circuit diagrams
↓
the laws of physics

In this next stage the algorithm is brought closer to standard form. We observe that every line contains (a.) one operator, (b.) one operand, (c.) reference to the accumulator @, and (d.) sometimes reference to the special variable ι. Furthermore, reference to the accumulator always occurs in the same way when associated with an operator; hence, no explicit reference to the accumulator in any line is necessary. Thus all lines are of the form "label: operation, operand, reference to ι," and they will contain only the operations given in Table 2.1 and a special operation that we shall find useful in the handling of loops:

26. $\iota \leftarrow \iota - 1$ and <u>if</u> $\iota > 0$ <u>goto</u> <u>else</u> continue   SIT

For symmetry we will include an additional operation:

27. $\iota \rightarrow$ STI

It is useful in describing the operations to specify the effect they have on the variables @, ι, and an arbitrary variable x. We shall discuss these operations in more arithmetic detail in a subsequent session. But note that there are just $27 < 32 = 2^5$ different operations that can occur in any of our algorithms!

TABLE 2.1

	Operation	Mnemonic	
1.	@ ←	CLA	
2.	@ +	ADD	
3.	@ −	SUB	
4.	@ ϕ −	RSB	
5.	@ /	DIV	
6.	@ ϕ /	RDV	
7.	@ ×	MPY	
8.	@ ≥	GRE	
9.	@ =	EQU	
10.	@ ≠	NEQ	
11.	@ >	GTR	
12.	@ <	LSS	
13.	@ ≤	LSE	
14.	@ ∧	AND	
15.	@ ∨	OR	
16.	~ @	NOT	
17.	− @	NEG	no operand is specified
18.	if	IF	
19.	goto	GO	
20.	goR	GOR	
21.	PRINT	PRT	
22.	READ	RD	
23.	HALT	HLT	no operand is specified
24.	ι ←	LDI	
25.	@ →	STO	

In the discussion of the computer that follows we shall confine our attention to a subset of the instruction list, (Table 2.1) and, for a reason subsequently clear, we shall divide the operations into two classes, those that do not utilize an arbitrary operand and those that do.

No arbitrary operand:

0.	~	NOT	
1.	−	NEG	
2.	HALT	HLT	
3.		SIT	(see Table 2.1)

Arbitrary operand:

4.	<u>goto</u>	GO
5.	<u>go</u>R	GOR
6.	<u>READ</u>	RD
7.	@ →	STO
8.	ι →	STI
9.	<u>if</u>	IF
16.	@ ←	CLA
17.	@ +	ADD
18.	@ −	SUB
19.	@ ×	MPY
20.	@ >	GTR
21.	@ =	EQ
22.	@ ∧	AND
23.	@ ∨	OR
24.	<u>PRINT</u>	PRT
25.	ι ←	LDI

(2.3)

Let us put a limit on the number of data that algorithms can manipulate. Indeed let us limit the sum that the number of data and the number of lines to describe an algorithm, including all its sub-algorithms and all of theirs, etc., to be no greater than $4096 = 2^{12}$.

The computer we are about to describe would probably be classified as a minicomputer by present-day standards.

For the present let us limit any datum to being a fraction m such that $m = 0$ or

$$2^{-17} \le |m| \le 1 - 2^{-17}$$

Integers will be handled as fractions, that is, be multiplied by (scaled by) 2^{-17}, and we shall remember this in any of our manipulations of integers in our algorithms. Of course we can't use integers $\ge 2^{17}$.

An operand may or may not be subscripted, modified by the value of the variable ι. The foregoing allows us to establish correspondence of the following kind.

1.   Between the identifier of any variable and an integer:

$$0 \le d \le 4095 = 2^{12} - 1$$

2.   Between any line of the algorithm and an integer:

$$0 \le k < 4096$$

for any line of the algorithm can be represented as a datum since its three parts (operation, operand, and index) can be combined into an integer c, satisfying $1 \le c \le 2^{17} - 1$.

Put another way, every algorithm can be represented as a vector of integers C, and every collection of data used by the algorithm as a vector of fractions D, and the two together as a single vector of fractions $M = C + D$. We propose to show how these correspondences are arranged. These vectors are the standard forms on which digital computers operate. An algorithm so represented is called a *machine code program*.

We shall now show how the correspondences are achieved. Every algorithm is a list of statements in standard form customarily called *commands* or *instructions*. We shall translate the algorithm into its numeric form as follows.

We define a *PASS* as a scan of the algorithm from its (lexical) beginning to its (lexical) end. We create a *symbol* table during the first PASS that will hold the correspondences between symbols occurring in the algorithm and integers. We shall use a variable *PLACE* that will point at the particular line of the algorithm being scanned. It will start at 0 and increment in steps of 1, until the entire algorithm (and its subalgorithms) have been scanned. Let us now look at two arbitrary lines in the algorithm:

```
ALPHA:    MPY X, ι
          GO Z + 5
```

For the first line we enter ALPHA into the symbol table, its integer correspondent being the current value of PLACE. If ALPHA is already in the table without an integer correspondent, we attach the value of PLACE as the correspondent. If X is not already in the symbol table, it is entered *without* an integer correspondence. If X is already present, nothing is entered for it. Since X is a vector (note the use of $ι$ as a subscript indicator), it would already have been entered with its extent into the table, via a declaration in the preamble. Since ALPHA is a (unique) label, it would not have been entered into the table with a correspondence prior to this line.

Then PLACE $\leftarrow$ PLACE $+ 1$, and we move to scan the next line. On arrival at the second line listed we make no changes in the symbol table. The correspondent of $(Z + 5)$ is to be 5 + the correspondent of Z. We shall assign that in a subsequent (second) PASS.

When we have examined all of the lines of the algorithm, we proceed to append to the algorithm the list of constants. We treat this list as though it consisted of a set of labeled lines of the form, say,

```
ONE:    1
HALF:   1/2
```

and we now proceed to assign these labels the successive values of PLACE. By this point in the PASS all of the unassigned symbols will already be in the symbol table (why?).

When the list of constants is exhausted, the symbol table should now contain, as its unassigned symbols, only those representing the variables of the algorithm. We now scan the symbol table and assign to these symbols of variables successive values of PLACE. In case a symbol had been entered as denoting a vector, say X, it would have been entered with the number of its components; for example,

```
symbol      extent  correspondence
  X    VCT    35
```

Scalars require no extent. After the assignment to X, PLACE is augmented by the extent of X, PLACE $\leftarrow$ PLACE $+ 35$. When the symbol table no longer contains any uncorresponded symbols, we proceed to the second PASS.

ARITHMETIZATION 2

general algorithms
↓
linear algorithms
↓
symbolic programs
↓
numeric codes
↓
which are executed by   general computer
↓
microcomputer
↓
logical diagrams
↓
circuit diagrams
↓
the laws of physics

Again we commence with the first line of the algorithm, though we could just as well march backwards from the last line. For each line we perform the following codings, constructing a binary fraction:

1. Discard any label, if present.
2. If there is an operation, replace it by the integer correspondent from the operation table (2.3).
3. If there is a variable, replace it by its integer correspondent from the symbol table. If the symbol is of the form, say, $Z + 5$ and Z has the correspondent 1732, replace the occurrence of $Z + 5$ by 1737.
4. If the variable ι appears, say, attached to a variable X, create a 1, otherwise a 0. Now juxtapose the three integers into one integer, 1 27 1546. This is the standard form of instructions.

```
    0
    or        27          1546
    1
  index    operation    variable
```

5. If the line holds a constant, no further work needs be done.
6. If the line is a declaration, discard it.

Actually, let us represent each line in binary rather than decimal, and we shall then find that every instruction will fit into 18 binary digits:

```
1    11011    011000001010
1     27         1546
```

We might say a word here about binary representation of integers. Each integer has a decimal representation that we have become so accustomed to using that we think of the representation as the number. Thus if we are asked how many bars are in the set ||||||||||||, we write "12." But we could also write 1100, which is "twelve" in binary. Thus we should, to be precise, write 12_{10} and, so that we don't have to write $12_{10_{10_{10}\ldots}}$, we agree that the base will always be written in decimal. Thus $12_{10} = 1100_2$. Let us compare three number systems.

	Decimal	Binary	Octal
base	10	2	8
digits	0, 1, . . . , 9	0, 1	0, 1, . . . , 7
packing	1	3.3	1.1

(About three binary digits are required for representing each decimal digit.)

An example of conversion is the following.

$139_{10} \rightarrow 10001011_2$
$\rightarrow 010001011_2 \rightarrow 213_8$
$\leftarrow 011101111_2 \leftarrow 357_8$
$239_{10} \leftarrow 2^7 + 2^6 + 2^5 + 2^3 + 2^2 + 2^1 + 2^0$

How to convert:
(decimal → binary)

```
              139
             -128     2⁷     1     128
                             0
                             0
               11
                             0
               -8     2³     1       8
                3
               -2     2¹     1       2
                1
               -1     2⁰     1       1
                0                   139
```

To convert between binary and octal, remember that each triple of binary digits is exactly one octal digit.

In the case of constants appearing in our algorithms:

$$0_{17} \quad 1 \quad \text{will represent 1}$$
$$0_{16} \quad 10 \quad \text{will represent 2}$$

and 10_{17} will represent 1/2, where 0_{17} means

$$\underbrace{00 \ldots 0}_{17}.$$

We must remember that integers are *scaled* by 2^{-17}, though this fact will not overly concern us here. In a subsequent section we shall discuss binary arithmetic.

In any event, we have now succeeded in transforming every algorithm into a vector of 18-digit binary fractions (or integers scaled by 2^{-17}), and we can now turn to the examination of the device that executes the algorithm in its 18-bit vector representation.

A machine-code program (Table 2.2) for the coin algorithm is shown, in which the instruction set (2.3) is used. We list the symbolic program, the resultant symbol table, and the ultimate program in decimal. Finally, the first four instructions are shown in binary. Should the reader wish, he can perform the tedious, but trivial, translation into binary of the remainder of the program.

In the following table PASS 1 1/2 refers to the assignments of integers to symbols made after PASS 1 but before PASS 2.

SYMBOL ASSIGNMENT TABLE

		PASS	
SYMBOL	<u>1</u>	<u>1 1/2</u>	<u>2</u>
START	0		
L			66
C		46	
ALPHA	2		
N			67
INDEX			68
ZERO		45	
P			69
J			70
T			71
BETA	12		
M		56	
GAMMA	15		
ONE		44	
MU	21		
EPSILON	35		
DELTA	37		

In Section 2 we mentioned that algorithms are executed one line at a time through a window, as it were. At any moment in time we examine one instruction through the window, perform its in-

TABLE 2.2

	Label	Operator Symbol	Comment
START:	RD	L	
	LDI	L	
2 ALPHA:	RD	C, ι	Read in coin denominations
	SIT	ALPHA	
	RD	N	Read amount
	RD	INDEX	Read index
	CLA	ZERO	INITIALIZE
	STO	P	STACK LEVEL
	CLA	INDEX	RESULT
	STO	J	
	CLA	N	
	STO	T	
12 BETA:	LDI	J	
	CLA	T	
	STO	M, ι	
15 GAMMA:	CLA	C, ι	BASIC REDUCTION
	EQ	ONE	CYCLE
	IF	DELTA	
	CLA	P	
	ADD	ONE	
	STO	P	
21 MU:	CLA	J	
	SUB	ONE	STACK DECREMENT
	STO	J	
	CLA	INDEX	
	GTR	J	
	IF	EPSILON	
	LDI	J	
	CLA	M, ι	
	SUB	C, ι	
	STO	T	
	CLA	ZERO	
	GTR	T	
	IF	MU	
	GO	BETA	
35 EPSILON:	PRT	P	PRINT RESULT
	HLT		
37 DELTA:	CLA	J	STACK INCREMENT
	ADD	ONE	
	STO	J	
	LDI	J	
	CLA	T	
	STO	M, ι	
	GO	GAMMA	
	END		PUNCTUATION TERMINATING THE ALGORITHM DESCRIPTION
44 ONE		1	
45 ZERO		0	
C		VCT 10	
M		VCT 10	

TABLE 2.3 DECIMAL CODE

Location	Index	Operator	Operand	Location	Index	Operator	Operand
0	0	06	66	23	0	07	70
1	0	25	66	24	0	16	68
2	1	06	46	25	0	20	70
3	0	03	02	26	0	09	35
4	0	06	67	27	0	25	70
5	0	06	68	28	1	16	56
6	0	16	45	29	1	18	46
7	0	07	69	30	0	07	71
8	0	16	68	31	0	16	45
9	0	07	70	32	0	20	71
10	0	16	67	33	0	09	21
11	0	07	71	34	0	04	12
12	0	25	70	35	0	24	69
13	0	16	71	36	0	02	00
14	1	07	56	37	0	16	70
15	1	16	46	38	0	17	44
16	0	21	44	39	0	07	70
17	0	09	37	40	0	25	70
18	0	16	69	41	0	16	71
19	0	17	44	42	1	07	56
20	0	07	69	43	0	04	15
21	0	16	70	44	0	00	01
22	0	18	44	45	0	00	00

BINARY PROGRAM

```
0 00110 0₅ 1000010
0 11001 0₅ 1000010
1 00110 0₅ 0101110
0 00011 0₅ 0000010
```

dicated command, and then move the window along the path indicated to the next step. The computer executes in much the same way, except that it keeps the window physically fixed and moves the algorithm, one line at a time, past the window. Whereas the lines of the algorithm move smoothly past the window, the data referred to in successive lines have little relationship with each other, and the data are usually characterized as "randomly accessed."

The subscript position in the vector M of either a datum, a constant, or an instruction is called an *address*. Hence, addresses range from 0 to $2^{12} - 1 = 4095$. The vector M is called the computer store or memory, and access can be had to any component of M and hence to the value held by that component, whenever necessary, but at any one time only one component will be accessible. Executing a line of an algorithm may require either 1 or 2 accesses to the store M, depending on whether the instruction has no or one operand, respectively.

The paradigm by which a computer executes a program is extremely simple:

INITIALIZE.   Load the program. Set LP ← 0, where LP is the line pointer.

FETCH CYCLE.   Place in the window the line $M[LP]$. The line is assumed to hold an instruction.

EXECUTE CYCLE.   Increment LP: LP ← LP + 1; do the instruction in the window. This instruction may require a transfer of a line, or address contents, from the store to the window. Such a line is assumed to hold a datum (variable or constant). The execution may indeed change LP (this is how goto and branching conditions achieve their effect).

If the instruction was not a halt instruction then goto Fetch cycle else stop this process.

Note that the computer cannot distinguish between an instruction and a datum by its form in the storage, since both are 18-bit integers. Indeed, if brought into the window on a *fetch cycle*, a line holds an instruction, whereas on the *execute cycle* it holds a value, no matter what the intent of the machine program.

Let us now turn our attention to the window. It is within the window that all the computer's work is done. The window contains a small amount of its own storage and a subcomputer to arrange the execution of each fetched line. The storage elements of the window are usually called *registers* and have names (instead of numbers or addresses) that help to explicate their function. They are connected to each other by *register transfer paths*, along which information is transferred during the different phases of the fetch and execute cycles.

Let us list these registers with their *precisions* (number of bits) and their (gross) functions.

(D)   Distributor (18 bits): Holds in the rightmost 12 bits the address of the instruction to be fetched. Then it holds the instruction fetched. Then it holds the address of the datum required by the instruction. Then it holds the datum. Then it participates by holding an operand in arithmetic operations. It's a very busy register!

(@)   Accumulator (19 bits): Holds the result of all arithmetic and logical operations. Every arithmetic operation requires that one operand be in the accumulator. LP (see below) is augmented by 1, and IDEX (the register corresponding to ι) is decremented by 1 in the accumulator. Indexing, the selection of vector components, is done by utilizing the accumulator.

(R)   Remainder (17 bits): Holds the 17 least significant digits of a product. It can be considered a (right) appendage of the accumulator.

(LP)   Line pointer (12 bits): Holds the address of the instruction to be fetched.

(IDEX)   Index register (12 bits): Holds a 12-bit increment that may be added to addresses prior to the fetching of their contents. Certain instructions load this register; one decrements its contents by 1.

(I/O)   Input-output register (18 bits): Holds an 18-bit number that is to go into storage (input) or has come from storage (output). We shall not concern ourselves with how this register is loaded and unloaded by the "outside world."

(C)   Carry register (18 bits): Holds the carries generated during addition.

COMPUTER:

WINDOW:

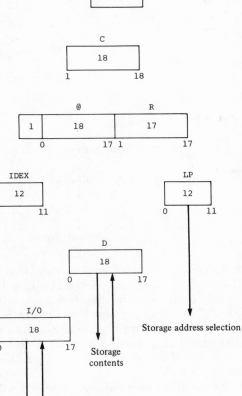

The view of the computer being presented here is one that deliberately uses very few registers in the window. A different computer with the same instruction code could easily be specified that would use one or two additional registers and would require considerably less shifting of information during the execute cycle.

It is useful in more complicated computers to exhibit maps of the paths between registers, for we may then consider for each path the circumstances under which it is used. Similarly, for each operation of the computer we can state which paths are used and in what sequence; that is to say, we can give a *program* for what each of the 26 instructions does, expressed in terms of even more elementary operations that we shall call the machine's *microcode*.

We must now turn to the issue of arithmetic. After all, our whole purpose in the reduction process has been to "arithmetize" algorithm descriptions so that we may "arithmetize" their execution. Now we shall see why binary representation is so natural to use in computers.

COMPUTER ARITHMETIC

general algorithms
$\downarrow$
linear algorithms
$\downarrow$
symbolic programs
$\downarrow$
numeric codes

which are executed by   general computer
$\downarrow$
microcomputer
$\downarrow$
logical diagrams
$\downarrow$
circuit diagrams
$\downarrow$
the laws of physics

Data in the computer, called *machine numbers*, are fractions. A datum X satisfies $|X| < 2^0$. Thus, $7/8$ is 0.1110_{14}, $5/16$ is 0.01010_{13}, and $11/152$ is 0.0_510110_8. Positive numbers have a 0 as their leftmost digit. The "." is imaginary and is written merely to separate the leftmost digit. How do we represent negative numbers? We define the complement of a machine number X to be $2 - X = \bar{X}$. The $\bar{X}$ is called the *2-complement* of X. Then $X + \bar{X} = 2 = 0$ (mod 2), meaning $X + \bar{X}$ gives a remainder of 0 on division by 2. Since $X < 1$, then $\bar{X} > 1$ and a leftmost digit of 1 will always indicate a negative number held in 2-complement form. We call the leftmost digit of a number its *sign digit*. Thus $3/4$ is 0.110_{15} and $-3/4$ is 1.010_{15}. How do we complement? Observe that

$$2 = 2^0 + 2^{-1} + \cdots + 2^{-17} + 2^{-17}$$

and

$$X = X_0 2^0 + X_1 2^{-1} + \cdots + X_{17} 2^{-17}$$

where X_i, the ith digit of X, is 0 or 1. Then

$$\bar{X} = (1 - X_0)2^0 + (1 - X_1)2^{-1} + \cdots + (1 - X_{17})2^{-17} + 2^{-17}$$

$$= \bar{X}_0 2^0 + \bar{X}_1 2^{-1} \cdots \bar{X}_{17} 2^{-17} + 2^{-17}$$

Consequently, we may obtain $\bar{X}$ from X in two steps:

1. Change each of the digits of X from 0 to 1 or from 1 to 0, respectively. Put another way, if $X_i = 0$ then $\bar{X}_i \leftarrow 1$ else $\bar{X}_i \leftarrow 0$.
2. Add 1 to the rightmost digit of the transformed number.

Examples: Since the above and ensuing analysis holds for any number of digits, to simplify descriptions, the examples that follow will use 5 digits instead of 18.

```
X = X₀.X₁X₂X₃X₄
Suppose X is 13/16 = 0.1101
Then    X̄ is 1.0010 + 2⁻⁴ = 1.0011 = 19/16 = 32/16 -
        13/16
```

and the complement of $\bar{X}$ is $(\bar{\bar{X}})$ is $0.1100 + 2^{-4}$ is $0.1101 = 13/16 = X$.

Let us examine in more detail the arithmetic operations of addition, subtraction, multiplication, and division. However, to keep things simple, our computer will not do division. Many early computers were similarly parsimonious, but experience and the availability of improved and cheaper devices have led to the inclusion of division as an operation in all modern computers.

In our computer, when arithmetic operations are to be performed, one operand, a, will be in the accumulator, @, and the other, d, will be in the distributor register D. The result z will always reside in the accumulator. We shall use a subscript r to denote the machine representation of the actual numbers and a subscript $0 \leq i \leq 17$ to indicate a bit position in the machine representation.

The operation of addition is best understood by a case analysis.

1. $a_0 = d_0 = 0$ (both operands are positive).
    a. $a_r = a$ and $d_r = d$, $z_r = a + d$ and $z = z_r$.
    b. If $z_{r_0} = 1$, a result has been obtained that is too large to fit in the machine and hence is not a machine number. In this case we say that an *overflow* has occurred.

The computer will usually signal in some way that this situation has occurred, by coming to a halt, or turning on a signal light, etc.

2. $a_0 = 1$ and $d_0 = 0$ (operands are of opposite signs).
$a_r = 2 - |a| = \bar{a}$ and $d_r = d$.
$a_r + d_r = 2 + d - |a| = z_r$.
   a. If $|d| > |a|$ the overflow is spurious, and $z = z_r \pmod 2$, which is to say that the overflow is discarded.
   b. If $|a| \geq |d|$, $z_r = 2 - (|a| - d)$, and the correct result has been obtained.

The case of $a_0 = 0$ and $d_0 = 1$ is treated the same way.

3. $a_0 = d_0 = 1$ (both operands are negative).
$a_r = 2 - |a| = \bar{a}$ and $d_r = 2 - |d| = \bar{d}$.
$a_r + d_r = 2 + 2 - (|a| + |d|)$.
   a. If we discard the overflow, should it occur, the result is $2 - (|a| + |d|) = z_r$.
   b. However, if $z_{r_0} = 0$, there is an actual, not a spurious, overflow since, if
$|a| + |d| = 1 + q \geq 1$, then
$a_r + d_r = 2 - (1 + q) = 1 - q < 1$, and
the sign bit $z_{r_0} = 0$.

The preceding analysis is illustrated in the following six cases.

1. 5/16 is 0.0101
   + 7/16 is 0.0111
   = 12/16 is 0.1100, the correct result (case 1a. with no overflow).
2. 9/16 is 0.1001
   + 10/16 is .01010
   = 19/16 is 1.0011 (case 1b. with overflow).
3. 5/16 is 0.0101
   + −7/16 is 1.1001
   = −2/16 is 1.1110, the correct result (case 2a.).
4. 7/16 is 0.0111
   + −5/16 is 1.1011
   = 2/16 is 10.0010, the overflow is spurious.
   2/16 is 0.0010 is the correct result (case 2b.).
5. −7/16 is 1.1001
   + −5/16 is 1.1011
   is 11.0100, the overflow is spurious.
   = −12/16 is 1.0100 is the correct result (case 3a.).
6. −9/16 is 1.0111
   + −10/16 is 1.0110
   = −19/16 is 10.1101, the sign digit is 0, and there is a real overflow (case 3b.).

The addition operation may be summed up as follows.

1a. $a_0 = d_0 = 0 = z_0$: z is the correct result.
1b. $a_0 = d_0 = 0 \neq z_0$: z is not a machine number, and an overflow has resulted.
2a,b. $a_0 \geq d_0$: z is the correct result when the overflow, if any, is discarded.   (2.4)
3a. $a_0 = d_0 = 1 = z_0$: z is the correct result when the overflow is discarded.
3b. $a_0 = d_0 = 1 \neq z_0$: z is not a machine number, and an overflow has resulted.

Subtraction is a special case of addition, since $z = a - d$ is obtained from $z_r = a_r + d_r - 2 = a_r + \bar{d}_r$. The d operand is complemented, and an addition is performed. The checks on the result, called for in (2.4), are performed by using the d operand after complementation.

Multiplication is more tedious, but only slightly more complicated, than addition. We observe that $z = |a| \times |d|$ if $a_0 = d_0$ and that $z = 2 - (|a| \times |d|)$ if $a_0 \neq d_0$. Consequently, multiplication is always performed on the absolute values of the operands, and the result is complemented if the signs of the two operands differ. The multiplication of two positive binary numbers is extremely simple, since each multiplier digit is either a 0 or a 1.

Consider the example $13/16 \times -10/16$. The respective numbers are 0.1101 and 1.0110. The second operand is complemented, and the multiplication unfolds as follows:

```
     0.1101
   ×0.1010
    ───────
     0 0000
    01 101
   000 00
  0110 1
 00000
 ─────────
 01000 0010
```

This, when complemented, is 10111 1110, or $-130/256$.

Either of the operands a or d may be considered the multiplier; in the computer we shall always take a to be the multiplier. The process (2.5) can be mechanized in a number of ways. Rather than do all additions after all the multiplications, we shall build the product as each digit of the multiplier is used. Thus we add, or do not add, d to the shifted partial product as the multiplier digit is 1 or 0, respectively. Instead of shifting the multiplicand left before adding, we shall shift the partial product right, and we shall use the R register to hold the multiplier and shifted partial products. With the example given above the following tableau shows how its multiplication unfolds. The underlined bit is the multiplier bit.

	@	R
	0 1101	0000
shift @ into R	0 0000	1101
add d	0 1010	1101
shift 1 place right	0 0101	0110
shift 1 place right	0 0010	1011
add d	0 1100	1011
shift 1 place right	0 0110	0101
add d	0 0000	0101
shift 1 place right	0 1000	0010

The complement of the last is 1 0111 1110, which is the correct signed product in 2-complement form. Since only the leading five digits of the result (18 digits in our computer) are a machine number and can be placed in storage, it is customary to *round off* the result by adding 1 to the most significant bit of R, treating @, R as a 9-bit register (for our example), and then throwing away the rightmost four bits of the result (the contents of R). Rounding off is done by shifting @, R one place left, adding 1 in the rightmost position of @, and shifting that result one place right. The unrounded product of largest magnitude is $15/16 \times 15/16 = (1 - 1/16) \times (1 - 1/16) = 1 - 2/16 + 1/256$. Rounding produces $1 - 2/16 + 1/256 + 1/32 < 1$, so that no overflow can result on rounding a product. In the example given above

0 1000 0010 becomes 1 0000 0100

and rounding gives

$$
\begin{array}{r}
1\ 0000\ 0100 \\
+\ 1 \\
\hline
1\ 0001\ 0100
\end{array}
$$

Shifting back gives 0 1000 as the rounded result in the accumulator.

Division is more complicated than multiplication. Given two machine numbers $a < d$, we seek two machine numbers q and r satisfying $a = q \times d + r$ where $|r| < d$. Let us again restrict our attention to 5-bit numbers.

Example: a is 10/16 and d is 13/16.

Using long division gives

$$
\begin{array}{r}
0.1100 \\
1101\,\overline{)\,1010\ 0000} \\
110\ 1 \\
\hline
011\ 10 \\
11\ 01 \\
\hline
0000\ 0100 \\
\end{array}
$$

(2.5)

or q is 12/16 and r is 4/256.

How can long division be mechanized? We observe that on each step:

1. An attempt to subtract d is made; if the remainder is non-negative (of the same sign as the divisor), a quotient digit of 1 is obtained, else a quotient digit of 0 is obtained.

2. The d is shifted one place to the right, and the cycle of steps 1 and 2 is repeated until four quotient bits are obtained.

We observe that, if the quotient bit is 0, we must undo the subtraction by adding back the divisor and then shifting the divisor one place to the right; but observe that

$$r + d - 1/2d = r + 1/2d$$

so that instead of adding back and *then* shifting and subtracting again, one merely needs to shift and then add on the next cycle. This is the gist of the method of "nonrestoring" division. Clearly, instead of shifting the divisor right one place, we may shift the current remainder left one place, thus multiplying the remainder by 2. Let r_i be the remainder at the ith step. Then

$$r_i \leftarrow 2r_{i-1} \begin{cases} -d \text{ if } q_i = 1 \\ +d \text{ if } q_i = 0 \end{cases}$$

or, as a single assignment statement,

$$r_i \leftarrow 2r_{i-1} + (1 - 2q_i)d$$

We commence the process with $r_0 \leftarrow a$ and terminate when i is 4. Our algorithm for division is:

```
START: r ← a
i ← 1
LOOP: if i > 4 then goto EXIT
qᵢ ← sgn(r) = sgn(d)
r ← 2 × r + (1 - 2 × qᵢ) × d
i ← i + 1
goto LOOP
EXIT: HALT
```

We have agreed to represent negative numbers in 2-complement form. How does this affect the algorithm? Let us look at an example.

Example: a is $-10/16$ and d is $13/16$.

Let us change the tableau somewhat:

$$
\begin{array}{llll}
r_0 = a = & 1.0110 & q_1 = 0 \\
+d = & 0.1101 \\ \hline
2r_0 = & 0.1100 \\
+d = & 0.1101 \\ \hline
r_1 = & 1.1001 & q_2 = 0 \\
2r_1 = & 1.0010 \\
+d = & 0.1101 \\ \hline
r_2 = & 1.1111 & q_3 = 0 \\
2r_2 = & 1.1110 \\
+d = & 0.1101 \\ \hline
r_3 = & 0.1011 & q_4 = 1 \\
2r_3 = & 1.0110 \\
+d = & 1.0011 \\ \hline
r_4 = & 10.1001
\end{array}
\tag{2.6}
$$

What is the quotient obtained by our algorithm? Take each equation for $i = 1, 2, 3, 4$, multiply each by 2^{-i}, and add them together,

$$
\begin{aligned}
r_0 &= a \\
2^{-1} \times r_1 &= \qquad\quad r_0 + (2^{-1} - q_1)d \\
2^{-2} \times r_2 &= 2^{-1} \times r_1 + (2^{-2} - 2^{-1}q_2)d \\
2^{-3} \times r_3 &= 2^{-2} \times r_2 + (2^{-3} - 2^{-2}q_3)d \\
2^{-4} \times r_4 &= 2^{-3} \times r_3 + (2^{-4} - 2^{-3}q_4)d
\end{aligned}
$$

to get

$$
2^{-4}r_4 = a + (2^{-1} + 2^{-2} + 2^{-3} + 2^{-4} \\
- (q_1 + 2^{-1}q_2 + 2^{-2}q_3 + 2^{-3}q_4))d
$$

or

$$
a = q \times d + 2^{-4}r_4 = q \times d + r
$$

The quotient q is $0.0010 - 0.1111$ or

$$
\begin{array}{ll}
& 0.0010 \\
q \ \underline{is} & +1.0001 \\ \hline
& 1.0011 \ \underline{is} \ -12/16
\end{array}
$$

What about the remainder?

$$
r_4 \ \underline{is} \ 0.1001 = 9/16
$$

and the remainder $\underline{is} +9/256$.

Note that $r_0 = 1.0110$ and $2r_0 = 0.1100$. Why should multiplication by 2 affect the sign bit? Simply because in 2-complement form there is no sign bit! All overflows are ignored because they do not influence the result that would have been obtained had we chosen to hold r fixed and shift d right instead.

Instead of complementing d, and adding $\bar{d}$, we could just as well complement r. Why? Because @ holds the current remainder, and we can then limit complementation to @. The q_i digits can be accumulated in the R register. The computation will be shown for the case a is $-9/16$ and d is $13/16$.

d		@	R		i
		10111	00000		
	shift	01110	00000	q is 0	1
01101 +		11011	00000		
	shift	10110	00000	q is 0	2
01101 +		00011	00000		
	shift	00110	00010	q is 1	3
complement @		11010	00010		
01101 +		00111	00010		
	shift	01110	00100	q is 0	4
complement @		10010	00100		
01101 +		11111	00100		
exchange		00100	11111	(shift q bits into @	
10001 +		10101		and remainder into R)	

The correct quotient is $-11/16$. The correct remainder is $2^{-4} \times 1.1111 = 1.1111\ 111\overline{1}$, since $2^{-4} \times (-2^{-4}) = -2^{-16}$ represented as $2 - 2^{-16} = 1.1111\ 1111$. Note that division would require the R register in our computer to hold 18 bits. Since we shall not discuss the divide operation in our analysis of the computer, we shall restrict the R register to the 17 bits required by the multiplication operation.

This completes our treatment of the way arithmetic is performed on our computer. We now proceed to a discussion of the mechanisms with which our computer performs both its arithmetic and its nonarithmetic actions.

We shall show that all arithmetic can be done by sequences of the five microoperations:

1. Half addition of @ and D (ha).
2. Carry clear (cc).
3. Set the jth carry to 1 (cj).
4. Carry propagate (cp).
5. Digit complement (cm).

Addition of two binary numbers can be looked upon as being done in two stages: the first is half addition, which forms a *partial sum* and creates carries, and the second is the propagation of the carries through the partial sum to create the correct sum. At any digit position the result of ha (and the following cp) may be symbolized as:

$0^{\leftarrow 1}$ becomes 1 (the carry stops).
$1^{\leftarrow 1}$ becomes $^{\leftarrow 1}0$ (the carry propagates).
$^{\leftarrow 1}0^{\leftarrow 1}$ becomes $^{\leftarrow 1}1$ (the carry stops).

A carry propagates only when ha produces 1: that is, when either, but not both, of a_i and d_i is 1. Carries never run into each other, because ha can never produce a carry at a position through which cp propagates one. A carry will propagate leftwards as long as successive partial-sum digits are 1 and will change each of them to 0. On encountering the first 0 the carry will change that 0 to 1 and propagate no farther. Thus all carries obtained in the first stage may be simultaneously propagated leftwards in the second stage, since they operate independently. For example:

```
         1 0110
ha     + 0 1111
        01 1001      partial sum
         0 0110      carries
cp      10 0101      sum
```

Note that the leftmost carry affects the three leftmost digits in the partial sum and complements them. In terms of these operations we can now define the operation + by the following algorithm:

```
U ← @[0]; comment save the sign of @
ha;
cp;
if U = D[0] ≠ @[0] then T ← 1 else T ← 0;
if T = 1 then halt.
```

COMPUTER-INSTRUCTION REPERTOIRE IN REGISTER TERMS

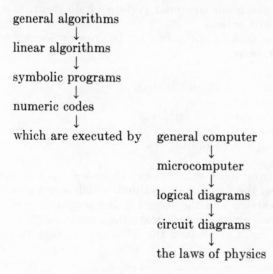

We now proceed to the next level of description of our computer. We shall develop a notation to describe the 26 computer operations in terms of their effect on the registers. It is very much like that of the algorithmic notation we have been using to describe algorithms in their successive simplifications. We commence with the description of the registers with the indices of their bit positions.

$D[0:17]$ Distributor for holding instructions and operands

$@[T, 0:17]$ Accumulator with the overflow bit T

$R|1:17]$ The right extension of $@$ used in multiplication

$IDEX[0:11]$ Index register whose contents regulate the accessing of vectors

$LP[0:11]$ Line pointer to the next instruction to be fetched from storage

$I/O[0:17]$ Input-output register

$Run[0]$ Holds 1 when the computer is running, 0 when it is halted.

$L[0]$ When it holds a 1, the overflow T does not set Run to 0 and stop the machine.

$U[0]$ Holds the initial sign of $@$ in arithmetic operations.

$M[Z][0:17]$ The storage location having address Z

Next, by using these registers the interpretation cycle of the computer can be succinctly described in algorithmic form by means of "conditional expressions." A conditional expression is a sequence of pairs of the form "condition $\rightarrow$ action":

$$c_1 \rightarrow a_1; \ c_2 \rightarrow a_2; \ . \ . \ .; \ c_n \rightarrow a_n$$

where the leftmost true condition invokes its corresponding action as the effect of the entire expression. Often the rightmost condition is one that is always true, which we may denote by true, so that the entire expression will always have a defined effect. If, on the other hand, no condition is true, the expression is undefined. The notation := will stand for a definition. Thus our first definition of the instruction interpretation cycle of the computer assumes the following simple form:

cycle := Run $\rightarrow$ ($D \leftarrow M[LP]$; $LP \leftarrow LP + 1$; next effective address calculation; next instruction execution); true $\rightarrow$ computer is halted;

A sequence of actions between nexts may be performed in any order or in parallel without effect on their results, but those following next are to commence only when all of the lexicographic predecessors have been completed.

We shall make two additional notational definitions: Let Z be $D[6:17]$ and OP be $D[1:5]$. Then the effective address calculation is $D[0] \rightarrow Z \leftarrow Z + IDEX$, and the instruction execution is as follows.

0. NOT := (OP = 00 → (@ ← complement @);
1. NEG := (OP = 01 → (@ ← complement @; <u>next</u>
   @ ← @ + 2^{-17});
2. HLT := (OP = 02) → (Run ← 0);
3. SIT := (OP = 03) → (IDEX ← IDEX − 2^{-12});
   <u>next</u> IDEX ≠ 0 → D ← M[Z];
   <u>next</u> LP ← D[6:17]);
4. GO := (OP = 04) → $\overline{(LP \leftarrow Z)}$;
6. RD := (OP = 06) → (M[Z] ← I/O);
7. STO := (OP = 07) → (M[Z] ← @);
8. STI := (OP = 08) → (M[Z][6:17] ← IDEX);
9. IF := (OP = 09) → (@17 ≠ 0 → LP ← Z);
16. CLA := (OP = 16) → (@ ← 0; <u>next</u> @ ← M[Z]);
17. ADD := (OP = 17) → ($D \leftarrow M[\overline{Z}]$; <u>next</u> @ ← @ +
    D);
18. SUB := (OP = 18) → (D ← M[Z]; <u>next</u>
    @ ← @ − D);
19. MPY := (OP = 19) → (D ← M[Z]; <u>next</u>
    @ ← @ × D);
20. GTR := (OP = 20) → (D ← M[Z]; <u>next</u>
    @ ← @ − D;
    <u>next</u> (@[0] = 0 ∧ @[1:17] ≠
    0 → @[17] ← 1;
    True → @[17] ← 0));
21. EQ := (OP = 21) → $\overline{(D \leftarrow M[Z]}$; <u>next</u> @ ← @ − D;
    <u>next</u> (@ = 0 → @[17] ← 1;
    True → @[17] ← 0));
22. AND := (OP = 22) → $\overline{(D \leftarrow M[Z]}$; <u>next</u>
    @ ← @ ∧ D);
23. OR := (OP = 23) → (D ← M[Z]; <u>next</u>
    @ ← @ ∨ D);
24. PRT := (OP = 24) → (I/O ← M[Z]);
25. LDI := (OP = 25) → (D ← M[Z]; <u>next</u> IDEX ←
    D[6:17]);

To keep matters simple, we have omitted the detailed description of <u>goR</u> and <u>return</u>, and we will not include the microcodes and registers to manipulate the return stack.

The preceding is an algorithmic description of what occurs in the execution of any instruction in a computer program stored in our computer. The reader is encouraged to follow through (to simulate) the execution of the first few lines of the detailed computer program for the coin problem (Table 2.2).

The preceding description of the computer is still not quite mechanical enough for our purposes: there are too many operations that have not been sufficiently defined. Our next step is to remove these anomalies by simplifying the computer and then following with a reduction in the number of operations that can appear in the conditional expressions describing each of the computer operations. Then we shall be in a position to look at a detailed logical description of the machine.

We shall insist that our computer be organized so that:

1. An element in storage is always selected by using the contents of LP for both instructions and data. In other words, M will only appear as $M[LP]$.
2. All arithmetic in the computer involves only @ and (sometimes) D and R.
3. All transfers of information from and to memory involve only transfers to and from the register D.
4. There is an operation, exchange (ex), that exchanges the contents of any pair of registers without loss of information.

With these four conditions in mind we shall now describe each of the computer operations, the address interpretation, and the instruction interpretation cycles in terms of simpler operations called *microoperations*.

Subject to the four preceding conditions, the basic interpretation cycle becomes:

$$Run \rightarrow (D \leftarrow M[LP]; ex(@[0:11], LP); L \leftarrow 1;$$
$$\underline{next} \ @ \leftarrow @ + 2^{-11};$$
$$\underline{next} \ ex(@[0: 11], LP), (D[0] \rightarrow ex(@[0: 11],$$
$$D[6: 17]);$$
$$\underline{next} \ ex(D[0: 11], IDEX); \ \underline{next} \ @[0: 11] \leftarrow \qquad (2.7)$$
$$@[0: 11] + D[0: 11];$$
$$\underline{next} \ ex(D[0: 11], IDEX); \ \underline{next} \ ex(D[6: 17],$$
$$@[0: 11]);$$
$$\underline{next} \ instruction \ execution);$$

MICROPROGRAMMING AND INSTRUCTION EXECUTION

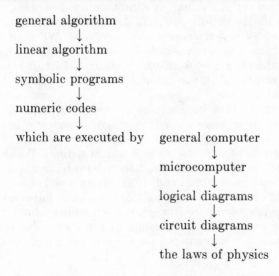

general algorithm
↓
linear algorithm
↓
symbolic programs
↓
numeric codes
↓
which are executed by   general computer
↓
microcomputer
↓
logical diagrams
↓
circuit diagrams
↓
the laws of physics

Before examining the instruction execution sequences let us comment on the role of microoperations. Microoperations provide us with another level of programming control over our computer and the algorithms it executes. In a sense they are more elementary data-processing operations than the instruction code of the computer, being more directly related to the devices that will actually perform the operations in the computer. As such, programming in the microoperations will permit us to conceive of families of computers, all of which are built from the same devices and use the same microoperations but which are combined into different microprograms, thereby realizing different operations and different computers.

In particular, the instruction set of a computer can be extended to provide more flexibility at the computer code level. With microcodes our 14-instruction computer can be extended to one having 50 − 100 instructions, the number of distinct instructions found in commercial computers.

Actually, the set of microoperations that we shall use is not that much smaller in number than that of the order code of our computer, but this is to be expected in a computer having so few instructions. Customarily, computers have from two to five times as many instructions as the machine described here.

A natural way to view the microcodes is that they are the order code of a microcomputer contained in, and operating, our computer. As such, the microcomputer, too, will have a memory, a line pointer, and a set of registers. The memory of the microcomputer will be much smaller than that of the parent computer, since it does not need to hold arbitrary programs with their data. It can be what is called a *read only memory* (ROM), since the execution of microprograms creates no change in the micromemory. The programs stored there are fixed, being the programs to execute the fixed instruction set of the parent computer. In describing the operations of this microcomputer we shall develop still another way of representing the execution process of a computer. We shall describe the microoperations in terms of *logical diagrams* utilizing logical devices that operate on boolean values: 0 or 1. In turn, these two values will correspond in the computer to direct-current electrical voltages, *low* and *high*.

You will note that the instructions in the microcomputer do not have arbitrary addresses—indeed only "go" does—and hence the storage needed for microprograms is significantly smaller than for computer programs of the same number of instructions. We shall assign a 4-bit code to the microinstructions, those having a code between 0 and 7 using no operand and those having a code between 8 and 15 requiring operands. Except for "go," which requires a full address within the microprogram storage, the other instructions will have a 4-bit code to specify the operands they require. The total number of microinstructions required for the microprograms of the

TABLE 2.4 MICROOPERATIONS

00.	ha	half—add
01.	cm	complement each digit of @
02.	cp	propagate carries
03.	cl	clear @, R and the carry register.
04.	sr	shift @, R right one place, and set @[0] to 0, R[17] is lost
05.	sl	shift @, R left one place, and set R[17] to 0; @[0] is lost
07.	fn	end of microprogram
08.	go	the program jump
09.	sk m	skip m lines of the microprogram; the next instruction will be m + 1 lines past the current one; this command is bypassed if C = 0
10.	tr m, n	transfer the contents of register n to m
11.	ex m, n	exchange the contents of registers m and n
12.	cs n	set the nth carry bit
13.	z m	zero set of type m; if _true_ _then_ C ← 1 _else_ C ← 0.
14.	lg m	logical operation of type m; if _true_ _then_ C ← 1 _else_ C ← 0

Multiplication will use a special counter K needed to count the steps in the multiplication process. K has the micro code 15:

15.	K m	apply the operation of type m to the counter K

instructions of our computer are less than 256, so that an 8-bit address will suffice to identify each line of the microprogram. Consequently, the "read only micromemory" (ROM) will consist of 256 8-bit words.

For instructions 10 through 16 the 4 bits denoting an operand have the following significance.

When their conditions are true, z and lg set C to 1 and, when they are false, to 0.

The microcode now completely defined, we can present programs in the microcode for each of the operations of our computer. Although we shall not go into any of the details of the fetch-execute cycle of the microcomputer at this point, we may assume that it functions in the same way as the fetch-execute cycle of the computer itself. Thus two cycles operate, the microcycle and the major, or computer, cycle, the microcycles operating within each major cycle. We shall present the microcodes for the computer operations both in a symbolic and in a hexadecimal form. The _hexadecimal system_ refers to number representation in base 16. The representing digits are 0, 1, . . . , 9, A, B, C, D, E, F. Each "hex" digit is representable by 4 binary digits.

TABLE 2.5

Code	Instruc-tion	Operand code	Significance
10	tr	0	Microrun ← C
		1	U ← @[0]
		2	L ← D[0]
		3	R ← @[1:17]
		4	I/O ← D
		5	M[LP] ← D
		6	@[17] ← C
		7	LP ← D[6:17]
		8	IDEX ← D[6:17]
		9	simultaneously: $\begin{cases} LP \leftarrow D[6:17] \\ D \leftarrow M[LP] \end{cases}$
		10	D ← M[LP]
		12	MLP ← MLT[D[1:5]]
		13	microrun ← 0
11	ex	1	@, D
		2	I/O, D
		3	LP, I/O [6:17]
		4	D[6:17], LP
		5	LP, @[0:11]
		6	IDEX, @[0:11]
		7	IDEX, D[6:17]
		8	LP, IDEX
		10	D[0:11], IDEX
		11	D[6:17], @[0:11]
12	cs	1	carry [12] ← 1
		2	carry [18] ← 1
		3	L ← 1
13	z		@[0:11] = 0
		1	@ = 0
		2(6)	@[0] = 0 (≠)
		3(7)	@[1:17] = 0 (≠)
		4	D[0] ≠ 0
		5	D[1] = 0
		8(9)	L = 0 (≠)
		10(11)	R[17] = 0 (≠)
		12(13)	U = L (≠)
		14(15)	@[17] = 0 (≠)
14	lg	0(1)	@ ∧ (∨) D
		6	U = D[0] ≠ @[0]
15	K	1	clear K
		2	K ← K + 1 and set C to 0
			set C = 1 when K reaches 17

TABLE 2.6

LABEL	Instruction	ROM address	Instruction	Comment
CLA	cl	52	3 0	clear
ADD	tr 1	53	A 1	save sign
	ha	54	0 0 ⎫	
	cp	55	2 0 ⎭	addition
	lg 6	56	E 6	test overflow
	tr 0	57	A 0	set microrun to 0 if overflow
	fn	58	7 0	end of addition
SUB	ex 1	5B	B 1	complement D
	cm	5C	1 0	
	cs 2	5D	C 2	
	cp	5E	2 0	
	ex 1	5F	B 1	
	go ADD	60	8 0	now do addition
		61	5 3	
MPY	tr 1	62	A 1	save sign
	tr 2	63	A 2	save D sign
	z 2	64	D 6	complement @ if negative
	sk 3	65	9 3	
	cm	66	1 0	
	cs 2	67	C 2	
	cp	68	2 0	
	z 8	69	D 4	complement D if negative
	sk 4	6A	9 4	
	ex 1	6B	B 1	
	cm	6C	1 0	
	cs 2	6D	C 2	
	cp	6E	2 0	
	tr 3	6F	A 3	multiplier in R
	cl	70	3 0	clear @
	K 1	71	F 1	clear multiplier counter
MPY1	z 10	72	D B	multiply loop
	sk 2	73	9 2	
	ha	74	0 0	add if multiplier
	cp	75	2 0	digit = 1
	sr	76	4 0	shift into R next digit
	K 2	77	F 2	increment multiplier counter
	sk 2	78	9 2	
	go MPY1	79	8 0	recycle if multiply counter < 17
		7A	7 2	
	sl	7B	5	do round off
	cs 2	7C	C 2	
	cp	7D	2 0	
	sr	7E	4 0	
	z 12	7F	D B	complement @ if signs of operands differ

TABLE 2.6   (*Continued*)

LABEL	Instruction	ROM address	Instruction	Comment
	sk 3	80	9 3	
	cm	81	1 0	
	cs 2	82	C 2	
	cp	83	2 0	
	fn	84	7 0	end of multiplication
GTR	ex 1	85	B 1	complement D
	cm	86	1 0	
	cs 2	87	C 2	
	cp	88	2 0	
	ex 1	89	B 1	
	tr 1	8A	A 1	the ADD function
	ha	8B	0 0	
	cp	8C	2 0	
	lg 6	8D	E 6	
	tr 0	8E	A 0	
	z 3	8F	D 3	skip if @[1:7] = 0
	sk 2	90	9 2	
	z 2	91	D 6	C ← 1 if @[0] = 0
	tr 6	92	A 9	@[17] ← C
	fn	93	7 0	@[17] = 1 iff @[0] = 0 ∧ @[1:7] ≠ 0 end GTR
EQ	ex 1	97	B 1	do the subtraction
	cm	98	1 0	
	cs 2	99	C 2	
	cp	9A	2 0	
	ex 1	9B	B 1	
	tr 1	9C	A 1	
	ha	9D	0 0	
	cp	9E	2 0	
	lg 6	9F	E 6	
	tr 0	A0	A 0	
	z 1	A1	D 1	test equality
	tr 6	A2	A 6	@[17] = 1 if @ = D
	fn	A3	7 0	end EQ
AND	lg 0	A6	E 0	
	fn	A7	7 0	end AND
OR	lg 1	A8		
	fn	A9	7 0	end OR
NOT	cm	AA		
	fn	AB	7 0	end NOT
NEG	cm	AC	1 0	Form 2-complement of @
	cs 2	AD	C 2	
	cp	AE	2 0	
	fn	AF	7 0	end NEG
IF	z	B0	D F	if true (i.e., @[17] = 1), skip

TABLE 2.6 (*Continued*)

LABEL	In-struc-tion	ROM address	In-struc-tion	Comment
	sk 1	B1	9 1	
	fn	B2	7 0	If end if <u>false</u>
GO	tr 7	B3	A 7	set LP
	fn	B4	7 0	end GO
PRT	tr 4	BF	A 4	
	fn	C0	7 0	end PRT
RD	ex 2	C1	B 2	transfer to D
	ex 3	C2	B 3	set storage address
	tr 5	C3	A 5	store data
	ex 3	C4	B 3	reset LP
	fn	C5	7 0	end RD
HLT	tr 13	C6	A 13	Microrun ← 0
	fn	C7	7 0	end HLT
LDI	tr 8	C8	A 8	Load IDEX
	fn	C9	7 0	end LDI
STO	ex 4	CA	B 4	store address in LP
	ex 1	CB	B 1	data into D
	tr 5	CC	A 5	store
	ex 1	CD	B 1	reverse the exchanges
	ex 4	CE	B 4	
	fn	CF	7 0	end STO
SIT	ex 6	D0	B 6	IDEX to @
	cm	D1	1 0	subtract 2
	cs 1	D2	C 1	
	cp	D3	2 0	
	cm	D4	1 0	
	z 0	D5	D 0	set C ← 1 if IDEX − 1 = 0
	ex 6	D6	B 6	
	sk 2	D7	9 2	
	go GO	D8	8 0	
		D9	A 3	
	fn	DA	7 0	end SIT
STI	ex 7	DB	B 7	
	ex 8	DC	B 8	
	tr 5	DD	A 5	
	ex 8	DE	B 8	
	ex 7	DF	B 7	
	fn	E0	7 0	end STI

The register structure of the microcomputer is extremely simple. Its registers are:

1. The read-only memory (*ROM*) of 256 8-bit registers.
2. The microroutine location table (*MLT*) of 32 8-bit registers.

3. The micro-line-pointer (*MLP*) register of 8 bits.
4. The micro-*D* register (*MR*) of 8 bits.
5. The condition register (*C*) of 1 bit.
6. The microrun register (*microrun*) of 1 bit.

The *ROM* of 256 registers holds the microprograms for each of the instructions of the computer. The microlocation table holds, for each computer operation, the starting location in the *ROM* of the microprogram for that operation. The micro-line-pointer points to the microoperation location whose contents are currently being executed. The micro-*D* register *MR* holds the data that trigger the actual microoperations being performed. The condition register *C*, set by *z* and *lg* commands, executes a *sk* operation only if the *C* register holds 1. The *microrun* register permits the computer to continue to operate as long as it holds a 1. The microoperation *fn* sets $MLP \leftarrow 0$ and the microoperation *tr* 12 sets *MLP* with $MLT[D[1:5]]$.

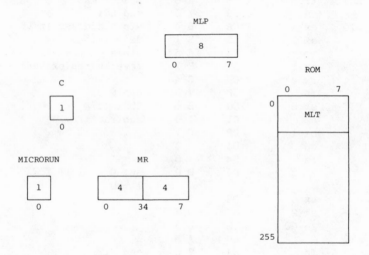

The fetch-execute cycle of the microcomputer is:

```
Microrun → (MR ← ROM[MLP]; next MLP ← MLP + 1;
next (MR = 8 → MLP ← ROM[MLP]; true →
microfunction execution (MR)));
```

The computer control (2.7) is expressed as the following microprogram.

Unfortunately, we cannot expect the control cycle of the microcomputer itself to be described in microcode, but we have succeeded in reducing the description of how all algorithms are executed to that of the microcontrol and the 16 microinstructions.

TABLE 2.7

LABEL	Instruction	ROM address	Instruction	Comment
	tr 10	00	A A	D ← M[LP]
	ex 5	01	B 5	LP ← LP + 1
	cs 3	02	C 3	L ← 1
	cs 1	03	C 1	
	cp	04	2 0	@ ← @ + 2
	ex 5	05	B 5	ex (@[0:11], LP)
	z 4	06	D 5	effective address calculation
	sk 2	07	9 2	
	go NDEX	08	8 0	no indexing required to obtain effective address
		09	1 0	
	ex 11	0A	B B	ex (D[6:17], @[0:11])
	ex 10	0B	B a	ex (D[0:11], IDEX)
	ha	0C	0 0 ⎫	form address
	cp	0D	2 0 ⎭	
	ex 10	0E	B A	ex (D[0:11], IDEX)
	ex 11	0F	B B	ex (D[6:17], @[0:11])
NDEX:	tr 12	10	A C	MLP ← MLT[D[1:5]]
	z 5	11	D 5	is D(1) = 0? (operand not required)
	sk 2	12	9 2	
	ex 4	13	B 4	ex (D[6:17], LP)
	tr 9	14	A 9	bring operand
	tr 12	15	A C	MLP ← MLT[D[1:5]]

The table MLT, which holds the initial addresses of all instructions, is:

0	AA	16	52
1	AC	17	53
2	B	18	5B
3	D0	19	62
4	B3	20	85
5		21	97
6	C1	22	A6
7	CA	23	A9
8	DB	24	BF
9	C6	25	C8
10		26	
11		27	
12		28	
13		29	
14		30	
15		31	

The empty entries are not used.

LOGICAL-ELEMENT DESCRIPTION

general algorithms
↓
linear algorithms
↓
symbolic programs
↓
numeric codes

which are executed by   general computer
↓
microcomputer
↓
logical diagrams
↓
circuit diagrams
↓
the laws of physics

We shall describe the operations of the microcodes and the fetch-execute cycle of the microcomputer in terms of logical diagrams describing how physical devices are to be combined to make our microcomputer. Thus the entire grand structure is now reduced to that of describing the devices and the fetch-execute cycle and operation codes of the microcomputer.

We shall begin with a discussion of the logical devices, so called because they manipulate single bits and because their operation is very like that of logical operations on the values <u>true</u> and <u>false</u>. Indeed, we should keep in mind the correspondences <u>true</u> ↔ 1 and <u>false</u> ↔ 0.

The computer may be thought of as having three power generators:

1. HIGH, which generates a steady high voltage that we may think of as representing 1 in the computer,

2. LOW, which generates a steady low voltage that we may think of as representing 0 in the computer,

3. CLOCK, which generates an endless, precise sequence of 1's, the successive elements (pulses) being separated by a time interval which, for all practical purposes, is constant. The time between successive 1's we shall call the *clock cycle* of the computer. Modern computers achieve a clock cycle of about 25 nanoseconds (25×10^{-9}) seconds. All actions in the computer occur at those times, and only those times, when the clock generator is producing a 1. The intervening time intervals are used to permit the physical devices to settle into their new equilibrium states if they have been affected in a preceding 1 step. We shall denote this clock output by P; see 2.8.

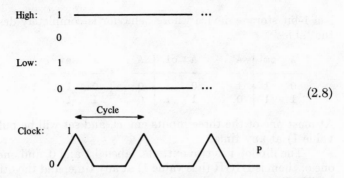

$$(2.8)$$

Aside from the storage of the computer and the *ROM* of the micro-computer, the computer is logically organized from combinations of exactly four devices, one of which performs a storage function, and all of which perform some logical function, as follows.

1. The AND gate represented by

and its function is completely described by the table

a	b	ab
0	0	0
0	1	0
1	0	0
1	1	1

2. The OR gate represented by

and its function is completely described by the table

a	b	a + b
0	0	0
0	1	1
1	0	1
1	1	1

3. The NOT gate represented by

and its function is completely described by the table:

a	$\bar{a}$
0	1
1	0

4. The flipflop represented by

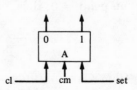

is a 1-bit storage device whose behavior is completely described by the tables

A	cm	A		A	cl	A		A	set	A
0	1	1		0	1	0		0	1	1
1	1	0		1	1	0		1	1	1

At most one of the three inputs cm, cl, and set will be pulsed (have value 1) at any time.

The flipflop has two outputs, labeled 1 and 0, and one and only one of them is HIGH (has value 1) at any time, and the other is then LOW. They will remain with one of the output lines at HIGH and the other at LOW until one of the three input lines is attached in some way to P. If more than one input line is pulsed, the resultant value is undefined. The three input lines are CLEAR (set the 0 line to HIGH and the 1 line to LOW), SET (set the 1 line to HIGH and the 0 line to LOW), and COMPLEMENT (set the HIGH line output to LOW and the LOW line output to HIGH). Whichever of the two output lines is set to HIGH may be said to specify the value held by the flipflop. Operations on flipflops will occur only when a 1 is being produced by the clock, and changes in the flipflop outputs will not be in evidence until the cycle following that in which the change was instigated. Put another way, if a flipflop is being changed on a clock cycle, the output of the flipflop on that same cycle is that which held immediately prior to the cycle, and the new value will first be available on the next clock cycle. As may be seen from the descriptions of the four devices, their behavior, and that of the circuits in which they participate, can be described by diagrams, by tables, and by logical equations. Furthermore it is quite mechanical to transform a circuit representation from one form to any of the other two.

Let us briefly examine some circuit realizations of these logical units. If we have a conducting wire on which there is a potential difference, the wire imposes a resistance R (and may indeed contain a specific resistor) to the flow of current, as described by Ohm's law:

$$\text{High} \quad \overset{R}{\wedge\!\wedge\!\wedge} \quad \text{Low}$$
$$i > 0 \rightarrow$$

$$\text{HIGH} - \text{LOW} = \Delta V = iR$$

Kirkoff's first law states that the algebraic sum of the currents at a junction point = 0; thus,

$$\text{High} \quad \overset{R_1}{\wedge\!\wedge\!\wedge} \quad \overset{E}{\quad} \quad \overset{R_2}{\wedge\!\wedge\!\wedge} \quad \text{Low}$$
$$i_1 \rightarrow \quad i \quad \leftarrow i_2$$

Ohm's law: $\text{HIGH} - E = i_1 R_1$
$\qquad\qquad\quad\;\; \text{LOW} \; - E = i_2 R_2$
Kirkoff's law: $i = i_1 = i_2$

or $\text{HIGH} - \text{LOW} = i_1 R_1 - i_2 R_2 = i(R_1 + R_2) = iR$, which is the law for resistors connected in series: current flows as if there were one resistor $R = R_1 + R_2$. Consider the circuit:

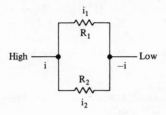

Here $\text{HIGH} - \text{LOW} = i_1 R_1 = i_2 R_2$ and $i = i_1 + i_2$.

    i = (HIGH – LOW)/R₁ + (HIGH – LOW)/R₂ = (HIGH – LOW)
    (1/R₁ + 1/R₂)

Let $1/R = 1/R_1 + 1/R_2$ and then $\text{HIGH} - \text{LOW} = iR$, which is the law for resistors connected in parallel. There is an equivalent circuit to the one above:

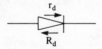

The *diode* is a type of physical device having the property that current flow in one direction encounters a small resistance r_d, whereas in the opposite direction it encounters a large resistance R_d: $R_d \gg r_d$. The standard notation for a diode is:

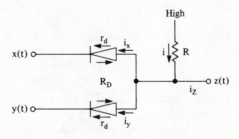

Consider the circuit:

The circuit is designed so that we may assume:

$i_z = 0$
$R_d \gg R \gg r_d$

Now, $x(t)$ and $y(t)$ are time-dependent voltages (HIGH or LOW). What then is $Z(t)$? Because of the symmetry of the roles of $x(t)$ and $y(t)$ there are only two cases to treat.

CASE 1. $x(t) = y(t) = $ HIGH. There is no flow of current, everything being HIGH, and $i_z = 0$; $\therefore Z(t)$ is HIGH.

CASE 2. Suppose $x(t) = $ LOW and $y(t)$ is LOW or HIGH. Then

```
i = iₓ + i_y   and   i = (HIGH - Z(t))/R
iₓ = (Z(t) - LOW)/r_d
        ⎧ (Z(t) - LOW)/r_d if y(t) is LOW
i_y =   ⎨ or
        ⎩ (Z(t) - HIGH)/R_d if y(t) is HIGH
```

so

$$\frac{\text{HIGH} - Z(t)}{R} = \frac{Z(t) - \text{LOW}}{r_d} + \left\{\frac{Z(t) - \text{LOW}}{r_d} \text{ or } \frac{Z(t) - \text{HIGH}}{R_d}\right\}$$

leading to

$$Z(t) = \left(\frac{1}{2R/r_d + 1} \text{ or } \frac{1}{1 + \dfrac{1}{r_d/R + r_d/R_d}}\right) \times \text{HIGH}$$

$$+ \left(\frac{1}{1 + r_d/2R} \text{ or } \frac{1}{1 + r_d/R + r_d/R_d}\right) \times \text{LOW}$$

Thus in either case the coefficient of HIGH is approximately 0 and that of LOW approximately 1; that is, $Z(t) = $ LOW. Thus the circuit has the table shown and is a realization of an AND gate.

x(t)	y(t)	Z(t)
LOW	LOW	LOW
LOW	HIGH	LOW
HIGH	LOW	LOW
HIGH	HIGH	HIGH

If we reverse the diodes and attach to a LOW line, we get the circuit shown.

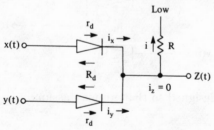

A similar analysis of this circuit shows its behavior to be summarized by the next table, which is a realization of an OR gate.

x(t)	y(t)	Z(t)
LOW	LOW	LOW
LOW	HIGH	HIGH
HIGH	LOW	HIGH
HIGH	HIGH	HIGH

The NOT gate can be implemented by means of two diodes and a transistor; see the figure. When $x(t)$ is LOW, the transistor is cut

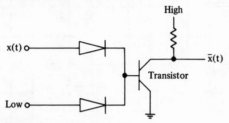

off and $\bar{x}(t)$ is essentially HIGH; otherwise, the transistor is in a "saturated" state, and its output voltage is LOW.

The flipflop can be implemented using OR and NOT gates.

The circuit is assumed to be in a steady state, i.e. at a HIGH (1) or LOW (0), and to remain in that state until both the input lines "a" and "b" are pulsed. Thus we may assume "a" and "b" both to be LOW unless pulsed. See the figure.

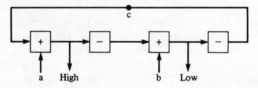

The diagrams for complement, set, and clear are as shown. Of course there are many additional circuits in a real computer, to

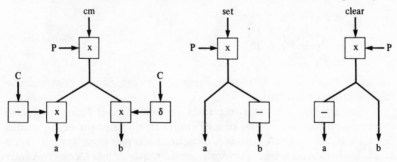

stabilize and amplify currents and shape pulses, but we shall ignore them since we are really more concerned here with the logical

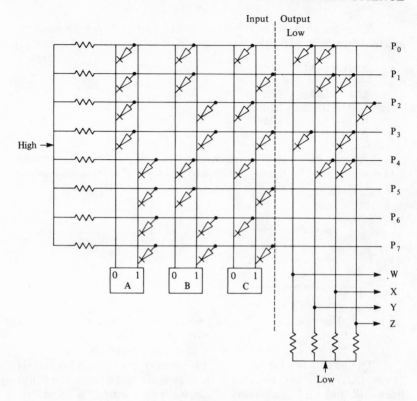

Figure 2.1

organization of the computer than its physical realization. However, there is one other circuit, constructed from AND and OR gates, that we shall find useful: the two-level diode network, an example of which is shown in Figure 2.1. The diodes on the INPUT (left) act as part of AND gates. Thus the horizontal line P_5 is HIGH if A is 1 and B is 0 and C is 1, that is, if the three flipflops hold $101 = 5$. However, the diodes attached to the OUTPUT (right) act as part of OR gates, so that

$$W = P_0 + P_3$$
$$X = P_1 + P_3 + P_4$$
$$Y = P_0 + P_1 + P_4$$
$$Z = P_2$$

act as outputs of the network. Such a network is the heart of the microcomputer control.

Storage in current computers is constructed from magnetic cores. Each core holds one binary digit. In our computer we would need 18×2^{12} cores. A core is a doughnut-shaped object about 1/20 of an inch in diameter. Through the annulus of each core run four wires, which we shall call X, Y, Z, and SENSE. The electric and magnetic behavior of the core is fully determined from its "hysteresis" diagram, shown. B is related to the magnetic flux in the core.

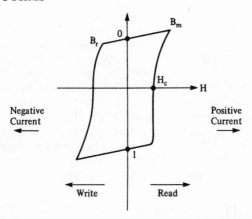

One direction, $(B > 0)$, represents a 0 being held in the core and, in the other, a 1. If sufficient positive current is applied on the X and Y wires to induce a magnetic field of intensity H_c, the magnetic flux in the core will jump from $-B_r$ to B_m, if it held a 1, and from B_r to B_m if it held a 0. A current is induced in the SENSE wire proportional to the change in B. Only if the core holds a 1 will the change induce a sufficiently large current to SET a previously cleared flipflop. Hence the information in the core has been transferred to the flipflop.

However, the information held in the core may have been altered from a 1 to a 0. Hence a "restore" cycle is required. If we reverse the magnetic field by applying current in the opposite direction but inhibit the application of this current if a 1 is not held by the flipflop (had not been produced in the SENSE line), the core will be returned to its original state and again hold a 1. The Z line inhibits the restore current.

The X and Y lines each carry 1/2 the current needed to switch the core, so both must be pulsed for switching the core. Hence they can function as coordinate identifiers, and we can lay out our cores in coordinate planes. Thus we may have 18 planes of 4096 cores each. Each plane has 64 rows of 64 columns.

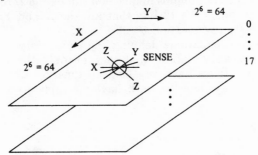

Suppose we wish to read out the contents of address

$$857_{10} = \underbrace{001101}_{X} \ \underbrace{011001}_{Y}$$

Since $857 = 13 \times 64 + 25$, X i̲s̲ 13 and Y i̲s̲ 25. Hence we pulse the 14th row and 26th column on all 18 planes. Each plane has *one* SENSE wire leading to, and *one* Z wire leading from, a flipflop. The contents of the 18 flipflops will then hold the contents of location 857_{10}. To restore the only core in each plane that has been changed, X and Y are pulsed with $1/2$ the necessary current in the negative direction, unless inhibited by Z (when the flipflop contains a 1).

To write in the core one merely provides $1/2$ the negative current on the X and Y lines and stores in the 18 flipflops the 18 bits to be read into the cores. The four possible states are shown in the accompanying diagram. We write into the 18 flipflops. Then we

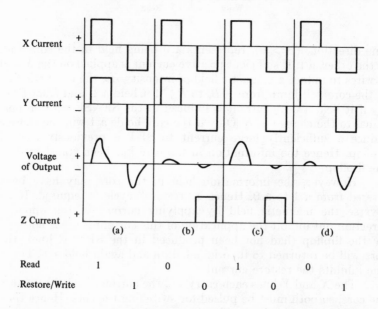

	(a)	(b)	(c)	(d)
Read	1	0	1	0
Restore/Write	1	0	0	1

write into the cores using the flipflops to trigger the Z lines. The 18 flipflops are cleared immediately preceding a read. The reader will note that the 18 flipflops in question can be the D register of our computer. LP holds the 12 bits that are the X and Y coordinates selecting the storage location.

Our logical equations defining the elementary devices relate variables, boolean variables, that take on only the values 0 or 1 (f̲a̲l̲s̲e̲ or t̲r̲u̲e̲). If we have any boolean function f of two boolean variables, we may describe its behavior completely by the table:

x	y	$f(xy)$
0	0	a
0	1	b
1	0	c
1	1	d

$$a, b, c, d = \begin{cases} 0 \\ \text{or} \\ 1 \end{cases}$$

The function f has only 4 values—at the 4 argument points $(0, 0)$, $(0, 1)$, $(1, 0)$, $(1, 1)$. There are only $16 = 2^4 = 2^{2^2}$ different ways of assigning 0 or 1 to a, b, c, d, so there are only 16 different boolean functions of 2 boolean variables. Two of them, the AND and OR functions, have already been described.

We define the function $\bar{x}$ (the inverse of x) by the table:

x	$\bar{x}$
0	1
1	0

From this table we deduce immediately that

$$x\bar{x} = 0$$

From the table for multiplication (AND) we get

$$0x = 0$$
$$1x = x$$
$$xx = x$$

From the table for addition (OR) we get

$$1 + x = 1$$
$$0 + x = x$$
$$x + \bar{x} = 1$$
$$x + x = x$$

Furthermore, multiplication and addition are associative and commutative:

$$x(yz) = (xy)z \qquad x + (y + z) = (x + y) + z$$
$$xy = yx \qquad\qquad x + y = y + x$$

Two additional important properties,

$$(\bar{x} + \bar{y}) = \overline{xy} \quad \text{and} \quad \bar{x}\bar{y} = \overline{x + y}$$

have become known as De Morgan's laws. Their truth can be verified from the defining tables of the operations AND, OR, and NOT.

The distributive laws are

$$x(y + z) = xy + xz$$
$$x + (yz) = (x + y)(x + z) \quad \text{(unlike ordinary arithmetic)}$$

Note that $x + \bar{x}y = x + y$.

Since only one of $\bar{x}\bar{y}$, $\bar{x}y$, $x\bar{y}$, xy are 1 for any assignment of values to x and y, any function f of two variables can be written as

$$f(x, y) = f(0, 0)\bar{x}\bar{y} + f(0, 1)\bar{x}y + f(1, 0)x\bar{y} + f(1, 1)xy$$

and one can, of course, suppress any of the terms for which $f(x, y) = 0$. Thus the function

x	y	$f(x, y)$
0	0	1
0	1	0
1	0	1
1	1	0

can be described as $f(x, y) = \bar{x}\bar{y} + x\bar{y} = (\bar{x} + x)\bar{y} = 1\bar{y} = \bar{y}$. This derivation of an equation from the table can be applied to functions of more than two variables. Thus for three variables x, y, and z any function $f(x, y, z)$ satisfies

$$f(x, y, z) = f(0, 0, 0)\bar{x}\bar{y}\bar{z} + f(0, 0, 1)\bar{x}\bar{y}z + f(0, 1, 0)\bar{x}y\bar{z}$$
$$+ f(0, 1, 1)\bar{x}yz + f(1, 0, 0)x\bar{y}\bar{z} + f(1, 0, 1)x\bar{y}z$$
$$+ f(1, 1, 0)xy\bar{z} + f(1, 1, 1)xyz$$

For example, if f is defined by

x	y	z	f
0	0	0	1
0	0	1	1
0	1	0	0
0	1	1	0
1	0	0	0
1	0	1	0
1	1	0	1
1	1	1	1

Then $f(x, y, z) = \bar{x}\bar{y}\bar{z} + \bar{x}\bar{y}z + xy\bar{z} + xyz = \bar{x}\bar{y} + xy$ and is independent of z.

A function we shall find useful is $x \oplus y = x\bar{y} + \bar{x}y$, and we shall assume it is available as an elementary function. We may translate this function into a block diagram, as shown. It is quite

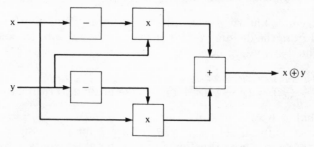

straightforward to perform the translation from an equation to a circuit. Recognizing that the output is available on the next cycle, the flipflop may be described by an equation from the table

cl(a)t	seta(t)	a(t)	a(t' = t + Δt)	
0	0	0	0	no change
0	0	1	1	no change
0	1	0	1	set
0	1	1	1	set
1	0	0	0	clear
1	0	1	0	clear
1	1	0	1	complement
1	1	1	0	complement

where $a(t)$ is the state of the flipflop at time t, and where we have used simultaneous clear and set to indicate complementation, $_{cm}a(t)$. The equation is $a(t + \Delta t) = \overline{a(t)_{cm}a(t)} + a(t)\overline{_{cm}a(t)}$.

In determining equations it is often much easier to solve for the complementation states of a flipflop. Consider a 3-bit counter, each line representing the state of three flipflops x, y, z resulting from the previous line on a pulse:

$$\begin{array}{ccc} x & y & z \\ 0 & 0 & 0 \\ 0 & 0 & 1 \\ 0 & 1 & 0 \\ 0 & 1 & 1 \\ 1 & 0 & 0 \\ 1 & 0 & 1 \\ 1 & 1 & 0 \\ 1 & 1 & 1 \end{array}$$

$$\begin{aligned} cmz &= (\bar{x}\bar{y}\bar{z} + \bar{x}\bar{y}z + \bar{x}y\bar{z} + x\bar{y}\bar{z} + x\bar{y}z + xy\bar{z} + \bar{x}yz + xyz)P \\ &= (\bar{x}\bar{y} + \bar{x}y + x\bar{y} + xy)P = (\bar{x} + x)P = P \\ cmy &= zP \\ cmx &= yzP \end{aligned}$$

The block diagram is also shown.

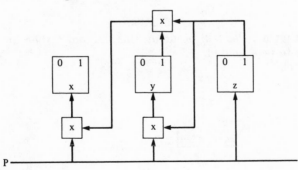

Using these simple logical devices, let us examine how some of the microcodes can be implemented (see the microoperations at the beginning of Section 8).

1. ha(0): Consider corresponding bit positions in @ and D. The table for ha is

Before		After	
D bit	@ bit	@ bit	C bit
$\emptyset$	$\emptyset$	$\emptyset$	$\emptyset$
$\emptyset$	1	1	$\emptyset$
1	$\emptyset$	1	$\emptyset$
1	1	$\emptyset$	1

where C is the carry bit. We see that, when $D = 1$, @ should be complemented. C is set to 1 when D and @ are both 1:

cm $@_{bit} = D$ bit
set $C_{bit} = D$ bit @ bit

The diagram for the kth bit position is as shown. The symbol $\overset{ha}{\rightarrow}$

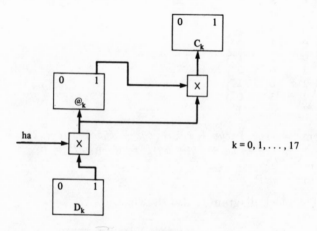

$$k = 0, 1, \ldots, 17$$

means that a pulse will occur on this line only when an ha command is to be executed.

2. cm(1):

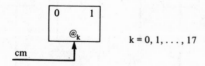

$$k = 0, 1, \ldots, 17$$

3. cp(2): Remember that a carry propagates leftward, complementing each digit encountered, but does not propagate past an $@_k = 0$, hence not past a stage generating its own carry.

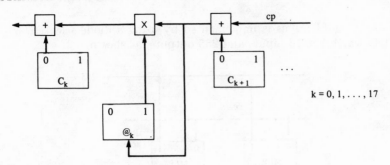

$$k = 0, 1, \ldots, 17$$

4. cl(3):

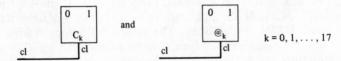

$$k = 0, 1, \ldots, 17$$

5. sr(4):

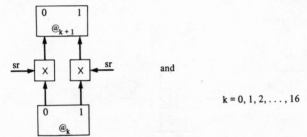

$$k = 0, 1, 2, \ldots, 16$$

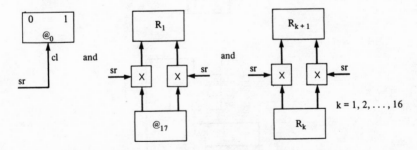

$$k = 1, 2, \ldots, 16$$

6. sl(5): This is much the same as sr except that $R_{17} \leftarrow 0$ and $@_0$ is lost.

7. fn(7):

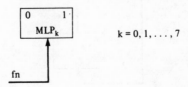

$$k = 0, 1, \ldots, 7$$

8. go(8): This is implemented by using a diode-selection matrix which has 16 inputs and 255 outputs, as shown.

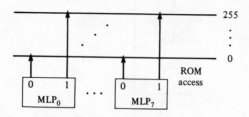

9. sk n(9): The skip command causes, if $C = 1$, the 4-bit integer in $MR0$, $MR1$, $MR2$, and $MR3$ to be added into MLP_4, MLP_5, MLP_6, and MLP_7, respectively. The circuit for accomplishing this is precisely the same as that for doing ha followed by cp. The skip command thus takes two clock cycles, and only after the second cycle is a finish signal to be sent.

10. tr(10):

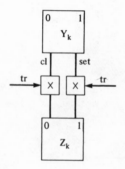

11. ex(11):

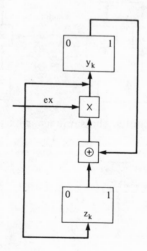

Thus $MR0$, $MR1$, $MR2$, and $MR3$ contain 4 bits, one of the integers from 0 to 15, and a diode network selects a line that triggers the appropriate exchange, for example, 1000 ($= 8$) would trigger the exchange of LP, $IDEX$.

12. cs(12):

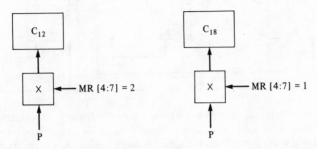

13. $z(13)$: There is a selector network that selects one of 15 lines, depending on the value in $RM[4:7]$. Consider in more detail $z = 1$, set C if $@ = 0$; see the figure.

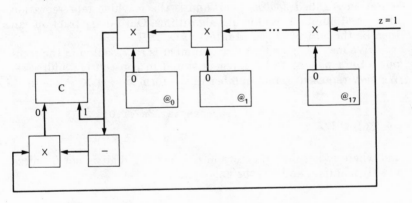

14. lg(14):

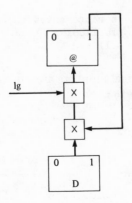

15. $K(15)$: K is a 17-counter; see the figure.

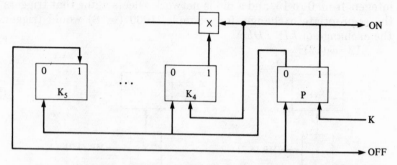

Our computer accepts and operates on binary fractions. As is easily seen, if x and y are such numbers, $x + y$ need not be. The computer "overflows" and halts in such case. Actually this case would occur often enough in most computations as to be embarrassing. Hence most computers have an alternative number representation and also operations on these representations that greatly diminish the frequency with which such overflows occur. This representation is called *floating point* and is the machine representation of the real numbers used in our algorithms. Our binary fraction can then be thought of as scaled integer $k \times 2^{-17}$.

We may imagine that a real number is represented in the computer by a pair of 18-bit integers stored in consecutive addresses. We may represent a real number in the form $x = m \times 2^c$ where

<u>if</u> m = 0 <u>then</u> c = 0 (representation of 0)
<u>else</u> $1/2 \leq |m| < 1$

and where m is called the normalized (leading digit is not 0 unless $x = 0$) mantissa and c is the exponent.

Example:

the number	is represented as
101.11001	.10111001 × 2³
−.0011	−.11 × 2⁻²

In the computer real numbers are called *floating-point numbers* and are represented as the pair

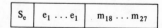

where S_m is the sign of the mantissa, $m_1 \cdots m_{27}$ are its digits, S_e is the exponent sign, and $e_1 \cdots e_7$ are its digits. Negative mantissas and exponents will be represented in 2-complement form.

The largest magnitude representable is

$$(1 - 2^{-27}) \times 2^{2^7-1}$$

and the smallest nonzero magnitude is

$$1/2 \times 2^{-(2^7-1)}$$

Note that

$$2^{127} = 10^{(\log_{10} 2)\,127} \simeq 10^{40}$$

Let us write a floating-point number x as the pair (x_e, x_m) of its exponent and mantissa. Consider now what the computer must do to multiply two floating-point numbers x and y, when $x \neq 0$ and $y \neq 0$:

1. Multiply the two mantissae in the way we have already described for multiplication of fractions.
2. Normalize the product by at most a single left shift, since more than one is never required.
3. The exponent of the product is the algebraic sum of the operand exponents, diminished by 1 if a normalizing shift is required in step 2.
4. Round the normalized product (after shifting).
5. The magnitude of the result is then

$$|m_r| = (|m_x| \times |m_y|) \times 2^{\delta} + 2^{-28}$$
$$e_r = e_x + e_y - \delta, \quad \text{where} \quad \delta = 0 \quad \text{or} \quad 1$$

Addition and subtraction are somewhat more complicated, since the number with smallest exponent must be right-shifted to make the exponents match before the addition can take place. The postnormalization may require a variable number of shifts owing to the loss of precision that can occur in subtractions.

In real computers exponent bases other than 2 are often used. This permits the representation of larger exponents but makes normalization of results somewhat more complicated.

MACHINE	EXPO-NENT BASE	MAN-TISSA LENGTH	EXPONENT RANGE
IBM 7090	2	27	−128 to 127
CDC 6600	2	48	−1023 to 1024
IBM 360	16	6	−64 to 63
IBM 360 (double precision)	16	14	−64 to 63
DEC PDP–10	2	27	−128 to 127

The set F of machine floating-point numbers is intended to represent real numbers, but the latter is a continuum and the former is finite. There are gaps in F, and reals in those gaps are erroneously represented by numbers in F. Thus the true results of many arithmetic operations will be numbers not representable in F. Instead, the computer will represent that number in F nearest in some sense to it. In subsequent operations the cascading of such "rounding" errors may lead to ultimate results that are surprisingly distant from the correct result.

Each number in F represents an interval of real numbers. Usually the two real numbers x and y will be represented by the same member of F when

$$\epsilon = \frac{|x - y|}{|x|} \leq \frac{1}{2} \times 2^{-27}$$

The representant from F may not even be the number in F closest to the true result. Instead it may be the member of F that is closest to, *and* not greater in magnitude than, the true result.

HISTORY OF ELECTRONIC COMPUTERS

The ENIAC (Electronic Numerical Integrator and Computer), built circa 1945 under the direction of Eckert and Mauchly for the U.S. Army, can reasonably be called the first electronic digital computer. The Army Ordnance Corps had responsibility for computing the firing tables that guide the accurate use of artillery and bombardment. The enlargement of technique for missile development— tonnage, range, speed, and accuracy—demanded an increase in firing-table precision and preparation rates. The merging of adequate technology (reliable vacuum tubes), adequate funding (wartime spending), energetic managers (in a large, rigid organization such as the army, melting under the impact of an all-consuming war, it was inevitable that dedicated managers, many flushed up in the chaos, would welcome a new technology that promised their organization's relief from the awesome burdens placed upon it), and superb, well-supported, highly appreciated scientists and engineers provided the perfect environment in which to develop a device that was physically complex and logically simple: the electronic computer.

Almost from the beginning those associated with the early computers *understood* what they had created. Their claims and intentions were conditional: "If the devices will be reliable, if we can keep the machine cool, if we can develop a large storage unit, then we can build a larger or a faster machine, but not an essentially different one." The development of electronic computers shows a highly accelerated selective breeding but not a struggle for domination between amazingly different mutations. Computer development is characterized by a good many bastards but, except for the ENIAC, no immaculate conception. Computers as a technological species seem to be quite stable, even though they have a very compressed life cycle (five years) and are hostage to an exceedingly diverse "tissue and nerve building" technology.

The ENIAC represented such an unheard-of concentration of vacuum tubes, about 18,000, that it was inevitable that scholarly predictions would arise to prove it could not function, pessimistic statistics on tube failures in a machine where *everything* must go right. Yet it worked well for almost ten years, from 1946 to 1955.

The ENIAC was not a stored-program computer. Programs required physical plugging of cables between units. The idea of storing the program as data in the computer probably was due to John Mauchly and appears in notes of his lectures at the University of Pennsylvania in 1945 and in the proposal for a successor to the ENIAC, the EDVAC (Electronic Discrete Variable Computer) in 1945. The ENIAC itself was modified to allow program storage in 1947.

The ENIAC having been proved successful, the history of computers is best traced from three developments: the improvement and invention of equipment, the enlargement of function, and the growth of an industry.

The Invention and Improvement of Equipment

Critical to the development of the computer has been the speed and reliability of the material from which gates, flipflops, and computer memory have been constructed. The crucial issues for gates and flipflops are reliability, "switching time," cooling required, and size. We summarize some of these issues in the following table:

DEVICE	SWITCHING SPEED, SEC	COST, $/BIS/ SEC	SIZE, REL. TO VACUUM TUBE
Vacuum tube	10^{-3}	10	1
Transistor	10^{-5}	1	.1
Integrated circuit	10^{-8}	.01	.01

The characteristics of computer memories are listed in the following table:

DEVICE	ACCESS TIME (RANDOM), (MICROSEC)	CAPACITY, BITS	COST, $/BIT
Magnetic tape or card	10^5	10^9	10^{-4}
Magnetic drum	10^4	10^7	10^{-3}
Slow core	10	10^7	10^{-2}
Primary core	1	10^6	10^{-1}
Integrated circuit	10^{-2}	10^3	10

The random access time is the time required to find any piece of data, and the capacity indicates average sizes of such stores found on computers. Magnetic cores, introduced about 1955, are still the principal primary memory of computers. Technology has increased their speed and reduced their size by (approximately) a factor of 10 over a period of fifteen years.

The Enlargement of Function

The codevelopment of patterns of use and improved technology enlarged the computer, not only in the number of its gates and the size of its memory, but in the set of directly programmable functions supported by the hardware. Some early computers did not provide a divide instruction. The circuitry for divide was complicated and expensive, and studies of common calculations showed that, among arithmetic operations, less than 10% were divides. Hence divide could be provided by means of a subprogram. A method widely used in subroutines for accomplishing divide was Newton's method:

$$a_{n+1} = a_n(2 - a_n a) \qquad n = 0, 1, \ldots$$
$$\text{and } a_0 = (a + 1)/2$$

It rapidly yields a good approximation to $1/a$, since the number of correct digits doubles at each iteration. If a_0 is correct to 1 place, a_k is correct to 2^k places, so that, for our computer with 18 bits, 4 or 5 iterations suffice. However, note that $|b/a| < 1$ doesn't guarantee $|a| < 1$, so scaling is required, and so are 2 multiplies per cycle. Consequently division, implemented in circuitry through successive subtractions, was soon in the repertoire of almost all computers.

The stored program is now accepted as an integral part of the digital computer. An important consequence of the stored program was the ability of programs to manipulate themselves. Thus programming a cycle—say, adding 80 numbers stored in locations 1500 to 1579 and placing the sum in 0810—might have looked like this:

LOC	COMMAND		
800	CLA	0806	Generate a variable command
801	ADD	0811	
802	STO	0806	Plant a variable command
803	SUB	0809	
804	IFG	0813	
805	CLA	0810	
806	ADD	1499	
807	STO	0810	
808	GO	0800	
809	ADD	1579	
810		0	
811		1	
812			
813	continuation		

Let us assume that 810 contains 0 when the program starts. Note that the command in 806 is changed on each cycle. When the program is completed, 806 contains ADD 1580 and cannot be re-used without a resetting of the contents of 806. Thus 812 might contain ADD 1499, and the program would be preceeded by an initialization:

```
CLA     0812
STO     0806
```

It was to avoid such settings and alterations that the *index register* was introduced. The invention is credited to scientists at the University of Manchester, England, and first appeared in a computer designed there. All modern computers use index registers, and programs are almost never modified during the course of execution.

From the earliest days of electronic computers it was recognized that floating point was indispensable for widespread use of the computer. Consequently, when reliable and inexpensive circuitry became available, built-in floating point was provided as standard equipment, at least on scientific computers. Actually another factor in the inclusion of floating-point hardware was the shift in relative cost of the various computer units. The introduction of large core memories, 32,000 to 65,000 words, of many magnetic tape drives (4 to 12 in number), multiple printers, and magnetic drums reduced the proportional cost of the central processor (as the arithmetic and logical processor came to be called) from 70% to 20% and hence made it possible to add additional instructions to the machine repertoire without changing the total cost of a computer system by more than a few percent. Floating-point hardware increased the speed with which some important scientific calculations could be done by factors of 10 or 50.

As the number of users on a computer increased, the efficient control of program traffic became an increasingly important issue. If the period 1955–65 concentrated on indoctrinating as many new users as possible through the development of good programming languages and procedure libraries, that from 1965 to the present could be characterized as being concerned with traffic control. The computer is now seen as a system composed of an increasing number of communicating parts that work in harmony to process a continuous stream of tasks. Individual tasks use fractions of the total computer resources, and the computer systems are capable of processing several tasks simultaneously. Computer storage then must be partitioned into segments, so that tasks may be isolated and protected from each other. Programs and data must become *relocatable*, since they must share storage with those of other tasks in a usually unpredictable manner. This had led to the development of complicated addressing schemes in modern computers. The simplest scheme was that of indirect addressing. In such a scheme a command such as CLA∗2000 would involve, not the contents of 2000, but that of the contents of the contents of 2000. If 2000 held 1527, it would be as though CLA 1527 had been written. Somewhat akin to indirect addressing is the use of base registers. A base register is like an index register, except that the base register contents change, in a program, almost not at all. Instead, individual instructions contain increments or offsets. Thus CLA 3 17 would mean "add 17 to the contents of base register 3 to determine the address whose contents are to be moved to a cleared accumulator." Most programs are now written in this style, which makes program relocation straightforward. Computers, as they have evolved, have not changed the repertoire of their instructions as radically as they have expanded the modes of addressing by which programs access organized data and by which programs are accommodated into dynamic collections of cooperating and competing tasks.

In their awareness of demands placed on their resources computers are like jugglers. Like jugglers, they know that most of the time a program is following a smooth trajectory away from the perils of collision, and they know that they must be *interruptable* when a collision is about to occur so that extremely close attention can be paid for a very short time to demands for storage or time or input-output. Modern computers have elaborate signaling conventions, so that a program called the monitor (the "juggler") can respond to infrequent, but critical, demands placed on the system by programs being executed. The signal processor is known as *interrupt processor*.

The Growth of an Industry

Few modern American industries have exhibited the growth and chaotic development of the computer industry. The potential of the industry, like that of its chief product, seems to be bounded only by the imagination and energy of its entrepreneurs. On closer examination products and applications fall into their profit-making place only with enormous effort and large expenditures applied over unexpectedly long times. Perhaps this is why so many industrial giants, such as RCA, GE, and Bendix, as well as so many exuberant infants, have entered, invested heavily in, and then withdrawn from, the computer field.

As important as the manufacture of computers has been the production of supporting equipment: transistors, cores, magnetic tape and drum memories, solid logic circuits, typewriters, and graphics displays. The support industry is phenomenal. Both it and the computer manufacturing industry owe much of their success to the American "middle technology" which so ably supports precision electronics.

Although IBM now dominates the electronic computer industry of the world, it was not always so. UNIVAC was at one time in a competitive position with IBM. In the early computer days, 1951–55, UNIVAC had an excellent business computer in the

UNIVACI and an excellent scientific computer in the ERA 1103. However, each effort was separately engineered, and the sales organization was never equally competent in marketing both machines.

Throughout the short history of computers important technological developments have come at moments embarrassing to some manufacturers. The development of the magnetic-core memory aided IBM but caused UNIVAC, successful with delay-line memories, to stumble.

However, UNIVAC has continued to produce excellent computers ranging from small data-processing computers to the very large scientific variety. UNIVAC has had a great deal to do with making the Minneapolis–St. Paul area an important center of computer manufacture.

In Minneapolis a group of former ERA people left UNIVAC to form Control Data Corporation (CDC) in 1957. They marketed their first computer, the 1604, in 1960. This was an excellent scientific computer with a 48-bit word, was very reliable, and was a workhorse for scientific computing for five to eight years. The success of this computer directed CDC into focusing their talents on the design and manufacture of computers that were capable of operating at speeds at the limits of known technology. The existence in industry and government of well-supported problem areas in which answers to important problems are "computer-bound" and not "data-bound" has helped to fund the development of a line of "supercomputers" of which we are justly proud and on which, in some key problem areas, we strongly depend (nuclear weaponry, weather-forecasting, geophysics, and nuclear-physics research). Their latest machine, the STAR, is expected to perform about 15×10^6 operations per second. From the ENIAC's 10^3 operations per second we have increased by 4 orders of magnitude in about 100,000 years (binary, of course).

CDC, along with many other manufacturers, later produced stripped-down versions of its fastest computers for sale at significantly lower prices. These "seconds" have proved to be a great bargain for computing environments where the computer load is high and the income low. Universities fall in this category. The CDC 3300, 3400, 6400, and 6500 are examples of this kind of machine.

IBM dominates the industry. Competing with IBM is not easy. It is so large and so dedicated to finding and marketing the ultimate in computers that it often appears deceptively easy for its competitors to exploit a gap in IBM's equipment or a tactical error in its development and marketing. These errors generally arise because not even IBM can accurately predict or quickly react to the sequence of explosive changes that occur in computing. The errors do not arise because of any fundamental misunderstanding of the goals and roles of the computer industry in our technological society. As such, IBM can and does quickly react to exploit impressive markets it did not invent or foresee.

As befits a behemoth, IBM generally moves with deliberate care and often appears as a reactive force intent on maintaining the status quo—except when a decisive step is required, and then its momentum makes a shambles out of enclaves carefully nourished by its smaller competitors. IBM was stampeded into sinking a huge, poorly organized effort in time-sharing with its 360/67 and its operating system TSS. However, their concept of a compatible spectrum of computers from the small 360/20 to the large 360/95 with the use of identical componentry, peripherals, and software was a master stroke and correctly catered to the urgent needs of computer users for growth and stability in their computer and program investments as their needs grew. Few IBM computers are masters in their class. Nevertheless for most users IBM provides a shelter, a standard, and a blueprint that reduces their customer's preoccupation with choice and change, though admittedly at a cost. In 1971 IBM had about 70% of the value of installed computers. The runner-up firm had less than 10%. Shortly after the 360 series was announced, IBM had orders for more than 6,000 of the model 20 (rental about $2,000/month), almost 1,000 of the model 50 (about $25,000/month), and almost 100 of the model 75 (about $80,000/month).

IBM is now delivering the 370 series of computers that are compatible with the 360 and offer some lower prices over comparable 360 models.

Honeywell has chosen to compete with IBM in the business data-processing area. One of their early computers, the Honeywell 800, had eight program counters sharing one arithmetic and logic unit, so that eight programs could be simultaneously in execution. In 1963 they provided, with their 200, a compatible successor to IBM's successful, small, business computer, the 1401, which IBM did not choose to provide as an alternative to its 360 development. The 200 launched Honeywell into business data-processing, where it is now second only to IBM.

The National Cash Register Company entered the electronic-computer field with the purchase of a small firm building small magnetic-drum-memory computers. They have developed a line of medium to large business computers that have proved successful in providing centralized computing service for small banks and savings-and-loan associations. With their interest in cash registers they are naturally interested in developing point-of-sale communication and processing to link with computers.

Burroughs, too, entered the field with the purchase of a firm building magnetic-drum-memory computers. From that point on they have developed an excellent line of small to medium data-processing computers and medium to large scientific machines. Their scientific computers (B5000, B5500, B6500) are notable for their direct use of hardware stacks and use of ALGOL60 as machine code. Though it's not quite ALGOL60, programs written in ALGOL60 run very efficiently. The only machine code is at the microcode level, in which few programmers can successfully write codes. The computer was designed so that an ALGOL60 translator could operate efficiently and produce machine-code programs that run efficiently.

One of the success stories in the industry is that of Digital Equipment Corporation. Its DEC line of computers, the PDP-1, 8, 9, 11, and 15 in the small range and the 6 and 10 in the large range have been enormously successful. The reasons for DEC's success are many. Their computers are simple and reliable, inexpensive to operate, and relatively easy to alter. They have been marketed in environments of high technological competence. DEC has successfully exploited a number of advanced research efforts carried on elsewhere: time-sharing, graphics, and advanced software. If CDC is the monarch of the supercomputer field, DEC rules over the minicomputers.

A number of large firms entered the field and then retreated. General Electric produced some excellent medium-sized time-sharing systems and participated in the development of one large system, the consequences of whose success propelled IBM into developing the costly 360/67 time-sharing system. The continuing losses in its computer venture caused GE to sell its computer holdings to Honeywell in 1970.

RCA chose to copy the 360, in its logically compatible Spectra 70 series. Arguing that IBM defines industry standards, RCA saw themselves as offering a competitive standard computer at somewhat lower prices and somewhat better capabilities. Unfortunately the market chose to view the 360 as computer + service + software + future and not just as hardware. Most users preferred to pay the IBM insurance premium, considered to be small compared with the investment, and RCA was unable to make a sufficient dent in the market. In the face of continuing huge losses RCA left the computer field early in 1972.

Bendix had an enormously successful G-15 drum computer in the period 1956–60 and designed and marketed a large computer, the G-20 in 1959. This computer was, in many respects, ahead of its time. It was seen as a network of processors, and attention was paid to the problems of computer–computer communication. Bendix withdrew from the field because the G-20, if it were to be successful, would require marketing support and capital that Bendix did not choose to provide. CDC purchased the Bendix computer division but never chose to exploit or generalize the G-20 computer.

Ford entered the computer field through the purchase of Philco, which had built some excellent and very fast machines. However, Ford has never chosen to exploit its computer arm commercially. Xerox purchased Scientific Data Systems and has not yet clearly demonstrated the correct link between its copying activities and the digital computer.

An adequate history and analysis of the computer industry has yet to be written. When it is forthcoming, it should clarify the basic dilemma of the industry: the great demand for computers leads to enormous capital investment, the amortization of which is constantly endangered by technological advances. The advances promise not only to reduce costs but also to challenge the very nature of the computation that users will pay for.

REFERENCES

The literature on the computer and computer designs is vast. A valuable reference work is

G. Gordon Bell and Allen Newell, *Computer Structures: Readings and Examples* (McGraw-Hill, New York, N. Y., 1971),

which contains reprints of many of the key original articles on early computers. In particular, the paper

A. Burks, H. Goldstine, and J. Von Neumann, "Preliminary Discussion of the Logical Design of an Electronic Computing Instrument" (reprinted on pages 92–119 of the Bell and Newell book)

provides a fascinating insight into the computer-design problem as seen by three of the pioneers in the computer field. Von Neumann, in particular, is recognized, along with John Mauchly, as being one of the founders of electronic digital computers. Von Neumann, primarily a mathematician, made important contributions to almost every part of computer practice and theory. His was one of the great minds of our century, and his early death from cancer was a terrible tragedy.

No major text on assembly-language programming exists. Great insight into the problems that assemblers must face and solve is shown in the delightful, if slightly outdated, book

M. V. Wilkes, D. J. Wheeler, and S. Gill, *The Preparation of Programs for an Electronic Digital Computer* (Addison-Wesley, Reading, Mass., 1957).

Every computer has its own assembly language, and the manuals provided by the manufacturers describe the full range of capabilities assemblers have come to possess. An excellent article on the assembly process per se is

S. Gorn, "Standardized Programming Methods and Universal Coding" (*Journal of the ACM*, 4, July, 1957, pp. 254–273).

Diverse implementations of computer arithmetic are treated at great length in

I. Flores, *The Logic of Computer Arithmetic* (Prentice-Hall, Englewood Cliffs, N. J., 1963).

The general subject of digital-computer design is well treated in

Y. Chu, *Digital Computer Design Fundamentals* (McGraw-Hill, New York, N. Y., 1962),

Norman Scott, *Analog and Digital Computer Technology* (McGraw-Hill, New York, N. Y., 1960).

Digital electronic circuits are treated in an enormous number of texts. A good one is

A. W. Lo, *Introduction to Digital Electronics* (Addison-Wesley, Reading, Mass., 1967).

A superb book on the physics of computer hardware theory is

W. Poppelbaum, *Computer Hardware Theory* (Macmillan, New York, N. Y., 1972).

PROBLEMS

1. Given the array A, whose shape is $[-2:4, 0:15]$, and whose elements are to be laid out as the components of a vector B.

a. What is the formula that establishes the relationship between the element in the Ith row and Jth column of A and the Kth element in B?

b. What simple transformation of the formula is made if A is *transposed*—that is, if its shape becomes $[0:15, -2:4]$?

c. The nearest neighbors of the element $A[I, J]$ are $A[I, J-1]$, $A[I-1, J]$, $A[I, J+1]$, and $A[I+1, J]$. Can you find a simple formula for obtaining their positions in B, given that $B[K]$ corresponds to $A[I, J]$?

d. Suppose the matrix A is "bordered" by a single strand of additional elements to become a new matrix A'; see the figure. How

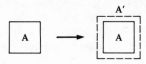

does K change? How do the neighbors change?

2. A program in assembly language has the same form as the following program:

```
START   RD    NUMBER
        LDI   NUMBER
CYCLE   SIT   DONE1
        RD    A, ι
        GO    CYCLE      ⎫
DONE1   CLA   S          ⎬ initialize
        LDI   NUMBER     ⎭
RPT     SIT   DONE2      ⎫
        ADD   A, ι       ⎬ test and loop
        GO    RPT        ⎭
DONE2   STO   W
        PRT   W
        HLT
S       00    0000       (octal digits)
```

a. What does this program do? (NUMBER is a positive integer.)

b. Replace the loop by the necessary code to store in W the maximum of all the numbers read in.

c. Create a symbol table, and "assemble" this program, starting at location 1000 and the data (A) starting at location 2000.

d. Replace the test and loop part by a code that will print a 1 if the data are all equal (all numbers the same) or a 0 if they are not all equal.

3. A subroutine named UMPH assumes that the @ register contains its input data and leaves its result in the @ register on exit. It has the form

```
UMPH    00    0000
        STO   TEMP
AGAIN   SIT   UMPH
        MPY   TEMP
        GO    AGAIN
```

What other piece of data does it use? Where is it? What does UMPH compute?

4. Alter UMPH so that it takes much less time if its input data have the value 0 or 1.

5. Can you find seven of the computer commands you can do without by having subprograms that do their work? Write four of these subprograms.

6. How would you represent the symbolic program in Table 2.2 as a character string? Using this kind of character-string representation of a program as input, give an algorithm that produces as output a string which is the assembled program. The algorithm is an elementary assembler.

7. A well-known piece of parlor magic is the "I can guess your secret number" game. There are N cards, on each of which is printed in orderly rows M distinct positive integers. All the integers lie in the range of 1 to L, and every integer in that range is on at least one of the N cards. The play is as follows. You pick a card at random, choose an integer appearing on it, and return the card to the deck. The N cards are now shuffled and shown to you one by one, so that both you and the magician see the cards. You say "yes" if the card contains your chosen number and "no" if it does not. When you have looked at all N cards, the magician immediately tells you which number you chose—he never misses. The magician does this by looking at *only the number appearing in the first column and row* of each card and summing those on the cards which you say contain the number you chose.

a. What numbers appear in the first row and column of each card?

    b.   Given N, what is the maximum value L can be?

    c.   What is the value of M?

    d.   What is the rule that determines which integers appear on any given card?

    e.   Why does this puzzle work?

8. Computer operations with complex numbers are usually performed by dealing with the real and imaginary parts separately and combining the two as a final operation. It might be an advantage in some problems to treat a complex number as a unit and to carry out all operations on such forms.

    The number system to be described permits the representation of a complex number as a single binary number, called a "binary complex," to a degree of accuracy limited only by the capacity of the computer. It is binary in that only the two symbols 1 and 0 are used; however, the base is, not 2, but the complex number $-1 + i$. The quantity $-1 - i$ would be equally suitable and, in fact, for real numbers it is immaterial which of these two we consider the base.

    The first few powers of $-1 + i$ are

1	$-1 + i$	5	$4 - 4i$
2	$-2i$	6	$8i$
3	$2 + 2i$	7	$-8 - 8i$
4	-4	8	16

We have, for example, the following equivalents:

-4	1 0 0 0 0	0		0
-3	1 0 0 0 1	1		1
-2	1 1 1 0 0	2	1 1 0 0 0
-1	1 1 1 0 1	3	1 1 0 0 1

    Every integer, whether positive, negative, or zero, can be represented uniquely in the form $a_0 + a_1(-4) + a_2(-4)^2 + \cdots + a_k(-4)^k$, where each a_i is 0, 1, 2, or 3. To represent an integer in base $-1 + i$, write it in powers of -4; the required representation will then be $a_k a_{k-1} \cdots a_1 a_0$, where the digits are 0000, 0001, 1100, or 1101, according as a_k is 0, 1, 2, or 3, respectively. For example,

$$46 = 3(-4)^2 + 1(-4) + 2$$

Therefore,

$$46 = 312_{(-4)} = 1\ 1\ 0\ 1\ 0\ 0\ 0\ 1\ 1\ 1\ 0\ 0$$

Initial 0's are neglected; for example,

$$19 = 0\ 0\ 1\ 0\ 0\ 0\ 0\ 1\ 1\ 0\ 1 = 1\ 0\ 0\ 0\ 0\ 1\ 1\ 0\ 1$$

The first few imaginary integers are

```
-4i  1 1 0 0 0 0    0              0
-3i  1 1 0 0 1 1    i              1 1
-2i        1 0 0   2i 1 1 1 0 1 0  0
 -i        1 1 1   3i 1 1 1 0 1 1  1
```

Every imaginary integer can be represented uniquely in the form $a_0 + b_0(8i) + a_1(8i)^2 + b_1(8i)^3 \cdots$, where $-6i \leq a_k \leq i$ and $-4 \leq b_k \leq 3$. To represent an imaginary integer to base $-1 + i$, write it in powers of $8i$ with appropriate a's and b's; the required representation will then be this number with the digits replaced by their binary equivalents. If the binary equivalent for any digit (except the first) contains fewer than six bits, 0's are prefixed to round it out to size. For example, $77i = (-1)(8i)^2i + 2(8i) + (-3)i$. Therefore $77i = 1\,1\,1\,0\,0\,1\,1\,0\,0\,1\,1\,0\,0\,1\,1$. Here $1\,1\,1$ represents $-i$, $0\,0\,1\,1\,0\,0$ represents 2, and $1\,1\,0\,0\,1\,1$ represents $-3i$.

The arithmetic operations $+$, $-$, and $\times$ can be performed on these numbers if we observe the following addition rules:

```
 0 +   0 = 0
 0 +   1 = 1 + 0 = 1
 1 +   1 = 1100
11 + 111 = 0
```

For example,

```
       46 = 1 1 0 1 0 0 0 0 1 1 1 0 0
      +13 = 0 0 0 1 0 0 0 1 0 0 0 1
           1 1 0 0 1 1 0 0 1 1 0 1
           1 1 0
       1 1 0 0 0 0
             1
       1 1 0 0
         1 1
   1 1 0 0 1 0
   1
   1 1 1 0
```

which gives $1\,1\,1\,0\,1\,0\,0\,0\,0\,1\,1\,0\,0\,1\,1\,0\,1$ and

$$59 = (-4)^4 + 3(-4)^3 + 2(-4)^1 + 3(-4)^0$$
$$= 1\,1\,1\,0\,1\,0\,0\,0\,0\,1\,1\,0\,0\,1\,1\,0\,1$$

Any complex number $a + bi$ with a and b integral can then be expressed as the sum of the real and imaginary parts. For example, $-2 = 1\,1\,1\,0\,0$ and $3i = 1\,1\,1\,0\,1\,1\,1$, so that $-2 + 3i = 1\,1\,1\,0\,0 + 1\,1\,1\,0\,1\,1\,1 = 1\,1\,0\,1\,1$. There is thus a one-to-one correspondence between the binary numbers of this system and the complex numbers $a + bi$ with a and b positive or negative integers of zero.

Give an algorithm for adding any two complex integers.

Design a logical circuit for performing such additions.

How would you treat subtraction? Multiplication?

Give conversion algorithms between complex "integers" represented as pairs of integers, $(5, -7)$ is $5 - 7i$, and "binary complex" integers.

What is the domain of complex integers that can be represented in 36 bits? (NOTE: This system of notation is due to Walter Penney.)

9. Design a multiplication algorithm that operates directly on 2-complement operands and in which all complementation is done only in @. Check the algorithm on $(0.001) \times (1.1010)$. How does one round and shift 2-complement numbers?

10. How should the division algorithm be extended to include rounding of the quotient? Many computers have two divide instructions: divide with remainder and divide and round.

11. Using the microcodes for our computer, program the division algorithm so that all complementing is done in @ and all adding is done with @ and D.

12. Using the microcodes of Tables 2.4 and 2.5, create a list of all the register transfer paths, and using the microprograms of Table 2.6, specify the circumstances under which these transfers take place.

The circumstances may be represented as boolean equations. An example is $LP \leftarrow D[6:17]$ on (tr 7) and (ex 4). These commands occur at microcode addresses B3, CA, CE, and 20. Hence, when MLP holds any of these addresses and a clock pulse occurs, the transfer will occur: $\mathrm{P}(MLP = \mathrm{B3}) \vee (MLP = \mathrm{CA}) \vee (MLP = \mathrm{CE}) \vee (MLP = 20)$ triggers $LP \leftarrow D[6:17]$

13. Devise a circuit to give

$X \oplus Y$	X	Y	$X \oplus Y$
	0	0	0
	0	1	1
	1	0	1
	1	1	0

14. Devise a circuit to give

$X \equiv Y$	X	Y	$X \equiv Y$
	0	0	1
	0	1	0
	1	0	0
	1	1	1

15. If we have

$X \rightarrow \boxed{/} \rightarrow X/Y$

$\uparrow$

Y

X	Y	X/Y
0	0	1
1	0	1
0	1	1
1	1	0

(Scheffer stroke)

we can build from it alone all other boolean functions of two variables. Build them.

16. Devise, with flipflops and OR gates, a 3-bit counter:

$$000 \rightarrow 001 \rightarrow 010 \rightarrow 011 \rightarrow 100 \rightarrow 101 \rightarrow 110 \rightarrow 111 \rightarrow 000$$

How would you modify it not to count from 0 to 7 to 0 but to count from 0 to 10 to 0?

17. Devise a counter whose behavior is:

FF1	FF@	FF3
1	1	0
0	1	1
1	1	0
0	0	0
0	1	0
1	0	0
0	0	1
0	1	0
1	1	1
1	0	1
1	0	1

18. (A little difficult.) Devise a circuit that counts the number of 1's held in the 18-bit @ register (that is, in its 18 flipflops).

19. A nonalgorithmic description of floating-point addition is given by the following examples, in which a 5-bit mantissa and a 3-bit exponent, both in 2-complement form, are used. We represent an operand by the pair (mantissa, exponent).

a.
```
  0 1 1 0 1 , 0 0 1
+ 0 0 0 1 0 , 0 0 1
  ─────────────────
  0 1 1 1 1 , 0 0 1
```

b.
```
  0 1 1 0 1 , 0 0 1
  0 1 0 1 0 , 0 0 1
  ──────────────────
  1 0 1 1 1 , 0 0 1
  0 1 0 1 11, 0 1 0
  0 1 1 0 0 , 0 1 0
```

c.
```
  0 1 1 0 1 , 0 1 1
  0 1 0 1 0 , 0 0 1
  0 0 0 1 0 , 0 1 1
  ─────────────────
  0 1 1 1 1 , 0 1 1
```

d.
```
  0 1 1 0 1 , 0 1 1
  0 1 0 1 1 , 0 1 1
  ─────────────────
  1 1 0 0 0 , 0 1 1
```

overflow

e.   0 0 1 1 1 , 0 1 0   f.   0 0 1 1 1 , 0 1 0
      1 1 0 1 1 , 0 1 0   1 1 0 0 1 , 0 1 0
  1 0 0 0 1 0 , 0 1 0   1 0 0 0 0 0 , 0 1 0
    0 0 0 1 0 , 0 1 0   0 0 0 0 0 , 0 0 0
    0 1 0 0 0 , 0 0 0

g.   0 0 1 1 1 , 0 0 1
      1 1 0 0 1 , 1 1 0
      1 1 1 1 0 , 0 0 1
  1 0 0 1 0 1 , 0 0 1
    0 1 0 1 0 , 0 0 0

Using these examples as a basis of experience, design an algorithm for binary floating-point addition and subtraction. The computer described in the text is altered so that floating-point numbers are represented in one word as

$$d_0 d_1 \cdots d_{12} e_0 e_1 \cdots e_4$$

with the mantissa in 2-complement form and the exponent in 2-complement form. What microcode operations would you add to the computer's repertoire for floating-point addition, subtraction, and multiplication?

20. A widely used method of communication between an algorithm and a subalgorithm or procedure is through a stack. The calling routine plants the return label on the top of the stack. The routine being called, on termination uses that label for an exit. The results of all actual parameter executions are also placed on the stack, where they are found by formal parameters.

Using this model, simplify procedure calls in algorithms. Assume the stack to be a vector $S[0:U]$, where U is some fixed value limiting the stack size.

Compare this model with the model in the text for their applicability in recursive algorithms.

CHAPTER 3

LANGUAGES

3

INTRODUCTION

In the first two chapters we focused on algorithms and machines: the former chapter described how something is to be accomplished, and the latter described the device for accomplishing it. The machine is specified in a simple way so it can be built easily and cheaply. One of its simplicities is that the machine can only accept ("understand") a small number of commands, each of these stated in a rather rigid sentence form, machine language. An algorithm expressed in machine language consists of a sequence of identically shaped sentences, each of which holds an indexing tag, an operator, and an operand, each of these having a fixed shape, expressed in the characters 0 or 1, and the whole compressed into 18 bits. Writing programs in such a language is nerve-wracking. One can become quite neurotic creating and scanning a sequence of 18-bit sentences! It should be mentioned that in the early days of computing this is precisely what programmers had to do. Naturally many became quite good at "machine programming," and some even used this hard-earned proficiency as an argument against the need for more flexible languages in which to express algorithms.

Somehow in using only machine code we are throwing away important levels of information-processing complexity that we can still mechanically and algorithmically control, and that make the writing and reading of programs more palatable to human beings. A programming language, then, is created to bridge the enormous gap between our ability and that of the computer hardware to manipulate symbols.

In (3.1) the large set A at the left is the set of all representations of symbol-manipulation algorithms that we might ever state. We may decompose this set into subsets so chosen that all the members (algorithms) in a particular subset are expressed by means of the same linguistic conventions. For the moment think of these conventions as specifying a language as for example, L1, in whose terms we state algorithms. Then for the subset L1 we must be able to "translate" any of its algorithms into an algorithm expressed in machine language, ML. And so must we as well for each of the other subsets. Why, we may ask, are there so many subsets? What determines, for an algorithm, in which subset it will reside? These questions possess no precise, nor even satisfying, answers. While we

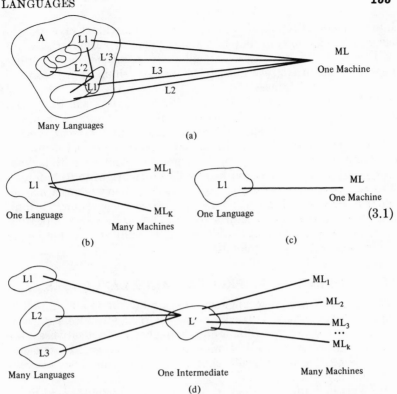

(a)

(b)

(c)

(3.1)

(d)

shall essay some answers, we must accept this plurality of algorithmic notations as a probably natural state of affairs: the invention and processing of diverse notations is a part of computer science. However, the very existence of so many notations impels some to seek a satisfactory encompassing notation, so that all algorithms not only can, but will, be expressed in this universal form. Thus far, at least, no satisfactory "omnibus" language has been found. We can only wonder if there ever will be one. Nevertheless some have been proposed, and it is the hope of their supporters that eventually all algorithms will be expressed in their terms. PL/I and Algol68 are the two latest candidates as of this writing.

Strong forces exist, some accelerating and others opposing, this trend to a single omnibus language. Having one programming language for all commerce with the computer would simplify computer design, programming education, and the communication of programs among computer users. However, programming languages are created in response to changing demands on computers and changing design of computers. New languages appear to offer more in improvement over current practice than will be lost from the increased turbulence they create in education and communication. However, one can already see the presence of a *lingua franca*, FORTRAN, whose use and development is so widely distributed in a large enough population—one million—that changes which creep into that language are attributable, not to individual invention or committee sponsorship, but to the inevitable evolution arising out of incessant use. In any event, all these notations have a great deal in common, and we must focus on their similarities before we analyze their differences.

In (3.1) are indicated the current situation, (a), and three fond hopes, (b), (c), and (d), of those who like tidy solutions to messy problems. One may argue that, since algorithms represent precise, well-organized renditions of thought processes expressed in precise symbolic form, there is an optimal notation and an optimal machine—which we haven't yet been sufficiently bright to have found. The rub, of course, is the word *optimal*. Optimality is not a mathematical concept; it is an economic one and, as such, requires technical, social, and political efforts to fix. Thus it is worth repeating that the current untidiness, while it will be subject to reduction, is likely to be with us for some time.

THE PROPERTIES OF PROGRAMMING LANGUAGES

What is a programming language? Let us try the following definition: A programming language is the set S of all finite strings of characters, constructed from a finite alphabet A, that satisfies a set of grammatical or syntactical rules and is such that each of its members possesses a semantically equivalent, finite computer program for some computer.

This definition has enough interesting, undefined terms in it for us to use it as a skeleton whose fleshing out will clarify what a programming language is and what purpose it serves. Thus we must seek to understand "alphabet," "string of characters," "satisfy a set of grammatical rules," and "semantically equivalent computer program."

Example 1: In Chapter 1 we described flowcharts. We described how to linearize a flowchart and hence how to write the "box and flow" structure of a flowchart as a string of characters. All such strings are not "legal" flowcharts; for example, the cut shown is not a "legal" flowchart. Can we give a finite set of rules for constructing all—and only all—legal flowchart structures? This

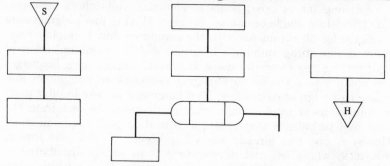

set of rules we may call the "box" and "flow" grammar. Let us give such a set of rules for a class of linearized flow charts:

Grammar FC1

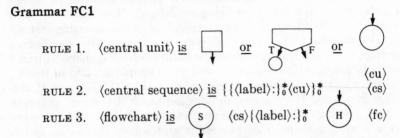

RULE 1. ⟨central unit⟩ is ☐ or T⟍⟋F or ◯   ⟨cu⟩

RULE 2. ⟨central sequence⟩ is $\{\{⟨label⟩:\}_0^* ⟨cu⟩\}_0^*$ ⟨cs⟩

RULE 3. ⟨flowchart⟩ is ⓢ ⟨cs⟩$\{⟨label⟩:\}_0^*$ Ⓗ ⟨fc⟩

Note that flowcharts in this grammar have only one Halt. We shall leave undefined the precise definition of ⟨label⟩, though we may think of one as being any string of characters made of letters and digits, such as A, B3, 2C5.

The notation we are using has become standard for describing a grammar. Thus "⟨central unit⟩ is" establishes that central unit is a grammatical type, as noun or verb is in a natural language, and that the text following is its definition. This notation is commonly called BNF, "Backus-Naur form," named after the two computer scientists John Backus and Peter Naur, who initiated its use to describe Algol60. The ⟨cu⟩ on the right is an abbreviation for ⟨central unit⟩ and will be used in subsequent definitions in the grammar. The grammar is defined as a set of rewriting rules.

In the definitions juxtaposition means concatenation in the linear representation of the flowchart. The notation "*c* or *d*" means one of its contents, *c* or *d*, and { }$_0^*$ means any number of replications of its contents, including 0 of them.

It is remarkable that an unbounded set of flowcharts is de-

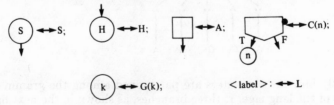

scribed by these three rules. Let us denote each of the object types shown in the figure. Then the following are legal flowcharts,

SH,	SLLH,	SAC( )ALLAC( )AH,	SALC( )G( )AAH
(a)	(b)	(c)	(d)

and

SALC( )G( )AAHLAG( )I.AOLH
     (e)

is not legal.

By "legal" or "not legal" we mean that the flowcharts can or cannot be derived from Grammar FC1. Because the particular label k that occurs in $G(k)$ and $C(k)$ is irrelevant in determining the grammatical correctness of a flowchart, we shall omit its use where only syntactic questions are being considered. Hereinafter we shall confine our discussion to the corresponding character string instead of the flowchart characters. There are only a finite number of strings of a given length that can be obtained from (generated from) rules 1, 2, and 3. Consequently we have a simple method of testing whether any string in the characters S, A, L, C(), G(), and H is a legal flowchart. If the string in question has k characters, generate all legal strings of k characters and test whether the string in question is among them. This process is grotesquely inefficient and is almost never used to test whether a string is grammatical.

Let us see how we might test the string (d). It is a flowchart if it is of the form $S\langle cs\rangle\{L\}_0^*H$. Hence it is a flowchart if ALC()G()AAH is of this form with S deleted. We continue by attempting to match the longest possible string from (d) with the syntax units occurring in the definition of flowchart as in rule 3. Thus we get:

ALC()G()AA matches $\langle cs\rangle$ because the string is a sequence of (possibly) labeled $\langle$central unit$\rangle$ s: A, C(), and G(), and H matches H.

The syntax analysis of this particular string may be represented as a *parse tree*, shown in the figure. The parse tree indicates

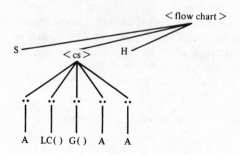

exactly how the characters are partitioned among the grammatical units of the language. If three branches, as shown in the next figure,

exit from a node, it means that the characters recognized of type α precede those of type β that in turn precede those of type γ. A grammar that permits more than one Halt is the following.

Grammar FC2

RULE	1.	⟨central unit⟩	<u>is</u> A <u>or</u> C()	⟨cu⟩
RULE	2.	⟨label sequence⟩	<u>is</u> {L}$_0^*$	⟨ls⟩
RULE	3.	⟨labeled central unit⟩	<u>is</u> ⟨ls⟩⟨cu⟩	⟨lcu⟩
RULE	4.	⟨central sequence⟩	<u>is</u> {⟨lcu⟩}$_0^*$	⟨cs⟩
RULE	5.	⟨labeled central sequence⟩	<u>is</u> ⟨ls⟩⟨cs⟩	⟨lcs⟩
RULE	6.	⟨terminal⟩	<u>is</u> G() <u>or</u> H	⟨trm⟩
RULE	7.	⟨labeled terminal⟩	<u>is</u> ⟨ls⟩⟨trm⟩	⟨ltrm⟩
RULE	8.	⟨tail element⟩	<u>is</u> L⟨lcs⟩⟨ltrm⟩	⟨te⟩
RULE	9.	⟨tail⟩	<u>is</u> {⟨te⟩}$_0^*$	⟨tl⟩
RULE	10.	⟨flowchart⟩	<u>is</u> S⟨lcs⟩⟨ls⟩H⟨tl⟩	⟨fc⟩

Grammar FC2 solves the problem of several Halts through the use of ⟨tail⟩. The grammar captures the idea that there is a path from S to an H in every legal flowchart. The string (e), illegal in grammar FC1, is legal in FC2. The parse tree for (e) is shown in the accompanying figure. The Θ denotes the "null" or "empty"

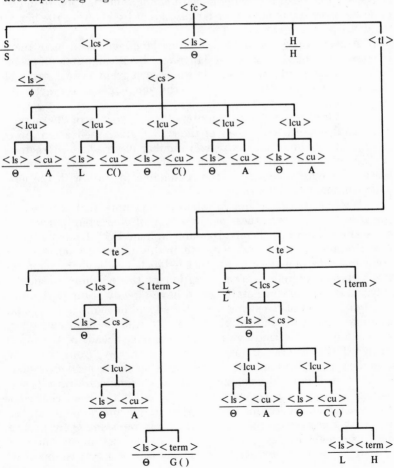

character. We should observe that the same set of strings can be generated by, or found grammatical in, different grammars. The choice of grammar is determined by other matters, such as ease of understanding and ease of parsing.

The purpose of parsing is twofold: to determine whether a string is grammatical and to yield a structure that will enable the meaning of the string to be determined from the meaning of its syntactic parts.

English is an extremely context-sensitive language: the meanings of words and sentences are often very dependent on the surrounding sentences in which they appear. The sentence "He used a table of logs" has many meanings, some because "table" and "logs" have several meanings and others because a "table of logs" can represent a flat-surfaced object known as a table that has been made from logs or even a pile of logs functioning as a table, and so on.

Computer languages, while not totally context-free, permit only very restrictive forms of context sensitivity, so that parsing comes very close to providing us with enough information to determine the meaning of computer-language text by knowing the meaning of its separate parts.

A goal of the use of programming languages is to have them processed (reduced to machine language) by a computer program. This program will be most simple when each grammatical string of characters has exactly one parse—the language is syntactically unambiguous.

By their very nature computers "scan" strings of characters. They have a worm's-eye view of the string, since their attention is focused at any one time on a small number of adjacent characters. We might as well take this small number to be 1. Since scanning must commence somewhere, it is reasonable to start with the leftmost character of the string.

We can design a simple abstract machine that determines the grammatical correctness of any string of characters purporting to denote a flowchart defined by our grammar FC2. Each syntactic unit is represented as a node, or state, in this diagram. Each directed arc connecting one state to another is labeled by a character from the flowchart alphabet. The operation of the machine is simple. Imagine we are in some state Q and have already scanned the first $r - 1$ characters of the string being tested and have discarded them. The first remaining character, the rth, we call the head character. We examine this leftmost remaining character (head) of the input string. If that character tags an arc leading, say, from the state Q to the state P, then move to state P and lop off the head character. If the state P is fc, the characters already examined form a grammatically correct string. On the other hand, if the head character does not tag an arc leading from Q, the string is ungrammatical. We repeat this process on the remaining string, replacing Q by P. The finish character ⊢ appears always only as the rightmost character of a string, so that only the entire string can ever be grammatical.

We always commence in state START, and the head character is the leftmost character of the original string. The machine is represented by its state-transition diagram (3.3). The same set of strings is recognized by the simpler finite-state machine in the diagram (3.4), which comes from the following grammar.

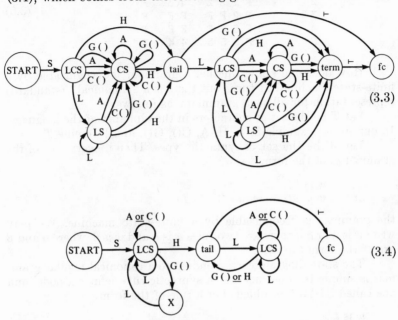

(3.3)

(3.4)

Grammar FC3

RULE 1.   ⟨lcs⟩ is {L or A or C() or G()L}₀*

RULE 2.   ⟨tail⟩ is {L ⟨lcs⟩ {G() or H̄}}₀*

RULE 3.   ⟨fc⟩ is S⟨lcs⟩H⟨tail⟩

Grammars recognizable by finite-state machines are called *regular grammars*. It is a simple matter to produce an algorithm in flowchart form from a finite-state-machine description. Indeed, the production process is quite mechanical, and there is an algorithm for the production process too! We have here a case of an algorithm producing another algorithm—a common occurrence in computer science.

Another convenient representation of the recognition process is the state-transition table. The rows represent states; the columns, the characters in the alphabet. Each entry is a row number (state identifier) or T, denoting a legal string, or F, denoting an illegal string. The action commences at row 1, and the character encountered isolates a table entry that identifies the next row (state), and the process repeats on the ensuing characters of the string.

Thus the smaller finite-state machine (3.4) has the following state-transition table.

Line character:	S	L	A	C()	H	G()	⊢
1	2	F	F	F	F	F	F
2	F	2	2	2	4	3	F
3	F	2	F	F	F	F	F
4	F	5	F	F	F	F	T
5	F	5	5	5	4	4	F

(3.5)

How does one know whether a grammar is recognizable by a finite-state machine? It turns out there is a "canonical" (standard) representation for all such grammars, as follows.

Let T be the set of characters in the alphabet of the language. In our simple example S, L, H, A, C(), G(), and ⊢ define T.

Let W be the set of syntactic types. Then if every rule of the grammar is of the form

$$w \underline{\text{is}} t \qquad\qquad t \in T$$
$$\text{or} \qquad w \underline{\text{is}} ut \qquad w, u \in W, t \in T$$

the grammar is recognizable by a finite-state machine. We may write $w \underline{\text{is}} \alpha \underline{\text{or}} \beta$ if there are two rules $w \underline{\text{is}} \alpha$ and $w \underline{\text{is}} \beta$, where α and β are of the form t or ut.

The state diagram corresponding to a canonical regular grammar is simple to construct. Each syntactic rule defines a node, and one called START is added. For a rule of the form

$$w \underline{\text{is}} t$$

an arc tagged t is directed from START to node w. For each rule of the form $w \underline{\text{is}} ut$ an arc is directed from u to w and tagged by t. The grammar FC3 has the canonical representation:

RULE 1. ⟨lcs⟩ $\underline{\text{is}}$ S $\underline{\text{or}}$ ⟨lcs⟩L $\underline{\text{or}}$ ⟨lcs⟩A $\underline{\text{or}}$ ⟨lcs⟩C() $\underline{\text{or}}$ ⟨x⟩L

RULE 2. ⟨x⟩ $\underline{\text{is}}$ ⟨lcs⟩G()

RULE 3. ⟨tail⟩ $\underline{\text{is}}$ ⟨lcs⟩H $\underline{\text{or}}$ ⟨lcs#⟩G $\underline{\text{or}}$ ⟨lcs#⟩H   (3.6)

RULE 4. ⟨lcs#⟩ $\underline{\text{is}}$ ⟨tail⟩L $\underline{\text{or}}$ ⟨lcs#⟩L $\underline{\text{or}}$ ⟨lcs#⟩A $\underline{\text{or}}$ ⟨lcs#⟩C()

RULE 5. ⟨fc⟩ $\underline{\text{is}}$ ⟨tail⟩

Conversely, the BNF grammar in canonical form can be derived from the state-transition diagram.

We have now defined a set of flowchart forms and have been able to test whether a form is a legal flowchart form: we have defined its grammar and constructed its recognizer.

Let us now extend our flowchart forms to include procedures. We add P() to represent a call and N() to represent a procedure name and formal parameter listing. R will denote the procedure "return," and each procedure has precisely one. D will denote the opening of a procedure definition and F its close. We use flowcharts to represent the bodies of procedure definitions. We can now appreciate the value of the BNF notation for describing grammars. Instead of describing the new rules in English we need merely list the new extended grammar. A flowchart with procedures is obtained from grammar FC3:

Grammar FCP1

$\langle$lcs$\rangle$ <u>is</u> $\{$L <u>or</u> A <u>or</u> C$()$ <u>or</u> G$()$L <u>or</u> P$()\}$

$\langle$procdef$\rangle$ <u>is</u> DN$()\langle$lcs$\rangle$R$\{$L$\langle$lcs$\rangle$G$()\}_0^*$F $\langle$pd$\rangle$

$\langle$tailp$\rangle$ <u>is</u> $\{$L$\langle$lcs$\rangle\{$G$()$ <u>or</u> H$)\}\}_0^*$ $\{\langle$pd$\rangle\}_0^*$

$\langle$fcp$\rangle$ <u>is</u> S$\langle$lcs$\rangle$H$\langle$tailp$\rangle$

Note that no procedure definition is permitted to contain another procedure definition. This is somewhat annoying, since procedures are obtained from programs which, of course, may have procedures, etc. Note that programs appear to have the possibility of many halts but that procedures have but one return. This is easily rectified by insisting that all programs have precisely one halt. To remove these inconsistencies we provide the grammar:

Grammar FCP2

$\langle$lcs$\rangle$ <u>is</u> $\{$L <u>or</u> A <u>or</u> C$()$ <u>or</u> G$()$L <u>or</u> P$()\}_0^*$

$\langle$pd$\rangle$ <u>is</u> DN$()\langle$lcs$\rangle$R$\langle$tailp$\rangle$F

$\langle$tailp$\rangle$ <u>is</u> $\{$L$\langle$lcs$\rangle$G$()\}_0^*\{$pd$\}_0^*$

$\langle$fcp$\rangle$ <u>is</u> S$\langle$lcs$\rangle$H$\langle$tailp$\rangle$

Thus to convert syntactically an $\langle$fcp$\rangle$ program to a procedure is merely to convert S to DN$()$, H to R, and $\vdash$ to F.

However, our grammar FCP2 can no longer be recognized by a finite-state machine. The definitions $\langle$procdef$\rangle$ and $\langle$tailp$\rangle$ "use" each other. The other parts of this new grammar can still be recognized by a finite-state machine, but the new definitions of $\langle$procdef$\rangle$ and $\langle$tailp$\rangle$ cannot be. If we strip away the regular part of the grammar, we are left with the problem of recognizing strings obeying a grammatic rule of the form

$$\langle Z\rangle \text{ } \underline{is} \text{ } \{D\langle Z\rangle F\}_0^* \text{ } \underline{or} \text{ } \alpha$$

where α is a regular grammar. If we replace all occurrences of D by [and of F by], then $\langle Z\rangle$ is the set of all nested parenthetical expressions: $\langle Z\rangle$ includes α, $[\alpha],[[\alpha][[\alpha][\alpha]]]$, etc. It is a theorem that $\langle Z\rangle$ cannot be recognized by a finite-state machine. Fundamentally this is because a finite state machine has only a finite memory, the set of its states, and hence can remember only a finite past. So if there were such a machine recognizing $\langle Z\rangle$, there would exist an integer M such that the machine could remember at most M marks and hence could not recognize $\langle Z\rangle$.

A way to recognize ⟨Z⟩ is to add a mark each time a [is encountered and to subtract one each time a] is encountered. If the number of marks is never <0 and is 0 when the end of the string is reached, the string is grammatical, if α is. We cannot perform this arithmetic process with a finite-state machine. Our extended flowchart language requires a machine with unbounded memory to recognize all of its legal finite strings. However, the required machine is extremely simple: we merely add a counter CTR and add the following states to our machine (3.4). The diagram is now as shown in (3.7).

SCTR   which sets the CTR to 0 and generates a null character

PCTR   which generates a character +1

MCTR   which generates a character −1

ACTR   which adds the current character to the CTR contents and outputs the character

RCTR   which generates the character 1, if CTR holds 0, and otherwise generates a 0

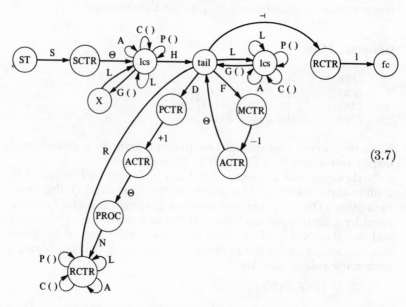

(3.7)

The flowchart language FCP2 we have defined is not very useful, since it says nothing about data or operations to transform data: the language does not allow us to write text about anything. However, it does perform an important delimiting function, since we have a general flow and control structure around which to define when we do decide what the language is to be about. We will flesh out our language by adding operations and data that still leave it context-free and then introduce an idea of limited context that seems appropriate for computer languages. Subject to reasonable definitions of A, C(), G(), and P(), the analysis of translation into computer code that we carried out in Chapter 2 tells us that our language FCP2 is algorithmically translatable into machine language.

As we become more familiar with programming languages, we become aware that an important distinguishing feature among them is the data types whose manipulation they permit. Our experience has taught us that certain problems induce algorithms that are most clearly understood, most easily written, and most efficiently executed when their data are represented in an appropriate way. Furthermore, each choice of data representation brings with it a set of adequate and satisfactory operators for manipulating the data. We are going to examine several languages chosen for their disparate data representation. Before we do, however, we shall look at one language, Algol60, and use it as a model for the fleshing out of our flowchart language FCP2.

ALGOL60

We must start with the data structures permitted by the language. Algol60 permits the direct use of integers, floating-point numbers called reals and booleans—variables taking on the values of true and false. These are the only simple variable types permitted. The only data structure permitted is the array. An Algol60 array is homogeneous—all its elements are of the same type—and its shape is essentially rectangular.

The operations on data are scalar operations on simple data only. Arrays in Algol60 merely provide a useful naming structure whereby a set of simple data can be gathered together under the umbrella of a single name. However, the operations on arrays must be performed element by element, since only array components can appear in A and C() statements.

The A-type boxes in Algol60 are called *assignment statements*, some examples of which are

1. $x \leftarrow 3 \times u + .4;$
2. $y[i] \leftarrow 5.46 \times u + w/g(r + s, y);$
3. $c[i, j] \leftarrow b \leftarrow d \wedge e \wedge (u > 7_{10} 2 \vee w \neq$
   $G(t \uparrow 2 - 1, y) \vee H(b, u));$
4. $w \leftarrow r +$ <u>if</u> $b \wedge c[j + 1, i]$ <u>then</u> $(u + 3)$ <u>else</u> $x + w;$
5. $y[j] \leftarrow j \leftarrow (i + 1) \div -2;$

and they mean that the expressions to the right of the $\leftarrow$ are evaluated and the resultant value (not values) becomes the new value of the variables to the left of any arrow, $\leftarrow$. A semicolon terminates each such assignment statement.

The examples illustrate nine features of assignment statements, as follows.

1. They contain references to variables, constants, and calls on procedures.

2. Constants are of a type indicated by their representation:

CONSTANT	TYPE
3, −2	integer
.4, 5.46, 7_{10} 2	real
true, false	boolean

3. A variable is represented by a name or identifier which does not, of itself, indicate the type of the variable. The type is specified in a declaration. Declarations induce a concept of context into the language, since the meaning of an assignment statement depends upon declarative information specified elsewhere. Every variable must be declared. The statements 1 through 5 might utilize the following declarations to set the types of all variables:

```
real u, w; integer t, r, s, i, j;
boolean b, d, e;
real array y[-2:7];
boolean array c[0:3, 1:5];
real procedure G;
boolean procedure H;
```

4. Expressions are evaluated from left to right, and the binding power of operators obeys the standard hierarchy given in Chapter 2. Parentheses can be used to obtain other execution orderings.

In assignment statement 5 the j for $y[j]$ is the value of j just prior to execution of the expression and is not the value assigned to j as the result of executing the expression $(i + 1) \div 2$.

Thus the evaluation of an A statement takes place in three steps:

a. Identify and fix the particular variables to be assigned values.

b. Evaluate the expression to the right of the rightmost ← from left to right.

c. Assign the value of the expression to the variables identified in step 1.

5. The expressions $a + b$ and $a - b$ are of the type integer if both a and b are of the type integer; otherwise they are of the type real. The expressions a/b and $a \uparrow b$ are of the type real. The expression $a \div b$ is only defined for integers a and b, and the result, of type integer, is the greatest integer in a/b.

6. When a real expression is assigned to an integer variable, as in assignment statement (a), its value is rounded to the nearest integer. Thus in $r \leftarrow 3 \times u + .4$ we have

u	r
1	3
1.1	4
.7	3

7. The procedures G and H yield real and boolean values, respectively. In Algol60 value-yielding procedures are called *functions*.

8. The conditional expression in assignment statement (d) adds to r

```
       u + 3 if b ∧ c[j + 1, i] were true
or     r     if it were not
```

and then adds w in either case. If, instead of $r + w$, it were $(r + w)$, the expressions would evaluate to

```
       r + u + 3   if b ∧ c[j + 1, i] were true
or     r + (r + w) if it were not
```

9. The boolean operations available in Algol60 are $\sim$ (not), $\wedge$ (and), $\vee$ (or), $\rightarrow$ (implication), $\equiv$ (equivalence). The truth tables of $\sim$, $\vee$, and $\wedge$ have already been given in Chapter 2; however, we include them here as (3.8), and a boolean variable can be assigned a truth value as in assignment statement (c).

x	y	$\sim$x	x $\wedge$ y	x $\vee$ y	x $\rightarrow$ y	x $\equiv$ y
F	F	T	F	F	T	T
F	T	T	F	T	T	F
T	F	F	F	T	F	F
T	T	F	T	T	T	T

$$(3.8)$$

We now see what A units are like in the language Algol60. As we have done with the $\langle$fcp$\rangle$ language, we can define the grammar of A units. We will see that this grammar is not a finite-state grammar. It will be convenient to introduce an additional kind of memory to our grammar to make parsing simple: the push-down stack.

An interesting aspect of this grammar is that we can imbed operation hierarchy directly in the grammar. Consider a simple subset of assignment statements of the kind $r \leftarrow a \times b + c$, $r \leftarrow (a + b) \times (c + d)$, $r \leftarrow a + b + c$, etc., involving the variables a, b, c, d, and r, parentheses, and the operators $+$, $\times$, and $\leftarrow$. Then define:

Grammar BEX

RULE 1. $\langle$baby variable$\rangle$ <u>is</u> a <u>or</u> b <u>or</u> c <u>or</u> d <u>or</u> r $\langle bv \rangle$

RULE 2. $\langle$baby primary$\rangle$ <u>is</u> $\langle bv \rangle$ <u>or</u> $(\langle be \rangle)$ $\langle bp \rangle$

RULE 3. $\langle$baby term$\rangle$ <u>is</u> $\{\langle bp \rangle$ <u>or</u> $\langle bt \rangle \times \langle bp \rangle\}$ $\langle bt \rangle$

RULE 4. $\langle$baby expr$\rangle$ <u>is</u> $\{\langle bt \rangle$ <u>or</u> $\langle be \rangle + \langle bt \rangle\}$ $\langle be \rangle$

RULE 5. $\langle$baby assignment$\rangle$ <u>is</u> $\langle bv \rangle \leftarrow \langle be \rangle$; $\langle bas \rangle$

Note that those definitions are not in the canonical form for a finite-state grammar and, indeed, cannot be expressed as a finite-state grammar: again there is the issue of counting parentheses. If we agree to scan a character string from the left, let us observe the parse of $r \leftarrow a + (b + c) \times d$, in (3.9). From the structure of the

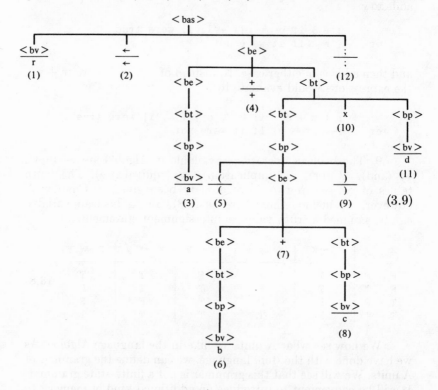

$$(3.9)$$

tree we may conclude that the order of operations is indeed first $b + c$, then its multiplication by d, then addition of a and assignment of the result to r. The grammar yields a parse tree that specifies an order for performing the operations that follows both the left-to-right scanning and operator-hierarchy rules. The tree shows that the order of matching and the rule for order of execution are simply:

An operation is performed when both its operands have been evaluated. A ⟨bv⟩, of course, is assumed to be immediately evaluable.

Let us now introduce a simple data-processing device for performing the parse of a string of characters by grammar BEX: the use of recursive procedures.

An ideal way to view the construction of our recognizer is that each syntax rule defines a procedure or flowchart for the recognition of the string of maximum length, starting at a given character— that is, of the syntax type defined by that rule. For our grammar

BEX there are five procedures that we name with the names of the rules themselves.

The set of procedures operates on the character string t to be parsed. We indicate the ith character by $t[i]$. Each procedure has one formal parameter, the position X of the head character in the string it is testing; and each procedure is integer-valued and returns $1 +$ the position of the rightmost character of t that it was able to recognize, or X if no recognition can be made. Recognition of the string fails or succeeds up to the leftmost-occurring ";." The additional procedure parse yields the value <u>true</u> if t is a ⟨bas⟩ or <u>false</u> if it is not.

procedure parse(X**)**

    <u>if</u> bas (X) = X <u>then</u> <u>return</u> (<u>false</u>) <u>else</u> <u>return</u> (<u>true</u>);

procedure bas(X**)**

```
y ← bv(X);
if y = X then return(y);
if t[y] ≠ '←' then return(X);
u ← be(y + 1);
if u = y + 1 then return(X);
if t[u] = ';' then return(u + 1) else return(X);
```

procedure be(X**)**

```
y ← bt(X);
if y = X then return(X);
while t[y] = '+' ∧ y + 1 < (u ← bt(y + 1))
    do y ← u;
return(y);
```

The procedure bt is the same as the procedure be, except that "×" replaces "+" and bp replaces bt in the definition.

procedure bp(X**)**

```
if t[X] = '(' then begin y ← be(X + 1);
if y = X + 1 then return(X);
if t[y] = ')' then return(y + 1) else return(X) end;
```

procedure bv(X**)**

```
if t[X] = 'a' ∨ t[X] = 'b' ∨ t[X] = 'c' ∨ t[X] =
    'd' ∨ t[X] = 'r'
then return(X + 1) else return(X);
```

The program to be executed is parse (1).

These procedures expose a problem that Algol60 resolves by the use of *local variables*. This refers to the multiple occurrences of the integer variables y and u in the cascade of procedure calls. The preceding set of procedures is clearly organized so that y and u are "local" to any procedure in which they are assigned values. A new y comes into existence on procedure entry and ceases to exist on procedure exit. To emphasize locality, we might write:

procedure bt(X)

```
integer y, u; y ← bp(X);
if y = X then return(X);
while t[y] = 'x' ∧ y + 1 < (u ← bp(y + 1))
   do y ← u;
return(y);
```

Even though Algol60 has a much more extensive syntax for its A statements than given by the grammar ⟨bas⟩, the recognizer for Algol60 A statements is only slightly more complex than that for ⟨bas⟩. The complete syntax is:

⟨left part⟩ is var	⟨lp⟩
⟨left part list⟩ is {⟨var⟩ ←}₁*	⟨lpl⟩
⟨assignment statement⟩ is ⟨lpl⟩⟨e⟩;	⟨as⟩

and ⟨expression⟩ is defined by:

⟨expression⟩ is ⟨ae⟩ or ⟨be⟩	⟨e⟩
⟨arithmetic expression⟩ is ⟨sae⟩ or ⟨ifc⟩⟨sae⟩ else ⟨ae⟩	⟨ae⟩
⟨if clause⟩ is if ⟨be⟩ then	⟨ifc⟩
⟨simple arithmetic expression⟩ is ⟨tm⟩ or ⟨aop⟩⟨tm⟩ or ⟨sae⟩⟨aop⟩ ⟨tm⟩	⟨sae⟩
⟨adding operator⟩ is + or −	⟨aop⟩
⟨term⟩ is ⟨fct⟩ or ⟨tm⟩⟨mop⟩⟨fct⟩	⟨tm⟩
⟨multiply operator⟩ is × or / or ÷	⟨mop⟩
⟨factor⟩ is ⟨pr⟩ or ⟨fct⟩ ↑ ⟨pr⟩	⟨fct⟩
⟨primary⟩ is ⟨unr⟩ or ⟨var⟩ or ⟨proc⟩ or (⟨ae⟩)	⟨pr⟩

and

⟨boolean expression⟩ is ⟨sbe⟩ or ⟨ifc⟩⟨sbe⟩ else ⟨be⟩	⟨be⟩
⟨simple boolean expression⟩ is ⟨imp⟩ or ⟨sbe⟩ ≡ ⟨imp⟩	⟨sbe⟩
⟨implication⟩ is ⟨btm⟩ or ⟨imp⟩ → ⟨btm⟩	⟨imp⟩
⟨boolean term⟩ is ⟨bfct⟩ or ⟨btm⟩ ∨ ⟨bfct⟩	⟨btm⟩
⟨boolean factor⟩ is ⟨bsec⟩ or ⟨bfct⟩ ∧ ⟨bsec⟩	⟨bfct⟩
⟨boolean secondary⟩ is ⟨bpr⟩ or ¬ ⟨bpr⟩	⟨bsec⟩

⟨boolean primary⟩ is ⟨logval⟩ or ⟨var⟩ or ⟨proc⟩
            or ⟨rel⟩ or (⟨be⟩))   ⟨bpr⟩
⟨logical value⟩ is true or false   ⟨logval⟩
⟨relation⟩ is ⟨sae⟩⟨relop⟩⟨sae⟩   ⟨rel⟩
⟨relational operator⟩ is < or ≤ or = or ≠
              or ≥ or >   ⟨relop⟩

Let us define ⟨var⟩:
⟨simple variable⟩ is ⟨id⟩   ⟨svar⟩
⟨subscript list⟩ is ⟨ae⟩{,⟨ae⟩}$_0^*$ ⟨sl⟩

For the moment we will leave undefined ⟨unr⟩ and ⟨proc⟩, standing for unsigned number and procedure designator, respectively. The only complexities that have been added to our scanning system are

1. additional brackets
2. lists

and, of course, more definitions. Neither the brackets nor the lists are terribly difficult to handle. For example, lists arise in $H[u, v, w]$. They would be reduced syntactically to $H[u]$ and then H. Similarly, $a \leftarrow b \leftarrow c$ is reduced to $a \leftarrow b$.

We shall not define all of the procedures for recognizing Algol60 A statements but merely indicate those that require somewhat different bodies than those used in bas. Thus, to the syntax construction

    {⟨var⟩←}$_1^*$

corresponds the procedure:

procedure leftside(X)

```
y ← var(X);
if y = X then return(X);
if t[y] = '←' then
while (y < (u ← var(y)) ∧ (t[u] = '←') do
  y ← u + 1; return(y);
else return(X);
```

The rule ⟨sl⟩ is of the form ⟨ae⟩{,⟨ae⟩}$_0^*$ and is handled much like ⟨bea⟩:

procedure sl(X)

```
y ← ae(X);
if y = X then return(X);
while t[y] = ',' ∧ y + 1 < (u ← ae(y + 1) do
  y ← u; return(y);
```

We may write the procedure for sl(X) with one return:

procedure sl(X)

```
y ← ae(X);
if y > X then
while t[y] = ',' ∧ y + 1 ≤ (u ← ae(y + 1)) do
   y ← u;
return(y);
```

Let us now turn our attention to C() statements in Algol60. They are of either of two forms: first,

```
if ⟨be⟩ then begin statement sequence 1 end
else begin statement sequence 2 end;
```

corresponding to the following flowchart structure,

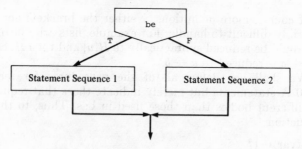

and next,

```
if ⟨be⟩ then begin statement sequence 1 end;
```

corresponding to the following flowchart structure,

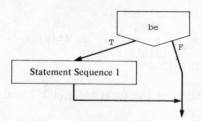

The Algol60 construct corresponding to G() is goto L, where L is a label.

The role of (START) and (HALT) is contained in the convention: An Algol60 program commences with the first begin and terminates when control reaches its matching end.

In the representation of algorithms using flowcharts no special construction for cycles was used. However, the occurrence of loops in programs is so common that most programming languages provide special constructions for defining loops. In Algol60 the principal statement form for loop specification is:

```
for ⟨var⟩ := ⟨ae⟩₁ step ⟨ae⟩₂ until ⟨ae⟩₃ do begin
statement sequence end;
```

where ⟨var⟩ is a real or integer variable, and the intent of the statement is that the statement sequence is repeatedly executed for successive values of ⟨var⟩. To see what values ⟨var⟩ would attain, consider the following examples, where S is some statement sequence in which i is not assigned a value:

1. `for i := 1 step 1 until 20 do begin S end;`
   i takes on the successive values 1, 2, . . . , 19, 20.
2. `for i := −1 step 2 until 10 do begin S end;`
   i takes on the successive values −1, 1, 3, 5, 7, 9.
3. `for i := 10 step −1 until 0 do begin S end;`
   i takes on the successive values 10, 9, 8, . . . , 2, 1, 0.
4. `for i := 1 step i until 20 do begin S end;`
   i takes on the successive values 1, 2, 4, 8, 16.
5. $X := 2;$ `for i := 1 step X until 18 do begin S; X :=`
   $X + 1$ `end;`
   i takes on the successive values 1, 4, 8, and 13, if we assume S does not alter the value of X.

The sequence S may contain for-type statements, permitting nested cycles, as in the example:

```
w ← a[1, 1];
for i := 1 step 1 until n do begin
for j := 1 step 1 until m do begin
if a[i, j] > w then w ← a[i, j] end end;
```

that finds the maximum value held in an array a of n rows and m columns.

There are other forms of the loop statement permitted in Algol60. A particularly useful one that has been added to some late versions of Algol60 is

```
while ⟨be⟩ do begin statement sequence S end;
```

that repeats the execution of S until ⟨be⟩ is no longer true. Naturally S should ultimately change the value of ⟨be⟩ from true to false. In standard Algol60 this very useful statement can be programmed by:

```
i := ⟨ae⟩ while ⟨be⟩ do begin statement sequence S end;
```

There is much more to Algol60 than we wish to scrutinize here. But enough has been described to establish a relationship between flowcharts and Algol60.

The coin algorithm is easily written, almost by transcription, in Algol60:

```
begin  integer N, index, P, J, t;
       integer array M, C[1:10];
       Read (N, C, index);
       P ← 0; J ← index; t ← N;
  L:   M[J] ← t;
       if C[J] = 1 then begin
          P ← P + 1;
  Z:     J ← J - 1;
       if J < index then begin
       Print (P); go to Q end
       else begin t ← M[J] - C[J];
       if t ≥ 0 then go to L
       else go to Z end end
    else begin J ← J + 1; go to L end
  Q:   end
Q labels an empty statement.
```

Note that we have used fixed bounds on the vectors M and C even though their size will vary with the amount N, the index, and the coin set C. Algol60 provides us with techniques for using variable-sized M and C, and we shall rewrite the algorithm to take advantage of this ability after we have studied block structure.

In a subsequent section we shall treat the important issue of procedures or subroutines in Algol60.

Algol60 has a well-defined syntax, and one masters it through use, though a great deal of use is not required. Although we do not wish to treat its full syntax in any further detail, it is instructive to examine a piece of Algol60 text with a plethora of syntactic errors. The notes following the text are numbered according to the lines of text and explain the errors. We might have written the text in an unindented format:

```
begin comment this is an algol60 program . . .          1
whose declarations are:                                 2
integer a,i,z,b,c                                       3
real f,g,y,x,u                                          4
boolean B,A                                             5
integer array D,C[-1:30, -20:50],[1:10],
respectively;                                           6
f ← SIN B + SIN 2 × B                                   7
D[1:15, -17:40] ← 0;                                    8
a + 4₁₀(2₁₀1) ← z + 3;                                  9
for i ← 1 . . . 10 do y ← y+i;                          10
x ← 2₁₀g;                                               11
15 := a × 2↑b;                                          12
```

```
goto L:                                                      13
if y > 7 then Z ← SIN(u) else cos(u);                        14
t ← B ∧ (A:=B) ∨ ↓B ∧ ↑B;                                    15
x ← 2 × (a↑(b–c); i ← 1;                                     16
L: for i ← step 3 until 10                                   17
u ← x + 7; if y > 7 then u ← u–1 else;                       18
D[1,u+3] ← C[if y < 7 then 3 else (i+2)];                    19
if y < 14 then if y < 11 then z ← 2 else z ← 1              20
else z ← 3; Di,j ← 3₁₀2.5;                                  21
end
```

Notes

7. SIN B is either the variable SINB or SIN operation B or the procedure call SIN(B).

8. $D[1:15, -17:40]$ is not a legal $\langle var \rangle$ but is a form used to indicate the shape of an array and appears only in a declaration.

9. An expression can occur as a left part only if it is a subscript of an array variable; $4_{10}(2_{10}1)$ is neither a legal expression nor a number. The exponent must not itself contain an exponent; $4_{10}20$ would be a legal number meaning 4×10^{20}.

10. The construction . . . has no significance in Algol60 and can occur only in a comment, as in line 1.

11. An expression cannot occur as the exponent of a number; $2 \times 10 \uparrow g$ would be a way of expressing this intent.

12. The 15 does not commence with a letter and hence is not a $\langle var \rangle$ and hence cannot appear as a left part in an assignment statement.

14. In a conditional statement the else clause must be an assignment statement and not an expression.

15. The $A := B$ is not a boolean expression, and $A =$ might have generated a boolean expression, but the form to the right of $=$ is not a legal expression. Nor are $\uparrow B$ and $\downarrow B$ legal expressions.

16. The parentheses are unbalanced.

17. The for statement is not properly formed, since i is not initialized, and the for clause does not terminate with do.

18. The first ";" converts the body into two statements and hence requires a surrounding begin end pair. The statement following the else is an empty statement and must be surrounded by a begin end pair, as in "else begin end;."

20. Only a simple statement can occur following then so that a matching begin end pair is required.

21. $D\overline{i,j}$ is not a variable; $D[i, j]$ would be. The exponent 2.5 is illegal since it is not an integer.

These are syntax errors. However, note that the opening comment probably should have terminated on line 1 with a ";." If this had been done, several forms in the original comment would show syntax errors.

Many Algol60 translators also treat as syntactic errors the

misuse of properly declared variables. In particular, violations of the following rules are detected during syntactic analysis by some Algol60 translators.

RULE 1.   In a given block an identifier can be declared only once and must thereafter be of its declared type (see Section 4 for a discussion of blocks).

RULE 2.   Every identifier must have been declared prior to its use.

RULE 3.   An identifier must be used properly in accordance with its declaration. An integer variable x cannot occur in the context if x then or $x \wedge \ldots$, a boolean variable B cannot occur as $B := c + d$, and an array variable must not occur without attached subscript, except as a parameter in a procedure.

The foregoing merely points out that the boundary between syntax processing and semantic processing by a translator is often chosen for the convenience of machine-code preparation. Certainly Rule 3 has nothing to do with grammar, but it is convenient to check for such errors while the text is being parsed.

The role of a programming-language grammar is to specify what text forms can be correctly translated into machine-language code; even more, which ones can be translated in a mechanical fashion (algorithmically) into machine code.

ALGOL60: SCOPE AND CONTEXT

Algol60 was the first language to possess a formal syntactic description. It also pioneered in establishing an elegant and uniform way of specifying and controlling scope or context. In our earliest version of flowcharts we made use of the construct shown in (3.10). We later

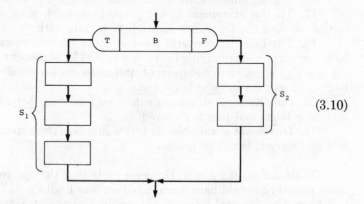

$$(3.10)$$

discarded it in linearized flowcharts. Algol60, certainly a linear language, retains this structure, using begin end bracketing to maintain it within a linear representation. The structure (3.10) is written:

> if B then begin S₁ end else begin S₂ end;

The brackets begin (open) and end (close) establish scope and do so
uniformly through the language: a succession of statements brack-
eted by begin and end behaves, syntactically, as a single statement.
Thus scope is jointly defined by punctuation and bracketing, and
the latter permits elegant nesting of syntactic units. But what
exactly is meant by scope?

    (Static) scope is that longest (contiguous) string of Algol text
over which some semantic or syntactic property holds, and the
property is said to have that scope. Generally begin and end permit
arbitrarily long strings of text to establish a scope. There is also a
dynamic scope that arises during the use of procedures.

    What are the properties for which scope is worth establishing?
The linearization of text makes scope-of-control properties important. In the ⟨conditional statement⟩ of Algol60, which text is the
scope of the T branch, which is that of the F branch, and which is
that of the common continuation of both branches? In a ⟨for state-
ment⟩ which text is to be repeatedly executed under the control of
the ⟨for clause⟩? What is the scope of an identifier declaration, and
if the scope is not the entire program, may one use the same identifier to denote more than one variable within a program text?

    Scope may also be seen as establishing a textual interval in
which some linguistic property remains constant. Whereas the
flexibility of a language is measured by what can be variable, the
efficiency with which its text can be processed on a computer is
measured by the control of constancy that can be specified in the
language.

    In programming languages scope is what we mean when we
use the word *context*.

    An important scope is the range of text in which a variable
exists. Declarations establish that identifiers have certain properties. Thus real x, y establishes x and y as naming real variables.
The scope of this property is the text enclosed in the innermost
matching begin end brackets containing the declaration in question.
What occurs when the end is attained? The declared property ceases
to hold. Algol60 treats this simply: When the property ceases to
hold, the variable having that property ceases to exist. Thus at the
matching end x and y cease to exist. Hence, after this end any
further occurrence of x or y must refer to different variables, but
having the same names as those that just ceased to exist. In the
following diagram b, e, r, and i represent begin, end, real, and
integer, respectively.

> b r x^1, y^1; ...x^1b i x^2; ...x^2 ...y^1e ...x^1 ...y^1 ...e

Occurrences with like superscript value have the same scope: the
real x is shadowed by the integer x as long as the latter exists but

reappears when the latter x "dies." Put another way, a b and matching e can introduce a new and private level of naming that, when it ceases, returns the state of naming to what had previously held. A level of naming commences at a block begin and terminates at a block end. Such is the Algol60 block concept.

A variable in a language is represented by an identifier that, in turn, is tied to one or more computer words that hold the value of the variable. Of four models, given below, Model A is the simplest useful one.

MODEL A. Each identifier is attached to a computer word; if two identifiers are different, so are their attached computer words.

It may be that two parts of a program are written separately and have individually chosen identifiers—after all, their choice is a personal one—and that, on combination, several distinct "identifiers" are found to name the same variable. Instead of laboriously changing "noncolliding" names, one may sometimes use a second model, Model B.

MODEL B. Each identifier is attached to a computer word. If, and only if, two identifiers name the same variable, they attach to the same computer word. The FORTRAN programming language utilizes such a synonym structure.

However, it may also be that independently written program parts use the same identifier to connote different variables, and hence they must be attached to different computer words. Furthermore, during the course of program execution a variable may be born and then may die; hence, its attachment to a computer word need not preclude the attachment of other distinct variables to that same word as long as attachments do not coexist in time. This view of identifier-variable-word attachments is followed in Algol60, as shown by Model C.

MODEL C. Each identifier is attached to a computer word. The attachment commences at its declaration and ceases when its matching block end is encountered. During the attachment period one and only one variable is attached to an identifier, and no two identifiers are attached to the same computer word.

The Algol60 block concept thus provides a means of control over the reuse of computer storage and over the confusion arising when the same identifier denotes several variables. However, Algol60 does not provide any attractive solution for Model B.

The control over identifier-word attachments in Algol60 can be handled in a simple and elegant way by using two structures:

a stack and an integer vector called the *display*. For our purposes
the computer words may be taken as having addresses 0, 1, . . . ,
N and will be treated as components of a vector M. $M[J]$ is the
value stored in the computer word having address J.

For the moment let us continue to ignore procedures. Then,
insofar as issues of identifier-address attachments are concerned,
any Algol60 program is representable in terms of its declarative
structure, for example, as

$$(C[5],x,y,z(A[x],y);(B[z],y,z,(B[z], v)))   \qquad (3.11)$$

where (and) denote <u>begin</u> and <u>end</u>, respectively, $C[5],x,y,z$ declares an array C of size $\overline{5}$ and three variables x, y, and z in the
outermost block, and $A[x]$ declares an array A whose size depends
on the value of x. Control dances through this program as it is
being executed, and the values of variables are changed. In particular, as x (which x?) and z change values, the sizes of the arrays
A and B change. But some features of the program do not change:

The block structure does not change. Hence the static level or
depth of any block is fixed.

The variables of the program with their types and the block
in which they are declared are fixed. The block nesting depth of
the given program is 3, so that the display vector D has three
components $D[1]$, $D[2]$, $D[3]$.

Each block has the static block level affixed to its opening
<u>begin</u> "(" and a unique identification tag:

level	1	2		2	3			
	(	(	)	(	(	)	)	)
tag	1	2		3	4			

For each block, associate each variable declared within it with the
variable's order of listing in its declaration list. Then the Jth simple
variable in a block at level k is uniquely named by $M[D[k] + J - 1]$,
and the nth component of an array that is the Jth variable declared
in that block is

$$M[M[D[k] + J - 1] + r - 1],   \qquad J = 1, 2, \ldots$$

where r is the position of the nth array element when the array is
linearly ordered as, for example, when the method described in
Chapter 2 is used.

The number of words used to hold the values of variables in
a block are used to construct a set of links connecting its storage
assignment to that of previously entered blocks. All attachments
are then dynamically regulated by the current values of $D[1]$, $D[2]$,
and $D[3]$. To see this let us treat our example (3.11) in more detail.

Suppose the passage of control causes the blocks to be traversed in the order

```
x:        3                      4   2
tag:      1 → 2 → 3 → 4 → 1 → 3 → 4
z:        5         4            2   5
```

The values of x and z are shown because they affect the attachments, through their determination of the sizes of A and B, respectively.

Table 3.1 shows what attachments are made in the block traversals and what values are assigned to the display. Note that $D[1]$ is 0 always, since 1 is the outermost block, and $D[2]$ is 9 always, since block 1 can never change the number of words attached to its variables. In the outermost block, arrays with variable bounds are not permitted. The attachment for y in block 3 is $M[D[2] + 1]$, always $M[10]$, while that for $B[3]$ in block 4 is

$$M[M[D[3]] + 2] \quad \text{or, first,} \quad M[21] \quad \text{and, later,} \quad M[18]$$

When and how are values assigned to the display?

TABLE 3.1

M	Traversal sequence						
	1	2	3	4	1	3	4
0	C 4						
1	x 3						
2	y						
3	z 5				z 2		
4							
5							
6							
7							
8							
9		A 11	B 12			B 12	
10		y	y			y	
11			z 4			z 5	
12							
13	y						
14							B 16
15							v
16							
17				B 19			
18				v			
19							
20							
21							
22							
D[2]	9						
D[3]				17			14

Suppose we enter a block at level k. Assume $D[k]$ already contains the base attachment for variables in that block. Then a count of the variables being attached at level k, $n(k)$, is used to assign a value to $D[k + 1]$: $D[k + 1] \leftarrow D[k] + n(k)$.

Hence when we next enter a block at level $k + 1$, $D[k + 1]$ will be set to the appropriate base.

When we exit from a block at level l to the interior of one at level k, $k < l$, $D[k + 1]$ is already set and waiting for a subsequent entry to a block at level $k + 1$.

The entire process commences with $D[1] \leftarrow 0$. This discipline for arranging attachments merely requires that entry to a block is always through its "head" wherein the declarations lie. This is easily arranged: all labels are (implicitly) declared in the innermost block containing the statement they label. Thus,

1. $(. . .$ goto $L. . . (x,y; L{:}S; . . .) . . .)$
   is illegal since the label L is "shadowed" by its block head.
2. $(. . . ; L{:}S; . . .(.(.(x,y; . . . ; \text{goto } L; . . .).).).)$
   is legal and the goto L will cause an exit from its containing block to that three levels shallower.
3. $(. . . ;L{:}S; . . . (x,y; . . . ; \text{goto } L; . . . ; L{:}S') . . .)$
   is, of course, legal. The goto L will cause a transfer to S' since L is locally defined in the inner block.
4. $(. . . ; L{:}(u,v{:} . . . ; \text{goto } M; . . .) . . . (x,y; . . . ; \text{goto } L; . . . ; M{:}S . . .). . .)$

The goto L is legal since L, even though it labels a block, is itself in a block containing the statement goto L. The goto M statement is illegal since M does not label a statement in a blcok containing the block labeled by L.

Now we are in a position to rectify the shortcomings of the algorithm (3.18). We merely imbed the algorithm in an outer block that reads N and the number of coins in the set C:

```
begin integer N, SIZE;
Read(N, SIZE);
begin integer index, P, J, t;
integer array M, C[1: SIZE];
Read(C, index);
P ← 0; J ← index; t ← N:
L: M[J] ← t;
if C[J] = 1 then begin
P ← P + 1;
Z: J ← J - 1;
if J < index then begin Print(P); goto Q end
else begin t ← M[J] - C[J];
if t ≥ 0 then goto L
else goto Z end end
else begin J ← J + 1; goto L end
Q: end end
```

ALGOL60: PROCEDURES

Algorithms are not easy to find; good algorithms are precious and of great value. While mentally challenging and of great educational value, the necessity of reinventing algorithms required for a problem impedes progress in computation. The "procedure" permits us to fit smoothly already existing algorithms into our programs. Every programming language admits a procedure structure.

Every highly organized use of the computer in an applied area as in for example, statistics, nuclear physics, chemical engineering, or economics, develops its own collection of procedures that are described in the technical literature of the field in question.

Algol60 has an excellent procedure structure. Several technical journals in computation devote space to publication of algorithms written in Algol60, such as *The Communications of the ACM*, and several hundred have been published there since Algol60 was invented.

Algol60 has two kinds of procedure: those that produce a scalar value of a certain type (real, integer, or boolean), called *functions* or *type procedures*, and those that produce no explicit value, called *procedures*.

Where do the procedures used in an Algol60 program come from? Many Algol60 computer implementations treat a program as a block immersed in one fixed encompassing block that already contains a collection of useful procedures called the Algol60 library. The given program may then "call" upon those procedures needed from the library. If a program is to use procedures that are not in the library, they must be defined (declared) inside the program.

In Algol60 procedures are declared much the same as other identifiers. A procedure identifier f is declared in a block heading and is thereupon coupled to the text of its definition. Calls upon f may then be made only from the interior of the block in which f is declared, since its identifying name disappears when the block in which it is declared is exited during program execution. As in the case of other identifiers, several different procedures may share the same name, but only in different blocks.

Variable declarations are simple:

```
real x, y;
integer array A, B[1: 10, n: m];
```

Procedure declarations are somewhat more complex in syntactic structure than variable declarations. Let us look at two examples:

```
1.    procedure UP(X,N); array X; integer N;
      begin integer I;
      for I ← 1 step 1 until N do
      Y[X[I]] ← I end
```

(3.12)

```
2. boolean procedure PRIME(X); integer X;
   begin integer I; boolean P;
   P ← X-2×(X÷2) ≠ 0                                    (3.13)
   I ← 3;
   while I↑2 ≤ X ∧ P do
   begin if X - I × (X÷I) = 0 then
   P ← false;
   I ← I + 2 end;
   PRIME ← P end
```

The first line of both declarations is the procedure "heading" containing the result type (if any), the name, and the list of formal parameters with a specification of their types. The procedure heading is followed by the procedure "body" that must be a statement and is usually a block, containing some declared variables, the local variables of the procedure.

Let us make some comments about the two examples.

First, every formal parameter must have a type specification, but no array-bound information is required in the parameter specification.

Second, procedures may contain identifiers global to them as, for example, Y in (3.12). Such procedures may then create "side effects" on variables not mentioned in a call. Their execution may change the value of a global variable, and the user of a procedure may not be aware of, or prepared for it.

Using global variables in procedures is a bad practice and should be avoided whenever possible. In (3.12) Y should have been a formal parameter.

Third, for a function the result is reported back as the current value, on exit from the function, of the variable having as its identifier the function name, as PRIME in (3.13). Furthermore, this variable must occur only on the left-hand side of one or more assignment statements.

Fourth, exit from a procedure is attained by reaching the end of the statement (or block) making up the procedure body.

A procedure is used in a program as a procedure call, as in the statement UP(IN,M+4×Q); or as a function call, as an operand, in an expression:

```
if PRIME(ENTIER(SQRT(M+2))) then . . .
```

Recursion is a powerful tool in defining functions, and Algol60 permits a procedure to be recursive, by which is meant that it may contain in its body a call on itself, as in

```
real procedure MAX(X,M,N); array X; integer M,N;
if N = M then MAX ← X[N]
else if X[M] ≥ MAX(X,M+1,N) then MAX ← X[M]    (3.14)
else MAX ← MAX(X,M+1,N)
```

This particular procedure reveals both an advantage and disadvantage of recursive procedures, due to the same phenomenon: the ability to do away with, or at least diminish, the need for local variables.

A first call on the function above might be MAX(W,1,SIZE). About 2 × SIZE calls on MAX are required. The number of calls can be reduced by introducing a local variable Y:

```
if N = M then MAX ← X[N];
else begin real Y; Y ← MAX(X,M+1,N);          (3.15)
MAX ← if X[M] ≥ Y then X[M] else Y end
```

though the procedure body (3.14) is somewhat more understandable than (3.15).

In procedure PRIME the formal parameter X is used several times in the procedure body. Indeed, a use is in a loop. More precisely, the value of X is used. The Algol60 rule for the use of a formal parameter is: When a procedure body is executed, at each encounter of a formal parameter, its corresponding actual parameter is evaluated. Hence, in the call PRIME(entier(sqrt(Y)), each encounter of X in the procedure PRIME causes the evaluation of entier(sqrt(Y)). This reevaluation is pointless, since this quantity remains constant during the entire execution of PRIME. A programmer could provide for this case by using a local variable, say, Z, and commencing the procedure body with

$$Z \leftarrow X$$

and using Z in place of X elsewhere in the body. This is such a standard technique that, by adding to the specification, value X, Algol60 "invents" the necessary local variable and makes it unnecessary for the programmer to do so. A formal *parameter*, for which a value specification is included, is said to be "called by value" and constrains its corresponding actual parameter to be evaluated exactly once immediately after the procedure is entered but before the formal parameter is first encountered in the procedure execution.

Those formal parameters not "called by value" are said to be "called by name" and are known as *name parameters*.

There is a significant difference between name and value parameters that accounts for much of the power of the Algol60 procedure concept. Let us consider a simple example. Let a procedure body be:

```
begin integer S; S ← 0;
for J ← 1 step 1 until 100 do S ← S + u;
SUM ← S end;
```

and consider two different headings that might be welded to the body:

(v)   <u>integer</u> <u>procedure</u> SUM(u, J); <u>value</u> u,J;
        <u>integer</u> u,J;
        <u>comment</u> leading to the (v) version of SUM;
(n)   <u>integer</u> <u>procedure</u> SUM(u, J); <u>integer</u> u,J; <u>comment</u>
        leading to the (n) version of SUM;

Now consider the program segment in which we insert for Q first the (v) version of SUM and later the (n) version.

```
begin integer i; integer array w[1:100]; integer a;
Q
for i ← 1 step 1 until 100 do w[i] ← i;
i ← 5;
a ← SUM(w[i],i);
end
```

What are the values of a when the two different versions of SUM are used?

Consider the (v) version:

u is evaluated to $w[5]$ which is 5.
i is evaluated to 5, which is never used.

The resultant value of SUM is $5 \times 100 = 500$.

In the (n) version, on the other hand, u is reevaluated, and i is too, in the sense that the i declared in the outer block is reassigned. Again the initial value of $i = 5$ is never used. The resultant value of SUM is $(100 \times 101)/2$, or 5050. The (n) version, in addition to causing the reevaluation of $w[i]$, causes the formal parameter J to behave as though it were a global variable.

Actual parameters are always evaluated in the context of the call. Recursion and call by name make it necessary to complicate the attachment rules by which identifiers and variables are related to addresses in the stack. However, we shall not treat the complications in this text.

Our discussion of Algol60 is now completed. For a further discussion the reader is referred to any of the standard texts on Algol60. The reader should note that Algol60 has no standard READ AND PRINT conventions. Each implementation provides its own version.

A list of some good Algol60 programming techniques follows:

1.   Knowledge of what you are computing often saves computing time.

    Example 1: To compute sinh $x = \frac{1}{2}(e^x - e^{-x})$:
    not $(\exp(x) - \exp(-x))/2$
    but $t \leftarrow \exp(x)$;
    $(t - 1/t)/2$

Example 2: To compute $\displaystyle\sum_{k=0}^{n} e^{-kx}$:

not

```
s ← 0;
for k ← 0 step 1 until n do begin
t ← exp(-k × x);
s ← s + t end
```

or not even

```
s ← 0; t ← exp(-x);
for k ← 0 step 1 until n do
s ← s + t ↑ k
```

or not even

```
s ← 0; t ← exp(-x); u ← 1;
for k ← 0 step 1 until n do begin
u ← u × t;
s ← s + u end
```

but recognize that the sum is indeed

$$\frac{(e^{-x})^{n+1} - e^{-x}}{e^{-x} - 1}$$

so that no loop is required:

$$t \leftarrow \exp(-x);$$
$$(t \uparrow (n + 1) - t)/(t - 1)$$

2. Do not waste computed information: if a quantity is used several times, try to compute it only once and assign its value to a (temporary or local) variable.

3. Do as much computing outside (for) loops as possible.

Example 3: To evaluate

$$f(x) = \sum_{k=1}^{n} (\sin kpx - qm)$$

given n, p, x, q, and m, do not write

```
sum ← 0;
for k ← 1 step 1 until n do
sum ← sum + sin(k × p × x)-q × m;
```

but write

```
sum ← -q × m × n; t ← p × x;
for k ← 1 step 1 until n do
sum ← sum + sin(k × t);
```

But, even better, use the summation formula for

$$\sum_{k=1}^{n} \sin kt$$

which can be obtained from that for $\sum_{0}^{n} e^{-kt}$.

HOW DOES ONE LEARN A PROGRAMMING LANGUAGE?

A programmer should never find it intolerable to learn a new language. While programming is done with, and in, language, much of it is quite language-independent. A good programmer should be able to make the bridge between one language and another with only modest difficulty. He should never think of himself as an "Algol60 programmer" or a "FORTRAN programmer." What steps, then, should be taken when, for one reason or another, he is required to program in a new language?

1. Establish which language the programmer knows is closest in "features" to the new language. Although each language has its own admirable features that account for its existence, approach the language comparison by using the standard features:

    a.   Primitive data types.
    b.   Open-ended data structures.
    c.   Primitive operations on primitive data types.
    d.   Expression structure.
    e.   Assignment: How do variables acquire new values?
    f.   Branching or conditionals.
    g.   Cycling or looping.
    h.   Procedures: How does the language acquire new data and operations?
    i.   Identifier communication: How do identifiers relate to each other?

2. Take a set of representative algorithms that you have programmed in the language that you know, and reprogram them in the new language, parroting as much as possible the algorithms with which you are familiar. In some cases this may not be possible without the creation of explicit procedures in the new language where none were required in the old. This is particularly so when the data structures of the old language are not contained in the new language. The writing of these procedures can be considered your first really creative use of the new language.

3. The set of algorithms, along with their added procedures in the new language, must now be improved. Presumably there are

features in the new language of which advantage has not been taken in your translation. At first the use of these features will create small changes in your programs, but ultimately they may lead to radical changes in the algorithms themselves.

4. Reexamine the new language. Of the features you have used, have you used them properly by obeying their syntactic and semantic definitions? Have you understood the generalities of the features you have used, even the generalities you have not required?

5. Probably there are features in the new language you have not used. But then what are their purposes? Under what circumstances are they to be used? Invent algorithms that use these newly uncovered features, and reverse the language acquisition process: write these new algorithms in the old language. Very possibly you will observe that the new is more felicitous, at least in some of these cases, than the old.

6. Commence to think in terms of the new language. Cast algorithms totally in its terms. Although one should not forget the old language, move it back into your "slow recall" memory and begin to think in terms of the new language.

To test these approaches we are going to consider in the following sections two languages, one of which is very much like Algol60, FORTRAN, and one that is rather different, APL.

FORTRAN

FORTRAN is the most popular programming language in the world. Every computer programmer should know how to program in one of the dialects of FORTRAN. Although no text in this book has been explicitly devoted to a description of FORTRAN, it is our purpose to show the student that he has, in fact, already learned FORTRAN, except possibly for a small number of details. There is an ancient quip that goes, "Learning French is trivial: *cheval* means "horse," and the rest follows in the same way." In fact, learning French is not trivial, and the rest does not follow in the same way! However, for the student who has progressed thus far in this book, learning FORTRAN is easy and, aside from input-output, grammatical trivia, and *patois* associated with implementations, the student already knows FORTRAN but probably is unaware of it.

Let us assume the student is familiar with Algol60 and now wishes to learn FORTRAN. We shall follow our points a to i.

What are the primitive data types? Not surprisingly they are much the same as Algol60:

ALGOL60   FORTRAN

```
integer  I, IMAX, KMIN, T;     INTEGER  I, IMAX, KMIN, T
real     J, X, POP;            REAL     J, X, POP
boolean  P,Q;                  LOGICAL  P, Q
```

FORTRAN provides a useful "default" condition for determining an identifier's type. If an identifier is not declared and commences with any of the letters I, J, K, L, M, or N, it is assumed to be an integer; otherwise, real. Thus the FORTRAN declarations above could be reduced to

```
INTEGER  T
REAL     J
LOGICAL  P, Q
```

the others being defined by default.

What open-ended data structures are available? Just as in Algol60, FORTRAN provides the array. The type of array is determined by the naming conventions used for simple variables. In FORTRAN all subscripts commence with the value 1. As in Algol60, arrays are homogeneous, rectangular, and must be declared. However, FORTRAN does not require a separate array declaration:

ALGOL60	FORTRAN
real IMAX;	INTEGER I(7), X(22,6), C
integer C;	REAL IMAX, Y(10)
real array Y[1; 10];	
integer array I[−3:3],	
X[1:22,1:6];	

Note that the Algol60 element I[C] would be I(C+4) in FORTRAN. FORTRAN permits at most three subscript positions in arrays. The subscript expressions must have integer value in FORTRAN, whereas in Algol60 real expressions are permitted and are automatically rounded. The form of subscript expressions is limited in FORTRAN to $\alpha \times \omega \pm \beta$, where α and β are integer constants and ω is an integer variable. The constant α may be omitted if it equals 1, and β may be omitted if it equals 0. FORTRAN arrays are stored by columns.

What primitive operations on primitive data types are provided?

FORTRAN provides operations on scalars and components of arrays. The basic operations of arithmetic are provided: $+$, $-$, $/$, $*$, $**$ (exponentiation). FORTRAN does not permit variables and constants of different types to be mixed in an expression, except that the exponent, in exponentiation, must be an integer, whereas the base may be real. FORTRAN provides automatic conversion between real and integer values on assignment: the result of the right-hand-side expression is converted to the type of the left-hand side.

Example: (using the foregoing declarations):

```
I = 3
J = 2.6
IMAX = J + 2.2
X = I + 1
```

assign to IMAX and X the values 4 and 4.0, respectively. The logical operations are .AND, .OR, and .NOT corresponding to Algol60's $\wedge$, $\vee$ and $\neg$, respectively, and the relations .GT, .GE, .EQ, .LE, .LT, and .NE correspond to $>$, $\geq$, $=$, $\leq$, $<$, and $\neq$, respectively.

FORTRAN uses E to correspond to Algol60's base 10 in representing constants using power-of-10 notation:

ALGOL60	FORTRAN
2	2
-2.3	-2.3
$5.46_{10}7$	$5.46E7$

FORTRAN obeys the same rules for determining the order of evaluation of operators in an expression and uses the same precedence rules for operators. However, FORTRAN has no conditional expressions.

How do variables acquire new values? The assignment statement is of the form

⟨variable⟩ = ⟨expression⟩

Multiple assignments are not permitted in a statement. Whereas Algol60 rounds on conversion, FORTRAN truncates.

What are the branching statements? The FORTRAN conditional statements are of two types.

A BRANCH ON A NUMERICAL EXPRESSION.

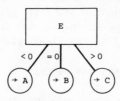

E is compared to 0, and a transfer to A or B or C occurs, depending on whether $E < 0$, or $E = 0$, or $E > 0$, respectively. The FORTRAN form is

    IF (⟨expression⟩) A, B, C

where A, B, and C are labels. In FORTRAN all labels are positive integers.

Example:

    IF (X**2 - 4) 7, 7, 8

causes transfer to that statement labeled 7 if $X^2 - 4 \leq 0$ and to 8 if $x^2 - 4 > 0$.

A BRANCH ON A LOGICAL EXPRESSION.

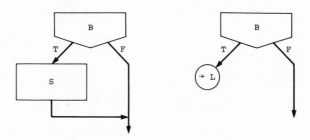

This is like the Algol60 conditional $\underline{if}$ B $\underline{then}$ S; FORTRAN has no general bracketing convention, so that S cannot be a compound statement. Indeed S must be either a GO TO or an assignment statement. The form is

```
IF(⟨logical expression⟩) {⟨assignment statement⟩ or
procedure call or ⟨goto statement⟩ or ⟨input–output
statement⟩}
```

Example:

```
IF (X.GT J + 2.0) I = IMAX - 3
```

UNCONDITIONAL BRANCHING, OR "GO TO" STATEMENTS.
The statements are of three forms, that we give by example,

1. GO TO 14.
2. GO TO (6, 12, 2, 25), IMAX. Suppose IMAX has the value 2; then the above is executed as GO TO 12. This is like the Algol60 switch and is called a COMPUTED GO TO.
3. GO TO IMAX, (6, 12, 2, 25). IMAX may only have one of the values in the list when this statement is executed. The transfer will be to that label.

Example:

```
I = 2
IMAX = I + 4
GO TO IMAX, (6, 12, 2, 25)
```

causes a transfer to the statement labeled 6.

How is cycling described? FORTRAN has a DO statement corresponding to Algol60's <u>for</u> statement. It is somewhat more restrictive than that of Algol60. We describe it by example:

```
DO 77 K = KMIN, IMAX, I
. . .FORTRAN statements of any kind, S, . . .
77 X = J - 2
next statement
```

The corresponding flowchart is

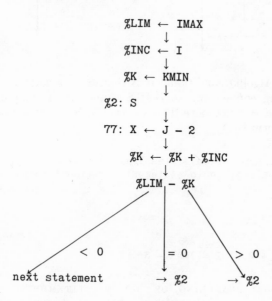

where %K, %LIM, and %INC are integer variables, and %2 is a label generated within the computer. The character % makes these identifiers illegal, and hence they cannot appear in a FORTRAN program. From the foregoing we see:

First, the increment and limit are integer constants.

Second, S cannot affect the control variable, the loop increment, or the termination value.

Third, $I \geq 1$, IMAX > KMIN, since the loop is always executed at least once. If $I = 1$, it may be omitted from the DO statement.

Fourth, the last statement must not be a transfer of control, though it may be a logical IF statement. FORTRAN provides a dummy statement called CONTINUE that is often used to terminate loops. Naturally DO statements may be nested.

What is the FORTRAN procedure structure? FORTRAN has both the procedure and the function in the Algol60 sense. When the function is a single arithmetic statement, it has a convenient abbreviated format and is called a *function statement*.

Example:

```
J(X,POP) = X**3 + POP**2
```

This is a declaration that should occur below the variable declarations but above the place of its first call. The formal parameters may be used as ordinary variables elsewhere in the FORTRAN program.

Example:

```
X = 10.0
POP = 5.0
I = 3.0 * J(POP,POP)     I is 450
POP = I                  POP is 450.0
T = J(-40., X)           T is -63,900
```

A *function procedure* is a procedure that returns a value. Thus a call on the function can occur as an operand in an expression. As in Algol60, within the procedure, the name of the function must occur as the left-hand identifier of an assignment statement, and the latest value assigned during execution is returned as the value of the function. A RETURN statement terminates the execution of a procedure. Syntactically, procedures open with the prefix FUNCTION or SUBROUTINE and conclude with the suffix END. The procedure heading is much like that of Algol60 and includes a specification of the type and dimension properties of the formal parameters. The formal parameters are identifiers representing arrays, procedures, or expressions. On a call of a procedure, FORTRAN passes the names of arrays and procedures and the values of expressions occurring as actual parameters. Thus arrays may be altered, and procedures called upon, by a procedure.

Procedures cannot contain procedure definitions but may have local variables that must be declared within the procedure. In the following example the parenthesized integers identify remarks that follow the algorithm description.

```
      SUBROUTINE ROTATE (ARRAY, B, R, C, I, J)          (1)
C     FORTRAN COMMENT. THIS PROCEDURE CYCLICALLY
C     ROTATES THE ITH ROW OF THE INTEGER ARRAY OF
C     R ROWS AND C COLUMNS, J PLACES LEFT.             (2)
      INTEGER R, C, I, J, K, S, T, ARRAY (R,C),B(C)    (3)
          J = MOD(C,J)                                 (4)
          DO 5 K = 1,C
    5     B(K) = ARRAY(I,K)
          DO 7 K = 1, C
          T = K - (J+1)
          IF(T) 6, 6, 7
    6     T = C + T
    7     ARRAY(I,T) = B
          RETURN                                       (5)
          END                                          (6)
```

1. ROTATE is the title of the procedure. The six formal parameters are ARRAY, B, R, C, I, J.
2. Lines commencing with a C in the left margin are comments and are ignored in processing.
3. The specification of the types of the formal parameters and the local variables can be combined. Note that ARRAY has R rows and C columns. FORTRAN permits use of variable array bounds only when the array bounds are formal parameters.
4. MOD is a built-in subroutine that gives the remainder when the integer C is divided by the integer J.
5. This RETURN statement terminates execution of the procedure.
6. This END statement closes the description of the procedure. CALL ROTATE (X,Y, 3, 14, 2, P) is a call on the procedure that might occur in a program. X must be an array having three rows and fourteen columns.

How do identifiers relate to each other? Algol60 uses the block concept to match identifier occurrence to identifier declarations. FORTRAN uses a different approach.

A statement called COMMON can be used to match identifiers in a procedure with those in the main program. In the main program might appear the declarations:

```
INTEGER C, Y(2,2)
COMMON T(3,5), X, C(2,4), Y
```

In a procedure might appear

```
INTEGER H
COMMON Q(4,4), H(4,3)
```

COMMON defines a mythical data area, and references to the same place in the data area refer to the same identifier. Thus

```
T(2,5)   is the same as Q(2,4)
X        is the same as Q(4,4)
C(2,3)   is the same as H(2,2)
Y(2,1)   is the same as H(2,3)
```

A COMMON statement may be used to serve the purpose of formal parameters in procedures.

Different identifiers in the same program can refer to the same variable by the use of EQUIVALENCE. Thus

```
EQUIVALENCE (X, C(2,1), A(5)), (A(6), B(3,2), U)
```

specifies that X, C(2,1), and A(5) refer to the same variable. Of course they must be of the same type. These pairings induce many others. Suppose the declaration

```
INTEGER X, C(3,2), A(9), B(4,5), U
```

accompanied the above. Then C(3,1) is the same as A(6) and A(7) is the same as B(4,0), etc.

Let us write our ubiquitous coin algorithm as a FORTRAN function, MANY:

```
INTEGER FUNCTION MANY (N, SIZE, COIN, INDEX)
INTEGER COIN(SIZE), M(SIZE), SIZE, N, INDEX
INTEGER T, J
      MANY = 0
      J = INDEX
      T = N
2     M(J) = T
      IF (COIN(J)-1) 4,3,4
3     MANY = MANY + 1
5     J = J - 1
      IF(J-INDEX) 6, 6, 7
6     T = M(J) - COIN(J)
      IF(T) 5,2,2
4     J = J + 1
      GOTO 2
7     RETURN
      END
```

It is considerably simpler to learn FORTRAN, once having learned Algol60, than the other way around.

THE APL LANGUAGE

We have examined a language, Algol60, that, while being a very general and powerful language, can be characterized as having the following major properties.

1. Programs are understood to be complete before they are executed. Algol60 was designed for execution in an environment where programs are processed through to completion (or to an error state) without human intervention. Furthermore, Algol60 programs are completely reduced to machine code before that code is executed to achieve the intent of the program.

2. A sophisticated control structure is provided, as revealed in the conditional statement and expression, block structure, procedure structure, and parameter passage conventions, and the for statement.

3. A reliance on the array as a data structure and a dependence upon scalar operations on elements to process arrays.

4. An accent on numerical rather than character or symbolic processing.

5. A reliance on type declaration to aid the code preparation process. Identifiers are of fixed (declared) type within the scope of their declarations.

Algol60 has been considered to represent the summit of algorithmic expressiveness for computer usage from 1960 to the present and has represented the acme of programming style during that period.

Our next language, APL, accents somewhat different properties. It is a computer implementation of a language developed by K. Iverson at Harvard University during the period 1958 to 1962 for the purpose of expressing a wide range of algorithms arising in numeric, combinatoric, and character processing. Its first computer implementation, on the IBM 360, coincided with the development of interactive terminal-oriented computer systems. Consequently APL has emerged as an "interactive" language supported by a time-sharing, terminal-oriented system.

APL programs may be created and executed in pieces. The programmer is quite able to alter programs, almost while they are in execution, and to submit input from a terminal upon request from the program during its execution. The programmer is assumed to be in the "execution loop" during computer processing of his programs.

APL's basic data structure is the array, and its operators facilitate operations on arrays in toto.

APL operations on arrays are carried out by efficient computer programs that generally involve a large number of machine operations per APL operation. The number of machine operations to scan, and determine the machine-code equivalent of, a statement can often be significantly less then those consumed in executing it; hence APL has developed as a statement-by-statement-interpretative, rather than a program-compile, language.

Two immediate consequences of statement-by-statement interpretation are exploited in APL.

First, program modification during execution involves little cost in undoing or redoing compiler operations. Consequently, the programmer can modify programs while they are in execution status without severe additional processing cost. APL can be interactive.

Second, arrays can be of variable shape, and the number of their elements during execution can vary. Thus they are not declared as to type and extent.

However, reliance on array operations has some negative effects. The processing of arrays is generally characterized by implicit natural control patterns induced by the operations. In adding element by element two arrays of identical shape, one does not proceed through the array elements in a chaotic fashion. Hence the language has not seen fit to provide elaborate control statements like the <u>for</u> and <u>if</u> <u>then</u> <u>else</u> statements of Algol60. Where this use would be convenient, and they often are, their absence makes APL programming offensively cumbersome.

Since APL's array operations generally apply to entire arrays, algorithms that involve selective scanning to find the first element having a desired property often turn out to be needlessly inefficient. While scanning can be programmed on the scalar components of arrays, the resultant programs are, because of interpretation costs, much less efficient than one would expect from a language of the power of APL. A related complaint can be made about processing sparse arrays, those having mostly zero elements. Thus, N linear equations take $\sim N^3$ operations to solve in general and only $\sim N$ operations when the array elements are 0, except for the elements on the main, first sub, and first super, diagonals, and yet there is no natural way to take advantage of this in APL without programming in scalars.

These deficiencies notwithstanding, APL is a powerful and enormously useful language and one that is well worth learning. One of the major advantages of APL is the improvement in one's expressive capabilities that arises in the artful use of arrays and the conciseness with which rather complicated algorithms can be expressed. An immediate consequence of both advantages is that the set of "elementary" problems that one uses to reveal the language powers are computationally more complex, though notationally no less concise, than their Algol60 counterparts.

Thus one does not choose to exhibit as an elementary example of APL programming an algorithm for sorting N integers in increasing order since, in APL, if X is the vector of the N integers, then $X[\triangle X]$ is the sorted vector. Finding all the primes $\leq N$, where N is a nonnegative integer, is given by the expression

$$(2 = +/[1]\ 0 = (\iota N)\ \circ.\mid\ \iota N)/\iota N$$

We begin our study of the APL language with the four classes of sentences, or statements, that we may execute. These sentences are executed in an environment called a *workspace*. When a computing session opens, a workspace is empty and contains neither program nor data until the successive transactions put program and data in the workspace. The sentence types are:

Immediate execution sentences
Function sentences
System sentences
Data sentences

Immediate sentences are executed as they are entered and, although they may change the values of variables, they disappear upon execution. Thus they may not participate in cycles.

Function sentences are not executed when they are entered but become part of a procedure or function definition that may be brought into execution at some later time.

System sentences are immediate sentences that communicate with the APL system. The APL system monitors traffic between the programmer and his data and programs.

Data sentences enter both numeric and character vector data as values for computation.

We should say something here about our use of the word *vector.* In APL usage a vector is merely a sequence of numbers or characters and is a special type of array.

The basic data type is the array. Arrays are homogeneous—all elements are either numeric or character—and regular in that they have the shape of rectangular parallelopipeds.

In APL all data are originally entered as vectors. Suppose

$$V \underline{\text{is}} \; 1 \; 2 \; 3 \; 4 \; 5 \; 6 \; 7 \; 8$$

then V may be reshaped into an array A by $A \leftarrow 2 \; 4 \; \rho \; V$. Here ρ is the reshape operator, and the value of V is reshaped into a rectangular array of two rows and four columns. The inverse of "ρ" ("reshape") is "," ("ravel"). APL permits the vector to be overused and underused so that the following are true:

```
V = ; 2 4 ρ V AND 2 5 ρ V is 1 2 3 4 5
                             6 7 8 1 2 (OVERUSE OF V)
  2 3 ρ V is 1 2 3
             4 5 6 (UNDERUSE OF V)
```

Shaping may be looked upon as always being preceded by a ravel of the structure being shaped. Ravel transforms scalars and arrays into vectors. Arrays are unraveled with the rightmost components of the shape changing most rapidly. Thus

```
3 3 ρ2 4 ρV is the same as
3 3 ρ, 2 4 ρ, V and is 1 2 3
                       4 5 6
                       7 8 1
```

Given an array A, the monadic operator ρ gives a vector that is the shape of A; thus

```
ρ 2 4ρ V is 2 4
```

Operations are performed from the right in APL, whereas in Algol60 they are performed from the left. With every array we associate its shape ρ A and its rank $\rho\rho$ A. Thus V and A as defined have shapes 8 and 2 4 and ranks 1 and 2, respectively.

Of course APL also permits the use of scalars and makes distinctions between scalars and arrays of one element. Furthermore, arrays containing no elements, null arrays, are also permitted.

A scalar is of rank 0, a vector is of rank 1, and a matrix is of rank 2. $V \leftarrow,1$ or $V \leftarrow 1\rho 1$ produces a vector of one component, while $X \leftarrow 1$ assigns X a scalar value of 1; ρV is 1 and ρX is blank or nothing—a scalar has no shape; $0\rho 1$ produces a vector of no components, and its shape is 0. It holds no values and yet has a shape! If X is blank, what is $\rho\rho X$? Since ρX is a vector of length 0, then $\rho\rho X$ is 1, since ρX is a vector. Any array, one of whose shape components is 0, is a null array.

One of the most widely used vectors is that holding the first N integers 1, 2, 3, . . . , N. This vector can be generated in APL by the use of the monadic index operator ι:

$\iota 7$ $\underline{\text{is}}$ 1 2 3 4 5 6 7

If N holds a scalar integer value n,

ιN $\underline{\text{is}}$ 1 2 . . . n

We have $\iota 0$ as a null vector. Then $\rho\iota N$ $\underline{\text{is}}$ N for $N > 0$; ιN is defined only for integral $N \geq 0$.

Naturally, in working with arrays it is important to be able to select subarrays. APL provides several operators for selection: index or subscription, take and drop, and transposition. We shall discuss the first two now and transposition later.

In Algol60 $A[k, j]$ selects the element of A in the kth row and the jth column. Since APL is an array-processing language, it is reasonable to assume that subscripting an array can give an array of any rank, not only an array of rank 0 (a scalar). Subscripts are a list of array-valued expressions, representing the selections in each dimension. Then, for an array A, $\rho\rho A$ is the number of subscripts, and $A[e_1; e_2; \ldots ; e_{\rho\rho A}]$ is the notation used for subscripting. Let $C \leftarrow A[e_1; e_2; \ldots ; e_{\rho\rho A}]$, or $C \leftarrow A[B]$. What is the shape of C? It is not determined by that of A, but by that of B: ρC $\underline{\text{is}}$ ρB except in the case that B is blank, in which case C is a copy of A. From now on we assume B is not blank. Then it must always be a ";"-separated list of $\rho\rho A$ entries. If an e_j is elided as, for example, e_2 in $A[3;]$, it is assumed to be $\iota(\rho A)[j]$, all possible subscript values in their natural order in that dimension.

All of the following predicates are true

$$\rho C = (\rho e_1), (\rho e_2), \ldots , (\rho e_{\rho\rho A})$$
$$C = (\rho C)\rho, A[e_1; e_2; \ldots ; e_{\rho\rho A}] \tag{3.16}$$

Thus if we use the identity (3.16), it is easy to see where every element of C came from in A, as in the following examples:

$$X \leftarrow 4\ 3\ 2\ 1$$
$$A \leftarrow 3\ 4\rho\iota3 \qquad\qquad\qquad\qquad (3.17)$$
$$D \leftarrow 2\ 3\ 4\rho,A$$

```
A = 1 2 3 1
    2 3 1 2
    3 1 2 3
D = 1 2 3 1
    2 3 1 2
    3 1 2 3

    1 2 3 1
    2 3 1 2
    3 1 2 3
      X[3] = 2
      X[ ] = X
      X[X] = X[4 3 2 1] = 1 2 3 4
      X[A] = 4 3 2 4
             3 2 4 3
             2 4 3 2
    ρX[A] = ρA = 3 4
    A[2;3] = 1
  A[2 2;3] = 1 1
 ρA[2 2;3] = (ρ2 2),ρ3
           = 2
 A[2 1 2; ] = 2 3 1 2
              1 2 3 1
              2 3 1 2
    A[ ] = A[ ; ]
         = A
    A[X;X]  UNDEFINED
    C←A[A; ]
    ρC = 3 4 4
    C[2;2;3] = A[3;3]
             = 2
```

Another important selector is that which selects subarrays. For example, if ρA is 4 6, to get the subarray consisting of rows 2 and 3 and columns 4 5 6, we could use the explicit row and column indicators as in A[2 3 ; 4 5 6]. This gets tedious if there are many rows and columns in the subarray. APL provides take ($\uparrow$) and drop ($\downarrow$) operators to facilitate subarray extraction. Let us give some examples and then the general definition. Again we shall use the arrays X and A, of (3.17).

All of the following predicates are true

```
    2↑X = 4 3
    7↑X = 4 3 2 1 0 0 0
   ¯2↑X = 2 1
   ¯7↑X = 0 0 0 4 3 2 1
  2 2↑A = 1 2
          2 3
  2 5↑A = 1 2 3 1 0
          2 3 1 2 0
```

Now we can state the definition of take ($\uparrow$):

C is $A \uparrow B$ means

1. That ρA is $\rho\rho B$.
2. That ρC is $|A$ (absolute value of each component of A).
3. That each element of A operates only on the corresponding coordinate of B, so we need consider only the case of A a scalar and B a vector producing a vector C:

If $0 < A \leq \rho B$, then C is the *first* A components of B.
If $\rho B < A$, then C is B concatenated on the right with $A - \rho B$ zeros.
If $-\rho B \leq A < 0$, then C is the last A components of B.
If $A < -\rho B$ then C is B preceded by $\rho B - |A$ zeros.

The operator drop ($\downarrow$) behaves in much the same way, except that A in $A \downarrow B$ specifies what of B is to be dropped. Dropping all or more than all in a given coordinate leads to a null-array result.

Arrays may be constructed by the reshape operator and also by catenation (binary operator ","). C is A,B for A and B vectors is just what we would assume:

ρC is $(\rho$,A$) + \rho$,B

for $k \leq \rho C$, $C[k]$ is $(k \leq \rho,A)A[k] + (k > \rho,A)B[k - \rho,A]$. In APL relations evaluate to 1 if <u>true</u> and 0 if <u>false</u>.

Arrays may also be catenated. The general form is $A,[K]B$. This use of bracketing in APL is to specify a coordinate along which an operation, in this case catenation, is to occur. If it is elided, then the maximum of 1 and $\rho\rho A$ is assumed for K. Since APL arrays are regular, conformability conditions must be satisfied when two arrays are catenated:

CASE 1. $(\rho\rho A) = \rho\rho B$. K must be in $\iota\rho\rho A$. $(\rho A) = \rho B$ except in the Kth coordinate.

CASE 2. $(\rho\rho A) \neq \rho\rho B$. Then either $1 = (\rho\rho A) - \rho\rho B$ and $\rho B = \rho A$ without its Kth coordinate or B is a scalar.

For example, using the array A of (3.17), we have the following.

Case 2 with $K = 2$ and B the scalar 0:

```
if C ← A,0 then C is 1 2 3 1 0
                    2 3 1 2 0
                    3 1 2 3 0
```

Case 2 with $K = 1$ and B the scalar 0:

```
if C ← A,[1]0 then C is 1 2 3 1
                       2 3 1 2
                       3 1 2 3
                       0 0 0 0
```

Case 1:

```
if D is 3 4 ρ ι 12 and B is 2 4 ρ ι 8
then D,[2]B is not defined but D,[1]B
   1  2  3  4
   5  6  7  8
is 9 10 11 12
   1  2  3  4
   5  6  7  8
```

It is appropriate to mention one of the more important features of APL. To an important degree it is naturally self-referential, and much of the discussion of the meaning and, hence effects of APL operators can be naturally stated in APL. One should get in the habit of stating facts about operators and operands using APL notation whenever possible. With that in mind let us restate the conformability conditions and meaning of array concatenation in APL terms.

CASE 1′.   The following all have value 1 (<u>true</u>).

a. $(\wedge/(\rho\rho A) = \rho\rho B) \wedge (K \epsilon \iota\rho\rho A) \wedge$
    $\wedge/((K \neq \iota\rho A)/\rho A) = (K \neq \iota\rho B)/\rho B$
b. If R ← A,[K]B then
    R[. . . ,$\iota(\rho A)[K]$; . . .] <u>is</u> A
          $\underbrace{\qquad\qquad}$
          Kth subscript
    and R[. . . ;$(\rho A)[K] + \iota(\rho B)[K]$; . . .] <u>is</u> B
c. ρR <u>is</u> $(\rho A) + (K = \iota\rho\rho B)/\rho B$

CASE 2′.

a. $\vee/(\rho\rho A) \neq \rho\rho B$.
b. $((\rho\rho B) = 0) \vee (1 = (\rho\rho A) - \rho\rho B) \wedge$
    $((\rho B) = (K \neq \iota\rho\rho A)/\rho A)$
c. If R ← A,[K]B then if $\rho\rho B = 0$
    R[. . . ;$\iota(\rho A)[K]$; . . .] <u>is</u> A
    and R[. . . ;$1+(\rho A)[K]$; . . .] <u>is</u> $((\rho A)[K])\rho B$
    whereas if $\rho\rho B \neq 0$:
    R[. . . ;$\iota(\rho A)[K]$; . . .] <u>is</u> A
    and R[. . . ;$1+(\rho A)[K]$; . . .] <u>is</u> B
d. ρR <u>is</u> $(\rho A) + K = \iota\rho\rho A$

The reader may bypass cases 1′ and 2′ until all of their operators have been defined. Then he should return to them and analyze what they say.

In addition to selection by indexing, APL provides selection by masking. The dyadic operator / ("compression") is used to select through a mask. Let $R \leftarrow A/[K]B$.

A is a vector each of whose components is 0 or 1; 1 is $\wedge/(0 = A) \vee 1 = A$. Let us call such a vector a mask. The following are true:

1. $(\rho A) > 1$ and $(\rho\rho B)[K] > 1$
    R[;ι+/A=1;] is B[;(A=1)/ι(ρB)[K];]
       K   K

    R contains those elements of B selected by 1 in the mask of A.

2. A = (ρB)[K]ρ1 then R is B
3. A = (ρB)[K]ρ0 then R is a null array with
    ((K−1)↑ρB),0,K↓ρB as its shape.
    if R ← 1 0 1 / [1] 3 4 ρ ι 12 then
    R is 1 2 3 4
         9 10 11 12

Arrays may be expanded by the dyadic operator \ ("expansion"). Let $R \leftarrow A\backslash[K]B$. Again A is a mask. It must be that $(+/A = 1)$ is $(\rho B)[K]$. Then

R[;(∼A)/ιρA;] is an array all of whose elements are 0
  K

and

R[;A/ιρA;] is B.
 K
while ρR is ((K−1)↑ρB),(ρ,A),K↓ρB.

APL OPERATORS

A formidable amount of new notation has just been introduced, and it is worth examining the APL operator structure at this time.

We have used the terms *vector* and *array*, but it is often better to think of APL data as organized into finite structured sequences on which operations are performed component by component. The terms *vector*, *array*, and *matrix* are conveniently used because their representation, and sequence representations in the computer, are alike. Although we use these terms interchangeably, APL operations are by and large sequence operations.

APL supports a collection of monadic and dyadic scalar operations, and they are extended to sequences by applying them component by component. Naturally, then, if A and B are two such sequences or arrays, they must be conformable: $(\rho A) = \rho B$ except when A or B is a scalar. The latter exception is an important convenience. If X is 1 2 7.5 9, then $3 + X$ is defined and is 4 5 10.5 12.

We need not say $X + (\rho X)\rho 3$. APL permits the standard dyadic operations:

addition $+$
subtraction $-$
multiplication $\times$
division $\div$
exponentiation $*$

In the following, A and B refer to corresponding components as well as to the entire sequence. In $A \div B$ (A divided by B), if A is nonzero, so must be B. If both are zero, the result is 1. As in Algol60, $*$ has the following constraints: In $A * B$, if A is positive, then B can have any value. If A is 0, then B must be ≥ 0. If A is < 0, the value of B must be a number of the form $P \div Q$, and Q must be an odd integer. If $A = B = 0$, then the result is 1.

Besides the standard arithmetic operations there are the relational operations $<, \leq, =, \neq, \geq, >$, leading to a value 1 (<u>true</u>) or 0 (<u>false</u>). In testing relations between real machine numbers exact satisfaction is usually not meaningful because of the loss of precision that occurs in many operations on numbers represented with finite precision. We have called this loss *round-off error*. In APL equality within a certain tolerance will lead to a <u>true</u> result. The tolerance, called *fuzz* in APL, is determined by the computer implementation. Fuzz is two types: relative (used in comparing two reals) and absolute (used to decide whether a number is close enough to an integer to be treated as such). Some examples of absolute fuzz are

```
⌈5 5.12 5.00001 is 5 6 5 and not 5 6 6
(ι4)[2.000005] is 2
while (ι4)[2.01] yields a DOMAIN ERROR!
```

Some examples of relative fuzz are

```
1 ε 1.000001 is 1
100000.1 ε 1 is 1
(A ← 100000.1 100000)ι100000 is 1
yet A[1] is 100000.1
```

There are also the usual logic operations defined for A and $B =$ 0 or 1, (<u>false</u> or <u>true</u>): $\sim$ (not), $\wedge$ (and), $\vee$ (or), $\not\wedge$ (nand), and $\not\vee$ (nor).

In addition to these standard dyadic operations APL has the following quite useful tools.

1. LOGARITHM. $A \circledast B$ <u>is</u> $\log_A B$ and is defined as $\ln_e B / \ln_e A$, which in APL is written as $(\circledast B) \div \circledast A$ with A and $B > 0$. If A is 1, then so must B be.
2. MAXIMUM. $A \lceil B$ <u>is</u> B if $B \geq A$ else A.

3. MINIMUM. $A\lfloor B$ is B if $B < A$ else A.

4. RESIDUE. $A|B$ is the least nonnegative number R such that for some integer Q, $B = R + A \times Q$. If $A = 0$, then B must be nonnegative and $R = B$. Let us look at this operation in more detail. What is $1|8.6$? $8.6 = .6 + 1 \times 8$, so it is $.6$. The 1 residue is the fractional part of a positive number. What about the residue of a negative number? What is $2|^-3$? $R = {}^-3 - 2 \times Q$. Hence one keeps adding 2 to $^-3$ until the result is first ≥ 0. Thus R is 1. Put another way, R is $A \times \lceil (|B) \div A) + \times B$. Since A may be negative, we say $A|B$ is the same as $(|A)|B$. The monadic, signum, will shortly be defined, in paragraph 6 below. APL assigns both a monadic and dyadic interpretation to many of its operator symbols.

5. Algol60 has a number of built-in functions, such as sin, cos, tan, cot, and others. APL uses one dyadic operator, $\bigcirc$, which encompasses many of these functions. B is expressed in radians for the trigonometric functions. A is the function of B, as follows, where R is $A \bigcirc B$:

A	R	RESTRICTION ON THE DOMAIN OF B
-7	arctanh	$1 > |B$
-6	arccosh	$B \geq 1$
-5	arcsinh	$B \geq 1$
-4	$(^-1 + B*2)*.5$	$1 \leq |B$
-3	arctan	
-2	arc cos	$1 \geq |B$
-1	arc sin	$1 \geq |B$
0	$(1 - B*2)*.5$	$1 \geq |B$
1	sine	
2	cosine	
3	tangent	
4	$(1 + B*2)*.5$	
5	sinh	
6	cosh	
7	tanh	

$R \leftarrow A!B$ computes the number of combinations of B things taken A at a time:

R is $(!B) \div (!A) \times !B-A$

Monadic "!" is the factorial function.

6. Algol60 has the monadic operators $-$, $+$, and $\rightarrow$; APL has many more. Thus, $R \leftarrow \pm B$ is $0 \pm B$. $R \leftarrow \div B$ is $1 \div B$, and $B \neq 0$. $R \leftarrow \times B$ is $(0 < B) - 0 > B$, 1, 0, or $^-1$, de-

pending on whether B is > 0, $= 0$, or < 0, respectively. $\times B$ is called *signum* of B. $R \leftarrow *B$ is $\exp(B)$, and $R \leftarrow \circledast B$ is $\ln_e B$. $R \leftarrow \lfloor B$, the floor of B, is the algebraically largest integer $\leq B$. Put another way, R is $B - 1 | B$. $R \leftarrow \lceil B$, the ceiling of B, is the algebraically least integer $\geq B$ or R is $B + 1 | -B$. $R \leftarrow | B$ is the absolute value of B, or R is $B\lceil -B$. Generating random numbers is an important computing activity. $R \leftarrow ?B$ is an integer randomly selected from the integers ιB. $R \leftarrow \sim B$ is $1 \neq B$, and $B = 1$ or 0. $R \leftarrow !B$ is $\times / \iota B$ if B is a nonnegative integer. It is also defined for other values of B as Gamma$(B + 1)$, where Gamma is the gamma function or generalized factorial, a function with whose properties we shall not be further concerned. $R \leftarrow \bigcirc B$ is $\pi \times B$.

Perhaps the reader has noticed that APL uses the same operator character to have both a monadic and a dyadic significance. Thus monadic "|" is absolute value and dyadic "|" is the residue operator. APL provides a monadic interpretation of dyadic operators in a much more complete way than does Algol60. Indeed, APL is an enormously operator-rich language, and many of its operators do not fit into the standard hierarchy or precedence order we have become accustomed to. Rather than assign an arbitrary precedence to these operators, APL dispenses completely with hierarchy as a method of assigning operand scope to operators. In Algol60 a$\times$b+c and c+a$\times$b are the same when a, b, and c are variables, but they are not the same in APL. The former is a$\times$(b+c), and the latter is c+(a$\times$b).

The right operand of every operator appearing in an expression is the entire expression to its right or to the nearest unmatched right parenthesis or bracket, whichever is closest. The left operand of every dyadic operator is the operand or parenthesized expression to its immediate left, whichever occurs. These rules imply that expressions are evaluated from right to left, and alterations in this "natural ordering" are achieved by use of parentheses. On the preceding pages this ordering was exhibited in many of the APL expressions. A few more examples will be helpful.

Example: To evaluate $4X^5 + 2X^3 - X^2 + 1$ we write

+ / 1 0 ⁻1 2 0 4 × X * ⁻1 + ι 6

The operator "/," called *reduction*, is one of the most powerful of APL's many operators, and a few applications of it will help us better appreciate why APL expressions are scanned from the right.

Scanning from the right tends on first trials to be annoying, since we write from the left. Many of the blunders made in writing APL programs arise from erroneous grouping of operands, but a little experience soon causes this source of blunders to vanish.

Reduction, as the name implies, reduces the rank of arrays.

Averaging the elements in a sequence is a very common operation, and it reduces a sequence of numbers to a scalar, the average. In the preceding example, evaluating a polynomial involves reducing a sum of products to a single number. Let δ be any of the dyadic scalar operators, and let B be a vector. Then, when we write δ/B, it is understood to mean

$$B[1] \; \delta \; B[2] \; . \; . \; . \; B[^-1 + \rho B] \; \delta \; B[\rho B]$$

evaluated from the right. The slash, $/$, always applies to arrays of rank 1. If we wish to apply it in arrays of higher rank, we must specify the coordinate along which reduction is to occur. $R \leftarrow \delta/[K]B$ specifies reduction along the Kth coordinate for $K \leq \rho\rho B$ and ρR is $(K \neq \iota\rho\rho B)/\rho B$ (note that this use of $/$ is as a dyadic operator and is termed *compression*). If $K = \rho\rho B$, it may be elided. Finally, if B is a scalar, δ/B is B.

Some additional examples of reduction are the following.

$\lfloor \; / \; 2 \; ^-5.2 \; 4 \; 1.6$ is $^-5.2$
$\wedge \; / \; 0 \; 1 \; 1 \; 0 \; 1$ is 0
$- \; / \; 2 \; 1 \; 3 \; 4$ is 0
$\div \; / \; 4 \; 1 \; 2 \; 4$ is 2

The last two examples, the alternating sum and alternating product, are consequences of right-to-left order of operation. Thus, $- \; / \; 2 \; 1 \; 3 \; 4$ is the same as, done left to right, $2 - 1 + 3 - 4$, and $\div \; / \; 4 \; 1 \; 2 \; 4$ is the same as $4 \div 1 \times 2 \div 4$ (done left to right). Another example comes from the alternating sum approximating π:

$$\pi = \frac{1}{4}\left(\frac{1}{1} - \frac{1}{3} + \frac{1}{5} - \frac{1}{7} + \frac{1}{9} \cdots\right)$$

Then $.25 \times -/\div^-1 + 2 \times \iota N$ yields such an approximation, whose last summand is $1/(2N - 1)$.

If B is the array $3 \; 4 \; \rho \; \iota \; 12$,

then $+/[1]B$ is $15 \; 18 \; 21 \; 24$
and $+/[2]B$ is $10 \; 26 \; 42$ as is $+/B$

An often useful approximation to a function is that provided by a continued fraction. Thus,

$$\exp(X) = 1 + \cfrac{X}{1 - \cfrac{X}{2 + \cfrac{X}{3 - \cfrac{X}{2 + \cfrac{X}{5 - \cfrac{X}{2 + \cfrac{X}{7 \ldots}}}}}}}$$

an initial segment of which is. in APL,

$$1+X \div 1-X \div 2+X \div 3-X \div 2+X \div 5-X \div 2+X \div 7$$

APL provides an elaborate reaction to the application of some dyadic scalar operators to a null array:

OPERA-TION	RESULT	
×	1	
+	0	
÷	1	right identity only
−	0	right identity only
*	1	
|	0	left identity only
∨	0	
∧	1	
!	1	left identity only
⌈	− ∞	(minimum representable number)
⌊	∞	(maximum representable number)
>	0	right identity only
≥	1	right identity only
<	0	left identity only
≤	1	left identity only
=	1	
≠	0	

Let us see how these values arise. Consider

$$\lceil/B = (\lceil/B)\lceil(\lceil/\iota 0) = \lceil/B$$

Since this holds for any B, then $\lceil/\iota 0 = -\infty$.
Consider also

$$*/B = */B, \iota 0 = (*/B)*(*/\iota 0) = */B$$

Hence $*/\iota 0 = 1$ as a right identity but makes no sense as a left identity.

For two sequences A and B we often wish to combine them, using a scalar dyadic operator on each of A with every one of B. Such a combination in APL is called the *outer product* and denoted by $°.\varsigma$, where ς is any dyadic scalar operator. For example,

$$(\iota 5)°.|\iota 5$$

gives the remainder on division of each of 1, 2, . . . , 5 by each of

1, 2, . . . , 5. The result is laid out as an array:

```
0  0  0  0  0
1  0  1  0  1
1  2  0  1  2
1  2  3  0  1
1  2  3  4  0
```

Thus, $4 \mid 1\ 2\ 3\ 4\ 5$ is the 4th row of the array. In general, if $R \leftarrow A°.\varsigma B$, then

$$\rho R \text{ is } (\rho A),\rho B \text{ and } R[I_1;I_2;\ldots;I_{\rho\rho A};I_{1+\rho\rho A};\ldots;I_{(\rho\rho B)+\rho\rho A}]$$
$$\text{ is } A[I_1;I_2;\ldots;I_{\rho\rho A}] \varsigma B[I_{1+\rho\rho A};\ldots;I_{(\rho\rho B)+\rho\rho A}]$$

Now we can see why

$$(2 = +/[1]0 = (\iota N)\circ.\mid\iota N)/\iota N$$

yields the prime integers $\leq N$.

The outer product is an extremely useful operation, because its application includes levels of implicit looping. The cycling through the elements of the left operand encloses the cycling through the elements of the right operand. Thus, if ρA is 2 4 and ρB is 3 5, the element $R[1;3;2;4]$ is $A[1;3] \varsigma B[2;4]$.

Another example is illustrative. Suppose we have a vector $Y \leftarrow {}^-10 + \iota 19$ and the linear function $X + 1$, the domain of X being $^-7 + \iota 13$. Then $Y°. = X + 1$ is an array, which is 1 where $Y = X + 1$ and is 0 otherwise. It yields the graph of $X + 1$ for $-6 \leq X \leq 6$. The outer product can be used in preparing plots of functions.

There is a specialization of the outer product that combines outer product with reduction. It is called the *inner product*, and the notation used is $R \leftarrow A \varsigma . \nu B$, where ς and ν are scalar dyadic operators. Suppose $\rho\rho A$ is n and $\rho\rho B$ is m. Then the inner product is defined as

$$\varsigma/[\rho\rho A]((\iota(\rho\rho A)-1),(\rho\rho A),(\rho\rho A),(\rho\rho A)+\iota^-1+\rho\rho B)\diamondsuit A\circ.\nu B,$$

providing $(^-1 \uparrow \rho A) = 1 \uparrow \rho B$. This turgid expression introduces another operator $\diamondsuit$, called *dyadic transpose*, about which we shall say more presently. Rather than understand the inner product through this expression we shall look at a few examples that will more easily clarify its intent. Consider

$$R \leftarrow (2\ 3\ \rho\ \iota\ 6) \lceil\ .\times 3\ 2\ \rho\ \iota\ 6$$

The result is an array whose shape is 2 2. In general, the shape of R is $(^-1\downarrow\rho A),1\downarrow\rho B$. The last coordinate of A must have the same number of elements as the first coordinate of B. In general,

$(\rho A)[\rho\rho A] = (\rho B)[1]$. The general element $R[I;J]$ is

```
ʃ/A[I;]νB[;J]
```

where I and J represent subscript lists. Thus the example yields

```
15   18
30   36
```

Let us look at an interesting application. Suppose we have a directed graph, by which we mean a set of labeled nodes (places) connected to each other by directed arrows (paths):

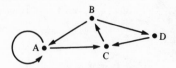

The graph may be represented by a connection matrix G whose rows represent "sources" and whose columns represent "destinations," and a 1 entry means there is a direct path from a source to a destination:

```
        A  B  C  D
      A  1  0  1  0
G is  B  1  0  0  1
      C  0  1  0  0
      D  0  0  1  0
```

Then $G[2;]$ specifies direct paths from B, while $G[;3]$ specifies direct paths to C. How do we find indirect paths of, say, two legs, as B to D to C? If X is any node so that $G[2;\text{column of }X] = 1$ and $G[\text{row of }X;3] = 1$, then there is a two-leg path from B to X to C. The set of all such two-leg paths is given by $G\vee.\wedge G$, and $G+.\wedge G$ tells how many there are of each kind:

```
GV.∧G is 1 1 1 0      G+.∧G is 1 1 1 0
         1 0 1 0               1 0 2 0
         1 0 0 1               1 0 0 1
         0 1 0 0               0 1 0 0
```

How would we compute the set of three-leg paths, four-leg paths, etc.?

The preceding operations are really the extension of scalar operations to scalars grouped in arrays, and the results are scalar results grouped in arrays. There is also a collection of useful operations on the structures themselves, whose results are most naturally described as vectors. In APL these are customarily called "mixed" functions. Some of them have already been described: monadic and dyadic ρ, monadic ι, ravel and catenate, $\uparrow$ and $\downarrow$. These operations are extremely valuable, since they allow us, in our programming, to

take advantage of, and extract information from, the structure of
sequences and the places in them where certain information resides.
We have already observed this phenomenon in programming: the
use of variables whose role in an algorithm is to specify places in a
data structure.

Two standard operations on structures are rotation Φ and
transposition $\mathbb{Q}$, for which both a monadic and a dyadic interpretation exist. In their full generality both of these operators are quite
complex. Let us first take up rotation:

$$R \leftarrow A\,\Phi\,[K]B$$

Rotation operates on vectors in arrays. ρR is ρB. Which vectors in
B are rotated? By how much? In what direction? Let us commence
with an example of vector rotation: $X \leftarrow \iota 5$.

```
2 ⍉X cyclically rotates X left 2 places:
2 ⍉X is 3 4 5 1 2
5 ⍉X is X
-2 ⍉X cyclically rotates X right 2 places
-2 ⍉X is 4 5 1 2 3
-5 ⍉X is X
17 ⍉X is 2 ⍉X
¯14 ⍉X is ¯4 ⍉X
2 ⍉X is ¯3 ⍉X
```

All rotations of an array B are merely collections of rotations of
vectors by a scalar amount. Let B be an array. There are two cases
to consider for A:

CASE 1. Scalar.

CASE 2. Array.

Consider case 1. The entire array B is rotated *uniformly* by the
amount of A along the Kth coordinate.

Example:

$$2 \; \Phi \; 3\,3\,\rho\,\iota\,9 \text{ is } \begin{matrix} \overset{\leftarrow+}{3} & 1 & 2 \\ 6 & 4 & 5 \\ 9 & 7 & 8 \end{matrix}$$

$$1 \; \Phi \; [1]\,3\,3\,\rho\,\iota\,9 \text{ is } \begin{matrix} \uparrow \\ + \end{matrix} \begin{matrix} 4 & 5 & 6 \\ 7 & 8 & 9 \\ 1 & 2 & 3 \end{matrix}$$

$$-1 \; \Phi \; [1]\,3\,3\,\rho\,\iota\,9 \text{ is } \begin{matrix} \_ \\ \downarrow \end{matrix} \begin{matrix} 7 & 8 & 9 \\ 1 & 2 & 3 \\ 4 & 5 & 6 \end{matrix}$$

Note that if $K = \rho\rho B$ it may be elided.

Consider case 2. A must satisfy $\rho A = (K \neq \iota\rho\rho B)/\rho B$. The array is rotated *nonuniformly* along the Kth coordinate in the following way:

Let I and J be subscript lists of $K - 1$ and $(\rho\rho B) - K$ elements; then the vector

```
R[I;;J] is A[I;J] Φ [K]B[I;;J] .
```

Example:

```
A is 2 3 ρ ι 4
B is 2 4 3 ρ ι 24
R is A Φ [2]B
```

Writing out the arrays:

```
R is  4  8 12
      7 11  3
     10  2  6
      1  5  9

     13 17 21
     16 20 24
     19 23 15
     22 14 18
```

The monadic use of "Φ" is reversal of a vector in an array: $R \leftarrow \Phi[K]B$. If B is a vector, then R is $B[1 + (\rho B) - \iota\rho B]$, and if B is an array of rank ≥ 2, R is $B[; \ldots ;\Phi\iota\rho B[K]; \ldots ;]$.

Example:

```
1. R ←  Φ 3 5 2 4. R is 4 2 5 3
2. R ←  Φ [1] 3 2 ρ ι 6. R is 5 6
                               3 4
                               1 2
```

The transpose $\bigotimes$ of an array is another powerful operation. Let $R \leftarrow A \bigotimes B$. A must be a vector for which $\rho A = \rho\rho B$. There are two cases:

CASE 1. $(\rho A) = +/(\iota \rho \rho B) \epsilon A$
Then $(\rho R)[A] = \rho B$

Example: Let B is 2 5 3 $\rho \iota$ 30 and $R \leftarrow$ 2 3 1 $\otimes$ B. Then
$\rho R[2\ 3\ 1] = \rho B$; that is, ρR is 3 2 5 or $\rho R = (\rho B)[\underline{\wedge} A]$, where $\underline{\wedge} A$
is the permutation of $\iota \rho B$ that puts A into increasing order.

CASE 2. $(\rho A) = +/(\iota \lceil /A) \epsilon A$ or, put another way, every integer from 1 to $\lceil /A$ is present in A. These lead to selections along
diagonal planes. Thus for

$$R \leftarrow 1\ 1 \otimes 3\ 2\ \rho \iota\ 6$$

R is 1 4, the elements of the array whose first and second coordinates have the same value, $B[1, 1]$ and $B[2, 2]$. For the first occurrence of each $I \epsilon \iota \rho A$ for which $1 < +/A[I] = A$, or duplicates
occur, let $S \leftarrow (A[I] \epsilon A)/\iota \rho A$. Then the $A[I]$ coordinate of the result is made up of those components of B whose Sth coordinate in-
dices are the same. Thus, if A is 1 3 2 1 2, then, for $I = 1$, S is 1 4,
and the first component of R is made up of those components from
B whose first and fourth components are the same. For $I = 3$,
S is 3 5. Therefore the third component of R is made up of those
from B whose third and fifth components are the same. All other
coordinates are structured the same as in the first case.
What is the shape of R? $\rho \rho R$ is $\lceil /A$. If $I \epsilon \rho \rho R$, then $(\rho R)[I]$ is
$\lfloor /(A = I)/\rho B$.
We have already seen how the inner product may be defined
in terms of a diagonal transposition of an outer product.
Examples of dyadic transpositions follow.

Example 1:
$R \leftarrow 1\ 3\ 2 \otimes 2\ 4\ 6\ \rho \iota 48$
ρR is $(\rho B)[\underline{\wedge} A]$ is 2 4 6[1 3 2] is 2 6 4
$R[I;J;K]$ is $B[I;K;J]$
$R[2;1;3]$ is $B[2;3;1]$ is 37

Example 2:
$R \leftarrow 1\ 2\ 1 \otimes 2\ 4\ 6\ \rho \iota 48$
$\rho \rho R$ is $\lceil /1\ 2\ 1$ is 2
ρR is $((\lfloor /(A = 1)/\rho B), \lfloor /(A = 2)/\rho B)$ is 2 4
$R[I;J]$ is $B[I;J;I]$

Example 3:
$R \leftarrow 2\ 1\ 1 \otimes 2\ 4\ 6\ \rho \iota 48$
$\rho \rho R$ is 2
ρR is 4 2
$R[I;J]$ is $B[J;I;I]$
$R[2;1]$ is $B[1;2;2]$ is 8

Monadic transposition: In the special case that

$$A \text{ is } (-2 + \iota \rho \rho B), \ (\rho \rho B), \ -1 + \rho \rho B$$

one may elide A and write $\lozenge B$. This elided notation is particularly useful when B is a matrix.

The dyadic operator "ι" ("index of"), as in $R \leftarrow A \iota B$, selects for each component of B, $B[J]$, the smallest index I such that $A[I] = B[J]$ and then $R[J]$ is I. A must be a vector. If there is no such $I \leq \rho A$, then $R[J]$ is $1 + \lceil / \iota \rho A$. If A is null, then R is $\iota 1$. This operator is very useful in finding leftmost positions in arrays holding elements satisfying certain conditions. It is often used in removing duplicates from structures.

The particular use of outer product in $R \leftarrow \vee / A^\circ. = B$ for A and B vectors can be looked upon as defining a vector R such that $(\rho R) = \rho A$ and $R[J]$ is 1 if $A[J]$ equals some component of B: R defines the membership of A in B. APL has an operator ϵ which extends the above to arbitrary arrays:

$$R \leftarrow A \ \epsilon \ B \text{ is } (\rho A) \rho \vee /(, A)^\circ. = , B$$

Ordering sequences is a standard and useful operation in programming. APL provides two operators, $\triangle$ and $\triangledown$, for ordering, as in

$$R \leftarrow \triangle B \text{ and } \triangledown B$$

$R[I]$ is the index of the Ith smallest and Ith largest component of the vector B, respectively.

Thus $X[\triangle X]$ is X sorted in increasing order, and $X[\triangledown X]$ is X sorted in decreasing order. If X is 2 5 3 2 1 4 7, then $\triangle X$ is 5 1 4 3 6 2 7 and $\triangledown X$ is 7 2 6 3 1 4 5.

A number B can be represented in a variety of radix systems A: 10 (decimal), 8 (octal), 2 (binary), 16 (hexadecimal), etc. We can look upon the representation as an encoding of B in the radix A. The encoding itself is represented in APL as a vector. Let us take some examples:

$(3\rho 10) \top 155$ is 1 5 5   (decimal encoding)
$(5\rho 2) \top 27$ is 1 1 0 1 1   (binary encoding)

But, note that

$(2\rho 10) \top 1576$ is 7 6

so leading digits can be truncated. Consider next

$(3\rho 5) \top 73.62$ is 2 4 3.62

so evidently a "pure" encoding in base 5 is not obtained. Consider next

$(3\rho 10) \top {}^-45$ is $(3\rho 10) \top 955$ is 9 5 5   (10 complement)

and

$(5\rho^-2) \top 13$ is 1 1 1 0 1

Finally, a mixed radix can be used, as in

   24 60 60 ⊤ 3723 is̲ 1 2 3

an interpretation of which is 3723 seconds is 1 hour, 2 minutes and 3 seconds.

Suppose A is̲ 0, C. Then $R[1]$ is the part of B that would have been truncated if C ⊤ B had been taken.

Now that we have this collection of phenomena associated with APL's interpretation of the operator ⊤ let us give its algorithm. Suppose ρA is̲ n; then R is computed by:

```
[1]            G←B
[2]            H←A
[3]            R← ι0
[4]  CYCLE:    G←(Gx(G≥0))-(G<0)xG-x/H   labeled statement
[5]            R←(F←⁻1↑H|G),R
[6]            G←⌊(G-F)÷⁻1↑H
[7]            →CYCLExιH←⁻1↓H            branch command
```

Note that this is our first example of APL program structure: the by now well-recognized sequence of statements, the use of assignment statements, and even nested assignments, the development of a cycle with its terminating branch, goto and attached label, and the use of local variables. We shall return to discuss program structure shortly, but you might ask, "On what principle does the branch command operate?"

The hexadecimal radix system is often used in computers because $16 = 2^4$ is the smallest power of $2 \geq 10$. Thus every decimal digit can be represented by its numeral as a hexadecimal digit, and six extra are needed to correspond to the decimals 10, 11, 12, 13, 14, and 15. The latter are usually represented as hexadecimal digits A, B, C, D, E, and F. We shall shortly see how to represent such hexadecimal sequences in APL.

Encoding represents a scalar as a vector in some (possibly mixed) radix notation. APL has an inverse operation ⊥ ("decode"), which maps vectors, presumed to be radix representations, into a decimal scalar: $R \leftarrow A \perp B$, where A and B are both vectors. As with encode let us first observe the APL behavior of ⊥ by example:

Example 1:   10 10 10⊥5 is̲ 555

Example 2:   3⊥4 5 2 is̲ 53

Example 3:   5 ⁻2 1.4⊥1 2 1 is̲ 1

In general, R is̲ B if A and B are scalars; otherwise,

$$R\leftarrow B+.\times1\downarrow((Z\rho,A)\times.\times(\iota Z)^{\circ}.\geq\iota Z\leftarrow(\rho A)$$
$$+(-1+\rho B)\times1=\rho A),1$$

This is another turgid formula. What actually is occurring is quite simple. A vector of weights W is created from A and then R is $B+.\times W$. The form of the vector W is easily seen from the examples:

Example 1:
$6\perp 1\ 3\ 1\ 4\ 0$
W is $6 * 5 - \iota 5$

Example 2:
$4\ 2\ 3\perp 5$
W is $6\ 3\ 1$

Example 3:
$4\ 2\ 3\perp 5\ 1\ 2$
W is as in Example 2.

Note that $A[1]$ plays no role in $A\perp B$. As an example $\perp$ can be used to convert units. Thus to convert a length of 2 miles, 5 yards, 3 feet, and 4 inches to inches we write: $2.4\ 1760\ 3\ 12\perp 2\ 5\ 3\ 4$.

Decode can also be used as a coding device. Consider the following example. Suppose we have a sequence X of integers. We wish to collect in separate sequences the indices of elements of X which are equal or share some other property.

Let us admit an extension to $\perp$ so that B may be an array as in

$$2\ \perp \begin{matrix} 1 & 0 & 0 \\ 0 & 1 & 0 \\ 1 & 0 & 0 \\ 0 & 0 & 1 \\ 1 & 0 & 0 \end{matrix} \text{ is } 21\ 8\ 2$$

Then $2\perp \mathbb{Q}(((\iota\rho X) = X\iota X)/X)^{\circ}. = X$ yields such a vector of codes.

$$(((\rho X)\rho 2)\top X[1])/\iota\rho X$$

gives the indices in X of the first sequence. For example, if X is $1\ 3\ 3\ 5\ 1\ 5\ 2$, then the code vector is $68\ 48\ 10\ 1$. The decoding of the second component is $((7\rho 2)\top 48)/\iota 7$.

We have now completed our description of the rich operator-operand structure of APL as revealed in the structure of its expressions.

Thus far we have neglected an important data type in APL: the character. Any legal APL character can be an array component. A character string is a sequence of characters. Thus,

$$A \leftarrow \text{'}APL/360\text{'}$$

assigns to A a sequence for which ρA is 7. All of the APL operations that do not depend on the arithmetic properties of values are defined on characters and character arrays. However, note that the homogeneity of APL arrays forbids mixing of character and numeric data in a single array. In some of the operations ' ' (space) replaces 0 when characters are the operands.

An example of the use of characters is the following. Suppose we have two character strings *KEY* and *TEXT* and we wish to find the places of all the occurrences of *KEY* in *TEXT:*

IDEX← (‾1+ρKEY)↓(∧/[1] (‾1+ιρKEY) ⌽KEY∘.=TEXT)/
ι(ρTEXT)

yields a sequence *IDEX* whose values are the leftmost positions of *KEY* in *TEXT*.

Suppose we wish to define a function that arranges the substitution of the sequence NEW for KEY in TEXT, wherever KEY occurs. Then all occurrences of *KEY* are cleared out by:

TEXT← (∼ (ιρTEXT)ε,IDEX∘.+‾1+ιρKEY)/TEXT

and space is made for insertion of *NEW* in corresponding places by

IDEX←IDEX+((ρNEW)−ρKEY)×‾1+ιρIDEX

The sequence of indices where *NEW* is to be inserted is

G← ,IDEX∘.+‾1+ιρNEW

Expansion provides room for the insertions, since spaces are inserted where there are 0's in the mask:

TEXT← (∼ (ι(ρTEXT)+ρG)εG)\TEXT

Finally

TEXT[G] ← (ρG)ρNEW

replaces the inserted blanks with the character string *NEW.*

Briefly, the following list of operations can be used with characters:

1. The operators = and ≠ have an obvious meaning for characters:

    A B C = C E C <u>is</u> 0 0 1

2. Reduction and outer product may be used with = and ≠. Inner product may be used, but the rightmost of the two operators must be confined to = or ≠.

3. The operators that refer only to the structure of arrays, ravel, dimension, reversal, monadic transposition, reshape, catenation, rotation, compression, expansion, dyadic transposition, take and drop, and indexing.

4. The operations index of (dyadic ι) and membership based on application of = between arrays.

It is important to be able to distinguish between numeric and character arrays. Let B be an array of unknown type. Then, since \ inserts ' ' (spaces) in character arrays,

$$0 = 0 \backslash 0 \rho B$$

will be 1 if B is a numeric array and 0 if it is a character array.

We shall now turn to the subject of procedures which, in APL, are called *functions*. APL functions do not provide quite as rich a structure as in Algol60, but they are far from primitive in their capabilities.

APL PROCEDURES

While APL does not support block structure, there are global and local variables in APL programs. Every APL function exists in an environment called a *workspace*, only one of which exists at any time. All functions are defined at this level. No function may be defined as being incarnated *only* when control is inside another function. Put another way, any function may be called from within a function: all function names are global. As in Algol60, functions may or may not produce a result (which, of course, may be an array of arbitrary rank). Unlike Algol60, functions that have more than two formal parameters may not be defined. Hence functions are called *niladic, monadic,* or *dyadic* if they have none, one, or two formal parameters, respectively. All parameters are called by value. Functions may be recursive and they may have local variables. The syntax of functions is quite simple:

$$\nabla \langle \text{Heading} \rangle \langle \text{Body} \rangle \nabla$$

Since functions are written from a typewriter-like terminal, the carriage return ⟲ serves as a line terminator. Then:

```
⟨heading⟩ is ⟨Result part⟩⟨Name-parameter part⟩
  ⟨local variable list⟩⟲
⟨Result part⟩ is ⟨empty⟩ or ⟨identifier⟩←
⟨Name-parameter part⟩ is ⟨function name⟩ or
  ⟨function name⟩⟨space⟩⟨formal parameter⟩ or
  ⟨formal parameter⟩⟨space⟩⟨function name⟩⟨space⟩
  ⟨formal parameter⟩
⟨local variable list⟩ is {;⟨identifier⟩}*₀
```

and

```
⟨empty⟩ is
⟨function name⟩ is ⟨identifier⟩
⟨formal parameter⟩ is ⟨identifier⟩
⟨space⟩ is {' '}*₁
```

The ⟨Body⟩ is not totally definable in BNF.

⟨Body⟩ <u>is</u> {⟨function line⟩}$_1^*$

But ⟨function line⟩ <u>is</u> ⟨inserted line number⟩⟨statement⟩ $\supset$ and ⟨inserted line number⟩ is supplied by the APL system and is the next of a set of consecutive integers always commencing with 1 and displayed in brackets. Let us give some examples.

Example 1:

```
     ∇ R←AVE X;T
[1]  R←(+/T)÷ρT←,X
     ∇
```

Example 2:

```
     ∇ R←X SUBST TEXT; IDEX;KEY;NEW
[1]  KEY←X[1;]
[2]  NEW←X[2;]
[3]  IDEX← (∧/[1](¯1+ιρKEY) ⌽KEY∘.= TEXT)/ιρR←TEXT
[4]  R[,IDEX∘.+¯1+ιρNEW]←((ρIDEX)×ρNEW)ρNEW
     ∇
```

where we have assumed $(\rho NEW) = \rho KEY$.
The algorithm for $(\rho NEW) \neq \rho KEY$ <u>is</u>

Example 3:

```
     ∇R←Z REPL T;K;NEW;KEY;J;IDEX;G;N
[1]  NEW←(K←Zι'□')↓Z
[2]  KEY←(¯1+K)↑Z
[3]  J←1-ρKEY
[4]  IDEX←(J↓∧/[1](N←¯1+ιρKEY) ⌽KEY∘.=T)/ιJ+ρT
[5]  R←((ιρT)ε,IDEX∘.+N)/T
[6]  IDEX←IDEX+((ρNEW)-ρKEY)×¯1+ιρIDEX
[7]  G←,IDEX∘.+¯1+ιρNEW
[8]  R←(∼(ι(ρR)+ρG)εG)\R
[9]  R[G]←(ρG)ρNEW
     ∇
```

In Z the data are supplied as $KEY,'\square',NEW$, where "$\square$" acts as separating punctuation.

Note how relaxing it is not to have to declare the size and shape of local variables.

Functions may be recursive, and the preceding example may be programmed recursively. This representation of the function is more concise and simpler to understand than Example 2.

```
     ∇ R←X SUBREC TEXT;KEY;NEW;H
[1]   KEY←X[1;]
[2]   NEW←X[2;]
[3]   R←0ρ0
[4]   H←(∧/[1](⁻1+ιρKEY) ⌽ KEY∘.= TEXT)ι1
[5]   R←R,(⁻1+H)↑TEXT
[6]   →0×ιH>(ρTEXT)+1-ρKEY
[7]   R←R,NEW, X SUBREC(⁻1+H+ρKEY)↓TEXT
     ∇
```

Of course, this particular use of recursion also lends itself to a third, nonrecursive, representation of the algorithm.

There are four statement types in APL:

1. Assignment
2. Procedure (call)
3. goto
4. Condition or branch

Statement types 1 and 2 are very much as in Algol60; goto in APL is either of the form →⟨label⟩, meaning that the next statement to be executed is that having the label, labels being either identifiers or integers (line numbers), or of the form →⟨expression⟩, meaning that the next statement to be executed is that whose line number is the value of the expression, if a scalar, or its first component if a vector. The ⟨expression⟩ is called the target of the → (goto).

Conditional statements in APL are quite primitive and represent one of the major weaknesses in the language. In point of fact, the branch command provides the following possibilities:

1. A branch to any of several explicit statements.
2. A branch to a specific statement or the statement following that containing the branch command.

Branches are controlled by predicates, as in Algol60. If the target is the empty vector, then the successor is the statement next in line. If the target is an integer, not included in the set of line numbers of the function containing the branch instruction, then the function is exited: control continues in the calling function at the point following the call.

Example 1: →k×ιt.

If t evaluates to 0, ι0 is empty as is k×ι0, so the successor is the next line of the function. If t evaluates to 1, then ι1 is the vector 1, so the successor is the statement in line number $k \times 1$, hence k.

Example 2: →k×t.

If t evaluates to 0 then the successor is an exit from the function to the caller, otherwise if t evaluates to 1, the successor is at line k.

The expression $\to k \times \iota a R b$, where R is a relation, can be looked upon as

<u>if</u> $a R b$ <u>then</u> <u>goto</u> k

Suppose we wish to program in APL control structures like those in Algol60:

1. <u>for</u> $I \gets 1$ <u>step</u> 1 <u>until</u> N <u>do</u> S
    [K] $I \gets 1$
    [K+1] $\to (L+3) \times \iota N < I$
    [K+2]·
       . $\Big\}$ S
       .
    [L]
    [L+1] $I \gets I+1$
    [L+2] $\to K+1$
    [L+3]   . . .
2. <u>if</u> B <u>then</u> S_1 <u>else</u> S_2
    [K] $\to (K+n+2) \times \iota \sim B$
    [K+1]
       . $\Big\}$ S_1
       .
    [K+n]
    [K+n+1] $\to K+q+1$
    [K+n+2]
       . $\Big\}$ S_2
       .
    [K+q]
    [K+q+1]   . . .
3. <u>while</u> B <u>do</u> S
    [K]   BEGIN: $\to$ END $\times \iota \sim B$
    [K+1]
       . $\Big\}$ S
       .
    [K+n]
    [K+n+1] $\to$ BEGIN
    [K+n+2]   END:

In APL all labels are local to the function in which they occur.

Thus far we have said little about input-output in APL. The operand $\square$ occurring to the immediate left of a specification arrow ($\gets$) causes the value of the expression just computed to be output.

The operand $\square$ appearing anywhere else causes execution to be interrupted until an expression to replace it has been entered from the terminal. The following dialogues exemplify the use of this operand.

The System Types	you type
$\square$:	$A \leftarrow 4 \times \square$
	6
	A
24	
$\square$:	$A \leftarrow 2\ 5\ \rho\ \square$
	'HELLODOLLY'
	A
HELLO	
DOLLY	
	ρ,A
10	

Note that only vectors can be input. Dyadic ρ must be used to reshape input data when desired. A single value or character is always treated as a scalar.

To enter a character string, surrounding quotes ''' must be used.

```
          A← □
□:
          'HELLO ⤸
          DOLLY'
          A
HELLO
DOLLY
          ρA
11
```

The carriage return is represented by a character in the text! How does one enter ''' into the text? Since two quotes delimit the text, two adjacent quotes represent one quote,

```
          A← □
□:
          'WON''T'
          A
WON'T
          ρA
5
```

and four adjacent quotes represent two quotes, etc.

Entering character strings is done so often that APL provides a special input symbol ⌑, "quote quad," in the use of which quotes stand for themselves:

```
                         A← ⌑
   ⌑ :
                         HELLO
                         A
   HELLO
                         A← ⌑
   ⌑ :
                         'WON''T'
                         A
   'WON''T'
                         ρA
   8
```

Whereas a matching quote terminates ☐ input, a ⌇ terminates ⌑ input. In ☐ input a quote opens up character input; hence, its absence is inference that a character string such as)*OFF* entered has an APL system significance, and one can use such to break out of an input state. But in ⌑ mode)*OFF* is assumed to be a string. Hence how could we break out of an input if we wish to? APL provides a special escape character made up of five typewriter strokes: "O backspace U backspace T," which then appear as Ⓤ on the page. When a function is executing, the entry of such a data character causes the function to terminate.

In APL, if an expression value is not assigned, it is as though ☐← were present.

```
   3+5
   8
```

Advantage can be taken of this to produce mixed output. The line

```
   'THE VALUE IS';4×5;'FEET'
```

prints out as

```
   THE VALUE IS 20 FEET
```

This completes our discussion of the APL language. We shall return in a later chapter to an examination of the APL system which supports the use of this language.

Though we have taken pains to describe APL as being much like Algol60—both being, as it were, programming languages for expressing flowcharts—in some important ways they are quite different. They make different demands on the expertise of the programmer. One achieves fluency in APL by imaginative use of arrays and operations on them which often lead to astonishingly concise programs. Very often a good APL program will be quite different in structure from an Algol60 program for the same problem. We shall consider some examples.

Example 1:   The Coin Problem

```
     ∇ P←G COIN C;T;M;J
[1]  P←1
[2]  →0×ι0=ρM←G[1]ρG[2]
[3]  C←G[1]↑C
[4]  →0×ι(ρM)<J←((T←M-C)>0)ι1
[5]  P←P+1
[6]  →4,M[ιJ]←T[J]
     ∇
```

C is the vector of coin denominations with the unit coin omitted and the coins in increasing order. G is the vector: index of maximum coin allowed, the amount.

Example 2:   The 8 Queens Problem

As in Chapter 1, let the vectors R, $NESW$, and $NWSE$ hold the disposition of the queens already placed. Then, for a given column J a queen may be placed in a row K, on or below row I, if and only if the following is true:

```
8 ≥ K←¯1+I+((0=(J-1)↓(J-I-7)↓ Φ NWSE)
V  (0=(J+I-2)↓(J-8)↓NESW)
V  (0=(I-1)↓R))ι1
```

If $K > 8$, then regression occurs, and the four vectors $NWSE$, $NESW$, R, and X must be corrected.

```
     ∇ QUEENS;NESW;NWSE;R;X;J;I;K
[1]  NESW←NWSE←1↓X,X←R←8ρ0
[2]  J←I←1
[3]  CYCLE: →OUT×ι(J<0)V(J>8)
[4]  →REGRESS×ι 8 ≥ K←¯1+I+((Ɔ=(J-1)↓(J-I-7)
     ↓ Φ NWSE)
     V  (0=(J+I-2)↓(J-8)↓NESW)
     V  (0=(I-1)↓R))ι1
[5]  ASSIGN: X[J]←K
[6]  R[K]←NWSE[8+J-K]←NESW[K+J-1]←1
[7]  ADVANCE: J←J+I←1
[8]  →CYCLE
[9]  REGRESS: J←J-1
[10] K←X[J]
[11] R[K]←NWSE[8+J-K]←NESW[K+J-1]←0
[12] I←X[J]+1
[13] →CYCLE
[14] OUT: →NOSOL.×ι(J<0)
[15] 'SOLUTION IS' ;X
[16] →0
[17] NOSOL: 'NO SOLUTION'
     ∇
```

A program with fewer lines is easily derived from this. With the same heading:

```
[1]   NESW←NWSE←1↓X,X←R←(8ρ0)
[2]   J←I←1
[3]   CYCLE:  →REGRESS ×ι 8 ≥ K←⁻1+I+((0=(J-1)
      ↓(J-I-7)↓φNWSE)
      ∨ (0=(J+I-2)↓(J-8)↓NESW)
      ∨ (0=(J-1)↓R))τ1
[4]   X[J]←K
[5]   →OUT×ι8<J←J+I←P←1
[6]   JOIN: R[K]←NWSE[8+J-(K-P)]←NESW[K+(J-P)-1]←P
[7]   →CYCLE
[8]   REGRESS: →NOSOL×ιP←0=J←J-1
[9]   I←1+K←X[J]
[10]  →JOIN
[11]  NOSOL: 'NO SOLUTION'
[12]  →0
[13]  OUT: 'SOLUTION IS' ;X
      ∇
```

Those who have been experienced in Algol60 and FORTRAN often find difficulty in adjusting to APL programming. Of course, it is not difficult to program in APL with the style to which one is accustomed, but developing an APL style requires practice. Since each APL statement is retranslated each time it is executed, and the array operations are executed with very efficient machine-coded programs, it is good APL practice, all else being equal, to maximize the use of array operations and to minimize the number of times statements must be translated. However, the statements that result may be extremely difficult to follow. Statements may become quite Germanic and involuted. Still, as with German, one can become adept at reading such heavy prose. For example, suppose one has an integer sequence X and wishes to find K, the position of the leftmost digit that is "out of order," not $\geq$ its predecessor, and J, the position before which its insertion would put it "in order." Then,

$$J←Q[;K←((+/[1]Q←(X°.\leq X)\wedge(\iota\rho X)°.\leq\iota\rho X)=\iota\rho X)\iota 0]\iota 0$$

will find K and J, assuming a K exists. With practice one can learn to read such involuted sentences. But before one learns to read APL, one learns to write it: it is easier to express one's thoughts in APL than to read someone else's. One develops a collection of expressions that mature into a stockpile of phrases in whose terms reading ability eventually develops. To aid in the development of a stockpile, a number of exercises are appended to this chapter. Acquiring a mastery of APL is an exhilarating experience and has a somewhat different effect on the programmer than does the acquisition of a mastery of Algol60. The latter seems to aid in the development of orderliness in laying out programs: one grows to depend on solving problems from the outside in, as it were. APL also leads to the use of this approach, but there is an accompanying development of complex phrase-making that allows one to wipe away many of the inner layers of the problem-solving process. One's intuition expands with practice, and APL permits us to express ourselves with conciseness as our expertise develops. We begin to think directly of the manipulation of patterns, and much of programming is just that.

A BRIEF SURVEY OF PROGRAMMING LANGUAGES

In this chapter we have examined two programming languages in some detail, Algol60 and APL, and a third, FORTRAN, somewhat summarily. An enormous number of other programming languages exist, and it is a rare person who is proficient in more than a few. However, as has been mentioned, most languages have enough similarity so that understanding or learning to write programs in a "foreign programming language" is not terribly difficult, once one has mastered one or two languages.

As with natural languages, there are families of programming languages whose members have strong similarities to—indeed, are often explicitly derived from—each other. FORTRAN, COBOL, and BASIC are members of a family. Algol60, Algol68, BCL, and PASCAL are members of another. PL/I is an offspring of three parents, FORTRAN, COBOL, and Algol60. LISP and APL are members of the same family, some enormous differences between them notwithstanding.

It is important to observe that languages arise, flower, go to seed, and die for a variety of economic, sociological, pedagogical and, of course, technological reasons. Hence we append here a small survey covering some of the more popular languages and the forces that have operated on (and for) them.

Computers can be used only through the execution of programs. Either programs are written at those individual installations which require them, or they are imported. Imports may be precisely what are wanted and work immediately, or a period of adjustment may be needed before such programs will work in a given installation. The adjustment period may be short (days) or long (several years). The variation in "shakedown" period can occur for many reasons: adaption from one computer to another, adaption from one language to another, adaption from one task to another and, of course, improperly trained personnel.

Since each computer has its own "machine" language, programs written directly in machine language are extremely difficult to transfer—they are not very portable. Machine languages must provide sufficient "richness" to express all programs that might ever be written for a given machine, and to do so using as few basic language constructions as possible. Consequently, almost all programs written in machine language require an enormous attention to details, all of which must be correctly handled. Many of these details play no essential role in the conceptual model being programmed but arise in profusion when the model is being adapted to a particular computer. Programs in machine language take a long time to write and are difficult to write correctly. However, it was observed, about twenty years ago, that:

1. Many important and frequently occurring problems arising in different problem-solving environments employed similar programming techniques.
2. The people most concerned with the results were unwilling or unable to write programs whose results they needed.
3. The creation of synthetic languages—that is, languages not natural and not directly associated with a machine—was possible and hence could be tailored to most commonly occurring problems and to the capabilities of those most directly concerned with the programs.

The first important synthetic language was IBM's FORTRAN, produced for the IBM 704 in 1956–57. FORTRAN continues to be the most widely used language, though there now exists such an enormous number of languages that they have acquired an identifying class name: high-level problem-oriented languages.

Since the advent of FORTRAN most programs have been written in high-level problem-oriented languages. Education in programming usually commences with the learning of at least one such language, and the job title of "programmer" has come to mean one who can write programs in FORTRAN, etc. Such people tend to see all programming tasks naturally reflected in the high-level language(s) they know.

It was inevitable that the success of FORTRAN would lead to the following developments in the period 1957–70.

1. FORTRAN-like languages more closely tied to particular manufacturers' machines appeared. None have achieved an importance comparable to FORTRAN.
2. Extensions and improvements of FORTRAN yielded languages more flexible in their capabilities and more graceful in their linguistic structure. Algol60 is the best example of this genre.
3. Languages oriented to the tasks and notations of specialized classes of user tended to reduce the educational problem in preparing people to bend the computer to their tasks. COBOL, SNOBOL, and LISP are examples.
4. As computers and modes of computer usage, such as time-sharing, changed, languages were created to exploit the increased capabilities reflected in these changes. APL and BASIC are examples.
5. Increased computer use led to new applications, in turn to new languages, whose proliferation led to the development of "omnibus" languages, in whose terms widely differing classes of problems can have their programs expressed in a natural way. PL/I and Algol68 are examples.

The consequences of the widespread availability of high-level program-oriented languages have been enormous:

1. The number of people writing programs is greater by a factor of at least 5 or 10 over what it would be if programming were continuing to be done in machine language.

2. The planning and programming time has diminished considerably. Put another way, in a given period of time more complex programs can now be written.

3. A more fluid labor supply of programmers has come into existence, since special technical-education requirements for beginning programmers have diminished, and since the same languages on machines of different manufacturers make both programmers and their programs portable.

4. Each new computer is weighted down with an enormous amount of language-processing capability in the form of manufacturer-supplied programs. The development cost for new computers—though not, of course, the manufacturing cost—is about evenly divided between programming support and hardware development.

5. The programming support service required to maintain a computer system in operating condition has increased.

High-level programming languages have, in the past fifteen years, revolutionized the use of computers. More people have been able to program; larger tasks have become practically programmable. We have, probably irrevocably, passed the point where our society can comfortably do without computers and their programmers. People have had to acquire a more logical, often called algorithmic, view of their problems so that they might be programmed. The languages have moved the usable power of the machines closer to people whose logical abilities lie closer to the human average. In the trio of man, language, and machine all will have to adjust in the coming years. Education, practice, and continued confrontation with computers will make us more aware, and more capable, of algorithmic activities. The languages will develop toward maximally important applications and toward forms in which more people are comfortably fluent. The machines for some time will develop along the gradient of purely technological breakthroughs in componentry. The order-of-magnitude improvement in computer cost performance will continue to depend on new hardware concepts and not administrative reorganizations of our present computers.

We have not yet begun to see the next generation of computer languages, languages whose statements are of goals and wishes rather than of means and methods. Those languages await the machines on which they can be efficiently run—a ten-power increase in memory size and speed.

COBOL: Common Business-Oriented Language

This language has a history of about a decade and is the only language that the U. S. Government requires on any of its general-purpose computer systems. COBOL is almost the only language that was created by a community of users and manufacturers with the direct intention of its becoming a standard for commercial data-processing. It has been well accepted, and a standardized version is almost universally available on medium and large computers.

A major goal of COBOL was to use a syntax and semantics that would be intuitively clear to programmers and their supervisors in data-processing installations—that is, to people who deal in data and numbers but who are not mathematicians or scientists. It was made to look like English, and it slightly succeeded in doing so.

Because data-processing problems are file-processing problems, COBOL, unlike most other languages, provides capabilities for describing the environment—the hardware resources—and the data formats to be employed in the processing of a program. Indeed, COBOL programs are separated into four parts: environment, data and procedure (on what, with what, and how), and identification (who).

The procedure division consists of sequences of executable statements and statements collected together, named, and parameterized, known technically as procedures.

The data division permits the easy description of hierarchical record structures. Data are organized as files, intermediate results, and constants. Each such is organized as a sequence of entries. These entries have a structural description as records, though COBOL requires a distinction between the physical attributes of a record—how it is represented, stored, and organized—and the logical attributes—how its information is structured and related. COBOL permits the programmer to specify for his files, by means of modifying clauses in file descriptions, the medium for, and the mode of, the file representation.

The environment division of a COBOL program allows the programmer to specify the hardware on which his program is to be compiled and run. This is of particular importance, first in making certain that sufficient hardware resources are available for the program and, second, in fixing file allocations to the appropriate units (tapes, discs, etc.).

Some important special features of COBOL, oriented towards data-processing, are the following.

1. SEGMENTATION. A large program can be divided into priority-rated segments, and a COBOL compiler will attempt an overlay strategy that attempts to fit high-priority segments with the same priority together in computer storage.

2. SORTING. Specific operations are included in the language for sorting certain files, called SORT files, on preselected keys.

3. REPORT-GENERATING. Since the object of much data-processing is the preparation of reports, COBOL has a REPORT SECTION, occurring in the data division, in which one can describe the format of a report, using information in a file.

Summarizing, COBOL has some outstanding virtues for business data-processing, which no doubt account for its widespread acceptance:

1. It has become a standard.
2. The federal government stands behind the maintenance of the standard and validation of new COBOL processors.
3. It is widely available.
4. The language is well matched to the training and abilities of the people who use it and use the results of its programs.

FORTRAN: Formula-Translation Language

This is the "daddy" of the class of languages being described here. It is almost twenty years old and has developed through a succession of dialects that have improved its value as a general programming language. We observe some interesting facts about the language.

1. It is the first problem-oriented language learned by almost every programmer. To most programmers the COBOL and FORTRAN languages are synonymous with the nature and content of computer programming. Consequently, textbooks, manuals, and problem books abound, treating the use of FORTRAN at every level of expertise and in almost every field of computer application.
2. It is the first high-level language processor produced by manufacturers for each of their computers. Any computer expecting widespread acceptance must have at least one FORTRAN processor.
3. As the modes of computer use have proliferated (batch, remote job entry, time-sharing, distributed minicomputer dependence), FORTRAN has remained the language of common usage in these environments.

Like COBOL, in its milieu, FORTRAN seems "right" and "adequate" to programmers in scientific and engineering environments. While there are languages that are more elegant, less verbose, and more flexible, none seems to fit the initial needs of programmers as well as FORTRAN. Furthermore, it is worth noting that FORTRAN has been the language chosen for many large programming projects central to specific disciplines, such as bubble-chamber analysis programs in high-energy physics, highway design and evaluation, nuclear power plant programs, and large linear programming applications in the oil and aircraft industries.

Even some specialized languages have been developed whose processors are written in FORTRAN, the rationale being that FORTRAN is the only language common to all commercial computers, making these specialized languages quite portable.

The gradual disappearance of FORTRAN has been predicted for the past five years, but no slackening in its appeal is as yet evident. As programming education spreads into new populations, such as in high school and junior college, it is FORTRAN that they learn first. Some would say that FORTRAN is not a flower but a weed: it is hardy, occasionally blooms, and grows in every computer.

Well worth noting is that the technology for constructing FORTRAN translators is so well understood and widely distributed that the manufacturer of any new computer can treat this piece of software much like hardware; that is, he can get realistic (accurate) estimates of cost in manpower and computer time for implementing a FORTRAN processor on a new computer. A large number of independent software firms can now produce cheap, efficient FORTRAN translators for any new computer approaching the market. FORTRAN processors can be constructed for computers as small as the popular minicomputers.

One dialect of FORTRAN, WATFOR, has become the most economical language for processing student problems in large university environments: for example, 15 to 25 cents per student job.

FORTRAN was originally developed by and for IBM. It has contributed enormously to the success of that company in placing computers in government, industry, research laboratories, and educational institutions. While IBM and SHARE, an IBM scientific users' organization, largely determined the early development of FORTRAN, the current picture seems to be that a computer manufacturer selects for implementation one of the standard FORTRANS as a base and adds a few features that increase his competitive stature in some zone of the computer field he is penetrating.

It is fair to say that no manufacturer has a competitive edge due to its FORTRAN processors. Decisions regarding computer acquisitions or computer development always take the existence of a FORTRAN processor as a necessary condition for choice, but it is rarely, if ever, a sufficient condition for choice.

FORTRAN is ubiquitous. Though the European computer-science community developed a great affection for Algol60, which they helped to develop, users of computers in specific disciplines have exerted increasing pressure on European manufacturers over the past decade to assign the same priority to FORTRAN processors on their computers that their American counterparts do. An interesting example is that of the Soviet nuclear physicists, who have adopted FORTRAN as their programming language because nuclear physicists elsewhere in the world use FORTRAN, even though Soviet computer specialists have been partial to Algol60 and to some lesser-known but Russian-created languages.

It is fair to say that in today's technical world, where commerce in ideas, technology, and notations is so widespread, the choice of a programming language is no longer determined solely by the manufacturer or computer scientists, but is also by the working environments in individual technical areas. FORTRAN is by all odds the most commonly understood and utilized programming language in the entire world. Even if IBM were no longer preeminent in computer manufacture, FORTRAN would remain the dominant programming language world-wide.

BASIC: Beginner's All-Purpose Symbolic Instruction Code

This language is an excellent example of a derivative of FORTRAN designed for a specific audience, a specific style of computing, and a specific type of hardware. The style has increased in importance; the audience, always potentially large, has accepted the language enthusiastically; and the type of hardware has become, through technological advances, increasingly cheaper and consequently more prevalent.

The audience is the set of people anxious to learn to program but unlikely to become programming specialists for a long time. Those who have occasional small applications and students early in their education sequence (high school and college) comprise the audience.

The style of computing is interactive via remote terminals, in particular the cheap, reliable, and widespread Models 33 and 35 Teletypes.

The hardware is the small to medium computer, in particular the new minicomputers. A BASIC environment has become so valuable that certain manufacturers (such as Hewlitt-Packard andWang Associates) market a system specifically advertised as processing BASIC (sixteen terminals for about $150,000 purchase).

Almost all commercial time-sharing firms now offer BASIC service for interactive computing at rather low prices.

BASIC is extremely easy to learn; a few hours usually suffice for this purpose. As interactive systems go, BASIC is relatively simple to implement. Textbooks with excellent sample problems exist. Thus it is not surprising that BASIC is available on almost all interactive computing systems.

Next to FORTRAN, BASIC is the most widely used first language for people learning to program. BASIC programs are almost transparent in their adaptability.

Algol60: Algorithmic Language

Algol60 is a competitor to FORTRAN and has been in existence for over a decade. This language was designed by an international committee, half of whose members were American. Recognizing that FORTRAN was a prototype of a class of languages, the committee

designed a language more elegant and more general than FORTRAN. }
It quickly became the favorite language in continental Europe, including the Soviet Union, and in China, and its structure became
the basis for much language development during this past decade.
Most of the current computer scientists and programmers in Europe
were educated in Algol60.

However, in the United States, Algol60 never became a serious competitor to FORTRAN for programming science and engineering problems. IBM never seriously supported it and was never
seriously pressured by its customers to do so. Among the manufacturers Burroughs alone took an active interest. Their B5000,
B5500, and B6000 lines of computers were designed so that Algol60
could be considered their machine code—though there was in the
background, for selective machine users, a hardware code. Burroughs users found Algol60 eminently satisfactory. Many of the
universities in their computer-science programs use Algol60, not
FORTRAN, as the fulcrum of language treatment and development.

Nevertheless, since IBM did not choose to support Algol60
vigorously, the language never became an important medium of
communication for the bulk of American users and machines. However, Algol60, rather than FORTRAN, served as the base for new
language developments in the United States and abroad that were
intended to replace both FORTRAN and Algol60.

The diffidence with which Algol60 was received in the United
States exposed for the first time in the computer field the importance, even the necessity, of marketing strategy and requirements
for creating widespread acceptance of a software product, no matter
how superior it may be to established usage. Some say the lack of
input-output capability was responsible for Algol60's rejection, but
the reason goes deeper: the acceptance (widespread usage) of a
programming language requires the explicit auxiliary support of
educational practices, reliable and well-documented systems on a
variety of hardware systems, the definition of a satisfactory standard, the establishment of strong, discipline-oriented groups (such
as nuclear physicists, highway engineers, and banking-procedure
specialists), who will use the language as their medium of communication with the computer and each other, and the establishment of an excellent library of standard techniques available to the
language users, among other things. What FORTRAN accumulated
through usage, language replacements must now provide ab initio.
There is, of course, an exception to the explicit, initial provision of
this supporting incubus required of languages: IBM, in its determination to support a new language development, insures the ultimate availability of these software necessities through a sequence
of "releases," and "insures" the existence of a large, diverse group
of users who will participate in the communication net, almost
from the beginning. While this insurance is only weakly guaranteed
contractually, the users of hardware and software accept IBM's
announced interests as tantamount to a guarantee of ultimate

availability. Although certain of its newer systems have somewhat tarnished this "guarantee," it remains the case that IBM alone is able to provide this assurance to a wide spectrum of computer users.

Returning to Algol60, it is fair to say that its main values have been:

1. The education of a generation of European computer users in the advantages and uses of high-level programming languages.

2. The provision of a base well suited to the development of those successor languages called for by more sophisticated equipment and more sophisticated users.

PL/I: "Programming Language I"

This is an IBM-inspired language developed as a successor to FORTRAN but using Algol60 as a base. PL/I is an attempt at an omnibus language, one that will be natural to use for a variety of programming tasks that previously found expression in different languages. Thus PL/I could be used in place of COBOL or FORTRAN or Algol60. For a variety of reasons it has not achieved universal acceptance as an omnibus:

1. No important and persuasive group of users (such as the federal government in the case of COBOL) has insisted on its use as a standard medium of exchange.

2. Computer manufacturers, other than IBM, have not strongly pushed the use of the language.

Until recently fast compilers processing useful subsets of PL/I have not been available for education, experimentation, or specialized production tasks on large computers, to say nothing of the fact that an efficient PL/I compiler is out of the question for small and medium computers perfectly capable of processing FORTRAN, Algol60, and even COBOL.

PL/I is a language of its generation. Since it came into being at a time when multiprocessing and multiprogramming were being introduced on machines of great complexity (hierarchies of storage, multiprocessors, remote job-entry, and so forth), and operating systems were being created to manage the collection of resources at the programmer's disposal, PL/I includes important capabilities allowing the programmer to specify how his program is to interact with a complex resource environment.

On the whole, PL/I is a language of enormous flexibility requiring a processor of enormous complexity. For those programmers creating omnibus programs—and most programs are not of this kind—PL/I is appealing. At this time the future of PL/I is tied to the development of hardware technology: new minicomputers may be cheap enough and profuse enough to change the nature of programming sufficiently to render PL/I obsolete before it has achieved widespread acceptance.

Algol68

Similar in intent to PL/I but far less likely to achieve success is the IFIPS (International Federation of Information Processing Societies) effort that culminated in Algol68. Like its predecessor Algol60, the development of this language has been mostly pushed by the Europeans, although a few Americans have participated in its development. The definition of Algol68 has been ostensibly a committee activity, but the language that finally emerged is largely the child of one man, A. A. Van Wijngaarden, of the Netherlands, and should properly be regarded as an important piece of individually inspired research, even though others have cooperated in the language's creation.

Although PL/I is a development heavily triggered by what people often did—and often not easily—with FORTRAN, Algol60, and COBOL, Algol68 developed, not so much from Algol60 practice, but through a search for generalizations and simplifications of Algol60 language structure. The increased sophistication in the general understanding of language that arose from prolonged and intelligent contact with Algol60 heavily influenced Algol68.

The reluctance of FORTRAN users to use PL/I is paralleled in Europe by that of Algol60 users with respect to Algol68. Whereas IBM is devoting considerable resources to PL/I development and marketing, Algol68 implementation and marketing is in the hands of isolated, though splendidly qualified, groups of computer scientists in Europe. These groups communicate loosely, the implementations are separately organized, and their equivalence is not easily determined.

At present it is unlikely that Algol68 will be the language to supplant Algol60 as the working programming language in Europe. Nevertheless, it is a testament to harmonious and general language design and is far more appealing than PL/I as an omnibus language. Terminal-oriented computation, when it develops in Europe, may well prove the undoing of Algol68.

SNOBOL

This language is included here, not because it is so widely used, but because it illustrates how languages have been developed for purposes far removed from the initial ones for which computers were created and put into widespread use. The importance of the applications will undoubtedly grow. SNOBOL was developed by a team at Bell Telephone Laboratories in 1962, and over the past ten years several improved versions have been produced. It is a direct descendant of COMIT, a language previously developed at MIT.

SNOBOL is most useful for specifying text-processing algorithms—not manipulation of numeric data, like FORTRAN and others, or of files, like COBOL. The basic unit of data is the character string, such as a paragraph of text, and the basic operations are the detection, isolation, and modification of those pieces of text that fit some pattern. For example, a search can be made in a text for all dates written in a certain format, say "2/171" or "month, day, year," and they can be, for example, transformed into a standard form, or information attached to the dates can be listed in chronological order. The patterns on which search may occur are quite general and lend themselves to a variety of text-processing applications. Of course, numerical calculations are also possible, since they are often required as auxiliary activities in text-processing, as in acquiring statistics.

It is important to appreciate the role of languages like SNOBOL. Any assessment of the ultimate value of computers in business, government, or social activities must include language-processing by computers. Consider the creation of contracts, manuals, directories, compendia. Indeed, consider the task of creating voluminous organizations of data that are intended for human processing on a scheduled basis but that change slightly in successive issues. Then an appreciation of the ultimate role of SNOBOL-like languages emerges.

SNOBOL has been implemented on a wide variety of computers—but it has not yet achieved the status of being required from computer manufacturers by their customers. Although there are several groups of system programmers who have implemented SNOBOL processors on their machine, most of the design expertise still resides with the group at Bell Telephone Laboratories.

LISP

LISP, like SNOBOL, seems on first glance to be esoteric, an elegant curiosity, and unlikely to be of value to anyone but the computer scientist. This is presently the case, but it is important to understand the nature and goals of LISP. This language chooses as its basic data structure the "list" or "binary tree." The important properties of this structure are the following.

1. The maximum number of elementary information units (called "atoms") attached to an identified list need not be a priori specified; that is, the course of computation may arbitrarily inflate and deflate these structures.

2. Substitution of trees for subtrees is extremely flexible, and the act of replacement does not alter the structure (hence the accessibility) of the tree complementary to that part replaced. In this sense LISP list behavior is quite different from the SNOBOL string.

3. The natural model for processing LISP trees is recursion. Since trees may bifurcate wildly during processing, any operation on trees is most naturally seen as a cascading of identical operations on sequences of subtrees, the cascading being performed as often as individual trees require.

It turns out that there are enormous numbers of problems associated with models of human problem-solving for which algorithms are naturally represented in LISP. These immensely important problems are associated with the dynamic creation of problem-solving strategies by programs. Programs of this kind turn out to be systems—integrated collections—of programs that are loosely organized and so much grow in number that program creators often lose their omnipotence concerning their program's behavior. This modeling of thought processes by programs is often labeled "artificial intelligence."

Many of the early systems created in LISP dealt with game-playing—the most complicated game now being studied being chess. However, other studies have been devoted to the understanding of natural language, the performance of (symbolic) mathematics, theorem-proving, design of complex structures, and the creation of vision, motion, and speech capabilities by automatons.

One program, DENDRAL, developed at Stanford, is now used by chemists as an analyzer of molecular spectra. This program examines a spectrum, makes reasonable hypotheses of chemical structures, computes their structure and theoretical spectrum, compares and improves until a satisfactory isolation of a set of compounds giving rise to the spectrum has been obtained.

In time, programs of this kind will dominate the activity of those computers dedicated most closely to management and policy functions. But this state of affairs is not yet here. No manufacturer supplies LISP other than as a courtesy when produced by one of its customers. At present, use of LISP is limited to an active, extremely sophisticated group of computer scientists clustered in universities and a few research laboratories.

APL: A Programming Language

Languages arise and acquire a dedicated following, not only because of the delineation of a problem area of importance, but also because of the emergence of a computing style of consequence. Such is the case with APL. The language is modeled on a sophisticated data-processing notation developed by Ken Iverson at Harvard in 1957–62. The computer language derived from his work, and whose creation was directed by him, was implemented at IBM as an interactive typewriter console language. APL is a beautiful example of a formidable language that has gained wide public acceptance because of its imbedding in a superb, dedicated system within IBM's operating system for the 360 line of computers. The stability and response of this system to the needs of as many as fifty simultaneous users on the IBM 360/50 has prompted programmers to study and master a language that under more normal circumstances (its imbedding in an unstable, sluggish system) they would have avoided because of its esoteric notations and complexity of operations. However, it is important to note that programmers, once they acquire some facility in APL, find its flexibility very satisfying, and a return to FORTRAN and COBOL, for example, stultifying when necessary.

APL directs a programmer to organize his activities on arrays of data characters or numbers. A large set of operators is provided for manipulating these arrays, and it is important to note that the operators abet data-processing as much as numerical calculations: that is, they deal as much with selection, rotation, transposition, reshaping, sorting, distribution, and testing of arrays as with addition, multiplication, and so on.

The variety of available operations permits programmers to express an amazingly large cross-section of useful algorithms in a concise and natural way. An interesting byproduct of this variety is the range of quite different correct programs that a group of programmers will create to solve a given problem. One has to go to rather immense FORTRAN programs to observe such individually distinct syntheses. Of course, the creation of such differences can be regarded as an undesirable trait of APL, if one is a manager of programmers, but it is also an advantage, since the language clearly has a wide range of useful tools for people who like such tools!

Since APL is interactive, editing programs is as easy as executing them. But this is only possible because APL is interpretive and not compiled. Interpretation and consequent flexibility do not come free; the execution of many programs is significantly slower than FORTRAN programs solving the same problem (ten or more times slower). Consequently, APL is often used during the creation and testing of algorithms, FORTRAN supplanting it in the production or full-scale version of algorithms.

It would be tempting to consign APL to the heap of "toy" languages unfit for serious computation. This would be a grievous mistake. With the advent of MOS circuitry, cheaper and faster semiconductor main memories, low-priced secondary memories, and low-priced minicomputers, machines that execute APL directly in hardware are not far off. The price performance of APL on such machines will be quite competitive with FORTRAN usage.

But an even more important aspect of APL's value is in the self-programming of "individual" systems. Manufacturers generally provide large, prepackaged systems having a variety of capabilities that require extensive overhead to maintain and rarely are precisely what is needed for a particular task. Most importantly, their use generally does not result in striking enhancement of an organization's ability to improve or generalize their data-processing etiquette. Use of APL seems to lead quite naturally to the development of systems individually conceived and created precisely for the purpose of enhancing an individual's ability to perform his data-processing jobs.

Although APL was developed at IBM, it is available on a number of machines of competing manufacturers. Indeed, it is the language closest in spirit to the machine language of the CDC STAR, the fastest commercial computer yet built.

Assembly Language

No catalogue of programming languages would be complete without a few words on machine assembly languages. Every computer has an assembly language—and they vary among makes of machines. The basic purpose of assembly language is to provide help in the creation of programs in machine code. When a new computer is designed, the first language associated with it is its assembly language. Assembly languages mainly make it possible for the programmer to use all the capabilities of the computer as effectively as possible while not requiring him to fix parameters of his program that do not affect its efficiency or correctness, such as location in memory of his program and data.

Almost all high-level language processors are written in assembly language. Almost all operating system programming is done in assembly language. Though most users never program in assembly language, it is bad practice to permit an organization to support a computer without possessing some capability for assembly language programming. Sooner or later a correction or alteration of existing programs requires it.

REFERENCES

Some excellent texts are available on the general subject of "mechanical" languages, of which programming languages like Algol60 and APL are examples. At an intermediate level the book

> Peter Wegner, *Programming Languages, Information Structures, and Machine Organization* (McGraw-Hill, New York, N. Y., 1968)

gives a reasonable survey. However,

> J. Hopcraft and J. Ullman, *Formal Languages and Their Relation to Automata* (Addison-Wesley, Reading, Mass., 1969)

is the standard reference text in the field.

Numerous texts describe Algol60. An excellent elementary text is

> T. Ekman and C. Froberg, *Introduction to Algol Programming* (Student Litteratur, Lund, Sweden, 1965).

An excellent description of the details of a program for translating Algol60 into machine code is provided in the excellent book

> B. Randell and D. Russell, *Algol60 Implementation* (Academic Press, New York, N. Y., 1964),

while the book

> D. Gries, *Compiler Construction for Digital Computers* (John Wiley, New York, N. Y., 1971)

provides an overview of the general problems associated with the building of translators. The *Communications of the ACM* publishes in each issue noteworthy algorithms in Algol60 and FORTRAN. For the serious student a study of some of these algorithms would nicely round off the material presented in this chapter. In any case, a scan of the list of algorithm titles will give the student a good sample of the range of computer applications in which Algol60 and FORTRAN are used.

So many texts are available on FORTRAN and its applications that it is hazardous to single out one for the additional attention of the student. However, the text

> P. Cress, P. Dirkser, and J. Graham, *FORTRAN IV with WATFOR and WATFIV* (Prentice-Hall, Englewood Cliffs, N. J., 1970)

on a dialect of FORTRAN is well written and covers most of the important issues of the language.

At this writing there are only a few books available on APL. Three exist that in their own way are excellent. No serious student of APL should be without the superb text

> K. Iverson, *A Programming Language* (John Wiley, New York, N. Y., 1962),

the standard reference work on APL. The paperback book

> S. Pakin, *APL/360 Reference Manual* (Science Research Associates, Chicago, Ill., 1968)

is a handy and inexpensive compendium on one particular, and the standard, APL computer implementation. An excellent APL primer is

> L. Gilman and A. Rose, *APL/360, An Interactive Approach* (John Wiley, New York, N. Y., 1970).

The various computer implementations of APL have operating manuals that also contain illustrative material on the language.

COBOL is adequately treated in

> N. Stern and R. Stern, *COBOL Programming* (John Wiley, New York, N. Y., 1970).

BASIC is a widely used language, and many texts describing it are available. Two excellent ones are

> J. Kemeny and T. Kurtz, *BASIC Programming* (John Wiley, New York, N. Y., 1971),

written by the creators of BASIC, and

> J. Gross and W. Brainard, *Fundamental Programming Concepts* (Harper & Row, New York, N. Y., 1972),

a book that treats both BASIC and topics in programming. PL/I is well treated in the text

> R. Sprowls, *Introduction to PL/I Programming* (Harper & Row, New York, N. Y., 1969).

A simplified version of PL/I developed at Cornell University (PL/C) is treated in the text by Conway and Gries, cited in the references for Chapter 1.

Algol68 is a complex language, and the reader could do no better than to study the nicely written and organized

> C. Lindsey and S. Van der Meulen, *Informal Introduction to Algol68* (North-Holland, Amsterdam, Netherlands, 1971)

so as to appreciate this "zenith" of programming language creation.

SNOBOL was created at Bell Laboratories, and the best text or the language is by people from Bell:

> R. Griswold, J. Poage, and I. Polonsky, *The SNOBOL4 Programming Language* (Prentice-Hall, Englewood Cliffs, N. J., 1971).

LISP can be quickly appreciated from a reading of

> W. Maurer, *The Programmer's Introduction to LISP* (American Elsevier, New York, N. Y., 1972).

Miss Jean Sammett has laboriously collected many of the numerous books and journal articles on programming languages:

> J. Sammett, *Programming Languages—History and Fundamentals* (Prentice Hall, Englewood Cliffs, N. J., 1969),

and her bibliography is a good departure point for a literature search.

A view of the programming process can be seen in

> B. Galler and A. Perlis, *A View of Programming Languages* (Addison-Wesley, Cambridge, Mass., 1970).

PROBLEMS

Algol60

1. The following Algol60 program is to be used in answering the questions below.

```
begin integer k,n,f,g; integer array B,C [1:4];
procedure MM (U,V,Z); integer array U,V; integer Z;
for Z := Z step - 1 until 1 do V [Z] :=U[Z] + V [Z];
integer procedure SS(n); value n; integer n;
SS := if n=1 then 1 else n+ SS (n-1);
for k := i, k+1 while k < 5 do begin
B[k] := k -1; C[k] := 2 × k end of for statement;
begin L1: n := 4;
L2: f := 2 × n/3;
L3: MM(B,C,n);
L4: g:= SS(f) end; L5; f := B[1] end of problem
```

Now answer the following questions. In questions 1 and 4 to 10, if the value cited is false, supply the correct value.

		TRUE	FALSE	COR- RECT VALUE
1.	At statement labeled L1 the value of $C[3]$ is 4.			
2.	Z is called by value in procedure MM.			
3.	n is a global variable in procedure SS.			
4.	The value of n immediately after statement L3 is executed is 1.			
5.	The value of n immediately after statement L4 is executed is 1.			
6.	At statement L1 the value of $B[1]$ is 1.			
7.	The value of $B[3]$ immediately after statement L3 is executed is 8.			
8.	The value of f immediately after statement L4 is executed is 1.			
9.	Immediately after statement L4, the value of g is 3.			
10.	Immediately before "end of problem" the value of f is 0.			

2. Below is a list of seven code pieces. Match each of the code pieces with one of the functions in the list following the code pieces.

Example:

```
ans := 0;
for l := 1 step 1 until n do      matches 6
ans := ans+1;
```

In the code pieces assume that

i, j, k, l, m, n are integers
r, s, t, y, z, ans. sum, term are real
A, B, C are real matrices of dimension $[1:n, 1:n]$
V is a real vector of dimension $[1:n]$

CODE PIECES

```
1.  for i := 1 step 1 until n-1 do
    for j := 1 step 1 until n do
    if V [i] < V [j] then begin
    t := V[i]; V[i] := V[j]; V[j] := t end;
2.  ans. := 0;
    for i := n step -1 until 0 do
    ans := ans × y + V[i];
3.  for i := 1 step 1 until n do
    for j := -1 step 1 until n do begin
    C[i,j] := 0;
    for k := 1 step 1 until n do
    C[i,j] :=C[i,j] + A[i,k] × B[k,j] end;
4.  real procedure sum (y,m,n,t); value m,n; real y,t;
    integer m,n;
    begin real r;
    r := 0;
    for y := m step 1 until n do r:= r+t;
    sum := r end;
    ans := sum (y,i,n,y↑2);
5.  term := y;
    sum := y;
    rrr := y↑2;
    for i := 3 step 2 until n do begin
    term :=-term × r/(i × (i-1));
    sum := sum+term end;
6.  ans := m;
    for k:= n÷m while n ≠ m × k do begin
    ans := n - m × k;
    n := m;
    m := ans end;
7.  real procedure H (J,k); value J,k; integer J,k;
    H := if J > k then 0 else J+H (J+1,k);
    ans := H(m,n);
```

FUNCTIONS

1. The greatest common divisor of two numbers by the Euclidean algorithm.

2. Evaluation of a polynomial of the form $\sum\limits_{k=0}^{k=n} a_k y^k$.

3. Matrix multiplication $C_{m \times n} = A_{m \times p} \times B_{p \times n}$ where the general element in C is

$$C_{i,j} = \sum_{k=1}^{k=p} A_{i,k} \times B_{k,j}$$

4. Sort a vector V into ascending order, i.e.,

$$v_i \leq v_{i+1}, \quad \text{for } i = 1, 2, \ldots, n-1$$

where the v_i are the components of V.

5. Sort a vector V into descending order, i.e.,

$$v_i \geq v_{i+1}, \quad \text{for } i = 1, 2, \ldots, n-1$$

6. Sum of the first n integers:

$$\sum_{i=1}^{n} i = \frac{n(n+1)}{2}$$

7. Sum of the first n squares:

$$\sum_{i=1}^{n} i^2$$

8.
$$\sum_{i=m}^{n} i = \sum_{i=1}^{n} i - \sum_{i=1}^{m-1} i \quad \text{if } n \geq m$$
$$= 0 \quad \text{if } n < m$$

9.
$$e^y \simeq 1 + y + \frac{y^2}{2!} + \frac{y^3}{3!} + \sum_{i=4}^{n} \frac{y^i}{i!}$$

10.
$$\sin(y) \simeq y - \frac{y^3}{3!} + \frac{y^5}{5!} - \frac{y^7}{7!} + \sum_{i=5}^{n} \frac{(-1)^{i-1} y^{2i-1}}{(2i-1)!}$$

11.
$$\ln(y) \simeq y - 1 - \frac{(y-1)^2}{2} + \frac{(y-1)^3}{3}$$
$$+ \sum_{i=4}^{n} \frac{(-1)^{i-1}(y-1)^i}{i}$$

12.

$$\cos{(y)} \simeq 1 - \frac{y^2}{2!} + \frac{y^4}{4!} - \frac{y^6}{6!} + \sum_{i=4}^{n} \frac{(-1)^{i-1} y^{2i}}{(2i)!}$$

3. Suppose two *real arrays* $A[1:10]$ and $B[1:15]$ each contain values that are arranged in ascending order, i.e.,

$$A[1] \leq A[2] \leq \cdots \leq A[10]$$
and $\quad B[1] \leq B[2] \leq \cdots \leq B[15]$

The following is a flowchart of a program that "merges" the contents of A and B into a *real array* $C[1:25]$, so that C contains all the values contained in A and B in such a way that C is also arranged in ascending order, i.e.,

$$C[1] \leq C[2] \leq \cdots \leq C[25]$$

Fill in the empty flowchart boxes. Do not add or delete any box or line.

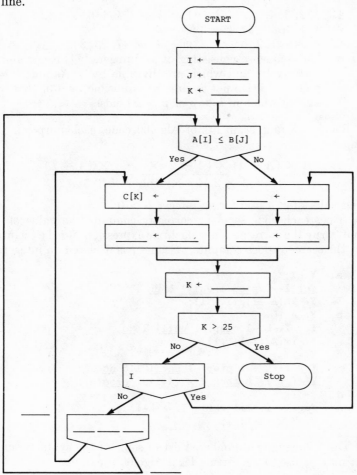

4. In the six parts given below fill in the blank in the <u>for</u> statement,

<u>for</u> i := _____ <u>do</u> print (i);

that would cause print (i) to print the successive values shown; print (i) is a specified procedure that prints the value of i. Note that ". . ." and "," in the sequences are not printed but stand for the values in the sequences not written on this page and a separator, used here for clarity, respectively. Also, the expressions in m and k are not printed, but their (integer) values are. The m, p, and k are Algol60 integer variables.

1. 1, 2, 4, 8, . . . , 2.
2. 1, 4, 256, . . . , $(2^m)^{2^m}$.
3. 1, 3, 5, . . . , $2m + 1$, $2m$, $2m - 2$, . . . , 0.

In No. 4, below, use only one for list element.

4. 1, 2, 3, 4, . . . , $k - 1$, k, $k + 2$, $k + 6$, . . . , $k + 3(n - 1)$, $k + 3n$.
5. 47, 16, 1, 2, 3, . . . , $m - 1$, m, 17, 23, 23.
6. The sequence consisting of all integers between k and p, inclusively, and which are divisible by 3. Assume $k \neq p$ and $k \div 3$. Do not assume p is divisible by 3 or that it is known which of $k > p$ or $p > k$ holds.

5. Below are four segments of Algol60 code, each purporting to compute

$$Y = \frac{A \times (A + 1) \times (A + 2) \times \cdots \times (A + L)}{1 \times 2 \times 3 \times \cdots \times L}$$

given values for A and for an integer $L > 0$.

Does each code segment correctly compute the value of Y? If not, write the corresponding algebraic expressions for the quantity that the segment does compute. Assume I is declared an integer.

```
a.  Y←1;
    for I←0 step 1 until L do
    Y←Y×(A +I)/(I + 1);
b.  Y←A +L;
    for I←L −1 step −1 until 1 do
    Y←Y×(A/(I+1) +1);
c.  Y←1;
    for I←L + 1 step −1 until 1.5 do
    Y←(if I≤L then Y × (A+I)/I else A);
d.  Y←1;
    for I←1, I+1 while I < L+1 do
    Y←Y × (A+I)/I;
```

6. The following is a numbered list of some of the syntactic units that may be used to construct legal Algol60 programs.

1. Number	6. For List Element
2. Label	7. Boolean Expression
3. For List	8. Arithmetic Expression
4. Boolean Simple Variable	9. Real Subscripted Variable
5. Arithmetic Assignment Statement	10. Compound Statement

In this problem a syntactic unit "may legally occur" in an Algol60 statement only if every specific example of that unit may legally occur there. In each of the underlined spaces below place the numbers of all syntactic units that may legally occur in that underlined space. See the example.

Place as many (correct!) numbers in each underlined space as possible; there always exists at least one correct number. The following declarations are to be assumed:

real A; real array $Q[1:100]$; integer I;

Example: A ← 1, 5, 8, 9;

a. _____ ← A;

b. for A ← 3 step _____ until I + 2 do _____ ;

c. if _____ , then _____ else A ← A + 2;

d. if A < _____ then goto _____ ;

e. for I ← _____ step 7 until A, _____
     while _____ do Q[I] ← 0;

f. for I ← _____ do Q[I] ← A + 1;

g. Q[_____] ← A ↑ I;

7. Consider the following Algol60 block for which X and Y are global integers:

```
begin integer Z, I;
for I := X - Y step 1 until X + Y do
if I < 2 then Z := X +I
else L : if X + Y < 3 + I then goto L;
end
```

Consider the following three propositions about the block:

A. The for statement body is executed precisely once.
B. The last value of Z will satisfy $-1 < Z \leq X + 3$.
C. The block cycles indefinitely by executing the statement goto L.

Give values of X and Y that on block entry would guarantee that

1. A is true, B is true, C is false.
2. A is false, B is true, C is true.
3. A is false, B is true, C is false.

8. The following are independent Algol60 programs. Each has some syntax errors. Locate and give a brief explanation of each error. You may assume that it is not a syntax error if a variable is used before it is given a value.

a. ```
    begin
    integer K, N; real Q, R, S, T, U, etc.
    Boolean YES, NO, T, P;
    X := 3 + N × N;
    LOOP: if Q > 10 then
    N := N + 1 and Q := Q + P;
    else goto NEXT;
    goto LOOP;
    end;
    ```
b.  ```
    begin
    integer A, BC, D, E, F, G, H, I;
    real array LIST [-5,10];
    Boolean STOP, go;
    for I := -2 step - 6 until 100 do:
    D[I] := LIST [I] + 10.6;
    go := true;
    if A GTR 7 then F = 6;
    ```
c. ```
    integer H, W, HABIT;
    Boolean MAYBE, true, false;
    integer array MORE, M[-6 : 12];
    MORE := 77.3 × SIGN (-17.82);
    M [-2] = H ** 2 $
    HABIT := 4 W $
    end;
    ```

**9.** The following are independent Algol60 programs. Each has syntax errors. Identify and give a brief explanation of each error. You may assume that it is not a syntax error if a variable is used before it is given a value.

a.  ```
    begin
    integer ALPHA, BP[i:10];
    real A, B, C, D, E, etc.;
    G := 3 + C;
    if C := 10 then D := D + 1;
    end;
    ```
b. ```
    begin
    Boolean YES, NO, T;
    integer I, J; real S, T, U, V, W, X, Y, Z;
    LAST: J := 10.3;
    for I := 3 step 2 × I until 15 do:
    if YES then X[2] := T-1 and Y := Z + 12;
    for J := -5 step -6 until 10 do
    if J LSS 5 then goto LOOP;
    else goto LAST;
    ```
c.  ```
    real R, 3.14;
    integer A, else, B;
    real array SKIP [-3 : 10], HERE [105 : 600];
    R := 17$
    else := SKIP [6.5] + SIGN [3.14);
    B = -77 + A ** 11;
    SKIP = 8; HERE (3) := 3R;
    end;
    ```

10. The Teach problem (TEACH 2) is as follows. Given 6 signed integers $A[1]$, $A[2]$, . . . , $A[6]$. Find, as the value of Q, the number of sign changes of the forms $+ - +$, and, as the value of P, the number of sign changes of the form $- + -$ in passing through all the numbers from $A[1]$ to $A[6]$.

Example: -3, 5, -1, 2, -4, -5 would give $Q = 1$ and $P = 2$.

The procedure TEACH 2 delivers a new set of data as values to A, P, and Q each time it is called. In this problem a fifth request causes the student's program to terminate.

A student (student number 101) submitted the following TEACH solution:

```
begin integer array A[1:6]; integer P, Q, I;
SY LIBRARY TEACH 2; Comment this Statement, not a part
of Algol60, appends TEACH 2 to the student's program as
though he had included it in his program as an
independent procedure;
L: TEACH 2 (101, A, P, Q); P := Q := 0;
for I := 1 step 1 until 3 do
if A[I] > 0 then begin
if A [I+1] < 0 then begin
if A [I+2] > 0 then begin Q := Q+1:
if A [I+3] < 0 then begin P:=P+1 end end
end;
goto L end;
```

Of four data sets supplied, the program failed on data sets 2 and 4. The student changed the program by altering the for clause to:

```
for I := 1 step 1 until 4 do
```

Now the program failed only on data set 2. The student now changed the program to:

```
begin integer array A[1:6]; integer P, Q, I;
SY LIBRARY TEACH 2;
L: TEACH 2 (101, A,P,Q); P := Q := 0;
for I := 1 step 2 until 3 do
if A[I] > 0 then begin
if A [I+1] < 0 then begin
if A [I+2] > 0 then begin Q := Q+1;
if A[I+3] < 0 then P := P+1 end end end
else if A[I] < 0 then begin
if A [I+1] > 0 then begin
if A [I+2] < 0 then begin P := P+1;
if A [I+3] > 0 then Q := Q+1 end end
end;
goto L end
```

The program then ran correctly on all but data set 4.

a. What are four data sets that would behave this way? You may give a data set as a sequence of 6 + and − signs; for example, $+++-+-$ would mean $A[1] > 0$, $A[2] > 0$, $A[3] > 0$, $A[4] < 0$, $A[5] > 0$, $A[6] < 0$.

b. Write a Teach procedure that is correct for any data set.

11. A mathematics professor got lost while walking in the woods one day. When he realized his predicament, he sat down by the nearest tree and decided upon the following algorithm for finding his way to one of the two roads which traversed the woods.

1. He would walk in straight lines from tree to tree until he found one of the roads. The woods were so dense that he would be able to see the road only when he was very close to it.

2. He had a piece of chalk in his pocket (of course). He would place a chalk mark on each tree he reached, so as not to walk in a circle. This chalk mark could be seen from any direction.

3. Starting at the tree where he was sitting, and at each tree he reached, he would:
   a. put a chalk mark on the tree, and then
   b. look around and decide which unmarked tree was closest to his position; then he would walk in a straight line to this tree. If, however, a road came closer to him than any tree, then he would walk directly to the road at its nearest point.

4. In deciding upon the nearest tree the professor could only be sure of distances with an accuracy of 1%. That is, if the distances of two trees differed by less than 1% of the larger of the two distances, then he judged them to be at equal distances. If it turned out that there was more than one tree at the closest distance (within the 1% error), he would decide among them by the following rule: he would take the one whose direction was most nearly north. He knew where north was from the position of the sun. If two happened to make exactly equal angles with north, he would take the more easterly one (since he was right-handed).

Our professor was lost in a forest of ideal trees with perfectly straight and infinitely slender trunks, all perfectly perpendicular to a plane surface. He was ideal, too, with negligible dimensions.

Assume a forest of N distinct trees whose (X, Y) coordinates relative to a fixed Cartesian coordinate system are given by elements $X[1:N]$ and $Y[1:N]$ of the real arrays X and Y. The professor is at tree T, with coordinates $(X[T], Y[T])$.

Write an Algol60 program to follow the professor's complete path from tree $(X[S], Y[S])$ where he starts until he reaches one of the roads. Assume the roads run north-south and east-west, with coordinates given by $X = 0$ and $Y = 0$, respectively. Given X, Y, S, and N, compute the following:

1. The integer NUMBER, the number of trees reached by the professor, not counting the tree where he starts,
2. The contents of an integer array PATH whose successive elements are the subscripts of the trees which the professor reaches, in the order in which he reaches them. That is, he walks from

   ```
   (X[S], Y[S]) to (X[PATH[1]], Y[PATH[1]])
   to (X[PATH[2]], Y[PATH[2]]), etc.;
   ```

   and finally to (X[PATH[NUMBER]], Y[PATH[NUMBER]]).
3. A real variable DISTANCE, the total distance he walks to reach a road.

12. A PROBLEM IN NUTRITION. This is both a problem and a lesson. We shall first learn and then program.

a. The equation $ax + by = c$ is a straight line in the plane. The values of (x, y) that satisfy the linear inequality $ax + by \geq c$ are called a half-plane. Why? Look at $3x + 4y \geq 12$. If two points are in the half-plane, so are all the points on the line segment joining them. This property is the property of *convexity;* a half-plane is convex. Suppose we have a number of such inequalities (note the change in notation because we are dealing with a number of such inequalities):

$$a_{11}x + a_{12}y \geq b_1$$
$$a_{21}x + a_{22}y \geq b_2$$
$$a_{31}x + a_{32}y \geq b_3$$

The values of (x, y) that satisfy each equation are *half-planes.* The values of (x, y) common to all the half-planes is called the *solution set* of the inequalities. The solution set is also convex; the intersection (the points in common) of a finite number of convex sets is also convex. Because the inequalities include equality, we say the half-planes are *closed.* The set of points common to all the closed half-planes is called a *polyhedral convex set.* The values (x, y) that satisfy the equality $ax + by = c$ are called the *bounding line* of the half-plane $ax + by \geq c$. The points lying on two bounding lines are called the extreme points of the polyhedral convex set.

Example:

$$2x + y \geq -9 \qquad \text{(L1)}$$
$$-x + 3y \geq -3 \qquad \text{(L2)}$$
$$-x - 2y \geq -3 \qquad \text{(L3)}$$

A sketch of the convex polyhedron showing the three extreme points is shown.

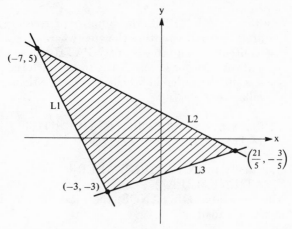

Given three equations in two variables, there are

$$\binom{3}{2} = \frac{3!}{2!(3-2)!} = 3 \text{ pairs of equations}$$

The solutions to these three equations are the extreme points. In this case they are $(-3, -3)$, $(-7, -5)$, and $(21/5, -3/5)$.

b. Suppose we are given a set of linear inequalities and a linear function $F = gx + hy + t$, where g, h, t are given constants. An important problem is to find the minimum (maximum) value that F can have when x and y range over a polyhedral convex set. It turns out that the minimum (and, for that matter, the maximum) value of F is taken on at (at least) one of the extreme points of the bounded polyhedral convex set.

If we wished to find the minimum of $F = 7x + 4y$ on the polyhedral convex set bounded by the lines indicated in the example given, it would be at one or more of the extreme points $(-7, 5)$, $(-3, -3)$, $(21/5, -3/5)$. Indeed, at these three points F is -29, -33, 27, respectively. Hence F is a minimum at $(-3, -3)$.

c. Now let us wander into higher dimensions. Instead of x and y as the coordinates of a point in the plane, let us use $x_1, x_2, \ldots, x_M$. Every point in M-space is said to have M coordinates. Our bounding lines are now called hyperplanes, and the inequalities are now

$$a_{11}x_1 + a_{12}x_2 + \cdots + a_{1M}x_M \geq b_1$$
$$a_{21}x_1 + a_{22}x_2 + \cdots + a_{2M}x_M \geq b_2$$
$$\cdots$$
$$a_{N1}x_1 + a_{N2}x_2 + \cdots + a_{NM}x_M \geq b_N$$

Generally $N \geq M$. These inequalities are often called "constraints."

The convex polyhedron is now a set of points in M-space. The function F is now of the form

$$F = g_1x_1 + g_2x_2 + \cdots + g_Mx_M + t \text{ (surprise!)}$$

and its minimum is taken on at (at least) one of the extreme points of the convex polyhedron. In the case of the N inequalities there are at most $\binom{N}{M}$ extreme points that are obtained by solving $\binom{N}{M}$ sets of M linear equations in M unknowns.

d. How can we solve M linear equations in M unknowns? We shall do it by example for three equations in three unknowns, and you can generalize it to arbitrary M. We use two facts: First, take any equation and multiply both sides by a nonzero constant; the new equation and the other two unchanged ones have the same solution as the original set of three. Second, take any equation and add to it one of the other equations; the equation so obtained and two of the others have the same solution as the original set.

Given now the three equations,

$$(A) \quad a_{11}x_1 + a_{12}x_2 + a_{13}x_3 = b_1$$
$$(B) \quad a_{21}x_1 + a_{22}x_2 + a_{23}x_3 = b_2$$
$$(C) \quad a_{31}x_1 + a_{32}x_2 + a_{33}x_3 = b_3$$

answer the following questions.

a. What do I multiply equation (A) by and equation (B) by, so that, when I form a new B as $B = sA + rB$, the resulting co-efficient of x_1 is zero?

b. Then what do I multiply equation (A) by and (C) by, so that, when I form a new C as $C = sA + rC$, the resulting coefficient of x_1 is zero?

Now note that in the new set of equations x_1 appears only in equation (A), since its coefficient is zero in B and C. The new set has the same solution as the original set.

c. How do we continue this approach so that x_2 also has a zero coefficient in equation (C)?

d. Then in how many equations does x_3 appear by itself? Do we not now know x_3?

e. If we know x_3, do we not know x_2, from equation (B), etc.?

Example:

$$2x_1 + x_2 - x_3 = -4$$
$$x_1 - 2x_2 + 2x_3 = 3$$
$$-x_1 - x_2 + 2x_3 = 7$$
$$2x_1 + x_2 - x_3 = -4$$
$$0x_1 + 5x_2 - 5x_3 = 10, \qquad s = 1, \quad r = -2$$
$$0x_1 - x_2 + 3x_3 = 10, \qquad s = 1, \quad r = 2$$

$$5x_2 - 5x_3 = -10$$
$$0x_2 + 10x_3 = 40, \qquad s = 1, \quad r = 0.5$$

$$10x_3 = 40 \quad \text{or} \quad x_3 = 4$$
$$5x_2 = -10 + 5x_3 = 10 \quad \text{or} \quad x_2 = 2$$
$$2x_1 = -4 - x_2 + x_3$$
$$= -4 - 2 + 4 \quad \text{or} \quad x_1 = -1$$

f. How do we generalize this process to the case of M equations in M unknowns?

Now we are ready to state the problem. There are N vitamins $V_1, V_2, \ldots, V_N$ and M foods $F_1, F_2, \ldots, F_M$, where $M \leq N$. A nutritionist must supply at least C_i units of vitamin V_i from the foods $F_1, \ldots, F_M$. Hence, if x_i is the amount of food F_i supplied (in pounds) and a_{ij} represents the number of units of vitamin V_i in a pound of F_j, then

$$a_{i1}x_1 + a_{i2}x_2 + a_{i3}x_3 + \cdots$$
$$+ a_{iM}x_M \geq C_i, \qquad i = 1, 2, \ldots, N$$

Furthermore, the cost of food F_i is u_i cents per pound. What amounts of food satisfy the vitamin requirement at least cost? The cost equation is

$$\text{cost} = u_1 x_1 + \cdots + u_M x_M$$

You are given a real array $A[1:5, 1:6]$ that will contain the coefficients of the set of constraint equations. N and M will also be given values, such that $1 \leq M \leq N \leq 5$. The cost function will be specified in a real array COST[1:5].

Your program should produce values for the following variables:

    a. P, the number of different solutions for the problem: the number of different sets of amounts of food that satisfy the vitamin requirement at least cost.

    b.   The array $FA[1:P, 1:M]$, whose ith row contains the amounts of each of the foods that satisfy the vitamin requirement for the ith such solution.

13.   You are given the following block:

```
begin integer i, k, j, z; boolean b; real y;
integer procedure upper (r); integer r;
begin real s; s := r + 2;
if s = entier (s/10) × 10 then
s := s/(r+1) else r/s;
upper := s end;
b := true;
k := 10;
y := 0;
for i := 2 × k - 1 step 2 until 2↑(2 × k) + 1 do
begin
y := y + sin (k) × cos (i-k); z := 0;
for j := 1 step 1 until 10 do
if b then z := z + j else z := upper (j+2) +z;
y := y +z; y := y + upper (i+2) end end;
```

The following table gives the time required for a real Algol60 compiler to execute basic Algol60 commands. If a command is not in the table, it takes negligible time.

ALGORITHMIC ENTITY	EXAMPLE	EXECUTION TIME, MSEC
Addition	$a + b$	0.12
Multiplication	$a \times b$	0.18
Division	a/b	0.21
Square	$a \uparrow 2$	0.18
Or	$a \vee b$	0.4
Power, Integer Exponent	$a \uparrow k$	
$\quad |k|$ (exponent) $= 1$		3.8
$\quad \leq 10$		5.5
$\quad \leq 100$		8.0
$\quad \leq 1,000$		10.0
$\quad \leq 10,000$		12.0
$\quad \leq 100,000$		14.0
$\quad \leq 1,000,000$		16.0

Step until element, constant
   Step and simple upper limit,
   step 1 until n each loop   0.6
Step until element, constant
   Step and variable upper, step 1 until f 0.6
   Limit, each loop $+$ time (f)
Block with simple variables, begin real a; end   1.4
Reference to formal parameter Called by name
Actual parameter:
   Simple   0.4
   Expression   3.2
Call of declared procedure having an empty procedure body
   No parameter P 3.8
   1 parameter $Q(a)$;   4.7
   2 parameters $R(a, b)$;   5.2
Call of standard procedure
   cos   cos (x) 6.0
   exp   exp (x) 5.8
   ln   ln (x) 5.6
   sin   sin (x) 5.8

Write an Algol block that computes the time required by the above-given block.

Estimate the time required (the nearest few milliseconds) for the execution of the given block.

Is it possible to reduce the time:

1. By 25%? How?
2. By 50%? How?
3. By more? How?

APL Exercises

The intricacies of a programming language such as APL are mastered through exercises. Write APL expressions to compute the following.

1. The first $N + 1$ terms of the McLaurin expansions for:

    a. e^x
    b. $\ln(1 + x)$
    c. $1/(1 - x)$

2. A diagonal array with $^-3$ on the diagonal.

3. An array of at least 3 diagonals with 1 on the first subdiagonal and superdiagonal and 2 along the diagonal.

4. Given two alphanumeric vectors S and T, determine whether S occurs in T (that is, produce a 1 if it does, and 0 if it does not).

5. Given two numeric vectors X and Y, determine whether they contain the same elements, except possibly as to order.

6. Given two alphanumeric vectors S and T, determine whether S contains only characters contained in T.

7. Rearrange the vector S, containing only alphabetic characters, so that its characters occur in alphabetic order.

8. From the character vector S remove all blanks.

9. A numeric vector X is in ascending sorted order. Find its median (the scalar in the middle, if ρX is odd, or the arithmetic mean of the two middle numbers, if ρX is even).

10. Insert the character "*" between each pair of adjacent elements of the vector X.

11. Find the second forward difference U of a vector X, defined as:

$$U_i = X_{i+2} - 2X_{i+1} + X_i \quad \text{for } i = 1, 2, \ldots, (\rho X) - 2$$

and

$$\rho U \text{ is } (\rho X) - 2$$

12. Given two vectors S and T, each with no duplicates, obtain the vector that contains:

    a.   All the elements of S and T with no duplicates.
    b.   All the elements common to both S and T with no duplicates.
    c.   All the elements in S but not in T.

13. Given a numeric integer literal of at most ten digits, create the number that it represents.

14. Find the longest consecutive string of nonblank characters in the alphanumeric vector X.

15. Concatenate a column to the right of a matrix X.

16. Concatenate a row to the bottom of a matrix X.

17. Construct a 5×5 matrix whose elements are random integers in the range 0 to 50.

18. Make an array whose two columns are the vectors X and Y. Assume $(\rho X) = \rho Y$.

19. Produce an array of three columns listing K, $!K$, and the number of factors of K for all integers $1 \le K \le N$.

20. Given an integer N and an array X, produce an array Y such that Y is an N-fold expansion of X. For example:

$$X \underline{\text{ is }} 1\ 3\ 2 \quad \text{and} \quad N \underline{\text{ is }} 2. \text{ Then}$$

$$
\begin{array}{l}
\quad\quad 4\ 6\ 8 \\
\quad\ 1\ 1\ 3\ 3\ 2\ 2 \\
\quad\ 1\ 1\ 3\ 3\ 2\ 2 \\
Y \underline{\text{ is }} 4\ 4\ 6\ 6\ 8\ 8 \\
\quad\ 4\ 4\ 6\ 6\ 8\ 8
\end{array}
$$

21. Define an APL function of two parameters X and Y whose value is the number of occurrences of the character X in the character vector Y.

22. Define an APL function of two parameters X and Y whose value is the "tail" of Y determined by X. X is a vector of 1s and 0s and, if

$$X = \underbrace{11 \ldots 100}_{k} \ldots 0$$

then the value is the last k elements of Y. If $k = 0$, the value is the empty vector. Assume $(\rho X) = \rho Y$.

23. In this problem A always refers to a square array of rank 2. You may assume ρA is (n, n).

a. Write expressions that evaluate to 1 if the following are true statements about A, or to 0 if they are false.

1. The value of the inner product of row k with row j is 0 for $k \ne j$ and 1 for $k = j$, where $k, j = 1, 2, \ldots, n$.

2. Tridiagonal, i.e., elements of A satisfy

$$a_{ij} = 0 \quad \text{for} \quad |i - j| > 1, \quad i, j = 1, 2, \ldots, n$$

3. Is symmetric, i.e.,

$$a_{ij} = a_{ji} \quad \text{for all} \quad i, j = 1, 2, \ldots, n$$

b. Write expressions that generate A such that every element of A is 0 except for:

1. 1 in each last column position, i.e.,

$$a_{in} = 1, \quad i = 1, 2, \ldots, n$$

2. 1 along the main diagonal, i.e.,

$$a_{ii} = 1, \quad i = 1, 2, \ldots, n$$

3. 2 along the 3 main diagonals, i.e.,

$$a_{ij} = 2, \quad i, j = 1, 2, \ldots, n \quad \text{and} \quad |i - j| \le 1$$

24. What do the following APL expressions compute?

a. $(2 = +/[1]0=(\iota N)\circ.|\iota N)/\iota N$
   $N>0$

b. $(+/X)\div\rho X$
   X is a nonempty vector.

c. $(((R\iota R)\iota\iota\rho R)\le\rho R)/R\leftarrow/(R=\lceil/R\leftarrow+/X\circ.=X)/X$
   X is a nonempty vector of positive integers.

25. Using "ρ" and "ι," construct an array of shape $n\ n$ that is a circulant:

$$A \text{ is } \begin{array}{l} 1\ 2\ \ldots\ n \\ 2\ 3\ \ldots\ n+1 \\ \ldots \\ n\ n+1\ \ldots\ 2n-1 \end{array}$$

26. Given a numerical array A whose shape is $m\ n$, left-justify its rows; that is, rotate to the left each row so that an element in the first column is only 0 if every element in its row is 0.

27. Compute the mode of a vector X. The mode is a vector, each of whose elements occurs the greatest number of times in X.

28. Given an array A, of arbitrary shape, construct an array B, each of whose rows is a subscript of A, and whose rows are ordered in the order in which A is raveled. Thus,

```
if ρA is 2 1 2.

          1 1 1
          1 1 2
  B is 2  1 1
       2  1 2
```

29. Given an array A, ρA is n n, which is zero above the diagonal, create the ravel of the lower triangular part.

30. Given an array A, ρA is n n, whose lower triangular part contains only 0 and 1, create two vectors X and Y that contain the corresponding row and column indices of the elements whose values are 1.

31. Calculate the area of a triangle by Hero's formula, given below in conventional notation:

$$\text{Area} = \sqrt{S(S-A)(S-B)(S-C)}$$

A, B, and C are the sides of the triangle, while S is the semiperimeter. In your algorithm use L as the vector whose components are the sides of the triangle.

32. The geometric mean of a set of n positive numbers X is the nth root of their product. Write an APL expression to calculate this for X is 1 7 4 2.5 51 19.

33. The Gregorian calendar provides that all years from 1582 to about 20,000 that are divisible by 4 are leap years, with the provisos

that of the centesimal years (1600, 1700, etc.) only those divisible
by 400 are leap years, and of the millenial years, those divisible by
4000 are not. Write a one-line APL expression to determine whether
a given year Y is a leap year.

34. January 1 falls on Thursday (the fifth day of the week) in
1970. Determine the day of the week on which January 1 falls in
any given year Y. For simplicity assume that any year divisible
by 4 is a leap year.

35. Construct an APL expression that will determine whether or
not the first N significant figures of two whole numbers X and Y
are identical.

36. Write an APL expression that rounds numbers down if the decimal part is less than .5 and up if greater than .5. For numbers end-
ing in .5, your expression should round to the nearest even integer.

37. Construct each of the following sequences:

$$1 \ {}^-1 \ 2 \ {}^-2 \ 3 \ {}^-3 \ \ldots \ K \ {}^-K$$
$$1 \ 2 \ 1 \ 2 \ 3 \ 1 \ 2 \ 3 \ 4 \ \ldots \ 1 \ 2 \ 3 \ \ldots \ K$$
$$1 \ 2 \ 2 \ 3 \ 3 \ 3 \ 4 \ 4 \ 4 \ 4 \ \ldots \ K \ K \ \ldots \ K$$
$$1 \ 0 \ 2 \ 0 \ 0 \ 3 \ 0 \ 0 \ 0 \ 4 \ \ldots \ K \ 0 \ 0 \ \ldots \ 0$$

38. Write functions that would approximate each of the following
series to N terms:

$$1 - \frac{1}{2} + \frac{1}{3} - \frac{1}{4} + \cdots + (-1)^{N-1}/N$$

$$\frac{1}{0!} + \frac{2}{1!} + \frac{4}{2!} + \frac{8}{3!} + \cdots + 2^{N-1}/(N-1)!$$

39. Select 100 random positive integers none of which is greater
than 10.

40. Make the scalar S a vector without using the ravel operation.

41. Define a monadic APL function that will take a vector V with
an arbitrary number of components ≤ 7 and insert as many zeros
in the front to make the result a seven-component vector; for example, 3 2 5 7 becomes 0 0 0 3 2 5 7.

42. Write a function WITHIN to select from a vector W those
elements that lie within an interval R on either side of the average
of W.

43. Write an APL expression to select those elements in a vector
that are integers.

44. Show how to select the elements with even indices in a
vector Y.

45. You are given a vector X whose components are all different
and arranged in ascending order. Write a program to insert a given
scalar S into the appropriate place in the sequence so that the result is still in ascending order. Be sure that your function is able to
handle the case in which S is identical with some element in X.

46. Write an APL expression to select the last element of a vector Y.

47. Write an APL expression that returns the index of the largest element in a vector W.

48. Define a function to remove all triplicates from a vector.

Example:

X is 2 3 1 3 4 2 5 3   turns into   2 1 4 2 5

49. Write a program SELECT that takes two arguments and will print out that element in the left argument X whose position corresponds to the position of the largest element in the right argument Y.

50. Write a function returning an explicit result that finds all the factors of a given integer N (that is, the integers that divide evenly into N).

51. Define a function COMFACT to print a list of common factors, if any, of two integers A and B.

52. The trinomial is $(1 + x + x^2)^N$, and N is a nonnegative integer. For $N = 2$ it is

$$1 + 2x + 3x^2 + 2x^3 + x^4$$

and the vector of coefficients is 1 2 3 2 1. Write a function that will yield the vector for any nonnegative N. HINT: Can you find a recurrence formula that will yield the vector for N from that for $N - 1$?

53. Generalize the function to give the corresponding coefficient vector for the multinomial

$$(1 + x + x^2 + \cdots + x^M)^N$$

54. There are sixteen binary boolean functions. Create an array M, ρM is 4 16, whose columns are the values of the sixteen functions. Write a function K BRED X that reduces the Boolean vector x by the Boolean function described in column K of M.

55. Given two arrays A and B, for which ρA is $a_1\ a_2$ and ρB is $b_1\ b_2$ and $a_1 = b_1$, produce an array C having the property that $C_{ij} = 1$ if and only if $A[;i] = B[;j]$ otherwise $C_{ij} = 0$, and produce C from a single expression. (HINT: use $\wedge$. = , $\lozenge$, and $\wedge/$).

56. Given an array M of 0 and 1. If $M[I;J] = 1$ then assume there is a point in $X\ Y$ space at I,J. Form the vectors X and Y of the X and Y coordinates of the 1 entries in M.

57. Given the vectors X and Y (as above) form the smallest array M for which $X[k] = I$ and $Y[k] = J$ implies $M[I;J] = 1$.

58. Write an APL expression for

$$\sum_{i=1}^{10} [e^{-p_i x_1} - e^{-p_i x_2} - x_3(e^{-p_i} - e^{-10 p_i})]^2$$

where $p_i = .1 \times i$ and x_1, x_2, x_3 have been previously specified as the three component vector X.

General Problems in Which Algol60 or APL May be Used

1. Write a program to find a "stable" set of marriages for a given group of N boys and N girls. Each boy has ordered the girls according to his preferences, and you are given the results as an array BOY, in which

$$\text{BOY}_{ik} = \text{(the number of the girl who is the } k\text{th choice of boy } i)$$

Similarly, the girls have indicated their preferences in an array GIRL, in which

$$\text{GIRL}_{ik} = \text{(the number of the boy who is the } k\text{th choice of girl } i)$$

A set of marriages is unstable if a man and woman exist who are not married to each other but prefer each other to their actual mates. If there are no such discontented couples, then the set of marriages is stable.

One possible algorithm for solving this problem is:

a. Each boy proposes to his favorite girl.

b. Each girl who receives more than one proposal rejects all but her favorite from among those who have proposed to her. She does not, however, accept him yet. Instead, she keeps him "on a hook" just in case someone better will come along later. A girl who receives only one proposal must put that boy on her hook. A girl who receives no proposals must simply wait her turn. Her Prince Charming will be along shortly.

c. All boys who were rejected by their initial choices propose to their second choices, etc.

d. Each girl receiving proposals chooses her favorite from the group of the new proposers and the boy on her hook, if any. All the rest are again rejected, and her favorite is again placed on her hook.

The algorithm is described in

D. Gale and L. S. Shapley, "College Admissions and the Stability of Marriages," *American Mathematical Monthly*, 69 (January 1962), pp. 9–15.

The marriages are indicated in the array PREFER. The value of PREFER[j] is the number of the boy married to girl j.

2. Given a decimal integer N of n digits, strike out $k < n$ digits, so that the remaining digits squashed together form a number as large as possible.

3. Write a nonrecursive procedure that computes the same function as

```
real procedure THETA (x,n); integer n; real x;
THETA := if n = 0 then x↑2 else THETA (x-1,n-1) +
x × THETA (x+1, n-1);
```

4. For each of the following write a simple statement in Algol60 that:

    a. Does not contain an explicit goto construction and yet when executed would not terminate.

    b. Would assign values 1, 2, 4, 8, . . . , 1024 to successive components of the vector y and yet has no arithmetic operators nor goto.

    c. Contains an expression with the constant .375 and yet contains no constructions containing a digit. You may assume the existence of a variable $x = .3149$, and no other.

5. Information about a set of circles is encoded in an array A: $A[;1]$, $A[;2]$, and $A[;3]$ are the values of the X coordinate of the centers, Y coordinates of the centers, and radii of the circles, respectively. Assume there are N circles. Find the area of the smallest convex polygon of K sides enclosing all the circles.

6. SNOWFLAKE. Compute the perimeters and areas of a sequence of figures obtained from an equilateral triangle by successively dividing the sides by 3 and appending new equilateral triangles, whose sides are of this reduced length, see the figure. Can you find a re-

currence formula for the perimeters and the areas?

7. This formula for determining the date upon which Easter will fall was derived by Karl Gauss, German mathematician, and is recorded in one of the essays of an English author named Christopher Morley.

    a. Divide the number of the year by 19; let the remainder equal A.

    b. Divide the number of the year by 4; let the remainder equal B.

   c. Divide the number of the year by 7; let the remainder equal C.

   d. Divide $19A$ plus 24 by 30; let the remainder equal D.

   e. Divide $2B$ plus $4C$ plus $6D$ plus 5 by 7; let the remainder equal E.

   f. Easter will be 22 plus D plus E and, if the number exceeds 31, the month will be April instead of March.

Express this formula as a single APL expression or a short Algol60 program.

BNF Problems

1. A class of strings of characters, ⟨a string⟩, is defined by the following BNF syntax:

    ⟨a string⟩ ::= ⟨rag⟩ <u>or</u> ⟨mop⟩ <u>or</u> ⟨mop⟩⟨rag⟩⟨mop⟩
    ⟨rag⟩ ::=a <u>or</u> b <u>or</u> cc
    ⟨mop⟩ ::=d <u>or</u> ee <u>or</u> fff

Write in dictionary order all ⟨a string⟩'s of exactly four characters.

2. Suppose the definition of ⟨rag⟩ is changed to

    ⟨rag⟩ ::= a <u>or</u> bb <u>or</u> a ⟨rag⟩

and ⟨a string⟩ and ⟨mop⟩ are as before. Write, in dictionary order' all ⟨a string⟩'s of exactly four characters.

3. The Dallas and Washington Railroad has had difficulty during various contract negotiations in defining what a train is. Our computer scientist in Washington, played by Gregory Peck, was given the task of defining what a train is. He listened to an old-timer, played by Boris Karloff, tell, on the front porch of the Treasury Building, what a train is: "Every train commences with a consecutive string of locomotives or terminates with such a string or has both. Any string of locomotives always commences with a diesel, though it may contain 2-4-4 Pacifics (o0Ooo) or 4-6-4 Hudsons (oo0O0oo). Trains are either freight or passenger. If the former, the last freight car is a caboose and the other cars are any of boxcars, tank cars, flat cars, and hopper cars. Of course, if there are hoppers, they all occur contiguously. If it is a passenger train, it may contain any of mail cars, passenger coaches, diners, and pullmans, and an observation car, but of course all pullmans, if they occur, are contiguous. The observation car, if there is one, must be last, and there must be at most one diner, and that separating all passenger coaches from all pullmans. Naturally the mail cars are behind the locomotive string and do not separate any passenger coaches from the diner."

    Using the following naming scheme, our hero defined trains by using a BNF syntax definition scheme—and was later promoted to Vice-President of the Railroad.

	(If you can draw)	(If you prefer)
LOCOMOTIVES		
Diesel		D
Pacific		P
Hudson		H
FREIGHT CARS		
Caboose		C
Box		B
Tank		T
Flat		F
Hopper		K
PASSENGER CARS		
Mail		M
Coach		S
Pullman		L
Diner		D
Observation		O

He also used the idea of the empty car (which was sneaky):

Empty		⟨empty⟩

Give a BNF definition of:

   a.   Freight trains
   b.   Passenger trains
   c.   All trains

CHAPTER 4

DATA STRUCTURES

4

INTRODUCTION

In the preceding chapters we have become aware that algorithms not only operate on data, but also operate on data structures. A data structure is composed of data elements, and we limit our attention to data elements that are any of the following:

Numbers
Logical values
Characters

Data structures are elements assembled together because they have common properties utilized by algorithms. Generally these common properties permit the algorithm to reduce significantly the number of different object identifiers that it must mention. This is particularly important when the quantity of objects to be manipulated is large or data-dependent. We have already mentioned that a vector X permits us to deal with all components at once, use of X, or any of its components, use of $X[i]$, and all other important differences among the components are processed by the algorithm.

In Chapter 3 it was pointed out that programming languages tend to have the same kind of data elements, but they differ somewhat in the data structures they can directly manipulate.

The issues that arise within algorithms in the handling of a data structure X can be separated into those intrinsic to the structure of X and those that arise from the representation of X in terms of some other data structure Y. The latter issue arises when the programming language does not permit direct use of X but does permit direct use of Y. The algorithms must then deal with both the structure and the representation.

Thus neither Algol60 nor APL has stacks as structures. Instead, stacks are representable in terms of one-dimensional arrays. Often a programming language suggests more than one representation for a structure X, and then the choice is made on the basis of efficiency or generalizability.

The choice of a data structure to hold a collection of elements is based on several factors:

Availability in a programming language.
Appropriate growth properties of the structure.

Appropriate   selection,   construction,   and   substitution
properties.

Appropriate data operations.

STRINGS

Let us consider, to put things into focus, the data structures called
strings. As we have already seen, a string is a sequence of characters.
The entire string is identified by the string name, that of a variable
whose value is a string. The uses to which strings are put make it
inappropriate to insist on an a priori upper bound for the number
of characters in a string, since in many algorithms this bound tends
to be elastic. Note that APL does not require such an a priori bound,
whereas Algol60 does require an upper bound.

For many applications an explicit, indexed scan of a string is
cumbersome; one is not really interested in examining the ith character and then the $(i + 1)$th, etc. Certainly one does not tend to
identify information by where it is in the string. The index position
of a character tends to lose all significance after some insertions and
deletions of characters have taken place during algorithm execution.

The natural construction operator for strings is catenation. If
A and B are strings, then C i̲s̲ A, B is the string formed by juxta-
posing the string B to the right of string A. In APL notation ρC i̲s̲
$(\rho A) + \rho B$ and $(\rho A) \uparrow C$ i̲s̲ A while $(-\rho B) \uparrow C$ i̲s̲ B.

The "$\uparrow$" and "$\downarrow$" are selection operators in APL, but they select
on the basis of lengths and number of characters and not on the more
desirable basis of patterns.

What is a pattern? Simply put, a pattern is a property that a
string possesses. Scans of strings search for the first (leftmost) or,
perhaps, all substrings that possess a given property. The concept
of a substring is an obvious one: If C is a string, then $1 \uparrow C$ and $1 \downarrow C$
are strings or, in particular, substrings of C, called the *head* and *tail*
of C. Any string isolated by a (meaningful) sequence of $H \uparrow$ and $H \downarrow$
applied to a string C is called a substring of C, where H is some positive integer.

Example:

```
C is 'ABCEDFGHUJKLMNOP'
3 ↓ 10↑C is 'DEFGHIJ'
```

Thus the decomposition of selection of strings is the identification and isolation of substrings. The purpose of the identification
and isolation may be any of the following:

Extraction

Replacement

Deletion

A condition for some computation

A pattern specifies the property to be possessed by a substring for which we search within a string. Although patterns may be defined in a multitude of ways, programmatically a pattern is a filter applied to a string X whose value is either a pair of nonnegative integers $0 \neq J \leq K$, representing the end positions of a leftmost substring of X possessing that property, or the pair 0, 0 if none such exists. In APL one could return a vector P of two elements. If one wishes to find all such (disjoint) substrings, one may use the following general routine.

```
     ∇ A←ALLP X;K;R
[1]    K←(A←0 0)[2]
[2]    LOOP: R←K+P K↓X
[3]    →0×ι0=K←R[2]
[4]    A←A,[1]R
[5]    →LOOP
     ∇
```

This will return an array of rank 2 holding in each row the end positions of all (disjoint) occurrences of the pattern P in the string X. $P Z$ is the function that isolates the leftmost position of the pattern P in Z.

What can we say about patterns? We may define patterns in the following constructive way.

Suppose $P_1, P_2, \ldots, P_r$ are primitive patterns. Then we may define our set of patterns by a recursive definition, very reminiscent of our use of BNF to describe language syntax:

$\langle$primitive pattern$\rangle$ is P_1 or P_2 or P_3 ... or
  P_r ... or $(\langle p \rangle)$ $\langle$pp$\rangle$
$\langle$basic pattern$\rangle$ is $\langle$pp$\rangle$ or $\sim\langle$pp$\rangle$ $\langle$bp$\rangle$
$\langle$conjunctive pattern$\rangle$ is $\langle$bp$\rangle$ or $\langle$cp$\rangle \wedge \langle$bp$\rangle$ $\langle$cp$\rangle$
$\langle$disjunctive pattern$\rangle$ is $\langle$cp$\rangle$ or $\langle$p$\rangle \vee \langle$cp$\rangle$ $\langle$dp$\rangle$
$\langle$pattern$\rangle$ is $\langle$cp$\rangle$ or $\langle$p$\rangle | \langle$dp$\rangle$ $\langle$p$\rangle$

The significance of the characters "$\sim$," "$\vee$," "$\wedge$," and "$|$" is what we might expect:

$\sim P$ means the largest (leftmost) string preceding a string satisfying P.
$P_1 \vee P_2$ satisfies P_1 or P_2.
$P_1 \wedge P_2$ satisfies P_1 and P_2.
$P_1 | P_2$ satisfies P_1 followed by a substring satisfying P_2.

Let us be quite clear what we mean by a substring satisfying a pattern P. If a substring σ of the string X satisfies P, this means that X is of the form $\alpha S_0 \sigma S_1 \beta$, where α and β are substrings, possibly empty, and S_0 and S_1 are characters, possibly null, and

  α does not satisfy P
  no substring containing S_0 satisfies P
  σ satisfies P but σS_1 does not.

We shall say that the string satisfying P "matches" P. Thus, if σ matches P, then αS_0 matches $\sim P$. Please note that $\sim(\sim P)$ is not the same as P. $P_1 \vee P_2$ is matched to the longest string that matches either P_1 or P_2. $P_1 \wedge P_2$ is matched to the longest string that matches both P_1 and P_2. $P_1 \mid P_2$ is matched to the longest string of the form $\sigma\tau$, where σ matches P_1 and τ matches P_2.

What are some useful primitive patterns?

Suppose we have a string X composed of characters from three alphabets A1, A2, and A3, represented as strings:

```
A1 is 'A B C D . . . X Y Z'
A2 is '0 1 2 3 4 5 6 7 8 9'
A3 is ' '
```

Then the pattern X OF A1 matches the string in X, all of whose characters are in A1, and correspondingly for A2 and A3. $\sim X$ OF A3 might be used to identify numbers and words from a text. The pattern X IS A1 matches the exact occurrence in X of A1. The pattern ANY is matched by anything, including the null string. Thus the pattern

```
X OF A1 | ANY | X OF A2
```

when applied to the string

```
X is 'MY AGE IS 21'
```

will yield the array

```
 1   2
 3  10
11  12
```

and X of A1 | ANY | ANY will yield the array

```
 1   2
 3  11
12  12
```

Once a substring is isolated by matching to a pattern, string processing is concerned with modifying the string in which the substrings have been found.

APL functions for the preceding primitive patterns are easy to write. Thus X OF A and X IS A are

```
     ∇ R←X OF A;K
[1]   R←0,0
[2]   →4×ι(ρX<K←(X∈A)ι1)
[3]   R←K,⁻1+K+(∼(K↓X)∈A)ι1
     ∇
```

and

```
    ∇ R←X IS A;K
[1]  R←0 0
[2]   →0×ι(ρX)<K←(∧/[1](⁻1+ιρA) ⌽X∘.=A)ι1
[3]  R←K+(0,⁻1+ρA)
    ∇
```

respectively.

More complicated than the preceding two functions is the function that matches the string against a catenation of two patterns, since backtracking may be required. Thus, suppose we seek to match X against the patterns $A_1 \lor A_2 \mid A_3 \lor A_4$, where A_1, A_2, A_3, and A_4 are primitive patterns. All four possibilities must be checked to find the longest substring of X that can be matched.

Suppose the matched alternates have been found and listed in two arrays L and R. Then the APL code segment produces, in LEFT and RIGHT, the index of the patterns in L and R that give the maximal match:

```
A←(1+L[;2])∘.=R[;1]
Z←A×(1+L[;2]−L[;1])∘.+(1+R[;2]−R[;1])
T←∨/Z=⌈/,Z
LEFT←(L[;1]=⌊/L[;1]×T)ι1
RIGHT←(Z[LEFT;])ι1
```

For example, suppose the pattern had been

$$A_1 \lor A_2 \lor A_3 \mid A_4 \lor A_5$$

and had led to

```
      6 14         15 28
L is  5 15   R is  24 39
      9 23         15 31
                   16 30
                   24 51

A is  1 0 1 0 0
      0 0 0 1 0
      0 1 0 0 1

Z is  23 0 26 0  0
       0 0  0 27 0
       0 31 0 0  43
T is 0 0 1
LEFT is 3
RIGHT is 5 and the best match covers from L[LEFT;1] to
R[RIGHT;2]
```

Some languages, like SNOBOL, are preoccupied with string manipulation and pattern matching, and their string functions can be described rather nicely as APL functions.

Once we adopt the technique of using constructive rules such as BNF for defining new patterns in terms of old ones and ultimately in terms of primitive ones, we face the problem of writing pattern-matching procedures of some complexity. The first method that suggests itself is to give a pattern-matching procedure for a pattern P in terms of the procedures for matching the constituent parts that compose P. Since these procedures communicate through their parameters, it is natural to adopt a standard method of communicating what is to be matched and, as a result, what has been matched. We identify a pattern with its procedure for matching and state:

Every pattern is a dyadic function whose arguments are a. the string to be matched and b. the character position in the string at which matching is to commence and whose result is c. the leftmost character position following a successful match, or d. 0 if no match is possible. These conventions are much like those used in syntax analysis in Chapter 3.

For example, suppose P is the pattern defined by

$$P \text{ is } P_1 \vee P_2 | P_3$$

Its procedure, defined in terms of P_1, P_2, and P_3, could be written in APL as

```
      ∇ R←X P J;T;U;K
[1]   T←1↑1,U←X
[2]   →6×ι0≠K←U P1 J
[3]   T←0
[4]   →6×ι0≠K←U P2 J
[5]   →,R←0
[6]   →0×ι0≠R←U P3 K
[7]   →4×ιT
[8]   →2×ι0< ρU← 1↓X
      ∇
```

A little thought will convince the reader that the method of procedure construction is so stereotyped that an alternative approach can be used. A single general procedure MATCH can be created that "interprets" any pattern definition to perform the matching function required by the pattern. The set of pattern definitions must be scanned by MATCH and the appropriate one selected and then parsed by MATCH to determine the proper sequence of "primitive" matchings to be made. This is the approach used in the language SNOBOL. In SNOBOL patterns are data types, and operations exist for manipulating them. We shall postpone further treatment of general pattern matching until the end of the next section.

APL does provide for the direct handling of string information, since strings are a basic data structure within APL. However, let us examine another data structure that is not indigenous to APL and must be counterfeited in APL: trees.

TREES AND LIST STRUCTURES

For some problems the substitution and scanning properties of strings make their use cumbersome. Suppose we have a character string holding a "formula" such as

$$A \text{ is } '3 \times Y + 7 \times (Z - \ln (Y)/92' \qquad (4.1)$$

The pivotal operation (last to be performed) is the "+." But how do we find it? A formula has an inherent "tree" structure whose nodes hold operators and whose "leaves" hold constants and identifiers of variables. Thus (4.1) is representable by the tree shown as (4.2), and the layout of the tree suggests how to manipulate the

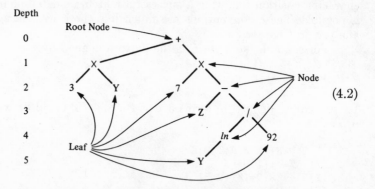

$$(4.2)$$

formula, whereas the string representation gives us little more than the picture of the formula. For example, the tree representation suggests that a dyadic operator has two branches descending from it, that operations are performed in the reverse order of their depth in the tree, and that those operations at the same depth can be performed in any order. You will note that this tree is the parse tree of the expression.

Thus the tree representation carries important explicit information, which the string representation does not. Following a path in the tree (hopping from node to node) is immediately relatable to answering questions such as "What is the right operand of the '−' at level 2?" and "To what operator is the leftmost 'Y' attached?" whereas scanning the string tells us almost nothing without executing a sequence of controlled "subscans."

Suppose we wished to substitute for all occurrences of "Y" in A the formula 'U−2×Z'. We could easily find all occurrences of Y in the string A by use of the pattern IS and substitute for each of them, obtaining the new formula

$$C \text{ is } '3 \times U - 2 \times Z + 7 \times (Z - \ln(U - 2 \times Z))/92 '$$

But this is probably not what we intended. Indeed, we should have surrounded the substituting formula by parentheses, obtaining

C <u>is</u> '3 × (U – 2 × Z) + 7 × (Z – ln((U – 2 × Z)))/92 '

which now has one set of superfluous parentheses.

But now, having made the substitution, we must reparse the string to determine the structure of the new formula.

However, the new tree shows that the substitutions have only a local effect and the original tree structure is still present; see (4.3).

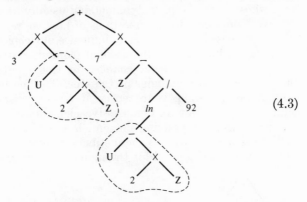

(4.3)

Even after entering the substituted formulas, all else in the tree is unchanged: trees are a more natural data-processing representation for formulas than strings. Indeed, strings carry very little structural information, since there are only two paths through a string: from left to right and from right to left. However, in a tree there are a multitude of traversal modes reaching each symbol in the formula.

Another important use of tree representation is in games where a tree represents a set of possible moves. Suppose we have a move game being played by two players denoted by ○ and □. Suppose □ moved first. Then denote the set of possible moves by branches emanating from the root node □, as shown in (4.4). Now whatever

Depth

```
0              □
            / | \
1        ○   ○ ··· ○          ○ would now move        (4.4)
            / \
2        □ ··· □              □ would now move
```

strategies guide the choice of □ on depth 0 are open to him again at depth 2, etc., and hence the algorithm for determining strategies that □ might use will be applied recursively. Of course, he might apply a similar algorithm to identify the moves ○ would choose were □ to choose, etc. We shall say more about this paradigm in the next section, but let us fix our attention on the point made above, that processing information in game trees is naturally done recursively: tree-processing is most naturally done with recursive algorithms. After all, if you examine any node of a tree, it is the root of the tree suspended from it. Since recursive algorithms are usually applied at the roots of trees, they are rarely, if ever, concerned with the actual depth and width of trees. Hence the processes of growth and withering during the course of an algorithm execution have little influence on the explicit description of tree-processing algorithms. Put another way, algorithms for tree-processing should not be explicitly dependent on tree shape, since most tree-processing involves trees whose shape is quite dynamic and usually unpredictable.

We come now to the questions of how we represent trees and how we process them. Two facts influence our choice: first, the representing medium is one-dimensional (computer storage, arrays, or strings) and, second, local changes in tree contents should not unduly affect the remainder of the tree. The method most widely used in programming is to represent trees as list structures. We define a list element as k successive elements of the representing medium or as corresponding elements in k copies of the representing medium. For our purposes the distinction between these two representations can be ignored for the moment. Consider the tree

(1)

We might also have written it in any of the forms

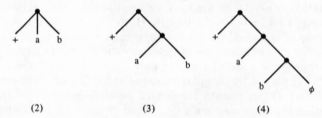

(2)   (3)   (4)

where Φ is a "rightmost end of tree" symbol. In all three representations only leaves hold data; nodes hold pointers to data or to other nodes. In (2) a node has three branches; in the others, only two. One can easily visualize the tree description for three summands, etc.; see (4.5). Note that an unnecessary "+" has been

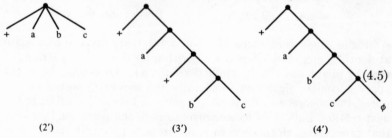

(4.5)

(2')   (3')   (4')

needed in (3′) to handle three operands. In (2′) we allow a variable number of branches to descend from a node. All four tree representations have many list-structure representations. For the moment let us ignore (2′), or (2), and concentrate on the (1), (3), and (4):

TYPE	CONTENTS		
(1)	center	left	right
(3), (4)		left	right

Center, left, and right are pointers or references and name either a datum or a subtree structure. Thus our original formula, (4.1), might be represented as an APL array F of two rows by using representation (3):

```
F is    -1  3 -2   -3 -2 -4 -5 -6 -7 11  -8
         2  5  4  -10  6  7  8  9 10 -9 -10
node:    1  2  3    4  5  6  7  8  9 10  11
```

The negative entries specify a pointer to a table of symbols (see Table 4.1). But how is the table represented? Since all the symbols are of fixed length, we may store them concatenated in a character string:

```
SYMBOL is '+ × 3 7 - Z / ln 92 Y U 2'
```

and the negative entries refer to entries in a symbol pointer vector:

```
SYMBOL POINTER is 1 1 2 2 3 3 4 4 5 5 6 6 7 7 8 9 10 11
12 12 13 13 14 14
```

Now to substitute $U - 2 \times Z$ for Y we alter the occurrence of -10 to 12 and concatenate to the given array the array G:

```
        -5 -11  2 -12
G is    13  14 15  -6
node:   12  13 14  15
```

TABLE 4.1

Code	Symbol
1	+
2	×
3	3
4	7
5	–
6	Z
7	/
8	ln
9	92
10	Y
11	U
12	2

obtaining F <u>is</u> F, [2] G. However, note that the structure is no longer a tree. (Why?)

We note that the entries in the representation are of two kinds: pointers to places or sites in the array and pointers to data (symbols).

In our processing of trees we wish to think in terms of trees and operations on them rather than in terms of their representation as lists that are in turn arrays containing pointers. We are not able to ignore totally the effects of representation, such as the treatment of storage we use, and we often do not wish to, since the choice of representation often improves processing efficiency. Nevertheless the separation is conceptually quite important.

The operations we program should be dictated by tree-processing and not list-processing or array-processing. Among the things we wish to do are to create trees, to display trees, to alter trees, and to search trees. We shall assume that, by a *tree*, we mean objects of type (4). How may we create trees? We may "bear" trees from a coded linear string representation. Thus, let our "trees" grammar be

$$\langle\text{atom}\rangle \;\; \underline{is} \;\; \langle\text{symbol}\rangle \;\; \underline{or} \;\; \varnothing \qquad\qquad \langle\text{at}\rangle$$
$$\langle\text{tree}\rangle \;\; \underline{is} \;\; (\langle\text{tr}\rangle,\langle\text{tr}\rangle) \;\; \underline{or} \;\; \langle\text{at}\rangle \qquad \langle\text{tr}\rangle$$

Then $((a,(b,c)), (d,(a,\varnothing)))$ is a linear coding of the tree; see the figure. We may call this "binary parenthesized coding." Every bi-

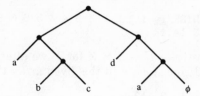

nary tree can be represented in this linear parenthesized coded form. There are many other codings of trees that are more useful than binary parenthesized coding, if the trees are not binary or do not have the same number of branches attached to each node. A parenthesized coding obtained from the grammar

$$\langle\text{atom}\rangle \;\; \underline{is} \;\; \langle\text{symbol}\rangle \qquad\qquad\qquad \langle\text{at}\rangle$$
$$\langle\text{tree}\rangle \;\; \underline{is} \;\; \langle\text{tr}\rangle\{, \text{ tr }{}^{*}_{0}\} \;\; \underline{or} \;\; \langle\text{at}\rangle \qquad \text{tr}$$

gives $(a,(b,c,d),e,f)$ as the coding for the tree; see the next figure.

Note that data reside only at terminal nodes.

If we use trees of type (1), where every node carries a datum, a tree may be coded by a pair of vectors d, c, where d holds the data and $c[j]$ holds the number of nodes (or data) in the subtree of the tree of which $c[j]$ is the root and the nodes are listed in a "tree traversal order." Thus if we take the tree of our formula (4.1), we can have

$$+ \times 3 \; Y \times 7 - Z \; / \; \ln \; Y \; 92 \qquad\qquad (4.6)$$
$$11 \; 2 \; 0 \; 0 \; 7 \; 0 \; 5 \; 0 \; 3 \;\; 1 \; 0 \; 0$$

We may call this *preorder depth traversal;* or we may represent the tree as

$$+ \times \times 3 \; Y \; 7 - Z \; / \; \ln \; 92 \; Y \qquad\qquad (4.7)$$
$$11 \; 2 \; 7 \; 0 \; 0 \; 0 \; 5 \; 0 \; 3 \;\; 1 \; 0 \;\; 0$$

in *left-depth traversal.* A variant of (4.6) is called *end-order (depth) traversal:*

$$3 \; Y \times 7 \; Z \; Y \; \ln \; 92 \; / - \times + \qquad\qquad (4.6a)$$
$$0 \; 0 \; 2 \; 0 \; 0 \; 0 \;\; 1 \;\; 0 \; 3 \; 5 \; 7 \; 11$$

The latter traversal scheme is particularly useful in representing formulas because it points out an extremely simple model for evaluating formulas by using a stack, as follows.

Each operator has an integer-valued weight that is the number of operands it requires. Scan the code from left to right. If the ith datum is an operand, place it on the top of the stack; if it is an operator of weight k, apply it to the top k elements on the stack, popping these k data from the stack and then putting the result of the performed operation on the top of the stack.

We may define these traversal schemes as follows.

PREORDER (DEPTH) TRAVERSAL

1. Visit the root.
2. Preorder traverse the left subtree.
3. Preorder traverse the right subtree.

END-ORDER (DEPTH) TRAVERSAL

1. End-order traverse the left subtree.
2. End-order traverse the right subtree.
3. Visit the root.

LEFT-DEPTH TRAVERSAL

```
for i←1 step 1 until max depth do
for j←1 step 1 until width (i) do
visit the jth root at depth i.
```

The roots are numbered from the left at each depth, and the depths are numbered from 1 at the tree root. Width (i) is the number of nodes at depth i.

Note that preorder and end-order traversals have succinct recursive descriptions of the traversal rules, whereas left-depth traversal calls for an Algol-like iterative traversal rule.

Trees may be easily reconstructed from any of the three coded forms. A reconstruction is simply a matter of identifying which segments of the code are the subtrees of a given datum and then recursively reconstructing trees from them. It is simple to reconstruct the tree from (4.6) by scanning from the right; see (4.8). The num-

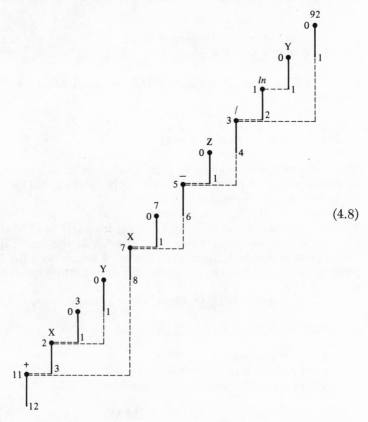

(4.8)

ber to the left of a node is the weight it requires from its subtrees, and the number to the right of the vertical line is the weight given to the tree. Turning the tree upside down, shaking it out, and trimming the branches gives back the original tree.

Actually the tree reconstruction is identical with answering the question: Given any datum element d, what is the code of the tree of which it is a root? It is the next w entries in the code.

What is the degree, number of branches, emanating from the root in question?

Let w be the weight of the datum at entry k. Scan to the right of the datum, and find the first set of weights w_{j_i} and integer n that satisfy

$$w = \sum_{i=1}^{n} w_{j_i} + n \tag{4.9}$$

where $j_1 = k + 1$ and $j_{i+1} = j_i + w_{j_i} + 1$.

Then there are n branches emanating from the datum, and the n segments $j_1 \ldots j_1 + w_{j_1}, j_2 \ldots j_2 + w_{j_2}, \ldots, j_n \ldots j_n + w_{j_n}$ are the subtrees. In the example the subtrees of $+$ are determined by

$$11 = w_2 + w_5 + 2 = 2 + 7 + 2$$

Hence segments $2 \ldots 4$ and $5 \ldots 12$ are the respective data of the two subtrees descended from "$+$."

Note that these codes do not make use of pointers or links. Hence they are more akin to string-structure than to list-structure representations of trees. Often internal pointers are a nuisance, and a more arithmetic representation, such as our codes, may be preferred. However, note that making copies of trees or substituting a tree for a datum involves considerably less work if pointers are used. Let us confine our attention, for the moment, to the coded form in (4.6). Suppose we have two trees T_1 and T_2 and we wish to replace a subtree of T_1 by T_2. A subtree of T_1 is a code segment uniquely identified by its root. Thus, to replace it by T_2, we

1. Excise the code segment T_3 of T_1 to be replaced.
2. Insert the code segment for T_2.
3. Add $1 + w(T_2) - w(T_3)$ to every datum that is on the path from the root of T to the root of the excised segment.

Thus, to replace the subtree

```
/  ln  Y  92   in  (4.6)
3  1   0   0
```

by

```
×  Z  +  ×  3  Y  Z
6  0  4  2  0  0  0
```

yields

$$\begin{array}{ccccccccccccccc} & & & & & & & & & & & & \text{path} & & \\ + & × & 3 & Y & × & 7 & - & Z & × & Z & + & × & 3 & Y & Z \\ 14 & 2 & 0 & 0 & 10 & 0 & 8 & 0 & 6 & 0 & 4 & 2 & 0 & 0 & 0 \end{array} \tag{4.10}$$

How does one find the path from the root to a node? It is simply the set of entries that defines the left edges of all the code segments con-

taining the node in question. In our example the root node being
excised is "/", node 9. The jth element, as a root, contains all elements, as nodes, whose position $k \leq w[j] + j$ (with $j < k$).

> 9 is certainly contained in node 1, since $9 \leq 14 + 1$.
> Node 1 contains nodes 2 and 5.
> 9 is contained in node 5, since $9 \leq 5 + 10$.
> Node 5 contains nodes 6 and 7.
> 9 is contained in node 7, since $9 \leq 7 + 8$.
> Node 7 contains nodes 8 and 9.
> $9 = 9$.
> The path is 1 5 7 9.

Thus far in our examination of coded trees we have seen the
need for algorithms to:

1. Create a tree.
2. Find a subtree.
3. Replace a tree.
4. Find the path to a node.

One is naturally tempted to ask, "How many algorithms are necessary to provide a basis for processing trees?" This question has no
useful or, at the same time, obvious answer. However, we do need
to work from some concept of an algorithmic basis for tree-processing. Let us take our primitive set of algorithms to be the four
following:

1. Find a subtree.
2. Replace a subtree.
3. Delete a subtree.
4. Fuse two trees.

and the predicates

5. Two data are equal.
6. A datum is a pointer.

If we create these algorithms as APL functions and represent trees as
APL arrays, we have a basis for a tree-processing system in APL. We
have mentioned that in copying a tree it is often much more efficient
to point to the tree being copied than to insert a full copy. Thus we
could have (at least) two trees referencing some third tree. We pay
for this increased efficiency in copying by some added problems that
we can call *responsibility* problems. Consider the state of affairs
represented in the accompanying figure, in which there is a pointer

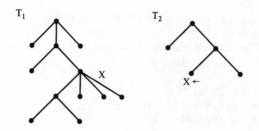

in T_2 to X. Can one change X in T_1 by processing in T_1 or T_2? For if we had copied X into T_2, then changes in X in T_2 would not affect X in T_1 and vice versa. In particular, can one erase X and recover its storage without the permission of both T_1 and T_2? The consequences of data-sharing are complicated and are rarely handled to the equal satisfaction of all algorithms that use the data. Many schemes for treating responsibility have been tried at one time or another with varying degrees of success. One widely used scheme is the following.

Each time a subroot of a tree T (and its attached subtree) is copied into another tree T', a counter for the subtree, kept at its root, is augmented. If the count is > 1, no alteration of the subtree is ever permitted until (a) it has been copied and (b) its count has been reduced. Naturally, when the count at a node reaches 1, responsibility becomes totally local. A marker at a node is used to keep these counts. Trees use space in the background (or representing) machine; the space used by a subtree can be made available for other processing purposes when no tree is connected to it.

The tree, represented as a pair of vectors, data and weight, admits of simple processing when the background machine is APL. Thus, the tree (4.2) can be represented by the vector pair (4.6), that is, as an array. Most of the tree operations are on the row of weights rather than on the row of data. So we will confine our attention to manipulation of the row of weights as a vector. Accessing corresponding elements in the data (vector) is simple, given the results of operations on the weight vector. Thus, the subtree of W whose root is at J is the segment $J+0,\iota W[J]$, and the path from the root to J is $(((\iota J)+J\uparrow W)\geq J)/\iota J$. For example, if J is 9, the path in (4.10) is 1 5 7 9. To find the number of branches leading from a root, we must solve equation (4.9) for n. An iterative calculation is used:

```
       ∇ K←W DEGREE J;T;L;S
  [1]    S←W[J]
  [2]    T←J+1
  [3]    K←0
  [4]    →8×ιS=0
  [5]    S←S-(L←W[T]+1)
  [6]    T←T+L
  [7]    →4,K←K+1
         ∇
```

K is the degree. It is straightforward to transform a tree from pre-order to left-depth form. The following function exhibits the transformation P as a permutation of the original weight vector W. Then $W[P]$ is the transformed weight vector:

```
    ∇ P←TSFM1 W;K
[1]   K←(((ρW),ρW)ρ↓ρW)×(↓ρW)∘.≤↓ρW
[2]   P←⋔(W+↓ρW)+∘.≥K
    ∇
```

The reverse transformation is much more complicated, and we will not include it here.

For (4.10) we get P is ⋔ 1 2 3 3 2 3 3 4 4 5 6 5

Given two weight vectors W and W', we may fuse them to a node by creating the weight vector

```
(W[1]+W'[1]+2),W,W'
```

To insert a tree W' after node J in W:

```
W←(J↑W),W',J↓W
W[P]←1+W'[1]+W[P←(((↓J)+J↑W)≥J)/↓J]
```

where P is, of course, the path vector from the root.

APPLICATIONS OF TREES

Let us now consider some applications of trees. Computer programs have been written to play two-person board games such as Tic-Tac-Toe, Nim, Kalah, checkers, and chess. We may assume the game pits a human, player A, against the program, player P. The general paradigm for such games is:

> Player A moves:
> Enter the new move of player A.
> Generate the new game position.
> If the game is over, then notify the players; else player P moves.
> Player P moves:
> Generate some or all successors of the current state which could be possible P moves.
> (*) Evaluate each successor.
> Move to that successor of greatest value to P.
> Display this move to A.
> If the game is over, then notify the players; else player A moves.

Let us examine (*) in detail. A way of evaluating each successor is to simulate its consequences by having P in successive steps alternately take the roles of A and P in order to compute a value for each successor move. Note that this simulation involves a recursive application of the paradigm to a set of simulated games in order to answer "If P did that and A did that, then if P did that and A did that, etc." The depth of the recursion is called the *look-ahead depth* of the game program. Each state of the game has a value for the mover. It is clear from the preceding that the treatment by P of both P and A is symmetric, except that the first move must always be P. We can represent the state of affairs by a move tree, (4.11). Thus we may write (∗) as: "(∗∗) If the look-ahead

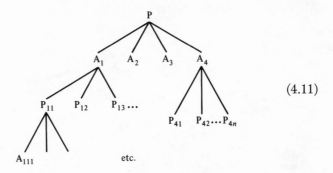

(4.11)

termination criterion is met, then use some fixed evaluation function to compute a value of the terminal move; else evaluate some of all successors by applying (∗∗)."

The value of a position is then computed by backing up from the terminal positions. If we assume that the value of a position is a positive integer, a natural strategy for P is to make that move that has maximum value and, for A, to make that move that has minimum value.

We report back from A to P the maximum value, since that dictates P's move and, from P to A, the minimum value, dictating A's move. If $S_1(M)$, $S_2(M)$, . . . , $S_K(M)$ are the contending successors of position M, then

```
val (M) is if terminal (M) then evaluate (M)
else max(val (S₁(M)),val (S₂(M)), . . . . , val(S_K(M)))
```

reports the value back from A to P and the min function is used to report back from P to A:

```
val(M) is if terminal (M) then evaluate (M)
else min(val(S₁(M)),val(S₂(M)), . . . ,val (S_K(M)))
```

The predicate, terminal (M), knows how deep the move tree is to be.

Clearly, an important question to decide is how the move tree is to be searched. Two obvious possibilities are: depth first and breadth first. The tree representation (4.6) is a depth-first one, and there is a corresponding breadth-first one. Thus the tree (4.6) has the breadth representation:

$$+ \times \times 3 \text{ Y } 7 - \text{ Z } / \text{ ln } 92 \text{ Y} \qquad (4.7)$$
$$11 \ 2 \ 7 \ 0 \ 0 \ 0 \ 5 \ 0 \ 3 \quad 1 \quad 0 \ 0$$

In the depth-first approach, from P are generated, in order, A_1, P_{11}, A_{111}, A_{112}, A_{113}, P_{12}, A_{121}, A_{122}, A_{123}, A_{124}, P_{13}, A_{131}, A_{132}, A_2, P_{21}, . . . , as in the tree of (4.13), where the integers at each

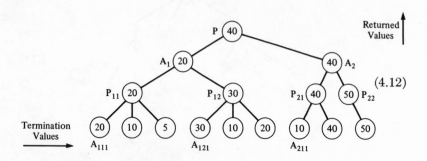

$$(4.12)$$

node are the values returned from the terminal evaluations. The final value is 40, so that P moves to position A.

An important modification of this depth-first search is called the α,β *search method*. Suppose we have the tree (4.13). The value α

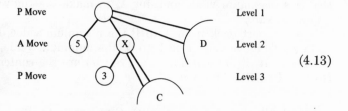

$$(4.13)$$

that will be reported to level 1 must satisfy $\alpha \geq 5$, and the value β ultimately reported back to level 2 must satisfy $3 \geq \beta$. The depth-first search plan now requires an examination of the moves in set C. But $\alpha \geq 5 > 3 \geq \beta$ tells us that at level 3 no moves in C need be attempted, since none could affect P's choice. After all, since level 2 will report a value no less than 5, and X will have a value reported to it no greater than 3, then C could produce no value that would change this state of affairs. Thus the next moves to be tested should be generated in set D. The number 5 is called an α *cutoff*. Similarly, consider the situation shown in (4.14). Suppose we have already

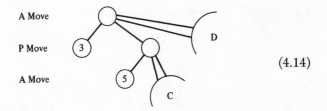

A Move

P Move   ③

A Move   ⑤

D

C

(4.14)

obtained the values 3 and 5. Then the value β ultimately to be reported to A on level 2 will satisfy $\beta \leq 3$, and the value reported to P on level 3 will satisfy $\alpha \geq 5$. The number 3 is called α,β cutoff. Therefore no moves in C need to be analyzed, since they cannot affect the choice made by A; hence the moves in D should be analyzed next.

Thus the move generation tree can often be significantly pruned by this simple approach. As moves are generated, successive cutoffs are determined to diminish (hopefully) the number of moves to the right that must be tested.

In such games the terminal value at a position is usually so chosen as to be easy to compute: for example, as a linear function of the form $V = w_1 f_1 + w_2 f_2 + \cdots + w_r f_r$, where the w_i are weights and the f_i are features of the game. The terminal value for a move is then $V(P) - V(A)$, the value for P minus the value for A.

How deep is the move tree? When are move trees terminated? Two obvious criteria are, first, a maximum depth is reached and, second, a game reaches a conclusion along that path. Each node of the tree contains a description of the game state and, on backup, the computed value of the position.

Our trees in depth representation are easily scanned. The predecessor P of the node at J is given by

```
K←¯1+J
P←( ⌽ (( ιK)+K↑W) ≥ J) ι1
```

though maintaining a pointer stack could be more efficient. The breadth successor, if one exists, of the predecessor at node J is given by

```
1+P+W[P]
```

which is useful in determining cutoffs.

To continue our tree example, let us look at the well-known game of tic-tac-toe. Let the features be

f_1: the unblocked one-in-a row advantage
f_2: the unblocked two-in-a row advantage
f_3: the three-in-a row advantage (a win)

For example, suppose the board state is

$f_1(P)$ <u>is</u> 2, $f_2(P)$ <u>is</u> 0, and $f_3(P)$ <u>is</u> 0
$f_1(A)$ <u>is</u> 2, $f_2(A)$ <u>is</u> 1, and $f_3(A)$ <u>is</u> 0

Row stands for row, column, or diagonal. Let the three weights be
1, 4, and 16. Then the position value is $F(P) - F(A)$, where

$$F = f_1 + 4f_2 + 16f_3$$

For the example, $F(P) - F(A)$ is -4.

Let us suppose the move tree is 2 deep. The board can, of
course, be represented by a character array B, for which ρB is 3 3
and an element of B is $'P'$ or $'A'$ or $' '$ and the record of every move
is kept in B with the position value recomputed on every move. A
somewhat better method is to keep a vector of 8 components representing the 8 winning paths, as shown in the figure, and letting the

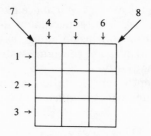

value of a component be the board state of its corresponding path.

Let the 8-component path vector be M, and let each of its
components have one of the values:

M VALUE	PATH HOLDS
-3	3 A markers and no P marker
-2	2 A markers " " " "
-1	1 A marker " " " "
0	Empty
1	1 P marker and no A marker
2	2 P markers " " " "
3	3 P markers " " " "
4	At least one A and one P marker

Then a move on a square changes the M value of each of the paths containing that square and the board value F by

M	-3	-2	-1	0	1	2	3	4	
P move	0	4	1	1	3	12	0	0	(4.15)
A move	0	-12	-3	-1	-1	-4	0	0	

Two computations are required:
Which paths contain a given square, and how are values affected by a move? Let us keep a vector C of 9 integers: 147, 15, 16, 24, 2578, 26, 34, 35, 367. Then a mark in square 6, $V \leftarrow (4\rho 10) \top C[6]$, gives the path indices 2 6, indicating the paths containing square 6. The constituents affected by a move are computed by using the array CHANGE:

```
0    6    5    1   1   1   0   0
0   -1   -1   -1   3   2   0   0
```

```
M[V]←M[V]+CHANGE[K;M[V]+8]
```

computes the new M values. K is 1 for a P move and 2 for an A move. The new value of F is

```
F←F++/ALTER[K;M[V]+8]
```

where ALTER is the array (4.15).
Thus each move establishes an M vector and a new board value, and our tree can contain, at the nodes, a reference to these quantities. Of course we must also keep a record at each node of the available squares into which a move may be made. Let us call this vector S. We may represent S as a vector of 9 bits, with a 1 to represent an open square and a 0 an occupied square. The triplet M, S, and F comprises the state of the game. At any node of the tree, $+/S$ is its degree. The move tree will contain at each node pointers to the M and S arrays and to the board value F. Thus the move tree is an array of 18 rows, each column representing a node. The rows are w (the node weight), F, . . . , $M[8]$, $S[1]$, . . . , $S[8]$. Having organized the data, we can now write our game-playing program.
We shall manage the computation by defining a depth-first generation of the tree, using four recursive functions. Let Degree(P) be the number of successors of P. The parameter n refers to the ordinal of a branch increasing from the right:

```
Maxmove(n,P) is if n = 0 then -∞
else max(Amove(succ(n, P)), Maxmove(n - 1, P))
Minmove(n, P) is if n = 0 then ∞
else min(Pmove(succ(n, P)), Minmove(n - 1, P))
Pmove(P) is if terminal (P) then eval (P)
else Maxmove(Rank(P),P)
Amove(P) is if terminal (P) then eval (P)
else Minmove(Rank(P),P)
```

Actually our programs will be somewhat different from this, since we are computing the changes in F as we generate moves and eval (P) is made somewhat simpler.

The parameter to Maxmove will be the node pointer (for P). The number of successors, Degree(P), will be computed from S.

```
        ∇ R←MAXMOVE J;K;H;V;L;U
[1]     R←⌈/ι0
[2]     →0×ι0=+/U←¯8↑T[;J]    𝕒 DO EMPTY SQUARES EXIST?
[3]     H←T[10+K←Uι1;J]←0     𝕒 FIND EMPTY SQUARE
[4]     V←(4ρ10)⊤C[K]         𝕒 AFFECTED PATHS
[5]     L←T[1+ι8;J]           𝕒 CURRENT M VALUES
[6]     L[V]←L[V]+CHANGE[1;L[V]+8]
[7]     H←L,H
[8]     H←T[2;J]++/ALTER[1;L[V]+8],H
[9]     T←T,[2](1+T[1;J]),H   𝕒 STACK THE NEW BOARD STATE
[10]    R←(AMOVE J+1)⌈R
[11]    →2
        ∇
```

Note that because of the generating strategy T need not be, and in this case is not, a tree but is, rather, a stack; hence no node weight need be kept. However, $T[1:J]$ will hold the depth of the move tree.

We shall not give the program for AMOVE, but we shall give Pmove:

```
        ∇ R←PMOVE J
[1]     →4×ι(0<+/3=|T[2+ι8])∨(2=T[1;J])∨(0=+/¯8↑T[;J])
        𝕒 TERMINAL CRITERION
[2]     R←MAXMOVE J
[3]     →0
[4]     R←T[2,J] 𝕒 OUTPUT THE BOARD VALUE
```

The program commences with PMOVE 1, and T contains the game state at that point. However, we have deliberately not included in the programs how P remembers which move was best for him. In what variable's values is this information available?

We could apply the α,β algorithm to our set of functions: α is reset on the A moves and β on the P moves. Thus, set α to the leftmost value of an A move. The values in the diagram shown affect α

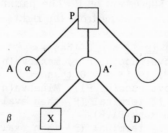

as follows: if $X \leq \alpha$, then omit D and evaluate the A successor of A'. If $X > \alpha$, then the new α is $\min(X, \mathrm{val}\,(D > \alpha))$. Similarly, in the next diagram β is affected as follows: if $X \geq \beta$, then omit D

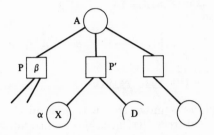

and evaluate the P successor of P'. If $X < \beta$, then the new β is $\max(X, \mathrm{val}\,(D < \beta))$.

Consequently, as we progress upwards and to the left, α increases and β decreases. It is even possible to combine the two programs AMOVE and PMOVE into one program! To see this, let us call the α,β version of Pmove "f" and that for Amove "g." $D(P)$ is the terminal value associated with a Pmove and $D'(P)$ that associated with an Amove. Then, using a pseudo-Algol notation, we have the following.

Let the direct descendants of P be numbered from left to right as $P_1, P_2, \ldots, P_{\mathrm{rank}(P)}$. Then $f(P, \alpha, \beta)$ is

```
if terminal(P) then begin
if D(P) ≤ α then return(α)
else if D(P) ≥β then return(β)
else return(D(P)) end
else begin
k ← 1
while (Y ← g(Pₖ,α,β)) < β ∧ k ≤ rank(P) do begin
α ← max(α, Y)
k ← k + 1 end
if k > rank(P) then return(α) else return(β)

g(P,α,β) is
if terminal(P) then begin
if D'(P) ≤ α then return(α)
else if D'(P) ≥ β then return(β)
else return(D'(P)) end
else begin
k ← 1
while (Y - f(Pₖ,α,β)) > α ∧ k ≤ rank(P) do begin
β ← min(β, Y)
k ← k + 1 end
if k > rank(P) then return(β) else return(α) end
```

Now $D(P) = D'(P)$, and observe that $-g(P, -\beta, -\alpha) = f(P, \alpha, \beta)$, so that, if we define median(D, α, β) to be the median of its three parameters, we need only use the single function MOVE:

```
MOVE(P, α, β) is
if terminal(P) then
return(median(P,α,β))
else begin
k ← 1
while (Y - MOVE(Pₖ,-β,-α) < β ∧ k ≤ rank(P) do begin
α ← max(α, Y)
k ← k + 1 end
if k > rank(P) then return(α) else return(β) end
```

An example of a move tree with α,β cutoffs is shown in the figure. Note the subtrees that need not be attempted.

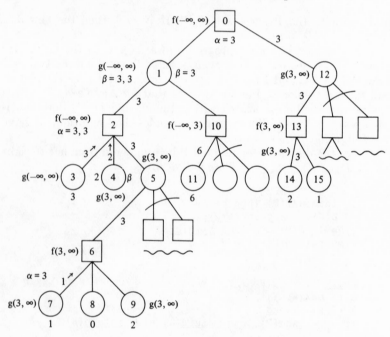

Matters are assumed to commence with a Pmove. Initially, one may set $\alpha = -\infty = -\beta$. Naturally one needs to keep track of which move at the top leads to a maximum value of R.

With simple games like tic-tac-toe simpler strategies of play exist, and a faster program could have been written. However, the paradigm described here is a model that can be applied to more complex games.

The preceding development of MOVE from f and g is our first example of operations on programs to produce equivalent programs.

Another important application of trees is in pattern-matching. Suppose we have defined the pattern

$$P \text{ is } (P_1 \lor P_2 \mid \sim P_3 \lor P_4 \mid P_5 \land (P_6 \mid P_7)) \lor P_8$$

where the P_i, with $i = 1, 2, \ldots, 8$, are primitive patterns. Then the tree shown will help us gain insight into the pattern-matching

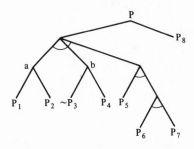

process. The notation $\bigwedge_{Q \quad R}$ means to match Q or R (an OR node), and $\bigwedge_{Q \quad R}$ means to match Q and R (an AND node). We may keep at each node the cursor value, the position in the string whence matching is to occur, using the pattern or the next branch to be followed. A pattern will report back (up) the position of the match it has obtained. Suppose we are attempting to match P_5 from string position S and cannot make the match. Then, if P_4 had not been attempted (because $\sim P_3$ succeeded), we must now attempt P_4 from the same point in S where $\sim P_3$ had been tested. If then P_5 still does not match, we must hope that P_2 has not yet been tried. If P_2 has been tried, then we must test P_8 to determine whether a match is possible.

The control of the pattern-matching process is describable in terms of a tree-walk. The pattern-matching process may be nicely described as a recursive backtracking algorithm. The standard paradigm described in Chapter 1 can be used when the following specializations are made.

1. The value of $X[k]$ is a tree.
2. The predicate $P(X[k])$ is a recursive application of the backtracking algorithm, unless $X[k]$ is a terminal node of the tree, in which case $P(X[k])$ is the matching program for a primitive pattern. Actually, the predicate is $0 \neq c \leftarrow$ Match (cursor,X[k]) or Backtrackmatch (cursor,X[k]), and each node of the tree carries a current value of the position of the cursor up to which a match has been obtained.
3. If the node of a tree is an OR node, there is one set (number of sets = 1) of as many choices as branches from the OR node.
4. If the root node of a tree is an AND node, there are as many sets (number of sets = degree(root node)) as branches.
5. progress(k) does:

$X[k]$ is the kth choice with cursor c.

Matching for the next subtree commences at cursor position $c(a \mid \text{node})$ or that at which the kth choice commenced (an $\wedge$ node):

$$k \leftarrow k + 1$$

6. regress(k) does: The cursor position for set(k) (a subtree) is reset to 0. Reset the choice counter for set(k) so that the first choice of set(k) (the leftmost branch of the subtree) will be the one next attempted:

$$k \leftarrow k - 1$$

7. Return c as the solution (unless one is also interested in knowing which primitive patterns were also matched), if there is one, or 0 if there is not.

In the algorithm that follows we dispense with $X[k]$ and deal directly with the pattern tree. If the rank of a node P is r, then $P(1), \ldots, P(r)$ are the r subtrees descending from P. If P is an AND node, its OR rank is 1. If P is an OR node, its AND rank is 1. In an expression of the form while $R \wedge S$ do g, S will not be tested if R is false.

```
Backtrackmatch (u,P) is
k ← 1
P ← leftmostsuccessor( P )
cursor ( P ) ← u
while k > 0 ∧ k ≤ ANDrank(predecessor ( P )) do
  while k ≤ ORrank( predecessor ( P )) ∧ 0 = c←
Backtrackmatch (cursor ( P ),P) do
      P ← nextsuccessor ( predecessor ( P ))
      k ← k + 1
if k > ORrank (predecessor ( P )) then
    cursor ( predecessor ( P )) ← u
    P ← nextsuccessor ( predecessor ( P ) )
else
    g ← cursor ( P )
    P ← nextsuccessor ( predecessor ( P ) )
    if nodetype ( predecessor ( P )) = '|' then
      cursor ( P ) ← c
    else
      cursor ( P ) ← g
    k ← k + 1
if k > ANDrank (P) then
  return (c)
else
    return ( 0 )
```

The data for many interesting computer problems is expressed in a "graph." A standard example is that of finding the shortest path from a source, say A, to a destination L in the graph; see, for example, the figure, where the number attached to an edge measures

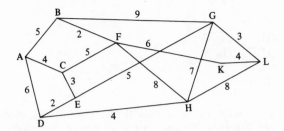

the distance between the two nodes connected by the edge. There are many convenient ways of describing a graph. We list three as follows.

1. THE CONNECTION MATRIX ⌈. Let the nodes A, B, C, D, E, F, G, H, K, L be numbered from 1 to 10. Then ⌈[i;j] is the distance between node i and node j. For example, ⌈[4;8] is 4. Since there is no path between G and F, we may define ⌈[6;7] to be ∞ (or any other very large number). Clearly, ⌈[i;j] = ⌈[j;i]. However, note that of the 55 entries ⌈[i;j], where $j \leq i$ (the lower triangular part of ⌈), only 16 of them have values ≠ ∞. For most graphs the number of actual edges is significantly less than the number of possible edges, so that it is often more convenient to use the node list (see below).

2. THE NODE LIST. For each node of a graph list the nodes and associated distances connected to them. To remove duplicates, order the nodes (for example, alphabetically), and only list those connecting nodes occurring later in the ordering.

3. THE EDGE LIST. List the edges as triplets: pre, post, distance, where pre never occurs after post in the imposed node ordering. The triplets can further be arranged in order in pre and then post:

1.	A, B, 5	9.	D, H, 4
2.	A, C, 4	10.	E, G, 5
3.	A, D, 6	11.	F, H, 8
4.	B, F, 2	12.	F, K, 6
5.	B, G, 9	13.	G, H, 7
6.	C, E, 3	14.	G, L, 3
7.	C, F, 6	15.	H, L, 8
8.	D, E, 2	16.	K, L, 4

Note that the node list and the edge list are really the same representation. For our example the node list is:

A: (B, 5), (C, 4), (D, 6)
B: (F, 2), (G, 9)
C: (E, 3), (F, 5)
D: (E, 2), (H, 4)

E: (G, 5)
F: (H, 8), (k, G)
G: (H, 7), (L, 3)
H: (L, 8)
K: (L, 4)

Another interesting application of trees is the generation of a *Huffman code*. Suppose we have an alphabet of five characters. Denote them by *a, b, c, d, e*. Suppose that, in the set of all strings we create with this alphabet, these characters occur with the frequencies

CHARACTER	FREQUENCY
a	.30
b	.07
c	.14
d	.09
e	.40

From this table we may derive, successively,

CHAR-ACTER	FRE-QUENCY		CHAR-ACTER	FRE-QUENCY
a	.30		*a*	.3
$\tilde{b}$	.16	and then	$\tilde{\tilde{b}}$	.3
c	.14		*e*	.4
e	.40			
and then				
$\tilde{a}$	.6	and finally		
e	.4		$\tilde{\tilde{a}}$	.1

The derivation takes the characters having the two lowest frequencies and assigns the sum of their frequencies to one new character. Since $\tilde{b}$ represents *b* and *d*, we distinguish between them by $\tilde{b}1$ <u>is</u> *b* and $\tilde{b}0$ <u>is</u> *d*. Continuing the distinguishing process, we get

$\tilde{b}1$ <u>is</u> $\tilde{b}$ and $\tilde{b}0$ <u>is</u> c
$\tilde{a}1$ <u>is</u> $\tilde{b}$ and $\tilde{a}0$ <u>is</u> a
$\tilde{\tilde{a}}1$ <u>is</u> $\tilde{a}$ and $\tilde{\tilde{a}}0$ <u>is</u> e

Unwinding, we can write

CHARACTER	CODE
a	$\tilde{\tilde{a}}10$
b	$\tilde{\tilde{a}}1111$
c	$\tilde{\tilde{a}}110$
d	$\tilde{\tilde{a}}1110$
e	$\tilde{\tilde{a}}0$

so that the string $a\ b\ b\ c\ e\ e$ would be represented as $\tilde{a}10\tilde{a}1111$-$\tilde{a}1111\tilde{a}1110\tilde{a}0\tilde{a}0$. One can prove that no code is the head of any other code, so that we can uniquely decipher the code even when the $\tilde{a}$ is not present! Our string would be 101111111111000. Since we have five distinct characters, each could be represented in three binary digits as

a	000
b	001
c	010
d	011
e	100

and we could decipher by counting off in threes. However, note that a b b c e e would require 18 bits in the latter code, whereas in the preceding one, called a Huffman code, only 15 were required. Huffman proved that such codes yield representations having the smallest number of binary digits, on the average. Our derivation process leads to a tree, as shown, and the code for a terminal element is

obtained by following the path from the root to the terminal. Thus the code for c is 110. The string is decoded by walking the tree until a terminal element is obtained and repeating on the substring remaining; see the figure.

We can define an APL function that will create the tree as an array A. Suppose the frequencies, in ascending order, are the components of a vector C. Then the array A created has the property that, if A[3;r] is 2 then A[1;r] is the frequency of one of the original characters, and if P is the path from r to the root, then $1{\downarrow}A[3;P]$ is the Huffman code for the character having the frequency A[1;r].

```
     ∇ A←HUFFMAN C;K;P;L
[1]    A← (3, ρC) ρC, (( ρC) ρ0), ( ρC) ρ2
[2]    LOOP: → (0= ρK←2↑ (A[3; ]=2)/ι ( ρA)[1])/0
[3]    A[3;K]←0 1
[4]    A← (+/A[1;K]), (P←2++/A[2;K]),2),A
[5]    → (( ρA)[1]<L← (A[1; (A[3; ]=2)/ι ( ρA)[1]]
          >A[1;1]).ι1)/LOOP
[6]    A←A[ ; (2+P), (P+2+ιL-P-3), ( ιP+1), (L-1)↓ι
          ( ρA)[1]]
[7]    →LOOP
     ∇
```

QUEUES

An extremely useful data structure is the queue. It may be looked upon as a string for which a new item is appended to the tail of the string and an item is always taken from the head of the string. This is often called a *first-in first-out discipline*. Queues permit no other accessing rights, by which we mean that in certain problems data would be handled only in this way, and a specialization of the data representation for just those accessing rights would be appropriate. Generally queues do not grow and do not collapse in large "chunks." We rarely take out, or add, a large number of particular entries without having added or taken out some others beforehand. Consequently our choice of data representation should mirror this behavior. Thus, suppose we attach an upper bound N to the number of elements in a queue. We might use a "ring" to hold the queue. We do this by subjecting all accesses to the queue to a modular indexing. Let us assume there are N places in the queue Q that we indicated by 0, 1, 2, . . . , $N - 1$. Call these N places the support of the queue.

We shall use two markers, H (head) and T (tail), to point to the head of the queue from which we take and to the tail of the queue into which we put, and a counter q that counts the number of elements in the queue. Clearly, it had always better be that $0 \leq q \leq N$. The functions for handling the queue Q are short and simple:

```
Initiate: T ← H ← q ← 0
Put  (x): if q < N then q ← q+1; Q[T] ← x;
                       T ← T+1(mod N)
          else sorry already full
Take (x): if q > 0 then q ← q-1; x ← Q[H]
                       H ← H+1(mod N)
          else sorry it's empty.
```

When the queue is empty, $H = T$, and when it is full, $T + 1$(mod N) $= H$.

Suppose we wish to lengthen the support by adding integers N, $N + 1$, . . . , $N + M$ to the support. We must be careful, since our queue might be in state (a) shown in the following figure, and we would not want to reach the state indicated by (c)

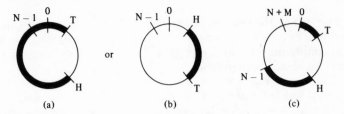

(a)   (b)   (c)

because the insertions that would follow would be incorrectly placed. To ensure that case (c) does not arise, we must determine whether $N - 1$ and 0 are both occupied for, if they are not, case (a) will not arise and we merely extend the support. However, suppose they are. Then a spurious gap will arise in case $H + q > N$, and a segment of queue members will have to be moved. Examining (c), we note two choices and will choose to move the smaller segment:

```
if H+q > N then begin
if N–H ≤ T then begin
for j ← N–1 step –1 until H do
Q[M+j+1] ← Q[j];
H ← H+M+1 end;
else begin
for j ← 0 step 1 until T–1 do
Q[j+N] ← Q[j];
T ← H+q end end;
N ← N+M+1;
```

It is not essential that the support be contiguous. We might maintain two vectors F and G, where $F[k]$ is the base of the $(k - 1)$th extension to the support, and $F[1]$) is the original support base, and $G[k]$ is the extent of the corresponding extension. Then Put and Take must use a modified subscript for H and T in Q[H] and Q[T], respectively.

The management of a queue is vested in the behavior of four functions:

Put(x)
Take(x)
Augment support (base, extent)
Delete support (extent)

The last-named function causes the total support to be diminished and is usually accompanied by a reduction, if possible, in ρF (and ρG, of course).

It is reasonable to treat the handling of queues in two levels:

1. Put and Take, independently of the support (queue logic)
2. Support processing, including accessing, augmenting, and deleting (queue data-processing)

Whether or not the four functions maintain this separation through use of function calls or some other programming device, it is good programming practice to design these four queue functions with the separation clearly understood.

The use of the word *support* in developing the representation for queues was intentional. The programs for processing data structures that have no a priori bounds must inevitably take into account their representation in terms of data structures that are a priori bounded, because real computer memory is made that way.

Consider the stack data structure. Access to a stack S is governed solely by its stack pointer $P(S)$ that points to the last item entered into the stack. The two operations on the stack are push(X,S) and pop(S,X),

```
push(X,S) is P(S) ← P(S)+1; S[P(S)] ← X
pop(S,X) is X ← S[P(S)]; P(S) ← P(S)-1
```

augmenting and diminishing the stack, respectively.

However, the support of a stack is often an array, such as integer array A[0:N], and thus we must not push past N or pop through 0.

No matter what the support is, we must not pop through 0. But what of pushing past N? The former is an error; the latter indicates a deficiency in the extent of support. One technique for handling this overflow situation is to use two levels of support, primary and secondary. Secondary support may be assumed to be significantly larger than primary support, but slow of access, while primary support, though bounded, is of much faster access.

We organize the primary support of the stack as two contiguous buffers. A buffer is a region of storage to which access is had at (at least) two very different rates. Typically, in a computer, buffers are used in handling input-output. In our particular application transfer of information to and from the secondary support is carried out in blocks, whereas stack operations are performed one item (word) at a time. See the figure. Each buffer load has an identi-

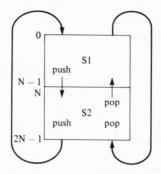

fying index $k = 1, 2, \ldots, M$. Let the index of the contents of S1 be k_1 and that of S2 be k_2.

1. $k_1 = k_2 + 1$
    Pop(S,X) <u>is</u> X←P(S):
    <u>if</u> P(S)=0 <u>then</u> P(S) ← 2N−1
    <u>else</u> <u>begin</u> <u>if</u> P(S)=N <u>then</u> <u>begin</u> empty S1 as load
    k_2 +1;
    load S1 with load k_2−1; P(S)←P(S)−1 <u>end</u>
    Push (X,S) <u>is</u>
    <u>if</u> P(S)=2N−1 <u>then</u> <u>begin</u> P(S)←0;
    <u>else</u> <u>begin</u> <u>if</u> P(S)=N−1 <u>then</u> <u>begin</u> empty S2 as load
    k_1−1;
    load S2 with load k_1 +1; P(S)←P(S)+1 <u>end</u>
    S[P(S)] ← X;
2. $k_1 = k_2 − 1$
    Pop(S,X) <u>is</u> X←P(S)
    <u>if</u> P(S) =0 <u>then</u> <u>begin</u> empty S2 as load k_1 +1;
    fill S2 with load k_1 −1; P(S)←2N−1 <u>end</u>
    <u>else</u> P(S)←P(S)−1;
    Push(X,S) <u>is</u>
    <u>if</u> P(S)=2N−1 <u>then</u> <u>begin</u>
    empty S1 as load k_2 −1; fill S1 with load k_2 +1;
    P(S)←0 <u>end</u>
    <u>else</u> P(S)←P(S)+1;
    S[P(S)]←X;

In modern computers one of the buffers may be filled or emptied from the secondary store while the other is participating in push and pop actions. Hence it is customary to initiate the empty and load operations before $P(S)$ reaches the critical boundary values of 0, $N − 1$, N, or $2N − 1$.

To return to queues, their processing by means of secondary storage would be more effectively organized with the use of four contiguous buffers, so that push and pop sequences near a boundary will not cause thrashing (excessive traffic with the secondary storage).

SEARCHING LINEAR LISTS

Linear lists, or tables, are organized to make it easy to:

1. Retrieve items
2. Insert (new) items
3. Delete items

By "easy" we mean that the amount of computation needed to do any of these operations is as small as we know how to make it. For most tables it is commonly the case that the number of times we perform the operations are in the relations

retrieve ≫ insert ≫ delete

so that it is most important to retrieve as efficiently as possible.

To make matters simple, we imagine a table entry is a pair KEY, POINTER, where KEY is a positive integer that uniquely identifies the table entry and POINTER is a positive integer that points to the arbitrary organization of data, that we can access by executing a procedure DATA(POINTER).

The analysis that follows ignores the nature of the associated data: structure, size, and type. Naturally the definition of a set of procedures to put and take these data is required. The issues arising in handling support for the data are similarly ignored. Therefore it may be assumed that we are concerned with only the two related tables: T and POINTER. If an item searched for has a key found in T[i], then POINTER[i] has an integer that, in some sense, "points to" the attached data.

Each KEY is a component of a vector T, and the retrieval problem is simply this:

Given an integer M which is a key, then where in T, or for what i, will we find an entry such that $M = T[i]$?

The insertion problem is to find an i such that T[i] is unoccupied and M (and its associated POINTER) can be inserted in the tables at i.

An obvious (and expensive) way of searching the table is to start at its beginning and search until the key is found:

```
integer procedure SEARCH(M); value(M); integer M;
begin integer i;
i ← 1;
while T[i] ≠ M ∧ i ≤ size(T) do i ← i +1
SEARCH ← if T[i] = M then i else 1+size(T)
end
```

On the average, size$(T)/2$ entries will be examined: that many probes of the table will be made.

A decrease in the expected number of probes can be made if the keys are ordered in size, for we may then use a binary search method epitomized by the recursive procedure:

```
integer procedure BINSEARCH(a,b,M); value a,b,M ;
integer a,b,M;
begin integer i;
i ← entier ((b−a)÷2);
if i=0 then BINSEARCH ← a
else BINSEARCH ← if M ≤ T[i] then BINSEARCH (a,i,M)
else BINSEARCH (i+1,b,M) end
```

The initial call is BINSEARCH(1,size(T),KEY).

The expected number of probes is approximately $\log_2(\text{size}(T))$. Since the table entries must be sorted in size, insertion of new entries requires shifting of old entries. Consequently, such organized tables are often supported by trees.

But we are interested in obtaining even more dramatic improvements if the keys are ordered in a different way. We will at-

tain this improvement by a method known as *hashing*. Hereinafter
let us reserve n to denote size(T). Suppose the keys are integers
$0 \leq \text{KEY} \leq M$, where $M \gg n$. For example, a key might be a
6-alphanumeric character NAME that can be represented by an
integer $\text{INDEX(NAME)} \leq 10^9$, since $26^6 = 10^{6\,\log_{10}\,26} \simeq 10^{8.5}$. In
APL language $36 \perp \text{'AB...Z0...9'} \iota NAME$ could be used for INDEX.
However, we might anticipate never using more than 100 different
"names" even though we do not know which ones we shall use.
Then how do we relate 10^9 possibilities with 10^2 actualities? One
obvious choice is to correspond 10^7 names with each of the $n = 100$
places in the table by a formula such as

$$M = \text{INDEX(NAME)} = Q \times n + R, \ 0 \leq R < n$$

and we put the key M in T[R]. However, T[R] may be already
filled with some other key. Many values of M will give the same
remainder on division by n; we say these values *collide*. What do
we then do? Clearly, we either put the new key somewhere else or
put the new key in T[R] and move the one already there somewhere else. The first suggests the following algorithm (written in
"APLgol60").

```
integer procedure FIND(NAME); value NAME; integer NAME:
begin integer M,Q,R,i;
M ← INDEX(NAME):
Q ← ⌊ M÷n;
R ← n|M;
i ← 1;
while(T[R] ≠ M) ∨ (T[R] ≠ 0)) ∧ i ≤ n do begin
R ←n|R + Q;
i ← i+1 end;
FIND ← if T[R] = 0 then −R
else if i > n then i else R
end
```

The arithmetic expressions in this algorithm obey APL evaluation
rules.

The procedure FIND then gives one of three answers:

1. M is in the table: $R > 0$ is returned.
2. The table is not full: M is not in the table and should be
   put at T[R]. $R < 0$ is returned.
3. The table is full, and M is not in the table; $n + 1$ is
   returned.

The procedure FIND both finds where M is located and tells where
to put M if it is not there. Of course, the algorithm, to be con-
sistent, defines the only places in T where M could be, those places
where FIND would tell where to put it.

The careful reader must now express some skepticism: although n entries may very well be examined, how do we know the

table is full? Might we not circle through entries more than once? Consider the example $M = 271$, $n = 9$. Then $Q = 30$ and $R_1 = R = 1$. The successive values of R are given by R_{i+1} is $9 | Q + R_i$,

$Q + R_i$	R_{i+1}
31	4
34	7
37	1

and then the values of R repeat. The table entries with indices 2, 3, 5, 6, 8, and 9 will never be examined at all! Even if the table were not full, FIND could never put M away if locations 4, 7, and 1 already contained other keys. Rather than modify the search pattern so as to examine the table entries by some other strategy as, for example, by searching consecutive locations, we shall put a mild restriction on the table size n. We note that, if n is prime and does not divide Q, this premature cycling cannot occur. For, suppose it did first occur in $k < n$ steps; then we would have $R_1 + kQ = R_1 + pn$ for some positive integer p. Hence $kQ = pn$. Since n is prime, it must divide either k or Q and cannot divide either. Therefore, $k \geq n$ and, indeed, $k = n$. Cycling will occur only after the entire table has been searched. The table size n should then be chosen to be a prime number. If n should divide Q, choose Q to be 1.

The desired feature of Q and R is that over the set of keys each value of R and Q (mod n) is equally likely to occur. A technical term for this behavior is that R and Q (mod n) are *uniformly distributed* over the values $0, 1, \ldots, n - 1$. In practice this rarely happens, so that values of Q other than the quotient may just as well be used. In particular, one may choose a Q so that $R + Q < 2n$, and then a subtraction of n replaces the division in the computation of R_{i+1}. Another suggestion is to use $Q' = 1 + m | Q$, where $m < n$.

Assuming the table has $c < n$ entries, what is the expected number E of probes that need to be made to find an empty place in which to put a new entry? This is the same as finding the location of a key that is not yet in the table. Let $\alpha = c/n$; then the expected value E_0 is

$$E_0 = \sum_{k=1}^{n} k \cdot (\text{probability of finding a 0 in } k \text{ steps})$$

Since α is the probability of finding a nonzero entry,

$$E_0(\alpha) = \sum_{k=1}^{n} k \cdot \alpha^{k-1} (1 - \alpha)$$

$$E_0(\alpha) = (1 - \alpha) \sum_{k=1}^{n} k\alpha^{k-1} \leq (1 - \alpha) \frac{d}{d\alpha} \left(\sum_{k=0}^{\infty} \alpha^k \right) = \frac{1}{1 - \alpha}$$

$$= \tilde{E}_0(\alpha)$$

The expected number of probes to find an entry E is the average of the number of probes to find a zero entry when there were no elements in the table, 1 element in the table, 2 elements in the table, etc., or approximately

$$E_f \cong \frac{1}{\alpha} \int_0^\alpha E_0(\beta) \, d\beta \leq \frac{1}{\alpha} \ln \frac{1}{1-\alpha} = \tilde{E}_f$$

The following table shows the behavior of $\tilde{E}_0$ and $\tilde{E}_f$:

FRACTION FULL, α	$\tilde{E}_0$	$\tilde{E}_f$
.20	1.250	1.116
.40	1.667	1.277
.60	2.500	1.527
.80	5.000	2.012
.90	10.000	2.558
.95	20.000	3.153
.99	100.000	4.652

An interesting variant of this method has been developed by Brent. Different keys collide at each R, and we may construct the following diagram shown. Suppose we wish to insert a new key, M.

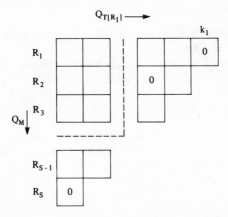

It would normally be placed at R_S after S probes; hence, to find it thereafter would require S probes. Since $T[R_1] \neq M$, then $Q[T[R_1]]$ loads to a path $Q_{T[R_1]}$ that reaches a 0 in k_1 probes. Hence for each $i = 1, 2, \ldots, S - 2$ we find k_i and then find the minimum of

$$1 + k_1, 2 + k_2, \ldots, S - 2 + k_{S-2}, S$$

which are the competing path lengths to a 0 for the keys that collide at R_1. In case of ties we choose the leftmost in the list.

Suppose the minimum is $j + k_j$. Then:

1. Place the entry now at R_j at $(R_j + k_j \times Q[T[R_j]])$ (mod n).
2. Place M at R_j.

Assuming M and the key formerly in R_j are equally likely to be probed for, a reduction in the number of probes for both, from $S + j$ to $2j + k_j$, has been achieved:

$$\Delta = S - (j + k_j)$$

E is the same as for the previous method, but $\tilde{E}'_f$ as shown by Brent is $\sim 1 + \alpha/2 + \alpha^3/4 + \alpha^4/15 + \cdots$. The following table compares this method with the preceding "linear quotient" method. The column labeled "advantage" gives the minimal number of accesses for a key for which this method is advantageous over the linear-quotient method:

FRACTION FULL	$\tilde{E}'_f$	ADVANTAGE
.20	1.102	2.9
.40	1.218	2.6
.60	1.367	2.5
.80	1.599	2.3
.90	1.802	2.3
.95	1.972	2.3
.99	2.242	2.4

Two deficiencies are associated with hashing methods. When deletions are to be made, an element cannot summarily be removed by being replaced with 0, because other colliding chains will also thereby be severed. Hence a special mark or tag must be used to indicate deletion. However, note that the usually much bulkier data attached to the key can be deleted and the data space easily recovered.

When the table becomes full, what can one do? It is unsatisfactory to create an extended overflow table, since new entries will pay a heavy penalty for insertion in this table: If we choose a new table of size n', where

1. n' is prime
2. $n' > n$
3. n' does not divide any key in the table

then we may map the old entries into their new table positions in two scans of the table, one to find n' and one to map the keys.

For example, consider the full table ($n = 7$) and tables for $n' = 13$ and $n' = 19$. Let ν be the number of probes needed to place an entry. Here 19 is the smallest value of n' that satisfies the conditions 1 to 3, but $n' = 13$ is almost as good.

Note how the modified method has improved the number of probes required over that required by the linear-quotient method.

TABLE 4.2

	n = 7				n' = 13		n' = 19	
	Lin. Quot.		Modified		Lin. Quot.		Lin. Quot.	
R	Key	ν	Key	ν	Key	ν	Key	ν
0	22	3	43	2	65	1		
1	43	1	22	1	40	1		
2	51	1	37	1	26	2	40	1
3	37	4	51	2			22	1
4	65	2	65	2	43	1		
5	40	1	26	1			43	1
6	26	6	40	4				
7							26	1
8							65	1
9					22	1		
10								
11					37	1		
12					51	1		
13							51	1
14								
15								
16								
17								
18								

SORTING: AN APPLICATION OF TREES

Suppose we have a tree, with numbers at each node, having the property M: each node has 0, 1, or 2 successors, and the value of each nonterminal node is $\geq$ maximum value of its successors. For such a tree the value at the root-node is the maximum of all the values in the tree.

Now we may append an element X to the tree at the leftmost node of minimum depth that has at most one successor and, through a series of exchanges only with the elements on its path to the root, maintain property M for this augmented tree.

Suppose we have a tree possessing property M. If we exchange the value at the root-node with that at the rightmost terminal node and then sever that terminal, we observe that the severed element has the largest value originally in the tree and the reduced tree no longer has the property M. However, by exchanging the new root value q with the maximum p of its two successors if $q < p$, and continuing this process on the subtree with q at its root until it can no longer be exchanged, the new tree is returned to the state of having property M. Obviously, this process can be iterated until the successive severings leave a tree with only one element. The sequence of severed values is then a sorted (in decreasing order) sequence.

Let us start with an arbitrary sequence of numbers. Let the first be the root-node of our tree, and let us append to the tree successive members of the sequence, exchanging upwards as necessary to maintain property M. When the full tree has grown, apply the reverse process, and successively sever the value at the root-node until the tree has been depleted. The resultant sequence of severed values is a sort of the original sequence.

We may measure the amount of work to sort N numbers by this method in terms of the number of comparisons we must make. In the worst case each element added must be compared with every element on its path to the root—the number of comparisons is the tree depth. Suppose there are K elements already in the tree. The tree has a depth $\lfloor 2 \circledast K$. The total work necessary to create the tree for N elements is proportional to

$$
\begin{aligned}
W &= +/\lfloor 2 \circledast 1 +_\iota N-1 \\
&\cong +/(_\iota q) \times 2 *_\iota q \leftarrow \lfloor 2 \circledast N
\end{aligned}
$$

The sum can be evaluated in closed form, since

$$
\begin{aligned}
W &\simeq 2 \left(\frac{d}{dx} \ +/X *_\iota q \right)_{X=2} \\
&\simeq 2 \left(\frac{d}{dx} \ (((X*1+q)-1) \div X-1) \right)_{X=2} \\
&= 2+(q-1)\times 2 \times q+1
\end{aligned}
$$

or W is proportional to $N \times \log_2 N$.

The same calculation suffices to measure the work for the tree-depletion phase. Hence N numbers may be sorted in $\simeq N \times \log_2 N$ comparisons. This is as bad as it need be. Suppose to sort an arbitrary set of N numbers takes $C(N)$ comparisons. But $C(N)$ comparisons have $2^{C(N)}$ different outcomes. For these N numbers there are $N!$ different sequences possible, and no two should yield exactly the same set of comparison outcomes, for the sorting method could then not distinguish between the two sequences. Hence $2^{C(N)} \geq N!$.

A good approximation for $N!$, the *Stirling approximation*, is

$$N! \simeq 2^{N \times \log_2 N}$$

Therefore

$$C(N) \geq N \times \log_2 N$$

These results tell us that this sorting method is, to within a multiplicative constant, about as good as we can hope for in the case of arbitrary sequences.

In programming this method we must observe that our tree is almost binary and we can scan it from both ends. There is a very neat and simple way of representing such a binary tree T as a vector X. Let $X[1]$ be the root. If $X[j]$ is a nonterminal node of the tree, then $X[2j]$ and $X[2j + 1]$ are its two successor nodes and $X[\lfloor j \div 2]$ is its predecessor for $j > 1$. If $(\rho X) < 2j$, then $X[j]$ is a terminal node. The leftmost node of minimum depth that has at most one successor is $X[\lfloor (1 + \rho X) \div 2 \rfloor]$. The node severed is always $X[\rho X]$ and, of course, ρX is then diminished by 1.

We may build and deplete the vector representation of the tree by operating directly on the given sequence.

Initially we have $X[1], X[2], \ldots, X[N]$, and finally we have $X[1] \leq X[2] \leq \cdots \leq X[N]$.

The algorithm is expressed as the following procedure.

```
procedure SORT (X,N); value N; integer N; array X;
begin integer j, k, ℓ;
create: j←2;
while j ≤N do begin
k←j;
while k>1∧X[ℓ←k÷2] <X[k] do begin
exchange (X,ℓ,k);
k←ℓ end;
j ←j+1 end;
deplete: j←N;
while j ≥2 do begin
exchange (X,1,j);
k←1;
while k≤j ÷2∧X[if X[ℓ←2×k] >X[ℓ+1] ∨ℓ+1≥j then ℓ
else (ℓ+1)] >X[k] do begin
exchange (X,k,ℓ);
k←ℓ end;
j ←j-1 end;
```

The reader should note the similarity of the two parts "create" and "deplete." The exchange(X, r, s) is a procedure or piece of program text that exchanges the contents of $X[r]$ and $X[s]$.

SUMMARY AND REFERENCES

The organization of data is an indispensable component of computer algorithms and is usually dealt with in two phases:

1. Organize the data to best match the input constraints and the requirements of the algorithm. Call this the abstract data representation.
2. Represent the data organization in terms of an available data structure in the programming language that will be used to express the algorithm. Call this the concrete data representation.

Two extreme positions can be defined for manipulating data organizations: interpretive and compiling. In the former all contact with data is through functions that alone work with the data representation. The program maintains the fiction of the abstract data representation: it is close to the original algorithm, and changes in the choice of concrete data representation will not overly affect the program. In the latter all contact with the data is through the language primitives. Changes in data representation must now be treated like any other reprogramming activity. One soon ignores the abstract data structure in working with the program.

Programs generally do not end up in either extreme position.

Many programming languages have been invented to narrow the gap between the two extremes. None is ideal over a wide range of data structures. This is primarily because it is difficult in these languages to describe how data structures are to be manipulated by the background computer on which the programs are to be run.

Every serious programmer should become familiar with a few of these data-structure-oriented languages. Some references follow. SNOBOL is beautifully described in

R. E. Griswold, J. F. Poage, and I. P. Polansky, *The SNOBOL4 Programming Language* (Prentice-Hall, Englewood Cliffs, N. J., 1968).

LISP is described in

W. D. Maurer, *The Programmer's Introduction to LISP* (American Elsevier, New York, N. Y., 1972),
C. Weissman, *LISP 1.5 Primer* (Dickinson Publishing, Belmont, Cal., 1967).

Algol68 is described in

C. Lindsey and S. Van der Meulen, *Informal Introduction to Algol68* (North Holland Press, Amsterdam, Netherlands, 1971).

Excellent general treatments of data structures can be found in

D. Knuth, *The Art of Computer Programming* Vol. I (Addison-Wesley, Reading, Mass., 1968),
B. A. Galler and A. J. Perlis, *A View of Programming Languages* (Addison-Wesley, Reading, Mass., 1969),
M. C. Harrison, *Data Structures and Programming* (Scott, Foresman, Glenview, Ill., 1973).

Computer science journals abound with technical papers treating various aspects of data structures. We single out a few here that exemplify the representation of abstract data structures in the data structures available in specific programming languages.

The representation of strings in trees:

E. Berkeley and D. Bobrow, eds., *The Programming Language LISP: Its Operations and Applications* (Information International, Cambridge, Mass., 1964). Note the chapter on METEOR.

Hash coding is described in an excellent paper,

R. Brent, "Reducing the Retrieval Time of Scatter Storage Techniques" (*Communications of the ACM*, 16, February, 1973, pp. 105–109),

and in the book by Harrison (cited above) that also includes an excellent bibliography of the subject.

PROBLEMS

1. Suppose you are given twelve seemingly identical balls. Actually, eleven are the same weight, and one is either heavier or lighter. Given an equal-arm balance, give a tree-diagram algorithm to identify the odd ball and to determine whether it is heavier or lighter in just three weighings.

2. Design a program that could decide what the "best" move would be for any given position in Qubic—three dimensional tic-tac-toe—played on a 4 × 4 × 4 cube. Your program should use a minimum-decision procedure with α,β pruning. For an evaluation function use the table shown, where $h(n)$ is the number of "2 in a

		Value to your program	
Number of "3 in a row" for program	Number of "3 in a row" for opponent	When it is opponent's move	When it is program's move
0	0	h(n)	h(n) + 2
	1 or more	–	–
1	0	h(n) + 2	+
	1 or more	–	+
2 or more	0	+	+
	1 or more	–	+

row" your program has, minus the number of "2 in a row" the opponent has. "N in a row" means you have N marks somewhere in a column, row, or diagonal in which the opponent has no marks. This evaluation function is fairly arbitrary, but that is irrelevant to the construction of the program.

Your program should search ahead to a depth D, accepting D as input parameter. Test your program for $D = 5$.

Your program should accept a given position as input, output the "best" move, output its backed-up value, and output the total number of positions to which the evaluation procedure was applied.

3. The Game of Four (or Fourpawn) uses a 4-by-4 checkerboard. Each player begins the game with four pawns located on his baseline. White moves first, with play alternating between black and white. The rules of the game are as follows.

  a. Either white or black, in his turn, can move forward one space to an unoccupied space.
  b. Or he can move diagonally one space to capture an opponent. A captured piece is removed from the board.
  c. The game is won by reaching the opponent's baseline with any one of your pawns.
  d. Or it can be won by leaving the opponent without a move. (NOTE: Two opposing pieces directly in front of each other are blocked from moving.)
  e. Or it can be won by capturing all the opponent's pieces.

(1) Show three plays of the game tree for Fourpawn, beginning with the first move of the game.

(2) Design a heuristic to be used to assign a value to each node of the tree. Fill in your tree from (1) with these values.

(3) Apply the minimax technique to determine an optimal branch to follow.

(4) Explain how tree-pruning is used: that is, which branches should not be searched further.

(5) After making the move for white dictated by (a), (b), and (c), repeat the 3-play evaluation for black, and move for black.

(6) Write an algorithm that plays Fourpawn by this technique.

4. CHESS-PLAYING PROGRAM (KING, ROOK, PAWN, VERSUS KING, ROOK, PAWN)

Chess is played on a square board subdivided into 64 smaller squares arranged as an 8 × 8 array. The board is always oriented so there is a light colored square at the lower right-hand corner of the board. We shall use usual matrix notation in referring to the board: thus, (1, 1), (1, 8), (8, 1), and (8, 8) refer, respectively, to the upper left, upper right, lower left, and lower right corners. In our game each side will have a king, a rook, and a pawn that will be situated as follows:

PIECE	SQUARE
white king	(8, 7)
white rook	(8, 6)
white pawn	(6, 7)
black king	(1, 3)
black rook	(1, 4)
black pawn	(3, 3)

MOVES OF THE PIECES. The pawn can only move forward (toward the opponent's end of the board) one square at a time. It is blocked from moving if any piece is directly in front of it; however, it may capture an opponent's piece to which it is diagonally adjacent. A pawn can capture an opponent's piece that is one square ahead and to the right or left of it.

A capture is achieved by moving into the square that holds the opponent's piece and then removing the opponent's piece from the board.

The rook can move forward or backward, left or right (either horizontally or vertically, but not both on the same move), for as many squares as the player wishes; thus a rook situated on an empty board of (4, 5) could on its next move go to any of the 7 squares in column 5. The rook is blocked by pieces of its own color; thus, if the rook was on (4, 5), and pieces of the same color were on (4, 3), (4, 6), (3, 5), and (7, 5), the rook could move only to (4, 4), (5, 5), or (6, 5).

The king can move one square in any direction, including diagonally.

SOME RULES. The king is said to be in check if it is under the threat of being captured on the next move. The king is said to be checkmated if it is in check and cannot avoid capture.

It is illegal to make a move that would render your king in check.

If your pawn can reach the end row of the board without being taken, it can be exchanged for any other piece (except a second king). (Usually the queen is chosen, because it is the most powerful piece; hence this process is called "queening.")

OBJECT OF THE GAME. The game ends when one player catches the opposing player's king. In our game (king-rook-pawn game) it will usually be enough to achieve either of the two following (in order to guarantee a win),

Have your pawn "queen"
Capture your opponent's rook
unless
You are checkmated on the next move
Your "queened pawn" (that is, the queen) is immediately recaptured
Your opponent "queens" too
In capturing your opponent's rook you lose your own rook

THE PROBLEM. Write an Algol60 or APL program to play out this chess game. The program should move for one side and then accept as input the opponent's move. (White always moves first,

and then the moves alternate.) To standardize things we shall enter
moves as

PIECE NUMBER   ROW NUMBER   COLUMN NUMBER

where the pieces are 1, 2, and 3 for white's king, rook, and pawn,
respectively, and 91, 92, and 93 for black's; thus the move 92 1 8
signifies that the black rook moves to square (1, 8).

A minimal program should (a) be able to play as either black
or white, (b) make only legal moves, and (c) detect illegal moves
made by the opponent.

BONUS PARTS.   Do not attempt these until you have a fully
operational minimal program.

Develop a set of strategic rules that govern the play.
Use a game tree analysis to "look ahead" several moves.
Use a minimax technique with α,β pruning on your game tree.

HINT: Normally your program should examine all possible legal
moves and,

If there is a winning move, make it
If the opponent has a winning move, block it
Adopt a "board position strength" rating scheme (for example, number of squares you control plus 5 divided by number
of squares your pawn is away from "queening" plus 3 times
number of capture threats), and select the move that leads to
the position with the highest rating

5.   Once upon a time there was a professor who was lost in a very
special wilderness. It seems that the professor decided to explore
part of this wilderness but quickly discovered that he was hope-
lessly lost. It is your job to produce a map of part of this wilderness
so that our professor can find his way home.

As it turns out, topographic information exists in the neighbor-
hood of where the professor is lost. This information has been ab-
stracted relative to altitude and, surprisingly enough, includes the
position of the professor and his home. Further, a two-dimensional
array, called MAP, contains this data in the following form.

a.   If $MAP[I, J] > 0$, then $MAP[I, J]$ represents the average
altitude of a small patch of land in the wilderness.
b.   If $MAP[I, J] = 0$, then the professor is standing on this
patch of land.
c.   If $MAP[I, J] < 0$, then the professor's house is on this
patch of land.

Produce a contour map of the area subject to:

1. MAP is a real array with the declaration

    <u>real</u> <u>array</u> MAP[1:50, 1:120];

    Further, within MAP there will be elements correspond-
    ing to the highest elevation, call it H, and elements corre-
    sponding to the lowest elevation, L. If N represents the
    number of contour intervals that are to appear, then
    $(H - L)/N$ represents the number of feet indicated by
    each interval.

2. The map should appear centered on a single page of
    printed output containing only the map. It should appear
    as a rectangle containing 50×120 adjacent character po-
    sitions, where each position represents an element from
    the array MAP. On the contour map should be included
    the characters:

    "/"   at the professor's position
    "*"   at his home
    "+" at the altitude of the highest point (there may be
          more than one such point on the map)
    "−" at the altitude of the lowest point (there may be
          more than one such point)

3. The contours should be generated by means of the follow-
    ing algorithm:

    a. If $(H - L)/N$ represents the number of feet in each
        interval, and we call it F, then the following intervals
        result.

        highest: $H \geq X > (H - F)$ interval 1
                 $H - F \geq X > (H - 2 \times F)$ interval 2
                                . . .   . . .

        lowest: $H - (N - 1) \times F \geq X > L$ interval N
        Intervals 2, 4, 6, . . . , $2 \times I$, . . . ,

        where $I \leq N \div 2$, are said to be even intervals. The
        remaining intervals are called odd intervals.

    b. Now look at the rows of MAP, and classify each ele-
        ment as to its interval number.

    c. Next count the number of elements of MAP that are
        in even intervals and the number that are in odd
        intervals; call these values E and O, respectively.
        Now, if $E > O$, then print "X" for each element of
        MAP which is in an even interval, and print a blank
        for each element which is in an odd interval. Other-
        wise, print "X" for each element in an odd interval and
        a blank for each element in an even interval.

Following the MAP itself, you should print the elevation of the highest and lowest points of the map.

6. POLYNOMIALS. A polynomial in N variables consisting of M terms has the general form

$$\sum_{I=1}^{M} \left\{ C_I \prod_{J=1}^{N} V_J{}^{E_{I,J}} \right\}$$

where C_I is the coefficient of the Ith term, V_J is the Jth variable, and $E_{I,J}$ is the exponent of the Jth variable in the Ith term. For example,

$$-2X + 3XY^2Z - 4Z$$

is a polynomial in three variables (that is, $N = 3$) and has three terms (that is, $M = 3$), where $C_1 = -2, C_2 = 3, C_3 = -4; V_1 = X,$ $V_2 = Y, V_3 = Z,$ and

$$\begin{aligned} E_{1,1} &= 1 & E_{2,1} &= 1 & E_{3,1} &= 0 \\ E_{1,2} &= 0 & E_{2,2} &= 2 & E_{3,2} &= 0 \\ E_{1,3} &= 0 & E_{2,3} &= 1 & E_{3,3} &= 1 \end{aligned}$$

Such a polynomial can be represented in Algol60 with an array of values in the following manner.

First declare <u>real</u> array P[1:M, 0:N], and fill the array using these rules:

$P[I, 0]$, where $I = 1, 2, \ldots, M$ should contain the coefficient of the Ith term (C_I).

$P[I, J]$, where $I = 1, 2, \ldots, M$ and $J = 1, 2, \ldots, N$ should contain the exponent of the Jth variable in the Ith term.

The polynomial appearing in this example would then be represented in an array P, as

here $M = 3$ and $N = 3$

	0	1	2	3
1	−2	1	0	0
2	3	1	2	1
3	−4	0	0	1

This is one way of representing a polynomial in N variables and is a reasonable way of representing a polynomial for this problem. *It is by no means the only way!!!*

Suppose you are given a polynomial described as an array; construct an algorithm for printing it. You may assume the variables of the polynomial are X_1," "X_2," etc. The printing should satisfy the following.

1. All exponents are on a line, all coefficients and variables are on the following line, and all subscripts (the 1 in X_1, etc.) are on a third line. Horizontal spacing between adjacent characters is doubled to balance the spacing between lines.
2. The polynomial is centered on the line.
3. The polynomial is printed as a sum (or difference) of terms with coefficient preceding. Variables of zero exponent are omitted, and exponents of 1 are not printed. For example,

$$3X_1X_3{}^2 + 4X_2X_3{}^3$$

You may assume all coefficients are integers and that the polynomial will fit in one printing line.

7. Another way of representing trees is to use local weights. For any node k, $W[k]$ is the number of branches descending from k. Give algorithms for translating between this representation and the representation, in which accumulated weights are used, developed in the text.

8. Give an algorithm for translating from breadth representation to a depth representation for trees. An example is the following.

From:

| D: | a b g h r m n p w t c u v d k x |
| W: | 15 6 6 6 0 5 0 4 4 3 0 1 0 0 0 0 0 |

To:

| D: | a b r p t o x u g m n w v d k h |
| W: | 15 6 5 4 0 1 0 0 6 0 4 3 0 0 0 0 |

9. Give an algorithm for transforming a tree with root node $D[1]$ into one for which $D[k]$ is the root node.

10. Find the unique path vector from node $D[j]$ to node $D[k]$.

11. Give an algorithm for transforming a tree when a branch is cut and one of the nodes of one part is connected to a node of the other part.

12. Over the collection of tree transformations for which you have found algorithms, do any advantages accrue in maintaining both a depth and a breadth representation for a tree?

13. Suppose on the average it takes T seconds to exchange the contents of a buffer of N components with secondary storage. Furthermore, suppose every t seconds, on the average, a push or a pop occurs. At what values of $S(P)$ should exchanges with secondary storage be initiated? How can a reasonably small value of N be estimated? Assume $t \ll T$.

14. An interesting application of the use of trees is the formal differentiation of arithmetic expressions such as $Z + 2 \times (Z \uparrow 3)$, $Z / (Z + 3)$, etc. These expressions may be represented as trees; for example,

```
+ Z × 2 ↑ Z 3      and      / Z + Z 3
6 0 4 0 2 0 0                4 0 2 0 0
     (a)                       (b)
```

Differentiation with respect to Z may be denoted by

```
D + Z × 2 ↑ Z 3      D / Z + Z 3
7 6 0 4 0 2 0 0      5 4 0 2 0 0
     (a)                (b)
```

The operation d/dZ can be performed by correctly dispersing D through the tree. Case (a) transforms successively to

```
+ D  Z  D × 2 ↑ Z 3          + 1  D × 2 ↑ Z 3
8 10 5 4 0 2 0 0       ⇒      7 0 5 4 0 2 0 0       ⇒

+ 1  + × D 2 ↑ Z 3 × 2 D ↑ Z 3
14 0 12 5 1 0 2 0 0 5 0 3 2 0 0       ⇒

+ 1  + × 0 ↑ Z 3 × 2 D ↑ Z 3
13 0 11 4 0 2 0 0 5 0 3 2 0 0       ⇒

+ 1  + × 0 ↑ Z 3  × 2 × 3 × ↑ Z - 3 1 D Z
19 0 17 4 0 2 0 0 11 0 9 0 7 4 0 2 0 0 1 0       ⇒

+ 1  + × 0 ↑ Z 3  × 2 × 3 × ↑ Z + 3 1 1
18 0 16 4 0 2 0 0 10 0 8 0 6 4 0 2 0 0 0
```

which, though it can be simplified, is the differentiated expression.

The tree operations that must be programmed are:

1. Find and delete first D.
2. Find the attached operator.
3. Find and delete left and right operands.
4. According to the attached operator, assemble new left and right operands, and insert them into the tree with the new attached operator.

Repeat these steps until no occurrence of D remains.

Write the algorithms for differentiation. Assume that $+$, $-$, $\times$, $/$, and $\uparrow$ are the operations and that integers are the numeric constants.

15. Write APL functions for matching the following patterns over strings composed of characters over an alphabet A:

1. $P1$:   matches any string.
2. $P2(j)$:   matches any string having j characters.
3. $P3(s)$:   matches any string having only characters in the string s.
4. $P4(P)$:   matches any string composed of consecutive substrings, each matching the pattern P.
5. $P5(a, b)$: matches any string commencing with the character "a" and terminating with "b" and having the additional property that, if $\nu(X) =$ number of 'a's and $\mu(X) =$ number of 'b's encountered up to the Xth character, then $\nu(X) - \mu(X) > 0$ for all X except the X associated with the last character matched, at which point $\nu(X) = \mu(X)$. This pattern is used for matching parentheses.

16. Consider the strings over the alphabet 0, 1, where X and Y are two such fixed strings. Let the following patterns be defined:

```
R1 is X ∨ Y
R2 is P4(R1) (see problem 15)
```

Write the pattern-matching function for R2.

17. Write APL or Algol60 functions to add, multiply, and take positive-integer powers of polynomials as represented in problem 6. Can you write each of these as a one-liner in APL?

CHAPTER 5

SYSTEMS

5

OVERVIEW

What is a system? In our context it is a set of cooperating programs or procedures designed to meet some goal. What does it mean to say they cooperate?

    1. They obey certain conventions regarding their shared use of global variables.

    2. They are linked to each other through the use of inputs and production of outputs.

    3. Each of the programs performs a specialized function which, although perhaps adaptable to a number of systems, in particular combination with the other procedures present in the system enables the system to meet its goals.

Generally we say more. A system contains certain particular functions:

    1. A monitor that controls which, and when, system functions are performed.

    2. An interrupt, or error-processor, that controls the system behavior when there is a departure from normal (error-free) behavior.

    3. An I/O processor that communicates with the system user—for example—at a terminal.

A system is characterized by being able to operate in a variety of modes and perform useful variations of its abilities, each of which is described as a program in a language we might call TSL (task-setting language). All of the normal tasks that the system performs should be easily expressed in a TSL.

A system is generally so complex that it possesses documentation that is more than a description of its component programs. Documentation generally includes:

    0.   What the system does
    1.   How to use the system
    2.   How the system works; expressed in terms of

a. how to understand it
b. how to repair it
c. how to extend it

Documentation is never perfect; there is usually too little rather than too much. Still, the latter situation may be as distasteful as the former. There is no standard way of providing documentations: flowcharts are not necessarily the best documentation. Since one can only understand a system through its performance of tasks, a good documentation device is a select set of carefully annotated system runs.

The development of a system goes through the stages:

1. Identification of need
2. Design, taking into account, first, simplicity and then adequacy, efficiency, and ability to evolve
3. Construction
4. Testing
5. Documentation
6. Use: which means its smooth imbedding in some larger, already existing, system

It is important in building a system to confine intellectual activity to an "intermediate" level of concern, leaving both an outer and an inner level, assumed already to exist, unchanged. Thus, in the examples that follow the users at the outer level, and APL at the inner level, will not be tampered with. Systems that bite off more than they can chew cause indigestion at all three levels.

For the moment we shall assume that a need for a system has been identified, so that we shall first consider the issues raised in design. Presumably there already exists a set of goals: requirements the system must meet in order to serve its purpose. A word of caution should be said concerning goals. They are rarely clear. Systems characteristically do not process precise goals. Often they are asked to perform a diffuse set of functions, and very often they suffer from a vexing lack of continuity: while the system adequately performs a task T, a second task T', slightly different from T, strains or exceeds the capabilities of the system.

Systems arise for any of different reasons: (a) an existing system needs to be copied into a new environment, (b) a generalization or specialization, or both, of an existing system seems appropriate, (c) a set of previously disjoint activities becomes related where they had not before been so. In the latter case it is often the emergence of new hardware that stimulates system development. However, in all cases it is the existence, or potential, of traffic that is the necessary condition for system development: a system must be expected to acquire heavy use.

Along with system use comes a pressure for system degradation: when a system is heavily used, most users will weakly use it, or poorly use it, or even misuse it. A system must expect to provide services to users of whom many will be ignorant of system nuances (how to take advantage of all the wonderful "hooks" and "gadgets" every system seems to accumulate), and almost all users will misuse the system (make blunders), at least in their initial stages of system use.

It is worth saying a word or two about these "hooks" that show up in every system. Once a system achieves a certain complexity, by containing enough cooperating processes many new and apparently worthwhile capabilities evidence themselves. Furthermore, many of these additions cost very little to include in the system, while their inclusion enhances the system for many users.

A related phenomenon noted in many systems is that some additions, seemingly but slightly different from capabilities already present and introduced at low cost, can be made only by drastic redesign of the system and, hence, at enormous cost. One is tempted to call this prevalent phenomenon "ultimate discontinuity in design."

It is probably true that people are more unforgiving of system behavior the less the understanding of the system that is required of them. All of the foregoing is a prelude to the statements that a system must expect its users to make errors and that the system components must be protected against such errors. Of course it goes without saying that the users must also be guaranteed that the system will accomplish correctly what it has been defined to do.

Generally systems are complicated—they contain a large amount of program code—and are built by many programmers. Both factors cause systems to be designed in a modular fashion. It is our purpose now to understand what we mean by modularization: the division of a complex into parts or modules. These modules represent data-processing functions that can be isolated and are often of use to other parts; note the plural. Generally the isolation of a module is accompanied by an ability to give, for its data-processing function, an adequate description that is significantly simpler to understand than its program listing.

What principles guide us in establishing modules?

1. Modules are chosen to be the functions that the outer environment understands the system to perform ("what" functions).
2. Modules are chosen to be the functions that make most natural, simple, and extensive use of the facilities of the inner environment ("how" functions).

In point of fact the first describes a decomposition that must be visible to the user, and the second describes the decomposition from which the system should be built. We might say that it is the task of the system designer to connect the two specifications, from "what must be" to "how it will be."

There are, of course, other aspects to this task that add art and spice to system design. For example, we do not always go solely from "what" to "how." Often we extend, or are forced to modify, what we will do by our knowledge of how things are to be done. The system is an information-organizing and action-organizing boundary between the outer and inner environments, and a fluid one at that. Fluidity is maintained by demanding that the "how" modules be kept well separated and that they communicate with each other in quite rigid ways, so that individual module alteration or deletion will affect other modules in quite limited ways.

In particular, no "how" module should be dependent upon how another module performs its function: their relation to each other must always be in terms of what they do, which must ultimately be expressed in terms of what they need (input) and what they produce (output). Nowhere is this more important than in the manipulation of data structures: each data structure (not each type of data structure) should be shielded from all modules but a select few, whose only functions are the data-processing functions associated with the structure. Why should this be so? In any system there are usually many data representations (in terms of inner system capabilities) from which to choose. The issues of simplicity, generality, and efficiency lead to a choice, but inevitably circumstances change—either in the outer or inner environments of systems—and thus representations change. When this occurs, the influence of the change must not propagate into the interior functions of those modules whose concern is with the use of data and not their representation.

Organizing the proper control and data communication between modules is extremely difficult and is best undertaken by using combinations of certain standard models. The most widely used models are procedures, coroutines, and cooperating sequential processes, and they are often organized into combinations of "virtual machines" or layered environments. We will appreciate the use of those terms by shortly considering some examples.

We have seen how procedures are defined in Algol60 and APL. All programming languages have some definition of procedures. In this chapter we are interested in their use as modules. Communication between procedures is via the call and the passing of actual parameters. If we avoid the use of global variables, each procedure is "opaque" to all others except for those (as in Algol60) defined within it. However, the use of procedures organizes control into a hierarchical structure: for example, "A calls B and B calls C" implies that processing commences with A and only when B is completed may A continue. On each call B commences at its beginning and proceeds to its end, calling on C en route.

System organization based on procedures is generally quite tidy, though it is often not as efficient as one would like. Thus if A calls on B but passes on each call incomplete data to be processed, so much at each call, how does B keep a record of where it is in the sequence of calls? Through global variables?

The classical example is in language compilers. Imagine we have two procedures, SYN and SEM. SYN has as its formal parameter a string A of characters and produces a parse tree T. SEM has as its formal parameter a parse tree Y and produces a code list C. Simple enough: execute the procedure composition

```
C ←SEM(SYN(A))
```

But the entire text A must be available, and the entire tree SYN(A) must be produced, and then the entire code C is generated; see the figure. Since SYN uses A while SEM does not, procedure com-

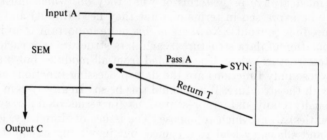

position obscures the cooperative nature of the processing of A to produce C.

Coroutines are a programming organization designed to facilitate the cooperation this kind of "stream" processing calls for. Even more, as coroutines, SEM and SYN can process pieces of A and produce subtrees of T and chunks of the code C. As coroutines SYN and SEM work as follows. A link holding an address or label is defined:

```
SYN–SEM LINK: α
```

Initially α points to the head of SEM, while control resides in SYN. Suppose a coroutine call from SYN to SEM is to be made; see the figure. SYN exchanges γ with the contents of the link and calls on

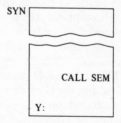

SEM at the address α pointed to in the link. The following diagram shows the flow of control in a sequence of such calls.

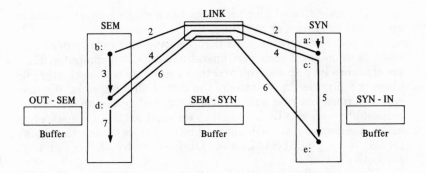

The contents of the SEM-SYN LINK at each step of the processing are:

1	b
2	c
4	d
6	e

In addition to the connecting link, data are passed between the two programs. We may think of the data as being the contents of the indicated buffers. The buffers are the actual parameters in all coroutine calls.

We may commence with control residing in any of the four programs that follow. The three buffers may be in any filled or empty state whatsoever.

```
SEM:
L1: if empty (SEM-SYN) then SYN:
if empty (OUT-SEM) then OUT-SEM ← createcode
  (SEM-SYN);
OUT:
goto L1
SYN:
L2: if empty (SYN-IN) then IN;
if empty (SEM-SYN) then SEM-SYN← createtree (SYN-IN);
SEM;
goto L2
OUT:
L3: if empty (OUT-SEM) then SEM;
printcode (OUT-SEM);
goto L3
IN:
L4: if empty (SYN-IN) then readtext (SYN-IN);
if terminal (SYN-IN) then halt;
SYN;
goto L4
```

The collection of four programs has a single control, vested in one of the programs at any time.

Suppose we now imagine that we have four independent controls, as we might if each were operating on its own computer. Each program has its own control, and they cooperate with each other by obeying rigid rules in their use of the three buffer registers. We shall call programs obeying such "social" rules of behavior *cooperating sequential processes*. To be specific, we shall attach a signal, often called a *semaphore*, to each shared buffer. Let us denote the signals for SYN-IN, SEM-SYN, and OUT-SEM by R, S, and T, respectively.

Let us confine our attention to the signal S. Signals R and T would be tested in similar ways. Two operations on S are postulated: grab S and release S. Two programs, possibly executing simultaneously, SEM and SYN share S and the associated buffer SEM-SYN. We shall assume that the buffer is organized as a queue. The operations grab and release are context boundaries like begin and end, and their behavior is defined by the following rules.

1. Only one program at a time can have its control pass grab S.
2. If a program control has moved past a grab S, it can only access and affect the variables q, H, and T of the buffer until it *reaches* the matching release S, and only until then and during no other times.
3. If a program P_1 reaches a grab S, and some other program P_2 is between a grab S and its matching release S, then P_1 must wait until P_2 reaches its next release S before it may continue—its operation is temporarily suspended. When a release S is reached, one of the suspended programs held up at a grab S is allowed to proceed. Nothing is known about the rule for determining which of the waiting programs is allowed to proceed.

SEM might contain the following program to read data from the SEM-SYN buffer to storage in SEM. The variables H, T, N, and q refer to the queue SEM-SYN as they were defined under "Queues" of Chapter 4.

```
Bring(a,ℓ,p):
L: grab S: c← q release S;
if p >c then goto L;
for j ← 0 step 1 until p-1 do a[ℓ + j] ←
SEM−SYN[H + j];
grab S: q← q - p; h←h + p (mod N) release S;
ℓ ←ℓ - p;
```

The program SYN has a corresponding program Deposit, which outputs from its storage into the buffer:

```
Deposit(b,ℓ,p);
L: grab S: c ← q; d← N release S;
if c + p ≥ d then goto L;
for j ←0 step 1 until p - 1 do SEM-SYN[T + j] ←
b[ℓ + j];
grab S: q ← q + p; T←T + p (mod N) release S;
ℓ ←ℓ + p;
```

We might observe that SEM might operate directly on the two buffers SEM-SYN and OUT-SEM, acting as a direct synchronizer between these two buffers:

```
SEM:
p ←treestate; comment how much tree is needed;
n ←codestate: comment how much code is to be produced;
L grab S: c ←q release S;
if p > c then goto L;
L1: grab T: d ← q; f ← N release T;
if n + d ≥ f then goto L1;
makecode(p,n);
comment makecode takes the tree data in SEM-SYN[H] to
SEM-SYN[H + p - 1] and produces code in OUT-SEM[T] to
OUT-SEM[T + n - 1] and produces new treestate and
codestate values;
```

We shall always terminate in the coroutine IN.

Actually, real matters are somewhat more complicated, since SYN may put less in the SEM-SYN buffer than SEM needs, and SEM may produce more than OUT-SEM can handle. Furthermore, SEM may require, in order to produce its code, an additional small piece of tree derived from some text that may be a long time in coming. One of the reasons that programming languages are made context-free is that such a situation may not arise. However, some algorithms do require, for example, forward references, as in Algol60 with goto K, since the statement labeled by K will possibly not have been encountered prior to the text "goto K." Please note, however, that a second pass over the text, if needed, could be processed in the same coroutine manner as the first.

Unfortunately, neither APL nor Algol60 includes a defined coroutine structure, though one can be implemented easily, albeit clumsily, in either language through the use of procedures.

Regardless of how modularity is achieved, the goal of limiting information flow between modules is a good one. We mean not only the information that must be supplied for the modules to cooperate but additional information that, if supplied, would contract or alter the mutual independence of the modules. With a decrease in mutual independence comes an increase in mutual responsibility that must be accepted at moments of crisis is a system's history. These crises principally occur when the system is under construction and when the system is modified.

Observe that the nature of Algol60 procedures is such that a collection of procedure definitions and calls can be combined into a procedure, but this is not the case of APL functions.

Modules share the inner system (machine) and, through that sharing, they possess only a simulated independence. It is the responsibility of the inner system to maintain this fiction of independence. An aspect of system design is the definition and complementation of mechanisms for maintaining "fictional" independence between modules. The resources being shared by modules are both hardware and program. For an example consider an APL function F that uses trees and so has defined a set of tree-processing functions, T. Suppose that another APL function G is to be created that also processes trees and that G and F communicate tree information with each other. Two models suggest themselves, as shown in the figures. We might prefer (b) because all tree-processing is concen-

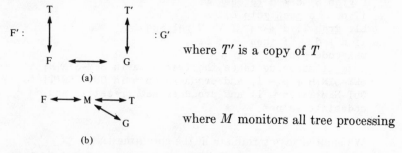

where T' is a copy of T

(a)

where M monitors all tree processing

(b)

trated in one module, M. However, should G go away, figure (a) would be more natural. At present transitions between styles (a) and (b) are not automatically accomplished by systems.

One aspect of systems is rarely spotlighted in individual programs: the systematic handling of errors. Systems are constructed from parts that are intentionally isolated from each other and are organized to provide a set of services to users who are not expected to understand how the system functions. Consequently, during system functioning demands on modules are often made that cannot be satisfied. The resultant error often reveals itself in a module that is not the source of the error and hence is unequipped to respond to it and certainly unable to recover from it, particularly since one of the prime desiderata of system design is that modules respond to anonymous calls for their services.

Hence we must find certain standard procedures for the processing of errors when anonymous coupling between modules occurs. We shall present such a model during the course of studying our examples.

THE APL SYSTEM

APL, as described in Chapter 3, was viewed as a programming language. There is also an APL system that manages or supervises the execution and handling of programs written in the APL language. And Algol60, too, has a system for the same purposes. We wish to examine in some detail the APL system as a system prototype, although actual APL systems may differ somewhat in detail from that described here. We commence by exhibiting a set of system flowcharts that show the data and control flow paths connecting the system functions. Insofar as the system is concerned, the user APL programs are merely data for the APL interpreter, and some of the program's results create control signals to the system.

APL is interactive. Programs are entered and activated from terminals. Input is requested by a program during its execution and is supplied from the terminal when requested. Moreover, the program's execution can be interrupted by a request from the terminal. It is in these two senses that APL is interactive.

The symbols in (5.1) refer to the following.

T_i: the ith terminal on which the ith user is in (continual) communication with the system
I: the interpreter that executes APL code
W_i: the ith workspace
LIB: the set of available workspaces, data, and functions
M: the system monitor
L: the system loader for putting information in workspace
I/O: the input-output handler

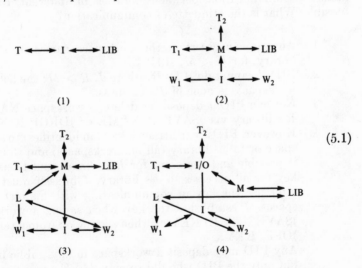

(5.1)

Note that only two terminals are shown. Clearly more are possible. The four figures represent increasingly realistic views of the APL system and, reveal through separation of functions, an increase in modularity. Often used system actions have been consigned to independent modules.

A good place to start our study of the APL system is the workspace: the working computer storage assigned to the terminal. The workspace contains:

Function definitions
Variables and their values
Execution status information

All information relating to the progression of the ith computation P_i is kept in W_i. Should W_i be altered, then W_j, where $j \neq i$, is unaffected, except for queries explicitly referencing W_i. Should the progress be interrupted for some reason other than a catastrophic breakdown in the system, then P_i can be continued at some later time without loss of information.

LIB holds a set of workspace collections available to the user population of an APL system. The users are distinguishable by a set of identification numbers, (PID), which we may take to be the integers M to N. For each PID there is a library of workspaces. Each of these is a private library. Generally there are also public libraries, to which any user may have access: the PID's 1 to M-1. Each of the workspaces in a user library has a unique name. There is, of course, a system command in TSL that enables T_i to ascertain which workspaces are in the associated library:)LIB.

In APL commands commencing with ")" are system commands. Communication between libraries of different PID's is possible. What is the etiquette of communication?

1. Anyone can ascertain the workspace names in a public library: for $K < M$,)LIB K.
2. PID J cannot do)LIB R, where $J, R > M$: the list of R's workspaces is none of J's business.
3. Nor can PID J deposit, or delete, a workspace NAME in R's library via)SAVE R NAME or)DROP R NAME.
4. However, PID J can attach a key (an identifier) to a workspace or to his library (all his workspaces) and thus make it possible and necessary for R to know, and to use, this key for all accesses to J's library. J himself must thereafter use the key in communicating with his own workspaces. J establishes the key when saving a workspace,)SAVE NAME: KEY or when signing off from a terminal,)OFF: KEY.
5. Any PID may deposit a workspace in any public library, but only the PID who did so may SAVE a new version of it or drop it from the public library.
6. The current workspace of any PID always has the name CONTINUE and the system saves the workspace under that name if a malfunction requires suspension of computer activity.
7. A new version of an existing workspace can be SAVEd,

but it must have the same name as the workspace it is replacing:

```
)WSID
CONTINUE
)WSID NEW
WAS CONTINUE
)SAVE
```

will deposit the current workspace as a new version of NEW. WSID assigns the identification NEW to the current workspace.

Of course it is often not useful to copy a whole workspace, since doing so replaces one's own current entire workspace. APL has a COPY command for gaining access to individual morsels in another workspace:

```
) COPY XXX:KEY ALPHA F G H
```

will copy from workspace ALPHA in library XXX the objects F, G, and H:

```
) COPY ALPHA F G H
```

assumes the user's library is involved.

What kind of objects are involved? They may be variables and functions, and their names refer to their values and definitions, respectively. A COPY stores over already existing objects of the same name. The notation)P COPY will not permit such overriding to occur: only an object having an identifier different from one in the workspace can be copied into it.

The command)ERASE F G will erase the values and or definitions associated with the objects F and G.

In summary, the APL system permits user privacy: a password that locks your library, or even only some workspaces, from access by anyone who does not know the password. However, the password is also a key with which the workspaces and their contents may be shared. A second level of control is provided by the PID: only the owner of a workspace or library may create or destroy within his controlled domain. Having given the right to share, the owner may revoke that right, whenever he chooses, by removing or changing the lock.

In any event, let us return to our overview examination of the APL system as shown in (5.1). The system function L is the only function that interfaces a workspace in the computer—but it does so in bulk, as it were. The interpreter I must also interface with the workspace, but it does so with more limited scope, usually one function line at a time. It seems reasonable that both L and I should interface with W_i, but should they interface separately or through a third system function? Here we observe that I reaches into W_i for each and every variable and every function line access—and hence such accesses must be made as efficiently as possible, consonant with the simplicity, correctness, and efficiency of the system. Both L and I must know how W_i is organized and, should that have to be changed, both L and I would have to be appropriately altered.

We have before us the central issue of all system work: efficiency versus the twin virtues of modularity and simplicity. In all organizations, made up of all kinds of components, be they live, mechanical, electrical, or abstract, and admitting reasonably complex goals, this issue is met and never permanently conquered.

Somewhat philosophically one might say that the changing balance that is observed in all systems is the meaning of system evolution. The struggle is differently labeled: centralization versus decentralization, constants versus variables, compilation versus interpretation. But it is always over the same issue. Needless to say, no one even knows what it means to have a solution to this problem—so we shan't try. Instead we shall describe a simple model, often useful in building programming systems, that addresses this problem in a simplistic way.

We observe that our problems arise from changes in the state of APL programs being processed and that these changes in state arise from the sharing of information by several processors. It is natural to look at systems by studying the sharing, by programs, of physical resources: the central computer, the peripheral devices such as printers and typewriter terminals, and the auxiliary storages such as drums, disks, and magnetic tapes. But there is also the sharing of data by (system) processes—the diverse executive groups of the system—that creates problems of synchronization for the system. For example, suppose APL is executing a function F. Then there is an execution state in APL in which F cannot be edited while execution is under way: F is pendant—awaiting a return from a called function G.

Two ways of organizing the control of sharing might be labeled the supervisory, or centralized, control and the distributed control through the use of organized interlocks. In the life history of particular systems both are found, usually the one as an antidote to shortcomings of the other.

We shall consider the following simple example of sharing a resource, an APL function line. APL is interpreted: the line being executed is, except for representation in the system, identical with that loaded from the terminal. We might conceive of a translator as also being present, whose task it is to transform the input line into a drastically different form, computationally equivalent to the input line but more efficient for the computer to execute and requiring a simpler interpreter than that of the current APL interpreter. We might call such a translator-interpreter combination an APL "compiler."

APL is an interactive language, and frequent editing of function lines occurs. Consequently, frequent recompilation occurs. Let us assume it can be done on a line-by-line basis.

Suppose some line u has been altered by the translator I_1 into a version v; see the figure. Successive interpretations made by I_2

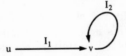

occur on v and not on u. However, suppose an editing E of u is accomplished, producing a line w to replace u; see (5.2). Then v is no longer a valid translation, and I_1 must reprepare u for I_2.

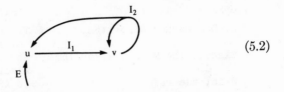

(5.2)

There are several mechanisms for controlling this synchronization between I_1, I_2, and E. One obvious approach is to use hierarchy by having a monitor processor M that controls E and I and to which both turn for permission to perform their function. M controls, as it were, the switches α and β, by selectively turning on I_1 and I_2; see (5.3). Otherwise M serves no important function for E, I_1, and I_2.

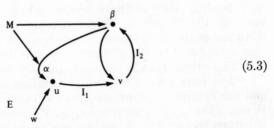

(5.3)

Instead of the utilization of M a discipline of cooperation can be defined between E, I_1, and I_2: they become three cooperating sequential processes processing a line of text in a register R and observing the behavior:

1. E may deposit w in R when neither I_1 nor I_2 is executing u or v, respectively, in R.
2. After E has deposited in R, I_2 must never function on R until I_1 has.
3. I_1 must operate on R if and only if E has occurred, and once for each such occurrence.

From these conditions we see that I_1 can be dispensed with as a separate process and may be included in E.

AN EXAMPLE: THE MARKOV ALGORITHM TRANSLATOR

As a detailed example we shall treat a system for processing Markov algorithms. This is a typical example of a symbolic system, created and organized to imitate the actions of one computer on another. Its constituent parts and resultant organization are quite illustrative of almost all symbolic systems.

We begin by examining what we are given: the outer environment through its initial view of the system's purpose.

USER	SYSTEM	APL
LOAD a Markov Algorithm.	Translate a	
Execute the Markov algorithm.	Markov Algorithm	Inner environment
Print the result.	to APL	

This is a "what" description of the system's purpose and clearly establishes intent. Of course, it is difficult (but by no means impossible) to proceed further in system design without establishing what Markov algorithms are and what it means to execute them. However, both of these issues can be settled quite quickly.

A Markov algorithm (MA) is a sequence of rules for transforming the symbolic contents of a single register, hereinafter called R. R holds a string of characters, is unbounded on the right, but has a specific left end. R, when not empty, has a first character and furthermore can be assumed to commence with any number of null characters, Δ. A string of characters may be substituted for any identified substring in R regardless of their respective lengths.

The rules specify which substitutions in R are to be made, and the control structure specifies the order in which they are to be done. Let us consider an example. We wish to count the number of occurrences in R of disjoint pairs of characters from the alphabet A, assumed to contain neither α nor β, and invert the characters in each pair. A sequence of rules for doing this is:

1. $\alpha\, \delta\, \eta \rightarrow \beta\eta\, \delta\, \alpha;$
2. $\alpha\nu \rightarrow \nu\alpha;$
3. $\nu\beta \rightarrow \beta\nu;$
4. $\alpha \rightarrow \cdot;$
5. $\quad \rightarrow \alpha$

What are δ and η? They are "generic" variables, whose domains are the alphabet A.

What does a rule state? Consider rule 1. Starting at the left end of R, a scan is made for the leftmost occurrence of α followed by any pair of characters in A. If such is found, the substring in R identified by the left-hand side is replaced by that specified by the right-hand side. The variables δ and η clearly play the role of local variables holding arbitrary characters from A. Suppose R had been #a*αba . . . and A were the alphabet of the 26 lowercase letters a, b, . . . , z. Then $\delta \leftarrow$ 'b', $\eta \leftarrow$ 'a', and the right-hand side of rule 1 causes the replacement of the leftmost occurrence of the triplet αba by β ab α.

In what order are the rules applied? Execution of the algorithm commences with the trial of rule 1. If the trial of rule i does not succeed in establishing a match between its left-hand side and some substring in R, then the trial of rule $i + 1$ is made. However, if the trial of rule i does succeed, then rule 1 is always the next to be tried. This process terminates when a rule succeeds, which contains the terminating . in $\rightarrow$. as in rule 4 in the example or when no rule can be found to succeed.

What roles do ν, α, and β play? The variable ν is the generic variable for a union of two alphabets, a, b, c, . . . , z, and # and *. The letters α and β are punctuation marks that serve as generic variables for alphabets consisting solely of themselves. Suppose originally

```
R is taab##c*acd
```

Let the underline show which substring of R participates in the match. Then the successive transformations of R and the rules that produced them are:

```
Δtaab##c*acd          (5)
αtaab##c*acd          (1)
βatαab##c*acd         (1)
βatβbaα##c*acd        (2)
βatβba#αc*acd         (2)
βatβba##αc*acd        (2)
βatβba##cα*acd        (2)
βatβba##c*αacd        (1)
βatβba##c*βcaαd       (2)
βatβba##c*βcadα       (3)
βaβtba##c*βcadα       (3)
ββatba##c*βcadα       (3)
```

Successive applications of (3) move β leftwards until

```
βββatba##c*cadα       (4)
βββatba##c*cad.
```

The string of β's at the left end is the desired count.

The following abbreviated schema also shows how the algorithm unfolds:

$$\overset{5}{R} \to \alpha R \;\underline{is}\; \underset{1}{\alpha\underline{tab}}: \;\to\; \overset{1}{\beta at\underline{\alpha}ab}: \;\to\; :\beta ba\alpha: \;\underline{is}\; :\underline{\alpha}\#: \;\overset{2}{\Rightarrow}\; :\underline{{}^*\alpha ac}:$$

$$\overset{}{\to} :\beta ca\alpha: \;\underline{is}\; :\underset{3}{\underline{\alpha}d}$$

$$\overset{2}{\to} :d\alpha \;is\; :t\beta: \;\overset{3}{\Rightarrow}\; \beta\beta: \;\underline{is}\; :{}^*\beta: \;\Rightarrow\; \beta\beta\beta: \;\underline{is}\; :\overset{4}{d\alpha} \to \cdot :d$$

The : refers to the omitted parts of R, and $\overset{k}{\Rightarrow}$ refers to a chain of successive applications of rule k. The $\underline{is}$ is used to specify the same string but with different parts accented.

We can write our algorithm in a more detailed syntax reminiscent of the APL function syntax:

$$R \leftarrow \text{COUNT } R \;/\; A(\delta,\eta,\nu)B(\nu)$$
$$[1: \quad \alpha + \delta + \eta \to \beta + \eta + \delta + \alpha;$$
$$2: \quad \alpha + \nu \to \nu + \alpha;$$
$$3: \quad \nu + \beta \to \beta + \nu; \quad 4: \alpha \to \cdot; \quad 5: \to \alpha]$$

The use of punctuation marks ";", "/", ":", ",", "+", "(", ")", "[", and "]" permits us both to treat the algorithm as a character string and to use identifiers for the punctuation, alphabet, and

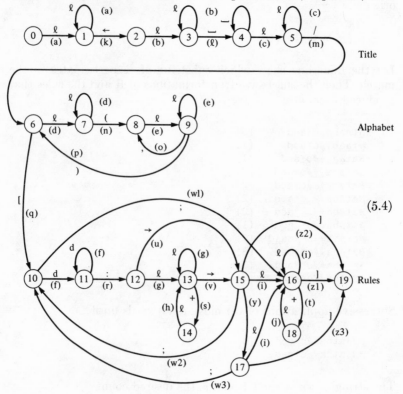

(5.4)

generic-variable names used in MA's. Note that rule numbers have been included even though they play no essential role in the algorithm execution; however, these rule numbers will be useful in editing algorithms. Note also that the alphabets A and B—that is, their constituent characters—have not been explicitly described.

The system we shall specify will process Markov algorithms by translating an algorithm, represented in the syntax described, into an APL function whose special purpose it is to execute the algorithm. The translator is a Markov algorithm "compiler."

We shall represent the syntax in the form of both a state-transition diagram and a state-transition table. From these a recognizer can be easily constructed and the "semantic" actions that arise from recognition of syntactic parts nicely isolated.

In (5.4) and Table 5.1 the lowercase letters refer to semantic states of the translator; the symbol ⊔ refers to a space; l and d refer to an arbitrary letter and arbitrary digit, respectively.

TABLE 5.1 STATE-TRANSITION TABLE

state＼symbol	l ⟨letter⟩	d ⟨digit⟩	←	⊔	/	(	,	)	[	:	+	→	·	;	]
0	1^a														
1	1^a		2^k												
2	3^b														
3	3^b			4^l											
4	5^c			4^l											
5	5^c				6^m										
6	7^d							10^q							
7	7^d					8^n									
8	9^e						8^o	6^p							
9	9^e														
10		11^f													
11		11^f							12^r						
12	13^g										15^u				
13	13^g									14^s	15^v				
14	13^h														
15	16^i											17^y	10^{w2}		19^{z2}
16	16^i									18^t			10^{w1}		19^{z1}
17	16^i												10^{w3}		19^{z3}
18	16^j														

The description of semantic functions consequent upon recognition of identifiers or unsigned integers follows.

- a. the name of the register where the MA results are to be stored
- b. the name of the algorithm
- c. the name of the register holding the data

d. the name of an alphabet
e. the name of a generic variable associated with the alphabet immediately previously named
f. the rule number
g. a rule left-hand-side variable
h. the first character of a (subsequent) left-hand-side variable
i. a rule right-hand-side variable
j. the first character of a (subsequent) right-hand variable

The punctuation marks in the MA description terminate and initiate identifier description and annotate important state changes in the compilation process, as follows.

	INITIATION	TERMINATION
k.	algorithm	result
l.	data	algorithm
m.	alphabet	data
n.	generic variable	alphabet
o.	generic variable	generic variable
p.	alphabet	generic variable
q.	rule sequence	heading
r.	rule variable	rule number
s.	rule variable	rule variable
t.	rule variable	rule variable
u.	right-hand side of a rule	left-hand side of a rule for blank left-hand side
v.	right-hand side of a rule	left-hand side of a rule for nonblank left-hand side
w.	rule number	a rule having blank left-hand side
x.	rule number	a rule having nonblank left-hand side
y.	right-hand side of a rule	$\rightarrow$
z.	next phase of compilation	algorithm

It generally turns out that we have a collection of tasks to do on an MA and several MA's are often undergoing these operations at the same time. A program is defined to monitor these tasks. Let us call it MON. This program communicates with the terminal T and both processes information arising from T and passed to T. In turn, MON communicates with the compiler C and a file storage F that is the bulk memory of this system. Communication between T and MON are by means of commands in TSL.

The syntax and semantics of TSL are quite simple, since most programs in TSL are single commands. A basic set of TSL commands might include the following.

1. SET R. Set the Markov register to contain some (initial) string of data.
2. REG. Display the contents of the Markov register.
3. HELP. Display the set of commands available to TSL.
4. EDIT. The editing options available to the user.
5. TO USE. The steps required for processing a Markov algorithm.
6. FILE. The steps required to connect the file system to the Markov system.
7. EXIT. To leave the Markov system.

All MON instructions are prompted with "$>$."
The EDIT command provides a number of options, as follows.

4.1 TYP -1. Display the algorithm.
4.2 TYP n. Display line n of the algorithm.
     TYP 0. Displays the heading of the algorithm.
4.3 REP n. $n \geq 0$ replaces line n, and $n < 0$ deletes it.
4.4 INS n. Inserts a line after line n.

Lines are automatically renumbered after an insert or delete.

4.5 ALF. Display an alphabet.
4.6 CHA. Change an alphabet.
4.7 CODE. Display the compiled code in APL.

All EDIT instructions are prompted with "$*$."
A carriage return, "$\wr$" terminates editing.
The TO USE command provides a number of options, as follows.

5.1 ENTER. Enter a Markov algorithm and compile it.
5.2 EX. Execute a compiled algorithm.
5.3 TRACE. The entering of a vector of line numbers will cause these lines, whenever executed, to display the register immediately after the line has been executed. The entering of a null vector terminates tracing.

All TO USE commands are prompted with "$\supset$." A carriage return "$\wr$" terminates TO USE.
The file command provides the following options.

6.1 LOAD. Load a Markov algorithm or a compiled version or a register from a file.
6.2 SAVE. Store a Markov algorithm or a compiled version or a register in a file.

All FILE commands are prompted by "$=$." A carriage return "$\wr$" terminates use of the FILE command.

The diagram indicates how TSL commands bring monitor functions into operation:

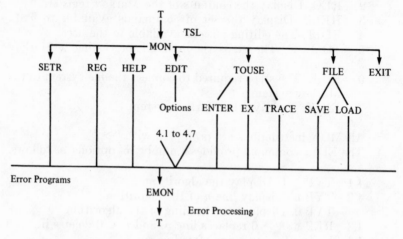

There are three APL data representations used by the inner system with which the system is concerned:

    APL character strings
    APL functions
    APL files

We can list the data transformations that some of the various routines perform:

1. ENTER: maps string into strings.
2. EX: maps a string into a function and arranges for its execution.
3. EDIT: maps strings into strings.
4. TRACE: maps vectors into APL function lines.
5. SAVE: maps strings into file elements.
6. LOAD: maps file elements into strings.

Let us now examine the program MON in more detail. Mostly MON reacts to TSL commands and, having arranged the processing of one such, asks for another. However, it is also the recipient of error messages from programs it calls into execution to carry out TSL commands, and it must arrange for a response to the occurrence of errors. Errors will, and do, occur for many reasons, and a good system is organized to respond sensibly to them. Whenever possible, the system should recover from errors without aborting an entire task or requiring excessive cooperation from the terminal. However, in all cases the terminal should be notified of the occurrence of an error and that a response has been taken to it. We shall return to the processing of errors in a later section.

An entry into the system, which we shall call MARKOV, is, of course, through the inner system, APL:

```
)LOAD MARKOV
```

The entire system is now accessible through the function MON, and a call on MON launches the monitor into control: the user is now working entirely in the middle system. The first action of MON is to apprise the user of the facilities available in the system and how to use them. We shall list the lines of the functions MON and EDIT and some of the editing functions:

```
      ∇ MON; X
[1]   ε')SAVE MARKOV'
[2]   'WELCOME TO THE MARKOV SYSTEM'
[3]   MCMDS
[4]   'FOR INSTRUCTIONS TYPE HELP'
[5]   '> □:'
[6]   →0×ι∧/'EDIT'=4ρX←☑,' '
[7]   →9×ι((ρMCMDS)[1])≥(MCMDS∧.=X)ι1
[8]   →5,1ρ□←'ILLEGAL MONITOR COMMAND'
[9]   →5,ε(X≠' ')/X
      ∇
MCMDS is the array
SET
REG
HELP
EDIT
TOUSE
FILE
EXIT
ρMCMDS is 7 5
```

Line [9] will execute the function whose name has been input.
The unary ε, known as *execute*, is an extremely interesting and powerful operator. Since APL translates and executes a statement each time it is executed, it keeps very little memory of its past translation efforts. Hence the creation, during execution, of new statements should not clash very much with the APL interpreter's normal functioning. Let us extend the diagram (5.2); see the accompanying figure. If we apply I_2, the APL executor, to a v of the form

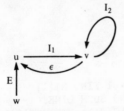

ε < character string>, the string is assumed to be an input representation of a legal APL expression or statement that must be translated and executed. Thus X holds a character string representation of a user-selected Markov command, permitting the system both to behave like APL and to use APL. Thus the system contains a compiler in the sense that it prepares, in the form of a string, an APL function and, through ϵ, arranges for APL to execute it.

Some of the system commands are:

```
       ∇ HELP
  [1]  'THIS IS A SYSTEM FOR EXECUTING MARKOV
       ALGORITHMS'
  [2]  'MONITOR PROMPTS WITH '' > '' COMMANDS ARE:'
  [3]  ' SET R    SET THE DATAREGISTER'
  [4]  ' REG      DISPLAYS THE DATAREGISTER'
  [5]  ' HELP     THIS MESSAGE'
  [6]  'EDIT      THE EDITOR COMMANDS'
  [7]  'TOUSE     THE STEPS TO PROCESS AN ALGORITHM'
  [8]  'FILE      THE STEPS TO FILE AN ALGORITHM'
  [9]  'EXIT      EXIT TO THE INNER SYSTEM: APL'
       ∇
       ∇EDIT;X
  [1]  'THE EDITOR PROMPTS WITH A ''*''. EXIT WITH
       CARRIAGE RETURN'
  [2]  'DO YOU WISH TO SEE THE MENU? Y OR N'
  [3]  '*'
  [4]  →13×ι'N'=⍞
  [5]  'TYP¯1    DISPLAY THE ALGORITHM'
  [6]  'TYP N    DISPLAY LINE N OF THE ALGORITHM'
  [7]  'TYP 0    DISPLAY HEADING OF THE ALGORITHM'
  [8]  'REP N    REPLACE LINE N ¯N DELETES LINE N'
  [9]  'INS N    INSERT AFTER LINE N. LINES ARE
                 RENUMBERED'
 [10]  'ALF      DISPLAY AN ALPHABET'
 [11]  'CHA      CHANGE AN ALPHABET'
 [12]  'CODE     DISPLAY THE COMPILED CODE'
 [13]  '*'
 [14]  →16×ι0<ρX←⍞
 [15]  →0,ρ□←'NOTHING TO EDIT'
 [16]  →18×ι((ρCMDS)[1]≥CMDS∧.=3↑X)ι1
 [17]  →4,1ρ□←'ILLEGAL EDIT COMMAND'
 [18]  →4,εX ∇
       ∇SETR
  [1]  'ENTER CONTENTS'
  [2]  DREG←⍞  ⍝ DREG HOLDS DATA
       ∇
       ∇ REG
  [1]  DREG
       ∇
       ∇ TYP N;C
  [1]  →5×ιN=¯1
  [2]  →4×ι0≠(C←1 FIND N)[1]
  [3]  →0,ρ□←'NO SUCH LINE'
  [4]  →0,ρ□←ALG[C[1],C[1]+ιC[2]]
  [5]  ALG
       ∇
       ∇ INS N
  [1]  C→FIND N
```

```
[2]    →4×ι0=C[1]
[3]    →0,ρALG←(C[1]+C[2])↑ALG,⊡,(C[1]+C[2])↓ALG
[4]    →0,ρ□←'THERE IS NO SUCH LINE'
       ∇

       ∇ REP M;C;K
[1]    →3×ι0≠+/C←1 FIND M
[2]    →0,ρ□← 'NO SUCH LINE'
[3]    →7×ιM<0
[4]    'PLEASE ENTER NEW LINE'; M
[5]    ALG←(C[1]↑ALG), (TM),'] ',(+/C)↓ALG
[6]    →0
[7]    ALG←(⁻1+C[1])↑ALG,(+/C)↓ALG
[8]    M←1+|M
[9]    →0×ι0=+/C←C[1] FIND M
[10]   K←(((C[1])↓(C[1]+C[2])↑ALG)=']')ι1
[11]   ALG←((C[1])↑ALG),(T⁻1+M),'] ',K↓ALG
[12]   →8
       ∇

       ∇ R←J FIND N;K;Z
[1]    K←(1=∧/[1](⁻1+ιρZ) Φ (Z←'[',(TN),']')∘.=
       (⁻1+J)↓ALG)ι1
[2]    →4×ιK≤(ρALG)−J+1
[3]    →R←0,0
[4]    →0,R←K,((K↓ALG)='⟩ ')ι1
       ∇

       ∇ TOUSE
[1]    'WHEN YOU TYPE ENTER YOU WILL BE PROMPTED FOR
        LINE [0]'
[2]    'WHICH IS THE HEADING: ALGORITHM NAME FOLLOWED BY
        THE ALGORITHM BODY'
[3]    'WHEN YOU TYPE LOAD THE ALGORITHM WILL BE
        COMPILED'
[4]    'WHEN YOU TYPE EX THE ALGORITHM WILL BE EXECUTED'
[5]    'WHEN YOU TYPE TRACE YOU WILL BE PROMPTED FOR A
        VECTOR OF LINE NUMBERS'
       ∇
```

We shall not complete the definition of TOUSE. Its layout follows the pattern set by the function EDIT.

We might now examine what a compiled MA looks like. It seems reasonable that it should be compiled as an APL function, since we are using APL as the inner system. The form of the compiled function will be, with the MA *COUNT* as an example,

```
       ∇ R←COUNT X;C;K;SW;N
[1]    ⟨ALF₁⟩←□
[2]    ⟨ALF₂⟩←□
[3]    N←0
[4]    ⎫
...    ⎬ Compilation of the first rule
[K]    ⎭
[K+1]  ⎫
...    ⎬ Compilation of successive rules
[L−1]  ⎭
[L]    EXIT: R←X ∇
```

Let us now examine the compilation of any rule, in which may occur generic variables, punctuation, and constants (explicit members of an alphabet). The compilation will, of course, depend on which of these is encountered. An encountered identifier ID is a generic variable if it was encountered in the algorithm heading. For each generic variable we postulate the existence of a character string, created during the scan of the algorithm heading text of the form GV $\underline{is}$ '$A_1A_2 \ldots A_k$'. Here GV is a generic variable for the alphabets A_1, A_2, ..., A_k and a string GVLIST $\underline{is}$ '$GV_1GV_2...GV_n$', generic variable identifiers. We also postulate a list of alphabet names: ALIST $\underline{is}$ '$A_1A_2...A_r$'. Now, if IDϵGVLIST is true, then ID is generic variable, else ID is in an alphabet and is a constant, or ID is punctuation.

We have the following possibilities for a rule.

1. Suppose the left-hand side of a rule is blank. The rule is then of the form $\rightarrow w_1 + w_2 + \cdots + w_Z$. The right-hand side must contain only punctuation or constants or both. Its compilation is

```
[1]   N←N+1
[2]   X←'ω₁','ω₂',...,'ωz',X
[3]    ←SW[1]
```

where the lines, of course, are relatively numbered. SW is a directory for determining successors and is useful if tracing is to occur; N records the ordinal number of the rule; the rule above is rule N; X is the register.

2. Suppose the left-hand side is nonblank and of the form

$$\omega_1 + \omega_2 + \omega_3 \rightarrow$$

Suppose ω_1 is a generic variable for alphabets A_1 and A_2, and ω_2 is punctuation, and ω_3 is a generic variable for alphabets A_2 and A_3. Then we would compile

```
          [1]   N←N+1+K←0
          [2]   H: →SW[N]×ι(1+(ρX)- left side number
                <K←K+1
          [3]   →H×ι~((C[K])∧(C[K+1])∧...∧C[K+left
                side number −1])
          [4]   X←((⁻1+K)↑X),R₁,R₂,...Rright side number−1,
                (K+left side number −1)↓X
either    [5]   →0,ρY←X for a terminal rule
   or     [5]   →SW[1],ZERO N for a nonterminal rule
```

Note that:

1. The compilation is the rule N.
2. "Left side number" is the number of entries on the left side of the rule.

3. X is the data register.
4. Suppose $X[k + m]$ is not a generic variable. Then

$$C[k + m] \underline{\text{is}} \ \delta = X[k + m],$$

where δ is the $(m + 1)$th entry on the left-hand side of the
rule. If $X[k + m]$ is a generic variable α_r, let $A_1, \ldots, A_s$
be its alphabets. Then

$$C[k + m] \underline{\text{is}} \ (\alpha_r \epsilon A_1) \ \vee \ \cdots \ (\alpha_r \epsilon A_{s-1})$$
$$\vee \ ((\alpha_r \leftarrow X[k + m]) \epsilon A_s).$$

5. Assume the right-side members are $\omega_1, \ \omega_2, \ldots,$
$\omega_{\text{right-side number}-1}$:

   If $\omega_i \underline{\text{is}} \ \alpha_r$, then $R_i \underline{\text{is}} \ \alpha_r$.
   If $\omega_i \underline{\text{is}}$ not generic variable, then $R_i \underline{\text{is}} \ '\omega_i'$.

6. Y is the result register.
7. ZERO N is a function that tests whether tracing is in
effect.

The only remaining difficulties involve preparing the various
strings that relate generic variables to alphabets, forming the
switching directory SW and representing the compiled function as
APL data.

We shall make use of our new unary operator "ϵ" and a new
unary interpretation of "$\top$." For our purposes "ϵ" executes a string
and "$\top$" converts a number into its representation as a character
string.

Now we are in a position to identify the actions performed by
the thirty semantic programs (a) through (z3) (Table 5.1). Most of
these functions are so simple that they can be deduced immediately
from the state diagram. At the start,

```
CID ← ' '
SW ← ι0
```

and, as the text of the MA is scanned, we shall accumulate identifiers and integer labels in a single variable CID. The current character being scanned is always in Q. The compiled APL function is
built up in the string FN.

A natural organization for COMPILE is to divide it into parts,
each representing a state. The transitions can be arranged as transfers, such as $\rightarrow S7$, meaning "transfer to state 7." Each state (except
the terminal state) is responsible for arranging for the next character to be in Q and for transferring to its successor state, as Table 5.1
requires.

Each state is of the form:

```
semantic action
NXTCHAR
transfer to next state
```

NXTCHAR is a function that puts the next character from the input string into Q. The function COMPILE has the gross structure

```
       ∇ COMPILE ⟨LOCAL VARIABLES⟩
  [1]  'PLEASE ENTER THE ALGORITHM TO BE'
  [2]  'COMPILED. SURROUNDING QUOTES ARE'
  [3]  'NOT TO BE USED. TERMINATE INPUT'
  [4]  WITH STANDARD OUT TERMINATOR.'
  [5]  ⟨ABSORB TEXT⟩
  [6]  ⟨PARSE⟩
  [7]  ⟨NXTCHAR⟩
  [8]  SO: ⟨SEMANTIC ACTIONS⟩
  ...
  [M]  ⟨TERMINATION ACTIONS⟩
       ∇
```

We shall not give the COMPILE function as explicit APL code. We merely remark that the compiling actions derive from the individual semantic requirements in the sequence laid down by the transition diagram. Thus, when (m) is reached, the heading of the compiled function should be appended to the string FN; (o) is the first semantic action of any subtlety. CID holds a generic variable identifier. We must put it in GVLIST unless it is already there. If it is not in GVLIST, we must create a variable whose name is the contents of CID and initialize its value to be an empty string. Then we must create an APL statement, as a string, and execute it to catenate the current alphabet, stored in CALPH, onto the list of alphabet names attached to the generic variable whose name is stored in CID.

In (p) the semantic processing associated with the heading is completed.

In (q) a "*" is planted in FN, where the directory SW is to be placed when the algorithm has been processed.

The APL statements that request the reading of the alphabets to be used in the algorithm must now be generated. The alphabet names, separated by spaces, are in the compiler variable ALIST. These names must be peeled off from ALIST and, for each, an APL statement of the form $\alpha \leftarrow \square$ must be created, where α is an alphabet name from ALIST.

In (r) we save the algorithm line number, accumulated in (f), which will be useful in case an error should arise in processing the line.

When we reach (v) or (u), the left side of the current rule will have been processed. In (u) we deal with the case of the blank left-hand side. On reaching (v) we shall have accumulated both the identities and the number of left-side elements. In (v) we shall compile the code required by the left-hand side of the rule.

In (w1), (w2), (w3), (z1), (z2), and (z3) the code required by the right-hand side is compiled. The (w2) and (z2) arise when the right-hand side is blank. The (y) indicates we are compiling a terminal rule. The (z1), (z2), and (z3) arise when we are processing the lexicographic last rule in the algorithm. Hence in the latter cases we plant SW and a function for trace control in FN.

The compilation now consists of SW, the switching directory, the trace control, and the compiled function. SW was inserted in FN where we planted the "*" in (q). In what form is it inserted? As an assignment statement:

$$\text{'SW} \leftarrow V_1, V_2, \ldots, V_K\text{'}$$

where V_i is the character representation of $1 +$ the ith component of SW.

Each component SW[i] is the last line number of rule $i - 1$. The compilation of the assignment statement is performed by

```
     K←1
     SD←'SW←'
L:   SD←SD,(⊤1+SW[K]),','
  →L×ι(ρSW)≥K←K+1
  SD[ρSD]←'⟩'
```

Finally, the planting is arranged:

```
P←('*'=FN)ι1
FN←((⁻1+P)↑FN),SD,P↓FN
```

The entire function is now imbedded in the string FN as APL code. Compilation is complete. COMPILE has produced a string representation of an APL function for executing the Markov algorithm.

The system function ENTER provides the character string to the function COMPILE. COMPILE controls the semantic routines through the syntax analyzer. There are 19 states, and processing commences with state 0. The function ZERO is provided for tracing. Whenever a rule is successfully applied during execution of the compiled code, the function ZERO intercedes if the trace test is on. The function ZERO is

```
     ∇ ZERO N
[1]  →0×ι0=∨/N=TTEST
[2]  'WE HAVE EXECUTED RULE';N
[3]  'THE REGISTER CONTENTS ARE';⟨CONTENTS OF CDATA⟩
     ∇
```

TTEST is the vector of line numbers to be traced. Compilation initializes TTEST to 0. TTEST is set by the system command TRACE. The function above is simply appended to FN when compilation of all the rules has been performed:

```
FN←FN,'∇ ZERO N⊃ →0×ι0=∨/N=TTEST ''WE HAVE
   EXECUTED RULE'';
   N⊃ ''THE REGISTER CONTENTS ARE'';',CDATA,'⊃ ∇'
```

Programming systems generally use one of two alternatives when editing has been accomplished.

1. Recompile the algorithm. This is by far the simplest to arrange.
2. Recompile only the altered parts. This requires keeping a record of information accumulated during compilation, such as the lists of generic variables and alphabets. This information should not be kept in the compiler but as an attachment to the compiled program.

Most systems would, on the grounds of simplicity, choose to recompile each time:

1. Erase the originally compiled function.
2. Compile the new Markov algorithm.

EDIT functions operate on the string representation of the algorithm. Searching of the string can be easily done by looking for syntactic patterns such as ";." However, searching time can be greatly reduced by keeping with the string a directory holding pointers to the syntactic units that can be altered. The directory can be prepared during syntax analysis.

We shall not comment on the issues arising in filing algorithms, since the techniques will depend on the nature of the file support available to the "inner system."

Systems not only provide a multiplicity of functions but also provide them to a multiplicity of users. When the number of functions and users is large, it is natural to experience "sharing" of resources within the system. The resources being shared are customarily programs, storage, and input-output devices. The sharing takes place over a span of time and creates both opportunities and problems for a system. The opportunity is the more efficient use of a resource by sharing it. The problem is to guarantee protection of one user's program, data and access to the system from either intentional or unintentional system misuse by another. Ultimately the design of a system comes down to the artful management of a scarcity.

The MA system becomes a very different system when it is being used simultaneously by several users. By and large, in this introductory treatment we have avoided all but the simplest consequences of simultaneity. However, it is a fact that systems can and do exist that serve one user and maintain a simplicity because of that.

We shall now turn to the system's response to errors. Errors may be of two kinds: syntactic and semantic. More pragmatically put, those errors observed during (a) syntax analysis and compilation and (b) execution, respectively.

Syntax errors are easy to identify: if the analyzer is in a state when it encounters a character for which that state has no defined transition, then and only then has a syntax error occurred. Less easy to specify is the response to a syntax error. The following approaches have been found useful in programming systems.

1. Excise text containing the error such that, if that text had not been present in the first place, the remaining text would be a correct MA if it had no further errors, and do a syntax analysis but no compilation of this remaining text. The purpose is to isolate as many syntax errors as possible before doing any further compilation.

2. Correct the error by making judgment of the programmer's intent. For example, in state 11a the notation "," might have been encountered. It is highly possible that a ";" was intended and a keying error made. Of course, all such inferences should be catalogued so that the programmer may disfavor the resulting program if the inference were incorrect.

3. Abort the entire task, requiring the system user to start over. This last approach is easiest for the system and least appreciated by the user. However, there is an alternative method which, in the case of terminal systems, is quite natural and easy to arrange: do the syntax analysis and compilation while the text is being entered. An error in the heading or in a rule will be ascertained before any additional text is entered and, hence, can often be corrected on the spot.

It turns out that there are few compilation errors or run-time errors other than those arising from excessive demands on resources, such as insufficient storage for the compiled text. This particular error occurs at the inner system level, in APL, and will cause an error message from APL, expressed in its terms and not in those of the MA compiler. Hence the compiler must make every effort to anticipate this error, so that a response can be made by the compiler rather than by APL itself. Of course, it would be better if APL made its error response to the MA system rather than to the terminal, but APL does not do so, because it has not been designed to take cognizance of which systems it is host to.

ERROR-PROCESSING

It is worth while now to look at the processing of errors by a system from a more general point of view. The more a user is buffered from knowing how a system works, the more intolerant he becomes of errors within the system. We may assume that the system is correct:

It does correctly what it is supposed to do. We are concerned with its behavior when it is asked to perform actions that it was not intended to perform but of which limitations the user, or even some internal functions, are not aware.

Errors may arise when any change of state of the system occurs, and it is sheer folly to test all changes for errors. However, there are certain actions that, when they occur, have a high enough likelihood of error, are quite critical, and yet are relatively infrequent, so that an error-checking of these actions is worth performing.

Two such error-prone actions are input by the user and calls on functions. Both represent possible erroneous behavior on the part of the "user." The possibility of error may be checked before the system has had to respond, or the system may be organized to cope with the error if and when it subsequently arises. Although both approaches are used, we shall focus on the second approach. Our approach is very simple.

Whenever a function F is called by a function G, it is the responsibility of the function F to test that the inputs from G satisfy the constraints set by F. Whenever a function F returns results (and control) to a function G, it is the responsibility of G to test the adequacy of these results and the response to be made to them. Put another way, the receiver must test all messages. A return from F is then like a *call* on F, since the results of F may be inappropriate and require another execution by F.

For example, suppose in the MA system a rule has been entered that has a generic variable on the right that does not occur on the left. The semantic routine (w1) should find, and report back to the calling function, this kind of error. The return must pass back an error indication. We illustrate the control flow by the diagram

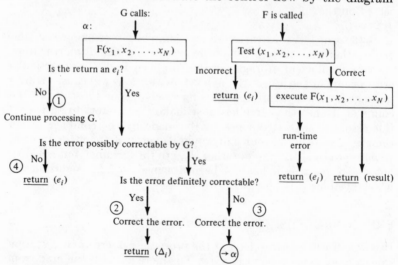

shown, where e_i denotes the ith error and Δ_i denotes the correction of e_i.

We note the following.

1. The transaction between F and G has been successfully completed.

2. F has notified G, and G has concurred, that the error is immediately correctable by G. The response of G is Δ_i and G returns Δ_i to F so that F may continue processing. Here F is the caller and G the function called.

3. F has notified G, or G has insisted, that the error requires a restart of F and that G can repair the data $x_1, \ldots, x_n$ so that a fresh attempt of F is possible.

4. F has notified G, or G has insisted, that the error requires correction by a routine that called on G. That routine, on correction of the error, can invite G to continue error-processing as though the error had been processed in G.

How do we mechanize this complicated communications process?

Assume the integer-valued variable CHECK holds 1 if the normal function output is character and 0 if the normal output is numeric. Then the line in G of the form

```
[k]...F...    where F is a function call
```

becomes

```
[j] E1 ← 1 + ι26
[j+1]...(H, → E×ιCHECK=0=0\0ρH←F)...
```

H holds the error message, if indeed there is one. $E1$ holds the line where the function call occurred. E is the entry point to the error function.

In APL the continuation of F, when an error has been corrected, is most difficult to arrange. APL is not designed to permit coroutine linkage between functions. Hence each invocation of a function reinitializes it. All its local variables lose their values, and execution always commences at the first line of the function. The inner system, APL, does permit function suspension, and a function can even suspend itself, but it cannot transfer control, once suspended, to anywhere in a "middle system." A solution practised in many systems is not to permit continuation of F when errors are found.

There now remains the issue of how to react to specific errors when they arise. Program execution involves a flow of control, and control constructions aid flow in one direction only: along a path from the start to the halt. The assignment operation and the use of the stack are generally handled in an irreversible manner. Although there are two possible exits from a branch, there are arbitrarily many entrances into a statement, and no record is kept, even of the last entry that actually preceded an error condition. A record of the last (incompleted) function call is, however, kept, since a return is necessary. Normal program execution is by and large information-diminishing, since each step involves a reduction in choice and is an irreversible process. However, it is possible to keep a history of all choices made, assignments and entries, and so forth, so that the program may be executed in reverse, as it were, from any execution state back to any state that actually preceded it in the time sequence of execution. This is done by keeping a record of predecessors, both statements and "stored-over" values. As might be guessed, this history is expensive both in storage and time, since the amount of retained information grows linearly with time. There are, however, some ways in which this growth of kept information can be slowed by trading storage for time. Clearly, we can start from any intermediate state, if we remembered it, and appear to move backwards by moving forward in spurts from this state. When an error is recognized as having occurred, the system must attempt to recover by taking the following steps:

1. Isolating the source of the error.
2. Returning the program to a state preceding the error source.
3. Marching forward to the error source, correcting the error, and continuing.

Step 2 might not seem necessary, since a local patch could "apparently" correct this error occurrence. However, other errors could arise in the future from the same source, and the patching might—and usually does—become unmanageable.

How are those steps to be carried out? It may be difficult to isolate the error source. The error may be intrinsic to the algorithm. For example, the algorithm, in order to be correct, requires a constraint on its data that is not explicitly tested for. Thus, the constraint may be assumed to be obvious to any user (the argument to a square-root algorithm should be nonnegative), may have been forgotten (to test for a zero or a small divisor coefficient of X^2 in a quadratic-equation root solver), or just may not be known to the creators of the algorithm. These are system errors that can only be corrected by surgery on the system. Such errors, alas, are present in the early life stages of all systems. However, system use tends to weed out most of these errors—algorithms are perfectable, but system and function users are not. At least in the early stages of system use a function call should be followed by a test of results returned, even when the called routine assumes it has functioned correctly. However, these tests should be easily excisable, since they may ultimately be removed from the system.

Let us return to those errors that are reported back by the routine called. The error routine in G has the responsibility of detecting error sources arising inside G and reacting to them. All other reported errors must be transmitted to the function that called G, and so on. If the error source is in G and can be corrected within the G, then G must correct it and arrange for F to be restarted or continued.

The Markov system does not have many levels of system administration. Consequently, most errors that arise will be processed at the terminal.

SUMMARY AND REFERENCES

All contact with the computer is mediated by software systems. Every user must master some such system to use successfully a computer for any task. Some systems are part of the operating style of the computer itself—they buffer the hardware from every other system—and are called operating systems. Thus on every computer on which the programming languages Algol60 and APL are available their systems cooperate with the underlying operating system of the computer on which they run. Below APL, our inner system, is yet another system, the computer operating system, and below that is, of course, the computer itself.

Layering is a natural mode of organization. Communication across established interfaces and through standard parts has some appreciated advantages:

1. The innermost (and earlier) systems are not altered by the invention of newer systems. The new must accommodate to the old.

2. The relative effectiveness of the innermost systems never diminishes. They use the computer resources better than do any of the outer systems.

3. The development of outer systems is often (but not always) simplified by the rigid constraints imposed by systems inner to it.

However, layering is rarely perfect; protracted use subjects every system to tensions that lead to change.

An example is provided by APL's response to errors. APL was not designed to serve as an inner system but merely to execute functions. When sufficient use of APL as an inner system occurs, we may expect a redesign of APL to provide for better error-handling. This redesign will be difficult, since it should be "upward compatible": programs correctly executed before APL redesign should be unaffected by the redesign, and the redesign should not drastically alter the APL style of programming.

System programming is more difficult than procedure programming, since more issues must be taken into account. The fundamental difference is one of degree rather than of kind. Systems provide a range of services, and this range introduces a web of interactions between parts of such complexity that their management usually exceeds the ability, memory, and energy of the individual programmer. Nevertheless, the specification of all systems is based on the premise that one programmer, hence many programmers, can comprehend the entire system at some level of description that contains both "what" and "how" descriptions of modules. No system should be designed, and no multiple programmer effort managed, by a programmer who would be unable to comprehend, for reasons of either intelligence or education, the technical details of module construction and interaction, should the need arise.

Some programming systems already exist that exceed 1,000,000 words of computer instructions. We have reason to believe that this number will be greatly exceeded in the near future, not regardless of, but because of, increased capabilities in computers yet to come. Consequently, demands on the system programmer will become more intense, and his proficiency must become more developed. This improved proficiency can be acquired in three ways:

1. Through an improved understanding of the techniques of programming.

2. Through an improved understanding of the techniques of system organization and communication links.

3. Through an improved ability to store and manipulate in the programmer's skull complex data structures and algorithms. The brevity of symbolic notations is most important in increasing the mass of procedural know-how that we can store in our skull and use as tools.

The last point is not often made, but its importance accounts for the heavy use of APL in this book. Programming languages such as FORTRAN, BASIC, and Algol60 are poor compared with APL in this respect.

Very few books on systems programming exist. One of the few good ones is

> John Donovan, *Systems Programming* (McGraw-Hill, New York, 1971).

Much of the concern of systems programmers is with specific types of systems, such as assemblers, language translators, and operating systems. In particular, the latter requires the study of parallel processing, a topic that has been avoided in this text. Two good introductory books on the subject of operating systems are

> M. Wilkes, *Time-Sharing Computer Systems* (American Elsevier, New York, 2nd ed., 1972)
>
> A. Colin, *Introduction to Operating Systems* (American Elsevier, New York, 1971).

An excellent paper on the design of a particular operating system is

> E. Dijkstra, "The Structure of the 'THE' Multi-programming System" (*Communications of the ACM*, 11, 1968, pp. 341–346).

PROBLEMS

1. Construct a library system that would keep track of

> Books held by the library
> Books on loan
> Overdrawn books
> Books to be placed in reserve when returned

The system can be understood by specifying what information is kept on file, what information can be input, and what information will be output. The system can be viewed in other ways as well.

THE FILES. The information can be factored into as many files as you wish. Remember that the shorter a file is, the easier it is to find something in it. In any event, you will need to store:

> The Dewey decimal numbers of every book in the library
> The number of each book
> The books on loan, and for each of them:

> Who has it
> When due
> Whether on reserve when returned

THE INPUTS

> Specification of a book taken out
> Renewal request
> Specification of a book return
> Addition of books: more old ones and new ones
> Specification of a book wanted

THE OUTPUTS

> Overdue-book announcements
> Unavailability of a wanted book:

> None available
> Available but on reserve for someone else
> Nonexistent

> Statistics of use

The system should have a single "control program" or monitor function with which all initial communication is made. Remember that the user of the system is a librarian who can type but does not know APL and cannot program.

Some good systems contain among the inputs one that explains how to use the system.

Remember that the system is not expected to respond to all possible queries a librarian might make.

A good system will identify when its own resources are exhausted: no file space left, etc.

2. We wish to design an algorithm to compute ($=3.14159$ . . .) one digit at a time, so that we may stop, for example, after M digits, save a "small" amount of information, and recommence some time later to compute the $(M + 1)$th digit, etc. Naturally, in computing the $(M + 1)$th and the following digits we do not wish to recompute many of the first M digits! What method would you use? Some references are the following:

> J. W. Wrench, "The Evolution of Extended Decimal Approximations to π (*Math. Teach*, 53, 1960, pp. 644–65).
> D. Shanks and J. W. Wrench, "Calculation of π to 100,000 Decimals" (*Math. Comp.*, 77, 1962, pp. 76–99).

3. Write an APL function SUPERWHILE that accepts as input a string definition of a function on a line by line basis but that allows the programmer to enter the additional structure

```
WHILE ⟨some APL predicate⟩ DO
```

and then (a) indents successive lines until coming across the string ELIHW that closes the line and the while loop and then moves the margin back to the left one level and (b) inserts the correct APL code to control the loop and (c) upon close of the function displays the "compiled function." NOTE: WHILE . . . . . . may be nested.

4. Describe an APL system you might create that writes business letters of various kinds, such as ordering items such as books, clothes, and records, making reservations for such as hotels, ships, planes, and making appointments to visit or see someone or something. Give both a "what" and a "how" description, but do not go into detailed function and data description.

5. A SYSTEM FOR MATHEMATICAL TEXT DISPLAY. The input is mathematical text in a reduced alphabet, such as ASCII. The output is a 0-1 array K to a dot printer that prints N dots to a line and R dots to a vertical inch. The system takes one line at a time from a file and produces the dot raster representation of that text.

The text is to contain representations in ASCII of an extensive alphabet: for example, Greek letters and mathematical symbols. One possible representation is to quote symbols representing characters in the extensive alphabet. Thus "CPHI" might represent Φ and "INT" represent $\int$. Formulas are to be represented as Algol60-like expressions and are to be displayed in a multiline form akin to that found in mathematics texts.

An approach is to translate a formula expression into a tree form and then analyze the tree to determine the spatial form of the formula.

6. The computer in Chapter 2 can be "simulated" by a system. The system can "imitate" the computer on several levels: machine-code, microcode, and logical-device levels. Design a system that simulates the computer on all these levels.

CHAPTER 6

THEORY

6

NONCOMPUTABLE FUNCTIONS

The algorithms we have examined and those we shall create can be expressed as procedures in a programming language. Let us now consider just the procedures that have positive-integer formal parameters and produce positive-integer values. To simplify matters further we can take each such procedure and replace it by one that computes the same function but has only one formal parameter, for we may easily represent n positive integers $u_1, u_2, \ldots, u_n$ by a single positive integer w, and from w we may uniquely recover $u_1, u_2, \ldots, u_n$. There are many ways of making this correspondence, but the simplest is due to Gödel. Let the first n primes be $2, 3, 5, \ldots, p$. Then let w be $2^{u_1} \times 3^{u_2} \times 5^{u_3} \times \cdots \times p^{u_n}$. Since every positive integer has a unique prime decomposition, the correspondence is uniquely defined. Let us write the correspondence w as $\langle u_1, u_2, \ldots, u_n \rangle$.

Every one-parameter procedure is described in a finite amount of text by characters from a finite alphabet, such as that of APL or Algol60 (see Chapter 3). Then how many procedures can there be? We can count them in the sense that there are only a finite number of procedures having a k character description for every $k = 1, 2, \ldots$.

If Algol60 is used to represent the procedures, the alphabet is understood to contain the characters begin, end, for, if, while, integer, procedure, etc.

After all, there are only a finite number of different character strings of length k, of which only some are legal procedures. Since we can count them, we can attach to each procedure P an index m. But we can do more: each positive integer may be such an index value, and we can resurrect the unique procedure that has that index. The index and its procedure are not only in a one-to-one correspondence, but there is an algorithm for making the correspondence: Among the legal procedures is one procedure (indeed there are many such) that resurrects a procedure description from its index. How can this be done? There is another procedure that can test any finite string of characters and determine whether the string describes a legal procedure. Such a procedure is called a *syntax analyzer*. Let us call it TEST. Let us call the procedure that can generate all character strings of k characters "GENERATE(k)." If the alphabet has, say, 99 characters, then any character string can be represented as a concatenation of 2-decimal digit integers, hence as an integer. If the character string is $n_1, n_2, \ldots, n_r$, where $0 < n_i \leq 99$, then we shall understand $\langle n_1, n_2, \ldots, n_r \rangle$ to mean the corresponding integer. Except for very small k, it is clear that many legal procedures of k characters can be generated. Thus, if we are given an index N, we need only look for its corresponding procedure among those that have $< C + N$ characters, where C is a constant depending only on the language in which the procedures are described. Let us agree to use GENERATE to help us assign indices to procedures in the first place. Let us now define two procedures.

1. INDEX($\langle P \rangle$), which, given P, finds P's place in the list of all procedures.
2. FIND(K), which, given K, finds the procedure that has K as an index. We may assume GENERATE(K) produces a new character string each time it is executed, for example, in order of increasing length and in alphabetic order for a given length. The boolean DONE is set to <u>true</u> whenever GENERATE can generate no additional strings of length K.

```
procedure INDEX (⟨P⟩);
begin Q ← 0; K ←0;
while ∼(TEST(Q) ∧ ⟨P⟩ =Q) do begin
K ← K+1;
Q ← ⟨GENERATE(K)⟩ end
INDEX ← K end
procedure FIND(K);
begin I ← 0; J ← 1;
while I < K do
if DONE then J ← J+1
else if TEST(Q ← GENERATE(J)) then I ← I+1;
FIND ← Q end
```

Thus for each integer K we have identified a corresponding procedure P.

Suppose the set of all mathematical functions that map positive integers into positive integers is denumerable. By *denumerable* we mean that the set of functions has no more members than there are positive integers. Hence each such function can be given an index. Call this set F. Let f_j be the jth function in F. Now consider the function HUH(n) that certainly maps integers into integers:

$$HUH(k) = f_k(k) + 1, \qquad k = 1, 2, \ldots$$

HUH cannot be a member of F. If it were, it would be one of the f_i. But this is impossible, since HUH differs from f_i at the value i:

$$HUH(i) = f_i(i) + 1 \neq f_i(i), \qquad i = 1, 2, \ldots$$

Since HUH satisfies the criterion for membership in F, the contradiction is removed only if we say that F is nondenumerable: the set of functions that maps integers into integers is not denumerable. There are integer-valued functions on the integers that we cannot write as procedures in Algol60 or APL or FORTRAN or any programming language.

Let us now exhibit an intended procedure that, it will turn out, *we cannot write!* Suppose we could program the following procedure by filling in the English description with precise algorithmic actions:

```
procedure HALT(⟨J,N⟩);
begin P ← ⟨FIND(J)⟩;
Q: comment Here we place the procedure text that
examines P and determines whether P(N) halts and sets a
boolean variable RESULT to 1 if it does and 0 if it
does not;
HALT ← RESULT end
```

The procedure $HALT(\langle J, N \rangle)$ determines whether the procedure P, whose index is J, halts when executed with the actual parameter N.

Then the following procedure ANTIHALT exists if HALT does:

```
procedure ANTIHALT(M):
begin
while HALT(⟨M,M⟩) = 1 do ANTIHALT ← 1;
ANTIHALT ←0 end
```

If ANTIHALT is a legal procedure, then

```
FIND (⟨ANTIHALT⟩) is B
```

where B is some integer. What happens when we execute $HALT(\langle B,B \rangle)$?

$$HALT(\langle B,B \rangle) = \begin{cases} 1 \text{ if } ANTIHALT(B) \text{ halts} \\ 0 \text{ if } ANTIHALT(B) \text{ does not halt} \end{cases}$$

But if $HALT(\langle B,B \rangle) = 1$, then ANTIHALT loops forever on its <u>while</u> statement. Hence it certainly does not halt, so $HALT(\langle B,B \rangle) = 0$. If, on the other hand, $HALT(\langle B,B \rangle) = 0$, the <u>while</u> statement cannot loop, and ANTIHALT has the value 0 and certainly halts, and $HALT(\langle B,B \rangle) = 1$. These contradictions are removed only if HALT is not a procedure that we can write in our programming language and that performs the service for which it was designed.

Now note that our argument shows that we cannot write HALT even if we ask less from it than to tell whether any procedure halts for any of its inputs. We cannot write a HALT that answers, for any P, whether P(INDEX(⟨P⟩)) halts.

Once we can represent any procedure P as data, we can define a single procedure UNIVERSAL that will execute P when given any of P's legal inputs. UNIVERSAL merely imitates such a given procedure P by doing whatever P would do on the data were P to be applied to it.

```
procedure UNIVERSAL (⟨J,N⟩)
UNIVERSAL ← EXECUTE (⟨FIND(J),N⟩)
```

EXECUTE is a tedious procedure to describe, but it is very much like an APL interpreter, if the APL interpreter were written in APL.

Having found one noncomputable function, one not representable by a procedure, we can find others by showing that their representation by procedures would imply that HALT also could be representable. Since we know that the latter cannot, neither can the former.

One well-known example of the use of this argument to show nonexistence is the equivalence problem.

Does there exist a procedure EQUIVALENCE(⟨M,N⟩), defined for every M and N, whose value is 1 if FIND(M) computes the same function as FIND(N)? (Both are defined over the same domain of actual parameter values, and they give the same value at each input); otherwise, EQUIVALENCE has the value 0.

Again we seek a contradiction arising from the existence of EQUIVALENCE. We can show it does not exist by requesting the comparison of simple functions to the function ZERO whose value for all inputs is 0.

Suppose we have the infinite set of procedures

```
procedure ISITK(X);
begin T ← UNIVERSAL(⟨K,K⟩);        ⎫
ISITK ← 0                          ⎬  K = 1, 2,...
end                                ⎭
```

Clearly ISITK, for those K for which it halts, is equivalent to ZERO, since, for any X, its value is 0.

If EQUIVALENCE exists, we can take any integer N, generate the procedure ISITN, find its index I_N, and execute EQUIVALENCE(⟨I_N,α⟩) where α is INDEX(ZERO). But now we can define a new version of HALT, NEWHALT:

```
procedure NEWHALT(N);
begin P ← ⟨CREATE(N)⟩;
K ← INDEX(P);
NEWHALT ← EQUIVALENCE(⟨K,α⟩)
end
```

where CREATE(N) produces the procedure ISITN. For every integer N, NEWHALT returns the value 1 if $P_N(N)$ halts (where

P_N is FIND(N)) and 0 if it does not. But we know that NEWHALT cannot exist. Therefore EQUIVALENCE cannot, either.

Such is the flavor of noncomputability arguments. The reader should not assume that, because there are functions that cannot be computed, those than can are either trivial or uninteresting. On the contrary, there are many interesting functions that are computable but that we do not yet know how to write or how to write well. The thrust of our efforts as programmers is to improve our abilities to do well what can be done, even though it is often very enlightening—and even disappointing—to know that there are functions for which we should not try to write programs since, alas, they do not exist!

PROGRAM CORRECTNESS

When we develop an algorithm and write a program to execute it, a number of abstract models undergo translation, one to the other. In some sense these models are different faces of the same thing, a mental abstraction. Naturally, we must ask ourselves: How do we make sure that they really are faithful translations?

While we do not know what people intend when they create algorithms, we do know what they create. Since algorithms have a precise intention and can be given a precise representation in flow-charts or Algol60 or APL, we can study their representation and attempt to prove that the represented algorithm does indeed solve the problem posed.

Very often the proofs are partial and include assumptions that are denied by reality, such as the infinite precision of numbers or the unbounded storage of computers. Nevertheless these proofs are quite valuable and often establish the logical correctness of an algorithm at a level of reality that is satisfactory enough for our purpose.

In some cases the logical correctness of our algorithm may lead us astray when we actually write a program, since the realities of the programming language and its host computer violate some assumptions we had made in our correctness proof. In such cases we must establish the real (reduced) circumstances under which our algorithm and its associated program are still correct.

How do we display a correctness argument? All arguments, to one degree or another, depend upon an a priori, agreed-upon, accepted set of truths. The language of mathematics is ideal for stating these truths and manipulating them according to accepted methods of argument.

That part of mathematical logic known as the predicate calculus is often used as the model for stating what is to be proved, what is to be assumed as initially given, and what arguments are to be used in the proof.

It has been customary among programmers not to give correctness proofs of programs for the following reasons.

1. It is too difficult for programmers to make them for the complex programs they write.

2. For complex programs the proofs are often as complex as the programs themselves. Whereas the computer can rapidly read and execute complex programs, who can do the same for proofs?

3. Mathematical proofs are clumsy for dealing with the time-varying values of variables and locus of control arising during program execution.

4. Testing the program with a number of test-data runs is assumed to be sufficient. After all, if the test data are chosen at random and the program gives correct results for those data, is it not quite likely to be correct for all data?

For each of these reasons a rebuttal can easily be given. The rebuttals derive their force from two arguments:

1. The proof of correctness of programs is an activity that proceeds apace with the creation of an algorithm, and each lends support to establishing the correctness and existence of the other.

2. Programs are not "random" objects, so a statement like "The program P is correct with probability α," meaning that out of every K runs of P, on the average αK will be correct, is not very helpful to the users who depend on the results of program execution.

Since programs contain loops, proofs must not enumerate what occurs during successive loop traversals. As with algorithms, proofs of correctness of algorithms should not have a descriptive length proportional to the number of execution steps of the algorithms. The natural analogue in proofs to the cycle in algorithm description is mathematical induction.

The most elementary statement of mathematical induction is as follows.

Suppose we wish to prove that a certain property P holds for all the nonnegative integers, that $P(n)$ is true for all integers $n > 0$. Then to do this it is sufficient to make just two arguments:

1. $P(0)$. The property holds for $n = 0$.
2. For an arbitrary $n > 0$, the assumption that $P(n)$ is true guarantees that $P(n + 1)$ is true.

How do we use induction in proofs of correctness in algorithms? Its use strikes at the very heart of our use of loops in algorithms. Suppose we take an arbitrary loop in some algorithm, as shown in the figure. X is the so-called loop variable; g is the result variable;

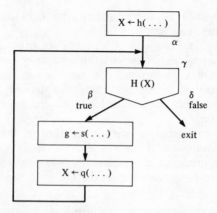

h(. . .) initializes X and q(. . .) varies X; s(. . .) varies g and usually depends on g and X; H is a predicate providing the termination condition of the loop.

An important property of loops is that they are executed differing numbers of times on passage, depending on the current data values. Yet the algorithm is solving the *same* problem in all such cases. Hence there is an important property of the algorithm variables that remains invariant through successive loop cycles. The induction argument now states:

1. We can prove that a property P holds, P <u>is true</u>, on first entry to the loop, that is, at point α.
2. From P's holding, on entry to the loop, at point α, we can prove that P holds at γ. Hence P is true *regardless* of the number of loop passages we make.

Thus, if this invariant property is true on first entry to the loop, it is true on exit δ, providing we reach there. To make sure that the loop terminates, so that exiting will occur, we establish another loop property that has a monotonous behavior, from which we may guarantee ultimate termination when this property achieves either a lower or upper bound.

To put matters more concretely, let us consider the following problem for which we wish to obtain an algorithm. Suppose we have an integer vector X, for which $\rho X = $ n. Suppose we are given two numbers, $\alpha \leq \omega$. We wish to find a rearrangement in X of its components so that all components $X[i] < \alpha$ lie to the left of all those $\geq \alpha$, and all those components $X[i] > \omega$ lie to the right of those $\leq \omega$. Furthermore, we wish to rearrange the components of X subject to the following constraints:

1. We may not use any data structure other than X, whose size depends on n.
2. We may not test the magnitude of any element of X more than twice.

The constraints are actually a help rather than a hindrance. We must rearrange within X, and we must separate those components we have examined from those we have not. The following picture presents itself:

$X:$ A D C B

    $A:$ The set of elements of X examined at most twice and found $< \alpha$.
    $B:$ The set of elements of X examined at most twice and found $> \omega$.
    $C:$ The set of elements of X examined at most twice and found $\geq \alpha$ and $\leq \omega$.
    $D:$ Elements of X not yet examined.

We have our cycle before us. Take from D a previously unexamined element of X. Our cycle invariant is simple to find. $Q(A, B, C)$: Each element we examine is appended to one of the sets A, B, or C, so that the new A, B, and C sets still satisfy their defining conditions. The monotonic condition is N, the number of elements in X not yet examined. Each time through the cycle that number will decrease by 1 and hence ultimately reach 0. Let Φ stand for the empty set.

An algorithm is:

```
A ←B← C ← Φ ; comment initially the sets are
empty;                                                        ①
D ←X;                                                         ②
while D ≠ Φ do begin
ε ← select (D); comment extract an element from D;
D ← D − ε ; comment ε is deleted from D;                      ③
if ε < α then A←A,ε
else if ε > ω then B←B,ε                                      ④
else C←C,ε end
```

This algorithm violates condition 1, so we must imbed sets A, B, C, and D in X without violating condition 2.

In terms of our conditions on Q and N we may reveal how the algorithm execution affects the condition Q and the integer N:

```
Q(A, B, C) is true                                           ①
N is n                                                       ②
while N ≠ 0 do begin
N is N–1                                                     ③
Q(A,B,C) is true end                                         ④
```

When N reaches 0, and it does, then $Q(A,B,C)$ is true.
The next phase in our correctness exercise is to represent our data and algorithm in a programming language such that our cor-

rectness proof remains valid and condition 1 is satisfied. We define our sets A, B, C, and D as follows.

Define pointers a, b, and c:

$i < a$ implies $X[i]$ in A
$i > b$ implies $X[i]$ in B
$c < i \leq b$ implies $X[i]$ in C and otherwise $X[i]$ in D.

With the new data representation the algorithm is

```
a ← 1; b ← c ← n
i ← 1;
while a < c do begin
h ← X[i];
if h < α then begin a ← a+1; i ← i+1; end
else if h >ω then begin
exchange (X[c],X[i]);
exchange (X[c],X[b]);
c ← c-1; b ← b-1 end
else begin exchange (X[i],X[c]); c ← c-1 end
end of algorithm
```

There are now additional matters, introduced by the representation, to prove.

However, on initiation it is clearly so, that Q(A,B,C) is true and $X = D$.

Within the cycle $c - a$ diminishes by 1 on each cycle, since either $a \leftarrow a + 1$ or $c \leftarrow c - 1$, but not both. But the elements of D are those $X[j]$ for which $a \leq j \leq c$, so that $N \leftarrow N - 1$ still holds in the program.

If $X[i] < \alpha$, then $a \leftarrow a + 1$; $i \leftarrow i + 1$ is the same as A $\leftarrow$ A, ϵ.

If $X[i] > \omega$, the exchange (X[c],X[i]) exchanges the rightmost unexamined element in X with that one just examined and then further exchanges the latter with the rightmost element that is not known to be $> \omega$. Both $b \leftarrow b - 1$ and $c \leftarrow c - 1$ establish that $B \leftarrow B$, ϵ.

Finally the last case establishes that $C \leftarrow C$, ϵ.

Thus $Q(A, B, C)$ is true on exit from the cycle. We do exit from the cycle, and the constraints are satisfied. We have found a faithful program representation for our algorithm.

Let us consider a second example. Suppose we have a set S of n points in the plane (X_i, Y_i), where $i = 1, 2, \ldots, n$. We wish to find their convex hull—the convex polygon of least area whose vertices are a subset of S and that contains (inside or on its boundary) all the points of S. A polygon is a closed figure whose sides are straight-line segments. When any straight line connecting any two points on the boundary contains only points on or in the polygon, the polygon is said to be "convex." We identify the hull by the set of its vertices.

Example. The set of points (1, 1), (2, 4), (2, 2), (3, 2), (0, 3), (1, 5), (4, 4), (2, 1), and (1, 2) have as their convex hull the area whose boundary is determined by the vertex set (1, 1), (0, 3), (1, 5), (4, 4), (3, 2), and (2, 1).

We shall consider two algorithms for this problem. Which one should we choose?

Algorithm 1: If all the n points are on a straight line, the hull is the line segment of minimum length containing all the points in S. Let us assume this is not the case. Then we can find four points, Q_1, Q_2, Q_3, and Q_4, not necessarily distinct:

Q_1: has the minimum x coordinate
Q_2: "   "   maximum "   "
Q_3: "   "   " y "
Q_4: "   "   minimum "   "

Three of these points must be distinct and not lie on a straight line. Call these three points P_1, P_2, and P_3. They are on the boundary of the convex hull. Suppose the situation is as in the figure: There

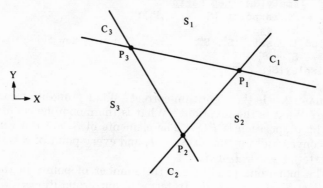

are no points of S in C_1, C_2, or C_3. We may partition S into five sets:

THE EXTERIOR SETS: S_0: P_1, P_2, P_3
S_1: All points in $S - S_0$ on the other side of the line P_3P_1 from P_2
S_2: All points in $S - S_0$ on the other side of P_2P_1 from P_3
S_3: All points in $S - S_0$ on the other side of P_2P_3 from P_1

THE NONEXTERIOR SET: I: $S - (S_0 + S_1 + S_2 + S_3)$

Let $S \leftarrow S_1 + S_2 + S_3$. S_0 contains three elements of the hull. The pattern of the algorithm is simple. We have given the initial phase.

The cycle is as follows (suppose S_0 contains k points P_1, P_2, . . . , P_k and we have found the corresponding exterior sets S_1, S_2, . . . , S_k):

In each set S_r find a point whose distance from the line seg-- ment $P_{r-1}P_r$ is a maximum.

Augment S_0 with each point found. Using the new S, define the new exterior sets S_1', S_2', . . . , S_j', where $j \leq 2k$.

Let $S \leftarrow S_1' + S_2' + \cdots + S_j'$.

The termination condition is: All the exterior sets S_1', S_2', . . . , S_j' are empty.

We may now write the algorithm in phases.

PHASE 1.

```
initialize S₀
Find S ← (S₁, S₂, S₃)
k ← 3
while ∼ empty(S) do begin
m ← k;
for j ← 1 step 1 until m do
if ∼empty(Sⱼ) then begin
S₀ ← S₀,maxpoint (Sⱼ, Pⱼ₋₁ ,Pⱼ);
k ← k+1 end
Find the sets (S₁', S₂', . . . ·, Sₖ' using new S₀)
S ← S₁' + S₂' + · · · + Sₖ' end
Display(S₀)
```

PHASE 2.   Is the algorithm correct? What propositions are we proving? What is the invariant? What is the monotone condition?

The proposition is $P(S)$: The elements of S_0 are the vertices of the convex hull for the set $S_0 + I$, and every point of S is either in an exterior set or I or S_0.

The monotone condition is the number of points in the exterior sets: $S_1' + \cdots + S_k'$. In terms of our propositions,

```
P(I)                      (1)
while N > 0 do begin
P(I)                      (2)
N ← N - δ end             (3)
```

The number δ is the number of points in S added to S_0 and I. Therefore $P(I) \wedge N = 0$. But if $N = 0$, then $S = I + S_0$ and hence $P(S)$.

Thus to prove correctness we must show that (1), (2), and (3) are indeed true statements when our algorithm is executed. At some stage or other we must say that a proof is obvious, by which we mean the truth follows from a logical argument applied to universally accepted mathematical truths. What are the theorems whose truth will support the correctness of the algorithm? Simpler theorems may lead to an alternative algorithm: Start with any triangle

S_0 and add one new point from S; then points may migrate from S_0 but only to I.

PHASE 3.   We must now decide on representations for our sets and on algorithms for our undefined functions, and we must then prove that each of these is "faithful." Regardless of whatever other propositions they induce, they must leave the truth of the invariance of $P(S)$ and the monotonicity of N unchanged. We leave this (and subsequent reductions) to the reader.

As so often happens in the creation of algorithms, an attractive possibility for improvement in our algorithm suggests itself, as follows.

Algorithm 2:   The first algorithm (p. 367) can, in a worst case, take $\sim n^2$ steps when S has n elements. Thus, if S is already a regular convex polygon of 3×2^k points, it can be the case that at each step S decreases only by 1 for each maximum found!

We know that we can sort n numbers in $\sim n \log_2 n$ steps, so that we might attempt to find an algorithm requiring that number of steps.

Suppose we take a point $\bar{P}$, for example $\bar{x} = 1/n \, \Sigma x_i$, $\bar{y} = 1/n \, \Sigma y_i$, as an origin and $y = 0$ as in axis. Let us then sort the points of S on the basis of their angles, measured from the axis and $\bar{P}$, in increasing order. Actually, we divide the points into seven classes. The table defines the classes, the successive sorting keys to be used to break ties, and the order of sort ($\triangle$ means increasing order and $\triangledown$ means decreasing order).

Let $\theta = \dfrac{|y_i - \bar{y}|}{|x_i - \bar{x}|}$, $x_i \neq \bar{x}$

CLASS		SORT ON
I.	$x_i - \bar{x} = 0$ and $y_i - \bar{y} = 0$	
II.	$x_i - \bar{x} > 0$ and $y_i - \bar{y} \geq 0$	$\theta,\ x_i - \bar{x}\ \triangle$
III.	$x_i - \bar{x} = 0$ and $y_i = \bar{y} > 0$	$y_i - \bar{y}\ \triangle$
IV.	$x_i - \bar{x} < 0$ and $y_i - \bar{y} \geq 0$	$\theta,\ x_i - \bar{x}\ \triangledown$
V.	$x_i - \bar{x} < 0$ and $y_i - \bar{y} < 0$	$\theta,\ x_i - \bar{x}\ \triangle$
VI.	$x_i - \bar{x} = 0$ and $y_i - \bar{y} < 0$	$y_i - \bar{y}\ \triangle$
VII.	$x_i - \bar{x} > 0$ and $y_i - \bar{y} < 0$	$\theta,\ x_i - \bar{x}\ \triangledown$

The points are now sorted and we take them in the order I, II, III, IV, V, VI, VII. The algorithm for finding the hull is now quite simple. Copy the first point to the end of the sorted list. We either keep or strike a point from the list by following the rule below.

Take three consecutive points. Strike out the middle point if it is on the same side as $\bar{P}$ of the line segment formed by the two other points.

Each time a point is struck out, backtrack one place to test for a new middle point. If the middle point is not struck out, advance and continue, until the last member of the remaining list is a middle point. This takes $2n$ steps at most. However, this second algorithm that takes $\sim n \log_2 n$ steps is more difficult to prove correct than the first algorithm given. Unhappily this is often the case: optimal algorithms often tend to be more obscure than nonoptimal ones.

Suppose we wish to prove the correctness of an algorithm written in APL. Since APL's expressive power permits algorithms to be stated with great conciseness, proofs often require an analysis of "one-liners." Let us look at two such.

Example 1: We state that if A is an array of rank 2, then the predicate

$$P \leftarrow \wedge /1 = + /A \wedge . = \lozenge A$$

is 1 (true) if and only if no two rows of A are the same. Let us decompose the one-liner:

$T_1 \leftarrow A \wedge . = \lozenge A$ and $\rho(T_1)$ <u>is</u> $2 \rho (\rho A)[1]$
$T_2 \leftarrow +/T_1$ and ρT_2 <u>is</u> $(\rho A)[1]$
$P \leftarrow \wedge/1 = T_2$ and P is scalar.

Then:

$T_1[I;J]$ <u>is</u> $\wedge/A[I;] = (\lozenge A) [;J]$
<u>is</u> $\wedge/A[I;] = A[J;]$
<u>is</u> 1 or 0
$T_2[K]$ <u>is</u>$+/T_1[K;]$
$P \leftarrow \wedge/1 = T_2$

Assume no two rows of A are the same:

$T_1[I;J]$ <u>is</u> <u>if</u> I = J <u>then</u> 1 <u>else</u> 0
$T_2[K]$ <u>is</u> $(\rho A) [1] \rho 1$
P <u>is</u> 1

Assume P <u>is</u> 1:
Then for all K$\epsilon \iota$ $(\rho A)[1]$, $T_2[K]$ <u>is</u> 1.
Hence $T_1 [K;]$ <u>is</u> 1.
Hence for $(J \neq K) \wedge (J\epsilon \iota (\rho A)[1])$,
$0 = \wedge/A[K;] = A[J;]$.
By De Morgan's law (see Chapter 2), $1 = \vee/A[K;] \neq$ A[J;].

That is, there exists an $L \epsilon \iota (\rho A)[2]$ for which A[K:L] $\neq$ A[J:L] for *all* K and J in range. Thus no two rows of A are identical.

Example 2: $R \leftarrow (2 = +/[1] 0 = (\iota n)$ $^{\circ}.|\iota n)/\iota n.$

We wish to prove that R is the vector all of whose components are the primes $\leq n$.

Since $R \leftarrow C/\iota\ n$ and C is a mask, the elements of R, if any at all, come from among the integers 1 to n.

Consider any component of C, $C[K]$, $1 \leq K \leq n$,

$$(2 = +/[1]\ 0 = (\iota n) \circ . | \ (\iota n))[K]$$

which is the same as ($\Leftrightarrow$):

$$2 = +/[1]\ 0 = (\iota n)\ \circ . | K$$
$$(\Leftrightarrow)\ \ 2 = +/\ 0 = (\iota n)|K$$
$$(\Leftrightarrow)\ \ 2 = +/\ 0 = (\iota K)|K$$

Therefore $C(K) = 1 \Leftrightarrow K$ has exactly two divisors among the integers ιK, that is, if K is prime. $C(K) = 1$ selects K in $C/\iota n$. R contains only primes $\leq n$.

Conversely, consider any prime $2 \leq p \leq n$. Then $p\epsilon\iota n$, and

```
2 = +/ 0 =(ιn)∘ . | p is 1
C[p] is 1 and p ε R.
```

TERMINATION OF ALGORITHMS

The monotone conditions are often difficult to specify, especially in the case of nested loop problems. A technique that is quite useful involves what mathematicians call "well-ordered sets." A well-ordered set of elements s is a set having two properties:

1. Between every two distinct elements of the set, a and b, a relation $>$ exists for which

$$\text{if } a \neq b \text{ then } a > b \text{ else } b > a$$
$$\text{and} \quad \text{if } a > b \wedge \quad b > c \text{ then } a > c$$

2. Every decreasing sequence of elements from S, (a_k), for which it is true that

$$a_1 > a_2 > a_3 , , , > a_n , , ,$$

has only *finitely* many members.

There are two very useful well-ordered sets:

1. The set of all nonnegative integers with their natural relation

$$N > N - 1 > N - 2 \ldots \quad 2 > 1 > 0$$

2. The set of all n-tuples of nonnegative integers for fixed $n \geq 1$, with the "lexicographic" ordering

$$(a_1, a_2, \ldots, a_n) > (b_1, b_2, \ldots, b_n)$$

meaning that

either $a_1 > b_1$

or there is some k, where $2 \leq k \leq n$, for which

$$a_1 = b_1$$
$$a_2 = b_2$$
$$\cdot \cdot \cdot$$
$$a_{k-1} = b_{k-1}$$
$$a_k > b_k$$

The use of well-ordered sets in proving termination is straight-forward. For an algorithm, identify all the steps that are branches within cycles and lie on a path to $\diagdown\!\!\underline{\text{H}}\diagup$. Call that set of steps F. Let D_α be the domain of the variables participating in the step α in F. Suppose we have a function g_α defined at each step α in F that (a) maps D_α into S_α, where S_α is well-ordered with respect to $>$, and that (b), on successive passages through step α,

$$g^{k\text{th passage}}(D_\alpha) > g^{(k+1)\text{ passage}}(D_\alpha), \quad \text{for all } \alpha$$

Then the algorithm must terminate. This is so because, if it did not, some branch (hence some α in F) would be executed an infinite number of times. But on each passage g_α would be diminishing in value. The sequence of values (g_α) is in a well-ordered set and is diminishing and must then be finite in number. Therefore we cannot pass through α an infinite number of times. Therefore the algorithm must terminate.

The converse is also true. If the algorithm terminates, such functions g_α and well-ordered sets exist for every cycle-participating branch node. This tells us that we can find such functions for every algorithm we write. Perhaps we should never write algorithms for which we cannot isolate such functions! However, it may be very difficult to find such functions. For example, given a positive integer N, the program segment

```
while N ≠ 1 do
if odd( N) then N ← 1 + 3 × N
else N ← N / 2
```

seems to terminate for every integer yet tested (up to 10^{40}), but no one has yet found a termination proof for all $N > 0$.

Let us consider another example: a sorting algorithm. Assume that we have an odd number of numbers, $a_1, a_2, \ldots, a_{n+1}$. We sort these numbers by comparing pairs of adjacent elements and exchanging, so that the left element of each pair is always the largest and alternately includes and excludes the first element of the sequence as a pair member. When two successive comparison runs result in no exchanges, the sort is completed. What termination functions do we define? The algorithm is

```
q ← true;
while q do begin
q ← false;
i ← 0;
while i < 2 do begin
k ← i+1;
while k < 2n+i do begin
if a[k+1] > a[k] then begin exch(k,k+1);
q ← true end;
k ← k +1 end;
i ← i +1 end
end
```

The flow of control through the cycles can be represented by the graph shown. The nodes are the conditions that control cycling.

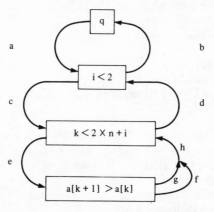

Along the paths are the assignments that change the values of variables participating in the conditions.

Let m be n minus the number of elements put in their proper place. Let p be the number of places that the largest number, not yet put into place, must move to be in place. Then define the monotone condition g as

$$(m, p, 2 - i, 2n + i - k)$$

that maps the domain of nonnegative integers into a 4-tuple of nonnegative integers.

On all cycles, g decreases because:

1.   On efh and egh, k increases.
2.   On cd, i increases.
3.   On ab, either m has decreased by 1 or p has decreased by 1.

Therefore the algorithm terminates. Even more, the minimum of g is $(0, 0, 0, 0)$, which says that, on termination, the sort has been accomplished ($m = p = 0$).

The use of well-ordering allows us to capture the idea that in our programs the execution of every cycle contributes to overall decreases, even though there may be some local increase, in components of our termination function.

Let us consider an example involving both termination and correctness. In Chapter 4 we described an excellent in-place sorting algorithm. Let us sketch out proofs of its correctness and termination.

Define a chain from $X[r]$, $_rX_k$, as the path from $X[r]$ through ancestors to an ancestor $X[k]$:

```
ᵣXₖ is X[r], X[r÷2], ..., X[(((r÷2) ÷2) ,,, ÷2)],
..., X[k]
```

The invariant is:

```
Q[j]:  for r < j all chains ᵣX₁ are nondecreasing
X[r] ≤ X[r÷2] ≤ ... ≤ X[1]
```

Suppose we had the program

```
j ← 2; Q[2] ← true
while j < n do begin
Q[j+1] ← if Q[j] then true else false;          (*)
j ← j+1 end
```

Its invariant is $Q[j] = $ true. The monotone g is $n + 1 - j$. Hence $Q[n + 1] = $ true, which is what we wish to prove. Consequently it remains only to show that (*) follows from the execution of the inner loop of the algorithm "create."

Let $_jP_k$ be the predicate: $_jX_k$ monotone implies $_jX_{k+2}$ monotone for $k > 1$. Then within the loop

```
Q[j ] ← true;
while k >1 ∧ ⱼPₖ do begin
ⱼPₖ ← true;
k ← k ÷2 end;
```

which, of course, terminates. If it terminates with $k = 1$, then $_jP_1$ and $Q[j]$ hold; hence $Q[j + 1]$ holds. With $k = r > 1$, $Q[j]$ and $_jP_r$ hold; hence $_jP_1$ holds, hence $Q[j + 1]$.

Our "proof" program for "create" is

```
j ← 2; Q[2] ← true;
while j ≤ n do begin
Q[j];
if Q[j] then ⱼP₁;
if ⱼP₁ then Q[j +1];
j ← j +1 end
```

which is, on execution, $Q[n + 1]$.

A similar proof can be given for "deplete." The invariant is

$$S[j]: X[n] > X[n-1] > \ldots > X[j].$$

If we take $S[n + 1]$ to be <u>true</u>, we seek to justify the proof program

```
deplete: j ← n; S[n+1] ← true
while j ≥ 1 do begin
if Q[j + 1] ∧S[j + 1]then begin
S[j] ← true;
Q[j] ← true end;
j ← j - 1 end
```

which leads ultimately to

```
create: Q[n+1] ← true
deplete: S[1] ← true
```

The use of the algorithm flow to organize a flow for the correctness and termination proofs is natural. The <u>while</u> and <u>for</u> loops then provide the natural algorithmic equivalents to mathematical-induction arguments. Seen this way, proofs flow naturally from innermost loops to outermost loops: The boolean-data type of the algorithmic language Algol60 is now used to carry the predicates arising during the proofs in our algorithmic condensation process.

SUMMARY AND REFERENCES

The practices and applications of programming draw heavily on mathematics and logic. Thus it is not strange that mathematical models of programming and computing should exist and be studied to shed light on the problems that arise in computation. In 1937 Alan Turing defined abstract devices, now called Turing machines, that could be studied in place of real computers. It was in their terms that the first noncomputable functions were displayed. In terms of this abstraction the subject of computability was defined:

What is the class of functions that can be represented as programs that terminate in a finite number of steps on these machines?

Are there functions that cannot be represented by programs in any language?

The logician Turing answered these questions with respect to his own particular kind of computer, the Turing machine. Consequent upon his work there has emerged a thesis,

> **Turing's thesis:** *No model of computation whatsoever will support a larger class of computable functions than Turing machines do.*

No mathematical proof of this thesis exists. It is somewhat like a general physical law: an increasing weight of evidence supports it, though its generality may be reduced in the light of future evidence.

However, all models of computation thus far developed completely support Turing's thesis. An excellent treatment of these and allied matters can be found in

M. Minsky, *Computation, Finite and Infinite Machines* (Prentice-Hall, Englewood Cliffs, N. J., 1967).

Methods of determining the correctness of computer programs were first published by Floyd:

R. Floyd, "Assigning Meanings to Programs," Mathematical Aspects of Computer Science (*Proc. Symposia Applied Math.*, 19, 1967, pp. 19–32).

The first treatment of algorithm termination was done by Manna in his Ph.D. thesis

Termination of Algorithms (Carnegie-Mellon University, Pittsburgh, Pa., 1968).

The particular proof of correctness techniques applicable to APL programs is described in

S. Gerhart, Ph.D. thesis, *Verification of APL Programs* (Carnegie-Mellon University, Pittsburgh, Pa., 1973).

An enormous amount of useful work is being done on algorithmic complexity: What are the resource demands, usually of time and storage, of an algorithm as a function of data complexity? For any particular program such an analysis usually requires a statistical analysis, since programs contain loops and conditional expressions. The books by Knuth contain many such analyses. For a particular problem—for example, the string-matching problem described in Chapter 1—it is desirable to fix bounds on the complexity that an algorithm should or must possess. Thus, any algorithm for a problem gives an upper bound, say for the time of computation. Much more difficult is to give a greatest lower bound, which says that no algorithm is possible that requires less resource than given by the bound, and to give an algorithm that comes very close to attaining that bound.

PROBLEMS

1. Another elegant in-place sorting algorithm is QUICKSORT, invented by C. A. R. Hoare and described in *Communications of the ACM*, July 1961, p. 321.

```
procedure partition (A,M,N,I,J); value M, N; array A;
integer M, N, I, J;
begin integer f; real X; f ← random (M,N); X → A[f]:
while M < N do begin
I ← M; J ← N;
while I ≤ N ∧ X > A[I] do I ← I+1;
while J ≥ M ∧ X < A[J] do J ← J-1;
if I < J then begin exch(A,I,J);
M ← I+1; N ← J-1 end
else if I < f then begin exch(A,I,f);
I ← I+1; M ← N+1 end
else if f < J then begin exch(A,J,f);
J ← J-1; M ← N+1 end
end
procedure quicksort (A,M,N); value M,N: array A;
inter M,N;
begin integer I,J;
if M < N then begin
partition (A,M,N,I,J);
quicksort (A,M,J);
quicksort (A,I,N);
end
```

Partition divides the interval of subscripts into three intervals:

1. $M \le r < J$ for which $A[r] < X$
2. $J \le r \le I$ for which $A[r] = X$
3. $I < r \le N$ for which $A[r] > X$

where X is the value of $A[f]$ and f is a random integer satisfying $M \le f \le N$.

Quicksort is recursively applied to intervals 1 and 3 until all intervals of type 1 and 3 are of length 1, at which point the original vector A is sorted.

Choose invariant and monotone functions for these two algorithms, and prove their termination and correctness.

2. Prove the termination and correctness of algorithms for the following problems:

    a. The coin problem.

    b. The 8-queens problem.

    c. The string-matching problem.

    d. The number of lattice points in the N-sphere.

    e. Convex hull of n points in the plane.

3. Given a BNF grammar, such as bas of Chapter 3, give an algorithm for generating all legal strings, in order of increasing length, and prove it correct.

4. Find, and prove correct, an algorithm for the "inverse" bowling problem: Given $0 \le n \le 300$, find a legal bowling game, using the minimum number of balls that has score n.

INDEX

75 76 77 7 6 5 4 3 2 1